Constitutional Law
and Young Adults

Constitutional
Law and
Young Adults

Peter G. Renstrom

Professor of Political Science
Western Michigan University

ABC-CLIO

Santa Barbara, California
Denver, Colorado
Oxford, England

Library of Congress Cataloging-in-Publication Data

Renstrom, Peter G., 1943–
    Constitutional law and young adults / by Peter G. Renstrom.
        p.   cm.
    Includes bibliographical references and index.
    1. United States—Constitutional law.   I. Title.
    KF4550.Z9R46   1991   91-47990

ISBN 0-87436-483-3

99 98 97 96 95 94 93   10 9 8 7 6 5 4 3 2

ABC-CLIO, Inc.
130 Cremona Drive, P.O. Box 1911
Santa Barbara, California 93116-1911

This book is printed on acid-free paper ∞
Manufactured in the United States of America

To Dan and Joey—
    May the Bill of Rights survive
        my generation to protect yours

Contents

4   The First Amendment, 87

8   The Eighth Amendment, 287

9   Equal Protection and Privacy, 313

A Note on How
To Use This Book

Constitutional Law and Young Adults is designed to introduce young people to the U.S. Constitution. The book focuses on the individual rights provided by the Bill of Rights and the Fourteenth Amendment. The issues featured should be of particular interest and relevance to young adults. The following suggestions are intended to enhance the value of this book to readers.

The best starting place is appendix A, which comprises the Constitution in its entirety. At the very least, the Bill of Rights (the first nine amendments to the Constitution), should be carefully studied, along with the Fourteenth Amendment. Readers should think about these words and try to imagine the intentions of the people who wrote them. It also is helpful to consider how the meanings of the words might have changed over time or how the words might lend themselves to different interpretations. These exercises establish a foundation of understanding and demonstrate how the choice of one interpretation over another, even regarding a single word, can have profound consequences.

Many chapters are organized around the constitutional issues that stem from the Bill of Rights. Chapter 6, for example, deals with issues grounded in the Fifth Amendment. The first two chapters, in contrast, are designed to serve several purposes: they establish a point of origin and provide a brief historical perspective of the U.S. constitutional experience; they introduce some essential concepts of U.S. constitutional law; and they describe the U.S. Supreme Court and the way that constitutional judgments are made through the Court's case decisions. It is helpful to read these two introductory chapters before proceeding to the others.

Chapters 3–9 may be approached in two ways because the material is organized into modules that link together. First, the chapters may be read from beginning to end to foster a better understanding of the scope of a particular constitutional amendment. This approach helps readers to discern differences or gradations in constitutional protections even within the same amendment. Second, the book is designed to serve as a quick reference source. If a reader has an immediate need to consider one specific issue, such as symbolic expression, he or she may refer to the module that addresses the particular topic (in this case, the relevant module is in chapter 4). The index provides access to each module.

All Supreme Court cases reflect a contest between two parties, each of whom has different views about an issue. In reading about the cases, it is valuable to imagine oneself as first one party and then the other. Try to envision as clearly as possible what each side is claiming and what is at stake in the case. The Supreme Court not only determines which party wins but also explains why. The Court's statement of rationale addresses the underlying question of law contained in the case. The principle established in a decision becomes the basis of future decisions. People look up cases in order to find out what they say about a particular point of law. Finding specific cases is possible by using citation numbers. Each Supreme Court decision has a unique set of numbers which refer to volumes of compiled cases. There are several series of volumes which contain Supreme Court decisions, but this book features the *United States Reports,* the only series produced by the U.S. government. A *United States Reports* citation number is provided for each case mentioned in this book: for *Roe v. Wade,* the citation number is 410 U.S. 113: 1973. The number before *U.S.* (410) refers to the volume in which *Roe* can be found. The number following *U.S.* (113) indicates the page number, and the number after the colon is the year in which the case was decided. It is helpful to look up one or more of the cases discussed in this book, using the citations provided, to see how a decision is reported and to read the opinion in its entirety. Some of the most recent cases have citation numbers from another series, the *United States Supreme Court Reports, Lawyers Edition.* This series is published by the Lawyers Co-operative Publishing Company of Rochester, New York. *Lawyers Edition* citation numbers follow the same format as the *U.S. Reports* citations: volume number, abbreviation to identify the series (L.Ed. or L.Ed.2d), and page number. The *Lawyers Edition* citation for *Roe v. Wade* is 35 L.Ed.2d 147: 1973.

 # Preface

This book is about constitutional law, which is the legal foundation of a political system. It is also the highest form of law, and all actions of government must conform to its provisions. Constitutional law addresses the basic organizational framework of government and the authority of those who exercise governmental power. It sets forth the general manner in which public matters are to be administered, which usually includes a statement of the principles that govern the relationship between the government and individual citizens. Constitutional law not only defines the powers of government but also establishes limits on those powers as well. In addition to the national Constitution of the United States, each of the 50 states has its own constitution. Using this book, readers can examine the limits on governmental authority as defined by the U.S. Constitution.

The U.S. Constitution is very general and requires continual interpretation. Constitutional law involves not only the words in the document itself but also the thousands of juridical interpretations of what those words mean. Because legal decisions are derived from the document itself, they carry full constitutional force. Final authority on the meaning of the U.S. Constitution resides with the U.S. Supreme Court; the highest court of each state performs a similar role with state constitutions. The supremacy clause of Article VI of the Constitution states that no provision of state law (even state constitutional law) and no legislative enactments (known as statutes) may conflict with the national Constitution. Courts safeguard the integrity of constitutions from improper legislative or executive action through the power of judicial review. Judicial review empowers courts to invalidate actions that conflict with constitutional provisions.

This book is limited to considerations of constitutional law because the book's primary objective is to introduce readers to the fundamental law contained in the Constitution, particularly as it relates to individual liberties. Much of U.S. substantive and procedural law is established by statutes and in common law, both of which fall outside the scope of this book. Though the book is written especially for younger readers, the focus is not on juvenile rights as such or on state substantive laws directed toward minors. The discussion of the protections afforded to citizens under the terms of the national Constitution includes an examination of constitutional freedoms.

The meaning of the U.S. Constitution ultimately rests with the U.S. Supreme Court. The ongoing interpretative process allows the provisions of the Constitution to change and adapt over time. Understanding what the Constitution says about individual rights requires examining the appropriate Supreme Court decisions. These decisions are the Court's responses to the questions raised by the cases that come before it. Case decisions are a window through which we come to understand our constitutional system. As readers learn about the decisions, they need to keep in mind the various influences on the Supreme Court. The foremost influence is previously decided cases. Generally, the justices allow prior decisions, called legal precedents, to dictate current responses. The social and political climate in which a case is considered, however, may require departing from or modifying precedent. As times change, the general guidelines of the Constitution are adapted to new situations by interpretation. This may require modifying a precedent, or even abandoning it in some instances. Court decisions also are affected by the predispositions of the current justices. No justice can leave these predispositions at the courthouse door. Pay attention to how a combination of these influences applies to specific cases. You can determine which justices are involved in a particular decision by using the date of the case to find the appropriate line row of justices in appendix C.

Several considerations were important in the selection of cases for discussion in this book. Certain cases were included because they are fundamental to understanding constitutional rights. Among these landmark decisions are *Miranda v. Arizona, Griswold v. Connecticut,* and *Schenck v. United States.* Cases dealing directly with the constitutional rights of minors also were sought. While the Supreme Court does not decide large numbers of cases involving minors, a serious attempt was made to address as many of these decisions as possible. Cases that reflect constitutional issues in an interesting fashion were another focus. Finally, recent decisions were used whenever possible. This was done to reflect the current thinking of the Supreme Court and to enhance representation of a series of decisions on a particular constitutional issue. Consequently, decisions of the Burger and Rehnquist Courts are heavily represented.

Acknowledgments

The material for this book was drawn exclusively from decisions of the U.S. Supreme Court. My knowledge of constitutional law, on the other hand, has come from many sources. I acknowledge the efforts of the many constitutional scholars whose work has influenced my thinking. Two require specific mention: the late G. Theodore Mitau, a remarkable political scientist and an extraordinary teacher of constitutional law who sparked my lifelong interest during my undergraduate years at Macalester College, and Harold J. Spaeth of Michigan State University, who introduced me to various valuable quantitative methods for explaining the decisional behavior of Supreme Court justices. I also acknowledge the stimulation and encouragement given by my department colleagues and my students at Western Michigan University; I especially thank Professor Ralph C. Chandler, as this book was his idea. I hope some of what I have learned from Ralph is reflected in these pages. I also thank Heather Cameron of ABC-CLIO for remaining confident that this project should and could be completed. Finally, a most special thanks to my wife, Bobbi Renstrom. Her support never waivers, and she is always willing to review chapter drafts. I could not get along without her help. These people have made this book a reality. I alone, of course, am responsible for errors of omission and commission.

— Peter G. Renstrom
Western Michigan University

Constitutional Law
and Young Adults

Introduction to Constitutional Law

Most political systems profess a commitment to the rule of law. This can mean either of the following: the rule of law may be enacted by an elected legislative body or "law" may be autocratically imposed by a dictator. Some political systems are governed by a fundamental or "higher" law that is different from any other type of law, such as the system in the United States. Fundamental law in the United States takes the form of a written constitution. Statutes are enacted by legislatures, doctrine is established by judicial decisions, and rules are created by executive agencies, but each must be measured against the provisions of the national Constitution. This commitment to constitutionalism provides the basis of government at both the national and state levels. The heart of the U.S. concept of constitutionalism is the principle that a government with limited power must act in accordance with the rule of law.

This book was written with the following objectives in mind:

1. To explore some general characteristics of constitutionalism.
2. To convey a specific history of constitutionalism as it has developed in the United States over the past two centuries.
3. To introduce some of the more significant questions that have arisen during the U.S. constitutional experience. The meaning of the Constitution's language is not always self-evident; this book is intended to represent the different ways particular provisions of the Constitution have been interpreted. In addition, an attempt has been made to introduce those concepts that are essential to understanding the interpretative conclusions that have been drawn in the past.
4. To generate a continuing interest in U.S. constitutional law,

3

especially among younger readers. An effort has been made to
emphasize how the Constitution, particularly the provisions
contained in the Bill of Rights, applies to everyday life. It is hoped
that this book will foster an appreciation of U.S. constitutional
heritage as the country begins its third century under the
document's terms.

This chapter focuses on the origins of U.S. constitutionalism, the U.S.
experience under the Articles of Confederation, the writing of the current
Constitution, the adoption of the Bill of Rights, and the matter of judicial
review.

The concept of constitutionalism involves several components. One, of
course, is legal. A constitution is the fundamental law of a political system;
it is superior to all other law. The structural component addresses the
organizational configuration of government. Constitutionalism also extends
to the institutional restraints on political and governmental power. This
component is designed to keep government from violating the rights of
individual citizens, and it is the primary component examined in this book.

The theoretical bases of constitutionalism have roots with the ancient
Greeks and Romans. The notion that government must be guided by a rule
of law was advanced by Plato. Aristotle subsequently developed further the
fundamental character of constitutions and distinguished them from the
more transitory and subordinate policies a political system might adopt
through the actions of governmental officials. Aristotle also spoke of
constitutions that provide "mixed" powers, which is something like the
concept we refer to as separation of powers. The Romans advanced constitutional theory in two ways. They gave the idea of government by law a
written and codified foundation, and, unlike the Greeks, the Romans recognized something akin to the natural law concept of equality. The second
development, coupled with the tenets of Judeo-Christian faith, substantially
elevated the standing of human rights.

U.S. constitutionalism had its origin in these ideas. It was also profoundly
influenced by the British experience. While the British do not have a written
constitution as such, the Magna Carta of 1215 unmistakably provided much
the same function, as it sought to make sovereign power subject to a higher
law. The desire to put a constitution in writing was distinctively American,
dating to such documents as the Mayflower Compact. By the time of the
American Revolution, the colonists believed strongly in having a written
constitution. As for the document's content, the colonists were quite familiar
with the work of such people as John Locke. Locke and other natural rights
theorists sharply focused the view that certain everlasting principles of

human rights and justice transcend any law established by humankind, a distinction critically important to the thinking of those who fashioned the U.S. Constitution. Locke believed in democratic processes where popular consent served as the basis of government. Locke saw government as something to be controlled by legal means and advocated integrating protections of individual rights into the written charter of government. This view was ultimately pursued when the First Congress adopted a Bill of Rights and sent it to the states for ratification.

Articles of Confederation

One of the first collective actions of the American colonists was to convene the First Continental Congress in 1774. The delegates were called together to fashion a statement of complaints against the British throne. Soon thereafter, the American Revolution began. It then became necessary for the colonists to form their own government. Up to this time, Britain had taken care of national defense and international relations on behalf of the colonists. When independence from Britain was declared, an action taken at the direction of the Second Continental Congress, a governmental vacuum was created at the national level. The Continental Congress generally acted as the national or central government, but had no formal authority to do so. It was out of the need to establish a national government that the first U.S. constitution, the Articles of Confederation, was written.

The Articles governed the fledgling nation from 1781 until 1789, when they were superseded by the new federal Constitution. The drafting of the Articles by the Second Continental Congress began in June of 1776. The battles at Lexington and Concord in early 1776 had made it clear that a full war of independence was inevitable, and a formal government for the colonies was needed, if only for military purposes. The Second Continental Congress rejected John Dickenson's first draft because it created too strong a central government. A second draft was approved by Congress in November of 1777, but the required ratification by all the states was not completed until Maryland's approval in March of 1781. During the interim, a central government created under the terms of the yet unratified proposal functioned as the national government.

Congressional debate over the proposed Articles had revolved around what kind of union was best for the 13 colonies. Although there was a wide spectrum of opinion, ranging from a monarchy to almost full state sovereignty, the delegates essentially divided into two groups. The first were the Federalists, who wanted a weak central government. (This group should not be confused with the Federalists of a decade later, who took the opposite position.) This group was led in the Second Continental Congress by Richard Henry Lee and George Mason. Thomas Jefferson, Patrick Henry, and Thomas Paine were sympathetic to the strong state/weak central government position as well, but they were not present at the Congress. The Nationalists (who later became known as Federalists) sought a strong central government; they were led by John Dickenson and subsequently James Wilson. The Nationalists included such figures as John Adams, John Jay, James Madison, Gouverneur Morris, John Rutledge, and George Washington. A combination of hatred for the tyranny of the British government, very strong feelings for individual state sovereignty, general distrust of politicians and rulers, and the self-interest of groups and regions won the day for the Federalists.

In its 13 articles, the final version of the Articles of Confederation laid out a close confederation of sovereign states over which the central government had only limited powers. Since provisions were made only for a weak executive and no judiciary, what powers the central government had were essentially vested in the Congress. Each state, represented by two to seven persons elected and compensated by the state legislatures, had one vote in Congress. Any important issue required the consent of nine states, and any amendment to the Articles had to be unanimously approved. When Congress was not in session, the daily business of the United States was to be conducted by a Committee of the States. The committee was composed of one representative from each state, with one of the thirteen members elected committee president for a one-year term. The Articles also permitted the establishment of any necessary congressional committees. The government was soon run by the four committees regulating finance, the army, the navy, and foreign affairs.

The enumerated powers of Congress included determining each state's share of the confederation's common expenses, although Congress had no power to collect taxes or compel individual states to do so. Congress was given procedural and moral authority to settle disputes between individual states, but it had no authority to enforce compliance with the settlements. Congress also had the exclusive power to declare war and peace, conduct foreign relations (except for commercial treaties that limited the rights of individual states to impose tariffs and embargoes), regulate currency and measures, run the postal service, appoint the highest officers in the military, and set limits on the sizes of the armies and navies of the individual states.

The structural arrangement under the Articles was fatally flawed from the outset. The states were so dominant that the central government was unable to protect the collective interests of the confederation against states acting in their own interests. The states preferred to act as independent entities, often with destructive consequences to other states. The insufficient strength of the central government under the Articles also contributed to substantial economic and political instability and, ultimately, to the need to abandon the Articles altogether. Two problems were particularly critical. First, the central government was virtually bankrupt. The only significant financial obligation faced by the national government during this period was the American Revolution, but it was unable to manage even that. A very small proportion of tax assessments against the states was actually collected, and it was necessary to obtain loans from private and foreign sources to sustain the war effort. By the end of the war, Congress could not even meet the interest obligations on the loans.

Second, economic conditions were generally terrible. Much of the population as well as the government was close to insolvency. Conditions were especially desperate for small farmers. Mortgages were held on their farms, and farmers were frequently unable to pay off their indebtedness. This problem was compounded because, under the terms of the Articles, states could issue their own money. As a result, the indebted farmers gained control of several state legislatures and adopted laws authorizing the printing of money. Creditors, however, often refused to accept this money. Such refusal was technically illegal, but it led to the loss of value for state-printed currency. While some retailers accepted the money, prices became highly inflated. Clearly, money printed by the states did not solve the farmers' problems. The indebtedness of landholders led to different difficulties in states where creditor interests controlled the state legislative process. In these states, the law was used to facilitate foreclosures. Armed conflicts were not uncommon; indeed, the famed Shays' Rebellion grew out of such a situation. Conflicts like those involving Daniel Shays also reflected the central government's inability to come to the assistance of states needing to maintain local order. Massachusetts had unsuccessfully sought federal aid before resorting to a state militia to handle the uprisings. Incidents like Shays's Rebellion fueled debate about the adequacy of the Articles.

The Second Constitution

The defects of the Articles had been apparent to people such as Alexander Hamilton and George Washington since before the end of the revolutionary war. In 1786, a serious attempt was made to convene delegates from all the states at a meeting in Annapolis, Maryland. The meeting was intended to address the shortcomings of the Articles, but was largely unsuccessful because only five states sent delegates. The delegates in attendance, however, did urge Congress to initiate efforts to convene another constitutional convention. Support for such a convention grew as economic and political problems worsened. Congress eventually recognized the need to reconsider the form of government, and it called for a constitutional convention to take place in Philadelphia in the spring of 1787.

The Philadelphia convention started slowly, and proceedings had to be delayed nearly a month for the lack of a quorum. Delegates from 12 states eventually arrived and work commenced. As a group, the delegates were not a representative sample of the general population. All were white males, of course, and many were quite wealthy. They were also men of some distinction, as many had been the leading political figures since before independence. A large number had been delegates to one or both of the first two Continental Congresses. The most famous delegate was George Washington, who had been the military leader during the American Revolution. Washington, albeit reluctantly, presided over the convention. Other very notable convention participants included Alexander Hamilton and Benjamin Franklin, but James Madison was probably the most influential in producing the constitutional proposal submitted to the states.

The delegates were essentially divided into two groups: those who favored a substantially stronger central government and those who favored making the central government only marginally stronger. This was a serious difference, but a difference of degree. The delegates all agreed that the Articles were irreparably defective and that major changes were in order. However, this view was not necessarily consistent with the expectation of the state legislatures that sent the delegates to Philadelphia. As a result, the adoption of a secrecy rule for the convention was key to the deliberation and to recommendation of a wholly new constitution. The proceedings were closed to the public, and the delegates were not allowed, by virtue of their own rule, to discuss the progress of the convention with nondelegates. Many scholars believe the deliberations that produced the new constitution were sufficiently delicate that public exposure would have seriously affected the content of the document. Without the secrecy rule, the convention might have arrived at a substantially different result. Great insight into the convention's proceedings has been gained from James Madison's comprehensive logs and other notes.

The delegates also agreed that a basic function of government was to protect certain natural rights. Thomas Jefferson had labeled rights such as life, liberty, and the pursuit of happiness as "unalienable" in the Declaration of Independence. It was of paramount importance to convention delegates that a government be able to effectively protect such rights. The delegates were trying to achieve a delicate balance by establishing a government powerful enough to be effective but not oppressive, and they seized upon several commonly shared principles to further their pursuit. One was the principle of republicanism, which describes a form of government in which the people elect representatives to act on their behalf. Republicanism gives the people the capacity to hold public officials accountable, because unresponsive or otherwise poorly performing officials can be removed at the next election. Firsthand experience (most local government officials of the time were elected) had taught the delegates that this simple mechanism was effective, and they sought to apply the concept on a larger, national scale.

The delegates also turned to the Baron de Montesquieu's concept of separation of power. With separation of power, the authority of government is divided among several branches to prevent potentially troublesome concentration of control. The distribution of powers embodied in the Constitution distinguishes functionally between the people and the government and among legislative, executive, and judicial tasks. While the Constitution creates three separate branches, it assigns them overlapping responsibilities that make them interdependent. This interdependence makes the checks and balances system operative. The Congress is assigned the responsibility for passing laws, but those laws must be implemented by the executive. Interpretation of what the laws mean falls to the judiciary. The president controls the executive branch, but the laws to be executed and the funding for implementation come from the Congress. The system of checks and balances simultaneously softens and augments separation of powers. The softening is due to the fact that checks and balances require the concurrence of one branch in the functions primarily assigned to another branch. The presidential veto, for example, makes the president a participant in the legislative process. Separation of power is augmented because checks and balances specify the controls each part of government has over the other parts. Separation of power, in concert with checks and balances, is designed to limit improper exercise of governmental authority by dispersing control to several locations. As a result, governmental power is restricted and decentralized, and no branch can dominate the processes of government for a protracted period. A drawback is that separation of power may create fragmentation or disunity for government if sufficient interbranch conflict exists.

The issue that divided the Constitutional Convention was the extent to which the central government needed to be strengthened. The Nationalists, who had become known as the Federalists, had numerical advantage, and their set of proposals, the Virginia Plan, essentially became the basis of the constitution recommended by the convention. (A counterproposal, called the New Jersey Plan, was advanced by the Anti-Federalists.) Virginia Plan provisions of the most consequence were those calling for a single chief executive, establishment of a federal judiciary, and substantial additions to the powers of the Congress. An effective taxation power, capacity to regulate interstate commerce, and the notion of federal supremacy topped the list of legislative changes. The Federalists subsequently compromised with the small states on the matter of legislative representation. The Virginia Plan had proposed a two-chamber legislative branch with representation in both chambers based on population, but the proposal that emerged from the convention provided for one chamber to have representation by state regardless of population.

The constitution presented to the states for ratification also embraced the concept of federalism. Federalism divides authority between a central government and constituent units, with each level governing the same people and the same territory. The U.S. system under the Articles of Confederation had been a federation, but what came out of the convention had not been seen in previous federations. The central government was much stronger, and the document contained language such as the supremacy clause of Article VI that might allow the central government to become even stronger relative to the states as time passed. Federations historically have not survived for long periods but have tended to disintegrate or pull apart under stress. The federation established by the U.S. Constitution has mechanisms designed to pull in the opposite direction: inward.

The delegates worked through the summer of 1787, finishing in September. While the vote to send the proposal to the states was not unanimous, the dissenting delegates did agree that the proposed constitution was sound. In setting the ground rules for ratification, the delegates were sufficiently satisfied with the proposed constitution that they rejected a suggestion for a subsequent convention to make further revisions. The proposal sent to the states was the "last and best" version, so to speak. The delegates also required that ratification be considered at special state conventions rather than by state legislatures, because they believed that elected representatives to a special convention would be more receptive to the strengthened central government than would members of state legislatures. The delegates virtually assured ratification by deciding that the new proposal would take effect when approved by 9 rather than all of the 13 states.

Even though the convention did its best to ensure ratification, substantial opposition existed in many states. Most of it focused on the absence of a bill of rights, though some opposed the proposal for economic reasons as well. For example, in states where political power was held by interests that supported liberal insolvency laws and state currencies, there were serious misgivings about placing power over these matters with the national government. These obstacles were eventually overcome, and the document was ratified by all 13 states. Particularly important to ratification in New York were the arguments advanced in the *Federalist Papers,* a series of essays written by Alexander Hamilton, James Madison, and John Jay that represent Federalist thinking on the proposed constitution. Ratification in some states was secured on condition that a bill of rights would be taken up by the first Congress.

The Bill of Rights

The difficulty encountered by the delegates at the Constitutional Convention was structuring effective government while at the same time protecting individual rights. Balancing these two interests requires that the rights of individuals in a democratic society be viewed in other than absolute terms. Individuals must be subject to a degree of regulation for the good of the social order, even if some regulations impinge on personal freedom. On the other hand, the exercise of governmental authority must be limited to the least possible interference with the enjoyment of rights. The principal problem is achieving the proper balance between effective governmental power and individual rights. The idea of individual rights is reasonable only in a political system where governance occurs under law. While one might recognize "natural rights" possessed by all individuals in the abstract, such rights are not automatically held by all individuals in reality. Thus, a primary function of government is protecting individual rights, yet the government itself must be limited so that it does not become the very medium through which rights are threatened.

The Federalists had the votes to prevail on most of the questions that arose at the Constitutional Convention. This was certainly true with respect to the most critical issue, a stronger central government. The Federalists also prevailed on the question of whether or not to formally enumerate individual rights that would be protected from governmental interference. The Federalists opposed inclusion of a bill of rights, and, indeed, the Constitution was ratified by the states without such an enumeration. Some argue the Federalists simply were not interested in protecting individual rights, but this position is generally regarded as overly harsh and inaccurate. No bill of rights emerged from the Constitutional Convention for several reasons.

First, one must keep in mind the reason the convention was called: The central government under the Articles was ineffective. The Federalists did not want the issue of individual rights deflecting them from establishing a central government with enough authority to govern. Second, and more important, the Federalists believed that the federal government created under the Constitution was one of limited delegated powers. As such, the government could not exercise power beyond what was formally conveyed by the document. The government was not, for example, empowered to enact any law that abridged free speech or religious freedom. The mechanism of separation of powers was utilized by the framers to protect both the public good and individual rights from the arbitrary exercise of governmental power. Third, many Federalists viewed a bill of rights as superfluous and possibly counterproductive. Extensive protection of individual rights was already in place at the state level. The existence of state bills of rights made a parallel approach at the federal level redundant. Some Federalists, including Alexander Hamilton, believed that enumerating rights might suggest that any list of such rights could, or later would, be considered fixed or final. Hamilton believed such an interpretation to be not only erroneous, but also dangerous in that rights not specifically listed might be violated by government. Hamilton argued that social diversity and watchfulness were the ultimate guarantees of personal rights. Finally, the Constitution did contain several specific provisions with a direct bearing on individual rights. Examples include the Article I, Section 9 language on *habeas corpus* and the prohibitions on bills of attainder—legislative acts that declare guilt and impose punishment—and *ex post facto* laws, which define certain conduct to be criminal after the fact, or retroactively. The unamended Constitution also requires juries in treason trials (Article III), protects the privileges and immunities of citizenship (Article IV), and prohibits religious tests as a condition for holding federal office (Article VI).

It was during the ratification process that absence of a bill of rights emerged as a major problem. Indeed, ratification in several of the larger states was achieved only through assurance that a bill of rights would be immediately added to the Constitution. Upon becoming president, George Washington directed the first Congress to promptly attend to the issue. The Congress, however, was preoccupied with other governance questions; James Madison finally took the initiative and guided a set of proposals to adoption. Though Madison had originally shared Hamilton's view that a bill of rights was not necessary, he was moved by the tremendous expression of popular sentiment. He was also a very pragmatic politician who wanted to preserve the Constitution as it emerged from the Federalist-controlled convention. Holding another convention to consider the bill of rights question was a strategy of the Anti-Federalists, and Madison feared such a convention would make more substantial revisions in the document.

Madison submitted a number of proposals to Congress that substantially resembled the bill of rights adopted in Virginia. He proposed that the changes be integrated into the body of Article I, since most were directed at the legislative branch. This approach was rejected by the House, which preferred to append each limitation to the document as a separate amendment. It was argued that the latter approach would underscore each independent phrase. Twelve House proposals were ultimately approved by the Senate and submitted to the states. Sufficient support existed to ratify 10 of these proposed amendments, and they became effective in December 1791. The First Amendment, which was designed to cover belief and expression, specifically protects the freedoms of speech, press, assembly, and religion. The Second and Third Amendments deal with the right to bear arms and the quartering of troops in private homes, respectively. Both amendments emerged from the unique post–revolutionary war context and have limited current impact, notwithstanding reference to the Second Amendment by opponents of gun control. Amendments Four through Eight focus on rights of those accused of criminal conduct, as well as touching on other areas. In addition to the self-incrimination, double jeopardy, and grand jury provisions, the Fifth Amendment protects property owners from the use of the eminent domain power without "just compensation." The Ninth Amendment provides that rights not otherwise itemized are retained for the people; it was intended to preserve any natural rights not specifically enumerated. The Tenth Amendment states, "The powers not delegated to the United States by the Constitution, nor prohibited by it to the States, are reserved to the States respectively, or to the people." The amendment was included largely to alleviate concerns of the Anti-Federalists by reiterating division of power between the national and state levels.

Judicial Review

The Declaration of Independence first asserted the primacy of individual rights when it made reference to people's natural rights—those rights that are "unalienable." The use of a written constitution creating a federal government of limited power was heavily driven by the concern for securing such rights. The Bill of Rights was added to the Constitution because most politicians of the time believed that explicit enumeration in the document itself made these rights more secure. But rights may not be fully secured by enumeration alone. The protections are not self-executing, nor is their meaning always clear. A vigilant and independent judiciary is needed to authoritatively interpret the words and to act as guardian of the integrity of the Constitution. The power of judicial review was claimed by Supreme Court Chief Justice John Marshall to better equip the judiciary to fulfill this function.

Judicial review varies depending on whose actions are under review. One situation involves review of administrative actions, which is both common and relatively limited in policy impact. Two more significant types of review were cultivated by Chief Justice Marshall in the early 1800s. The first involves the Supreme Court's role as umpire of the federal-state relationship. This kind of review allows the courts of the national government to review actions of the constituent states and invalidate those that collide with national authority or interfere with the authority of other states. The power to perform this kind of review can be derived from the supremacy clause of Article VI of the U.S. Constitution and from language of the Judiciary Act of 1789.

The remaining power involves judicial capacity to review actions of the other branches and carries the potential of placing the courts in a position of policy dominance. The argument for this function is that the integrity of the Constitution must be safeguarded from actions that conflict with it. This kind of judicial review is not mentioned in the Constitution, although it was debated at length by the framers. Judicial review authorizes courts to examine governmental actions, including those of the legislative and executive branches, and declare those actions unconstitutional if necessary. On the other hand, judicial review may ultimately uphold legislative or executive actions because most judges subscribe to the principle of judicial self-restraint. (More is said about judicial activism and self-restraint below.)

If judicial review is a generally recognized means for checking improper use of governmental power, why was it not expressly conveyed to the judiciary in the Constitution? Judicial review was debated at the Constitutional Convention, and several diverse proposals were advanced. One, offered by James Wilson and James Madison, would have created a council composed of the president and several judges with the power to veto legislation. These proposals, none of which provided for judicial review in its current form, were all defeated. This should not be interpreted as a repudiation of judicial review itself, however. On the contrary, a persuasive case can be made that most delegates viewed judicial review as useful, at least to some extent. Many felt such limited review was provided for in the Constitution. A sizeable number of the delegates would have supported explicit constitutional language giving the Supreme Court the power to invalidate any act of Congress that contradicted specific provisions of the Constitution.

It is also apparent that the Supreme Court assumed it could rule on the constitutionality of congressional acts virtually from the outset. The carriage tax case of *Hylton v. United States* (3 Dallas 171: 1976), for example, contained a clear challenge to the validity of a congressional enactment, and the Court took the case on those terms, though it found the tax to be constitutional. It was with the case of *Marbury v. Madison* (1 Cranch 137: 1803) that Chief Justice Marshall directly asserted that the Supreme Court is the ultimate authority for interpreting the Constitution. It was in *Marbury* that the Court first nullified a congressional act. *Marbury v. Madison* posed the question of whether James Madison, Thomas Jefferson's secretary of state, could refuse to deliver a judicial commission to a person who had already been confirmed by the Senate. William Marbury, the judge designate, sought to compel delivery of his commission by asking the Court to issue a writ of mandamus—an order from a court directing someone, usually a public official, to perform a specified act. The authority to issue such writs was conveyed to the Supreme Court by the Judiciary Act of 1789. The Court, however, ruled that the provision of the act dealing with mandamus was unconstitutional because it essentially amended constitutional language in its attempt to define the Court's original jurisdiction by statute.

The two most significant holdings in *Marbury* were the establishment of the Constitution's supremacy over statutory law and the definition of the Court's fundamental role in safeguarding that supremacy. Chief Justice Marshall cast the first issue in categorical terms. The Constitution is "either a superior paramount law, unchangeable by ordinary means," or it is "on a level with ordinary legislative acts" and alterable when the legislature "shall please to alter it." To Marshall, the answer was obvious. If the Constitution is supreme, then a legislative act "contrary to the Constitution is not law." Otherwise, the Constitution is an "absurd attempt" to limit power. The second proposition focused on judicial review; Marshall said that it is "emphatically the province and duty of the judicial department" to "say what the law is." Resolving a situation where a law "be in opposition to the constitution . . . is the essence of judicial duty." If the Constitution is superior to legislative acts, then the Constitution rather than statutes "must govern the case to which they both apply." Marshall took judicial review beyond explicit constitutional mandate. *Marbury* added the dimension of review for the coordinate branches to the power of judicial review that already existed. The kind of judicial review established by the decision in *Marbury* evolved to allow the courts to provide a critical check on governmental power and to function as an effective guardian of the Constitution. Consequently, the Supreme Court became a more active and vigilant guardian of individual rights as well.

Appellate judges have divergent views on when and how to exercise their authority. This is especially true when judicial review is involved. Two role orientations, judicial self-restraint and judicial activism, are useful in examining the behavior of Supreme Court justices. Judicial self-restraint is the self-imposed limitation used by judges who believe this approach is most compatible with democratic principles. Judges who subscribe to self-restraint will go to great lengths in deferring to the policy decisions of the elective branches. Such judges seek to limit their role to enforcing the norms established by those accountable to the electorate. Judicial self-restraint advocates that only where constitutional violations are flagrant should courts nullify actions of the elective branches.

The role orientation of judicial self-restraint directs judges to defer to the policy judgments of those in the elected branches of government. Judges who adhere to self-restraint tend toward a more restrictive definition of justiciability and adhere more strictly to judicial precedent. Self-restraint does not necessarily correspond to a conservative policy orientation, however. Deferring to legislative establishment of a minimum wage or to an aggressive pursuit of voting rights, for example, might yield a liberal policy result. According to judicial self-restraint, the exercise of judicial power should be limited because the legislative and executive branches are the appropriate sources of major policy initiatives, as both branches can be held politically accountable by the voters. A more aggressive or active role is considered inappropriate for several reasons. First, courts generally are not effectively accountable to the public. This is especially true of federal judges, who are appointed and enjoy life tenure. Second, courts seldom win confrontations with the other branches. Indeed, the courts tend to be vulnerable to reprisals aimed at limiting their power; judicial independence therefore may be threatened by activist and provocative decisions. Finally, self-restraintists argue that the courts are not a well-suited forum for decision making on broad and complex social questions.

Judicial activists, on the other hand, see the appellate courts as playing a substantial and affirmative policy role. Judicial activism prompts judges to entertain new policies, even those that would depart from adherence to established legal rules and precedents. Judicial activism can manifest itself in a number of ways, but most important is a court's adoption of its own policy preferences over those of the legislative or executive branches, which is exactly what occurs when a court declares a governmental action unconstitutional. Judicial activism may also extend legal rules to establish specific requirements for governmental action. While both judicial activists and self-restraintists acknowledge that a certain degree of policymaking is inevitable as a result of deciding legal questions, they differ on how aggressively and how extensively judges should pursue policymaking opportunities. Judicial activism is sometimes described as legislation by judges to achieve policy outcomes compatible with their own priorities. A judicial activist will find more issues appropriate for judicial response than a judge who subscribes to self-restraint. U.S. judges have engaged in judicial activism from the outset of U.S. history. The most obvious early example is Chief Justice John Marshall's establishment of the power of judicial review in *Marbury v.*

Madison. Activism need not coincide with a liberal policy orientation. Classic examples of judicial activism can be found in the 1930s, when the Hughes Court struck down numerous pieces of New Deal legislation in the interest of preserving laissez-faire economic doctrine. The judicial activist sees the Court as appropriately and legitimately asserting itself in the policymaking process even if its policy objectives differ from those of the legislative and executive branches.

Nationalizing the Bill of Rights

The ratification of the Bill of Rights and the assertion of judicial review by the Supreme Court in *Marbury* did not stimulate great amounts of activity for the courts. It was as though the Federalists had been right and the Bill of Rights had been unnecessary. Even the flagrant excesses of the Alien and Sedition Acts failed to find their way to the courts. History clearly records that the issues of federalism, commerce, power, and the protection of private property interests were of much higher priority until the Supreme Court extended the free speech protection to the states in 1925. Recourse to the Bill of Rights was not encouraged largely because of the widespread perception that states rather than the federal government were the principal protectors of individual rights. It was also true that actions of the states in the exercise of police power were a greater threat to individual liberties than anything coming from the federal government.

Another common view was that the federal Bill of Rights did not apply to the states at all. This position was officially adopted by the Supreme Court in the case of *Barron v. Baltimore* (7 Peters 247: 1833). John Barron owned a wharf that was rendered useless by actions of the city of Baltimore. To accomplish such public improvements as street paving, the city diverted streams, which caused sand and gravel to be deposited around Barron's wharf and thus prevented ships from docking. After unsuccessfully seeking compensation within the state courts, Barron turned to the Fifth Amendment of the federal Constitution for relief. He argued that Baltimore's action violated the Fifth Amendment provision that prohibits the "taking" of property without "just compensation." He claimed this provision ought to be interpreted as a restraint not only on the federal government but on the states as well. In a unanimous decision, the Court refused to apply the amendment to the states.

The opinion of the Court was delivered by Chief Justice Marshall. He referred to the question posed by the case as one of "great importance, but not of much difficulty." The Constitution, he said, was "ordained and established by the people of the United States for themselves, for their own government, and not for the government of the individual states." Each state, in turn, established its own constitution, with provisions restricting that particular government "as its judgment dictated." When the federal Constitution was created, powers were conferred on the federal government to be exercised "by itself," and the limitations on power were, "naturally, . . . necessarily applicable to the government created by the instrument." These were limitations on power granted by the instrument, not a "distinct government, framed by different persons and for different purposes." According to the decision in this case, none of the Bill of Rights provisions limit actions by state governments.

During this period, the Court seldom encountered individual rights issues. The few opportunities that did present themselves were not utilized to advance Constitution-based protections. Consider the Court's construction of the privileges and immunities clause of Article IV. The clause, available from the outset of U.S. constitutional history, was sufficiently vague to permit substantial shaping by the Court. One interpretation open to the Court and suggested by many Federalists of Marshall's time was cast around natural law, or fundamental rights. Under such an interpretation, the Court could have established national and potentially extensive standards to be applied to all the states over and above the rights protections that existed under state law.

The Court did not take that course, but instead handled the matter of citizenship and the privileges and immunities that flow from citizenship in a very narrow way. An example is the destructive decision in *Dred Scott v. Sandford* (19 Howard 393: 1857). In this case, the privileges and immunities clause was considered in the context of the volatile slavery issue, and the result was a very restrictive interpretation. Dred Scott, a slave from Missouri, had been taken to Louisiana Territory, a "free" area under provisions of the Missouri Compromise of 1820. When Scott returned to Missouri he sought to retain his free status. After failing to find relief in state courts, Scott tried the federal court. The Supreme Court held that Scott was not a citizen because of his race and, as a result, could not bring suit in a federal court. Aside from the rationale based on race, Chief Justice Roger Taney also held that the privileges and immunities clause could not help Scott. No state (or territory) could confer citizenship that would entitle a person to the privileges and immunities of a citizen of other states. To do so would have the effect of also conferring federal citizenship, something no state could do under Taney's dual citizenship doctrine. Thus, Scott (and all other blacks) could obtain no protection from the clause. Taney also characterized the nature of the protection afforded nonblacks, which was highly limited as well.

In short, protection of individual rights as a function of the federal Constitution progressed little prior to the Civil War despite formal adoption of the Bill of Rights and the establishment of judicial review. The *Barron* decision was in force until ratification of the Fourteenth Amendment in 1868. The Fourteenth Amendment created the opportunity to reopen the question of whether the federal Bill of Rights applies to the states (hereafter referred to as the incorporation question), because the language of the amendment was clearly directed to the states.

Several schools of thought have developed around how to resolve the incorporation question. The most sweeping recommendation was to apply all Bill of Rights provisions to the states through the due process clause of the Fourteenth Amendment. This clause prohibits a state from denying liberty without due process. Those advocating total incorporation viewed the term *liberty* as an all-inclusive shorthand for each of the rights enumerated in the Bill of Rights. This approach was vigorously advocated by Justice John Marshall Harlan and Justice Hugo L. Black, but this view has never been shared by a majority of any Supreme Court. A second opinion rejected any structural linkage of due process to the Bill of Rights and held simply that the due process clause requires states to provide fundamental fairness. Due process is assessed under this standard by criteria of "immutable principles of justice" or, as suggested by Justice Benjamin N. Cardozo in *Palko v. Connecticut* (302 U.S. 319: 1937), elements "implicit in the concept of ordered liberty." Application of such standards would occur on a case-by-case basis.

The third opinion, a hybrid of the first two, is known as selective incorporation. The selective approach resembles the fundamental fairness position in that it does not view as identical those rights contained in the Bill of Rights and those rights fundamental to fairness. Unlike the fundamental fairness approach, however, the selective view holds that rights expressly contained in the Bill of Rights, if judged fundamental, are incorporated through the Fourteenth Amendment and are applicable at the state level regardless of the circumstances of a particular case. If the self-incrimination provision of the Fifth Amendment were determined to be fundamental, for example, it would apply in full to any state case bringing whatever substantive standards it preferred into federal courts. The selective approach created an "honor roll" of Bill of Rights provisions, some viewed as fundamental and wholly incorporated and others as less important and not worthy of incorporation.

Incorporation focuses on the degree to which Bill of Rights guarantees apply to the states. The question assumed critically important dimensions soon after ratification of the Fourteenth Amendment in 1868, but the matter remained unresolved for several decades. In early decisions such as *Hurtado v. California* (110 U.S. 516: 1884), the Court refused to extend federal protections to the states. The Supreme Court eventually settled on the selective incorporation approach, starting with recognition of the free speech clause of the First Amendment in *Gitlow v. New York* (268 U.S. 652: 1925). This ultimately allowed the Supreme Court, especially the Warren Court, to apply most of the constitutional safeguards to the states. The Warren Court added many provisions to the list developed under the preceding fundamental fairness approach. The only Bill of Rights provisions that have not been incorporated are the grand jury requirement of the Fifth Amendment, the civil jury trial provision of the Seventh Amendment, and the excessive bail and fine clause of the Eighth Amendment. The incorporation doctrine is a central element in current U.S. rights policy; the process of incorporation has been especially important where state law did not provide protection of constitutional rights. Equally important, the doctrine made the U.S. Supreme Court the source of authoritative rules on rights policy. This had the effect of creating uniform rights policy across the states, thus providing for the "nationalization" of individual rights.

Parens Patriae

The final concept for this chapter, *parens patriae,* is not critical to understanding U.S. constitutional law generally, but it is helpful in discussing the state's relationship to minors. *Parens patriae* literally translates from the Latin as "parent of the country." The concept originated in medieval Britain and referred to the obligations of feudal overlords and, later, the monarch toward those with special needs, such as children or the handicapped. From a more current vantage point, the idea is that the government has a special role in caring for those not fully able to care for themselves.

The doctrine of *parens patriae* originally applied only to the physically disabled, the mentally incompetent, and minors who did not receive proper care at home. The philosophy was expanded by nineteenth-century reformers to reach juveniles who engaged in criminal conduct, in the belief that such conduct was the product of inappropriate care and treatment in the home. This view, in turn, provided the justification for government intervention in an attempt to "save" the minor from further delinquent conduct. *Parens patriae* evolved into the basis for legal codes that distinguished minors from adults and the foundation for a separate juvenile court. The reference to juvenile criminal conduct as delinquent was itself an outgrowth of the idea that minors, certainly those below the age of 15, were not fully responsible for criminal behavior. Commission of a crime involves more than merely an action. It also requires a criminal intent, or *mens rea* ("guilty mind"). Immature youth, it was argued, cannot possess such intent and thus ought not to be held accountable in the same way as an adult. Furthermore, consistent with this view, juveniles ought not to be punished for their behavior. Rather, the government should provide remedial treatment in an effort to stem the misbehavior.

Most states still subscribe to the *parens patriae* philosophy, although it has come under criticism in recent years. Chapter 3 discusses the juvenile justice system in more detail; suffice it to say here that *parens patriae* was responsible for the delinquency process looking more like a civil than a criminal process. Supreme Court decisions beginning in the mid-1960s have extended many of the constitutional protections afforded adults to the juvenile justice process, thereby making juvenile proceedings more like adult criminal proceedings. Nevertheless, the Supreme Court continues to adhere to *parens patriae*. In *Schall v. Martin* (467 U.S. 253: 1984), for example, the Court upheld a state law authorizing preventive detention for juveniles. In doing so, the Court made it clear that the state had a substantial interest in protecting the juvenile, already facing charges, from aggravating his or her situation by engaging in further criminal behavior.

Parens patriae faces greater opposition in other quarters, however. As some acts of delinquency have become more vicious, and as larger amounts of assaultive juvenile behavior have come from repeat offenders, states have been urged to take stronger, more punitive measures with juveniles. One way of separating repeat and violent offenders is to waive jurisdiction to adult courts. This makes it possible for some juveniles to face substantial prison sentences for their conduct while at the same time permitting the state to retain the *parens patriae* approach. How long *parens patriae* remains as a controlling influence on policy relating to juveniles is a judgment of legislatures and other policymakers at the state level. The doctrine's effect is substantial, however, because it has influenced U.S. thinking for almost a century. As a result, *parens patriae* underlies some of the discussion in succeeding chapters.

REFERENCES

Bowen, Catherine Drinker, *Miracle at Philadelphia* (Boston: Atlantic–Little Brown, 1966).

Chandler, Ralph C., Richard A. Enslen, and Peter G. Renstrom, *Constitutional Law Dictionary, Volume I: Individual Rights* (Santa Barbara, CA: ABC-CLIO, 1985).

Madison, James, Alexander Hamilton, and John Jay, *The Federalist Papers* (New York: Penguin, 1987).

Peltason, J. W., *Understanding the Constitution,* 12th edition (San Diego, CA: Harcourt Brace Jovanovich, 1991).

Rossiter, Clinton, *1787: The Grand Convention* (New York: Macmillan, 1966).

Wills, Garry, *Explaining America: The Federalist* (Garden City, NY: Doubleday, 1981).

Constitutional Law
and the Courts

The defining constitutional decisions that come from the United States Supreme Court are hard to read. The opinions are generally complex, and they focus on abstract legal questions. What is often blurred is that these decisions are based on real life contests that take the form of law cases. Each case that has led to a constitutional pronouncement was commenced in a court at least two levels below the Supreme Court. Full understanding of constitutional law requires familiarity with such things as the organizational structure of the U.S. court system and the decisional process used by the Supreme Court. It is also imperative to know how the law case serves as the medium through which landmark decisions may emerge. Succeeding chapters develop the substance of Supreme Court decisions as they define provisions of the Bill of Rights. This chapter is devoted to a discussion of what occurs before the Supreme Court is positioned to decide cases and the processes by which those decisions are made.

U.S. courts process literally millions of cases each year, only a handful of which will reach an appellate court, much less the U.S. Supreme Court. These cases begin in either federal or state trial courts, although very few of them result in actual trials. Only about 10 percent of the criminal cases in this country receive jury trials. The remaining 90 percent are concluded by plea agreements. The proportion of civil cases that are actually tried is even smaller, in the area of 2 to 3 percent. Virtually none of these settled cases ever goes beyond the court where the case was filed. It is from the small minority of cases that are tried that almost all appeals are initiated, and only a small fraction of these cases contain an issue that may involve the Constitution. So, it is important to recognize from the outset that a case that presents the Supreme Court with an opportunity to address a constitutional question is rare. But such cases do exist, and the following discussion tells how they progress through the judicial system.

Jurisdiction and Organizational Structure

One of the fundamental principles embedded in the U.S. Constitution is federalism, which divides political authority between national and state levels of government. Federalism was the main method used by the constitutional framers to decentralize control. One structural manifestation of U.S. federalism is the dual court system, where power is divided between federal and state courts. These judicial systems are quite separate—each has its own courts to discharge the trial and appellate functions. Once a case begins in either the state or the federal system, it virtually always stays in that system. More than 99 percent of cases are processed in state courts. Most criminal prosecutions, domestic relations matters, contractual and financial recovery disputes, to name a few categories, are governed by state law. Federal cases, on the other hand, are limited to matters of federal law or matters involving parties from different states. Federal jurisdiction is described in greater detail below; suffice it to say that it is not easy to "make a federal case" out of a dispute.

A small area of overlap exists where state and federal courts have concurrent jurisdiction. This permits litigants to initiate a legal action in either a federal or a state court. The only other real point of linkage between the federal and state systems is the U.S. Supreme Court. Provided federal jurisdictional requirements are satisfied, decisions of state courts of last resort may be reviewed by the U.S. Supreme Court. Otherwise, the federal and state court systems are independent. The independence of federal and state court jurisdictions was designed to maintain the respective sovereignties of the two levels of government. The main consequence of this dual judicial system is that it promotes some policy and doctrinal diversity. Though states may have similar constitutional provisions, statutes, and common law traditions, the state courts do not necessarily interpret them in exactly the same way. Different local attitudes as well as different social conditions account for some variations.

A court's authority to hear or decide a case is defined by its jurisdiction. It is through jurisdiction that the power of federal and state courts to "say the law" is distinguished. The overall jurisdiction of the federal courts is set forth in Article III of the Constitution; federal judicial power is further defined by Congress as courts located beneath the Supreme Court in the organizational scheme are established. Any action by Congress, of course, must be compatible with the general directives of Article III. Federal judicial authority extends to particular categories of cases defined by either substance or party. Cases that stem directly from the federal Constitution, federal statutes, or treaties or cases that involve admiralty or maritime issues can be brought to federal courts. Federal judicial power also extends to cases involving specified parties. Regardless of substance, federal jurisdiction includes actions where the federal government is itself a party, actions between two or more states, actions between a state and a citizen of another state, actions between citizens of different states, actions between a state and an alien, actions between a citizen of a state and an alien, and actions involving foreign ambassadors. In similar fashion, state constitutions and state statutes define the jurisdiction of the state courts. We now turn to the organizational configuration of courts in the federal and state systems.

The principal trial courts of the federal system are the U.S. district courts. These are courts of original jurisdiction, which means they hear federal cases first. Like other trial courts, they are designed to address disputes of fact. A court of original jurisdiction generally has no appellate jurisdiction, although district courts can entertain certain questions coming from other courts. The U.S. district courts were established by an act of Congress in 1789. The jurisdiction of district courts fits the general parameters established by Article III for all federal courts. More specifically, district courts can hear any federal criminal case and civil actions arising under federal law if the amount in controversy exceeds $10,000. U.S. district courts also have what is called diversity of citizenship jurisdiction, which allows them to hear cases involving parties from different states. In addition, U.S. district courts can review orders issued by certain administrative agencies.

A small portion of federal district court dockets (about 15 percent) is criminal cases, but most criminal prosecutions occur in state rather than federal courts because the federal government does not possess what is called police power. Conduct that is defined as criminal in federal law usually has an interstate dimension or involves federal officers or property. The remaining cases on district court dockets are civil. Three categories of civil matters stand out. First, a large number of cases involve application of the Constitution or federal statute and may have substantial policy consequences. This category includes cases concerning, for example, protection of civil rights. Second are diversity of citizenship cases, in which a party from one state is seeking some kind of judgment against a party from another state. Third are prisoner petitions, which are not criminal cases as such, but cases in which prisoners assert that their imprisonment violates some legally protected right. Most prisoner petitions result from the district courts' power to issue writs of *habeas corpus*. Congress may alter the jurisdiction of the U.S.

district courts as long as such action conforms to the provisions of Article III. All district court judges are appointed by the president with the advice and consent of the Senate. Some of the cases that make their way to the U.S. Supreme Court begin in a U.S. district court. These would be criminal cases initiated by the Justice Department based on violations of federal criminal law or civil matters that satisfy federal jurisdictional requirements.

Each state has at least one federal district court, with more populous states having as many as four. Ninety U.S. district courts are spread across the 50 states, plus one for the District of Columbia and one for the Commonwealth of Puerto Rico. There are also U.S. district courts in the territories of Guam, the Virgin Islands, and the Northern Mariana Islands. In addition to federal matters, district court judges in the territories handle local issues that would normally fall to a state court. U.S. district courts vary in size from one to thirty judges depending on the caseload. Congress may add district court judgeships at its discretion. Currently there are nearly 600 district court judges distributed across the ninety-five district courts. Cases decided by the district courts may be appealed to the U.S. courts of appeals.

There is a special form of U.S. district court called a three-judge district court. Three-judge courts were first authorized by Congress in 1903 to hear a variety of cases including those involving citizen challenges to the constitutionality of federal law. In such cases, three-judge courts were empowered to issue injunctions against enforcement of a challenged statute. Appeals of the decisions of three-judge district courts go directly to the Supreme Court. In 1976 Congress passed legislation limiting the use of three-judge courts to only certain kinds of civil rights litigation and legislative apportionment cases. Cases that do not satisfy the conditions for convening a three-judge court go before a regular U.S. district court. Though the number of cases going before three-judge courts is not large, the subject matter for which the courts may be convened makes them a disproportionately significant source of Supreme Court cases.

The federal judicial system also contains several specialized courts with very narrow or highly focused jurisdictions. A specialized court is established to reduce the caseload of the U.S. district courts and to provide heightened expertise of judges working in highly technical legal areas. Though specialized courts generally operate in the same manner as other trial courts, their narrow focus makes them resemble administrative agencies in some respects. Among the specialized federal courts are the U.S. Court of International Trade, the U.S. Claims Court, the U.S. Tax Court, and the U.S. Federal Circuit Court of Appeals. These courts are seldom a source of cases involving constitutional questions.

The federal judicial system has intermediate appeals courts, the U.S.

courts of appeals. These intermediate appeals courts are structurally located between trial courts and courts of last resort. In this instance, the U.S. courts of appeals are between the U.S. district and other specialized federal courts having original jurisdiction and the U.S. Supreme Court. The U.S. courts of appeals were established by Congress in 1891 to provide a first appellate review of cases brought from federal district courts and certain administrative agencies. (These courts were first called the circuit courts of appeal.) The United States is presently divided into 12 regions called judicial circuits, and each state is placed in 1 of 11 circuits. The twelfth is a separate circuit for the District of Columbia. All appeals from courts geographically located within the designated region go to the court of appeals for that circuit. Almost all the cases reviewed by U.S. courts of appeals come from U.S. district courts. The exception is the court of appeals in the District of Columbia, where almost half the cases originate with federal agencies. There is also a U.S. Federal Circuit Court of Appeals, which was established in 1984 and has a very specialized appeals jurisdiction. It reviews rulings from the U.S. Claims Court, the U.S. Court of International Trade, and administrative agencies such as the Patent and Trademark Office.

U.S. courts of appeals review more than 30,000 cases annually. As appellate courts, the courts of appeals engage in law interpretation and have substantial policy impact, though they have no organized jurisdiction. Their appellate jurisdiction is mandatory, which means they cannot refuse to hear any case seeking review. The courts of appeals may use abbreviated procedures on those cases viewed as presenting less substantial questions. The U.S. courts of appeals were first established to screen cases and thereby reduce the number of cases attempting to access the Supreme Court. The courts of appeals continue to perform that function, and only a relatively small proportion of cases decided at this level go on to the Supreme Court. Although some cases do go further, a U.S. court of appeals is typically the court of both first and final appellate review for most federal cases. Court of appeals judges are appointed for life by the president with the advice and consent of the Senate. Each circuit has from 4 to 23 permanent judges, depending on caseload. Each court usually reviews cases in panels of three judges but will occasionally sit *en banc,* which means all the judges in the circuit hear the case.

State court systems have the same general structural characteristics as the federal court system. States typically have a multiple trial court structure with one general jurisdiction trial court and several courts of limited jurisdiction. Rather than categorize under the general and limited jurisdiction labels, some refer to these courts as major and minor. A major, or general jurisdiction, trial court hears felony level criminal cases and civil cases involving monetary values in excess of a certain amount (usually $10,000) and possibly possesses limited appellate authority. Minor courts, on the other hand, deal with misdemeanors, traffic matters, small claims, and other civil questions of limited monetary value. The courts of limited jurisdiction are the courts with the heaviest caseloads. The matters before them, though high volume, are not particularly serious. Seldom do questions that reach the Supreme Court originate in minor state courts.

State systems typically have specialized courts to address juvenile and probate questions as well. Some states have separate courts to handle such domestic relations issues as divorce, child custody, and spousal and child support. Some states with domestic relations courts locate juvenile jurisdiction with these courts as well. Every state has a court that can hear matters involving minors. Juvenile courts have jurisdiction over minors accused of criminal conduct and minors who may be the victims of abuse or neglect. Each state specifies the maximum age for persons under the jurisdiction of the juvenile courts; the line is typically established at either 16 or 18 years of age. Juvenile courts are described in greater detail in chapter 3. Probate courts have jurisdiction over wills and estates and may also have power to appoint guardians as well as to perform certain functions regarding minors. The principal concern of probate courts is the proper distribution of assets from an estate.

State judicial systems have either one or two levels of appeals courts. About half the states, typically the more populous ones, have an intermediate court with jurisdiction that resembles that of the U.S. courts of appeals. These are appellate courts with mandatory jurisdiction: They must review all cases filed with them. Most cases go no further than this level, although a state court of last resort—a state supreme court—is structurally located above the intermediate appellate court. The cases reviewed by this intermediate court almost always come from the state's general jurisdiction trial court.

Every state has a court of last resort. Almost every state calls this court the supreme court, although several have other names such as the supreme court of appeals. Regardless of name, this court functions as the final appellate authority within the state system. It differs from the U.S. Supreme Court in that many state supreme court judges are elected rather than appointed. Some variation also exists in the structure and jurisdiction of state supreme courts. They range in size from five to nine justices, and like the U.S. Supreme Court, the justices sit *en banc* rather than in panels. The appellate jurisdiction of state supreme courts depends substantially on whether the state has an intermediate appellate court. Where an intermediate court exists, the supreme court typically possesses extensive discretion over the cases it reviews. This discretionary jurisdiction allows state supreme courts to control substantive law questions on their dockets. If the system does not have an intermediate court, the state supreme court provides the first-level function and is required to hear virtually all the cases that seek review.

Finally, a word about the Supreme Court's place in the structural configuration: The U.S. Supreme Court is the highest court in the U.S. judicial system. The Supreme Court is the only federal court established expressly by provision of the judicial article of the U.S. Constitution (Article III). It is principally an appeals court, although it has been assigned original jurisdiction over cases involving certain interstate or international matters. The Court exercises appellate jurisdiction "with such exceptions, and under such regulations as the Congress shall make." Such congressional authority over the Court's appellate jurisdiction is a part of the larger checks and balances approach to limiting governmental power. Appellate jurisdiction has been granted through various statutes, beginning with the Judiciary Act of 1789, but Congress has considered limiting the Court's power from time to time.

The Supreme Court has extensive power to make or influence the substance of policy. Through the exercise of its functions of judicial review and statutory interpretation, the Court can define the meaning of the Constitution. In doing so, the Court can determine the parameters of legislative, executive, and judicial authority. The Supreme Court receives its cases from two principal sources: the U.S. courts of appeals and state courts of last resort. The Court is headed by the chief justice of the United States, who presides over the eight associate justices. The size of the Court is set by Congress and has ranged from as few as five to as many as ten justices. All justices are nominated by the president and must be confirmed by the Senate. If confirmed, the justices have life tenure.

Selection of people to sit on the Supreme Court is a highly political process. When a president is considering a nomination, the most important criteria seem to be professional competence and policy compatibility. Generally, a president attempts to nominate a lawyer of distinction. An important element is the absence of any taint with respect to ethical standards. Of critical concern to the president is the political orientation of the prospective justice. A president brings to office an agenda, and no president knowingly nominates someone to the Court who will make fulfillment of that agenda more difficult. Though a justice may not always vote as the nominating president hoped, ideological compatibility produces judicial positions that are generally in accord with the appointing president's policy priorities. Beyond these criteria, presidents are cognizant of the practical political dimensions of a nomination. A president usually seeks to nominate someone who is "cost free," which means a person whose confirmation will be virtually automatic and will require the president to engage in little or no political "horse-trading." Similarly, a particular nominee may improve a president's standing with certain constituency groups. President Ronald Reagan's nomination of Sandra Day O'Connor, for example, was at least in part aimed at closing the so-called gender gap—Reagan's relatively unfavorable standing with women.

How Cases Begin

A case that reaches the U.S. Supreme Court for consideration of a constitutional issue begins in a state or federal trial court. A case at the trial level involves a fact dispute that requires resolution, usually through an adversarial process. If a trial actually occurs, the parties present evidence to an impartial judge or jury under basic rules of fair play administered by the trial judge. Once the fact dispute is resolved, an appeal may be pursued by the losing party, at which time any constitutional questions that may be present can be developed. How cases are begun at the trial level depends on whether the case is criminal or civil.

A criminal case begins with the government accusing a person of violating one or more provisions of the criminal code. It is the government, through the offices of a prosecutor, that initiates all criminal cases. A criminal case is an adversarial contest between the "State" or the "People" and the accused, who is called the defendant. The issue of fact in a criminal case is whether the state can prove beyond a reasonable doubt the guilt of the accused. No private party can take such a case directly into the courts. Once a criminal case is filed, it is the responsibility of the trial court to conduct a series of proceedings up to and including a trial to determine as a matter of fact whether the accused is guilty. Most criminal cases are not concluded by trial, however. Rather, the government and the defendant resolve the case by means of a plea agreement, which typically involves the accused admitting guilt in exchange for some consideration by the prosecution. The fact dispute on the matter of guilt is resolved by agreement. Cases settled in this way usually reflect the defendant's decision not to press any constitutional question the case may have contained. Indeed, the objective of the settlement is to close the case rather than pursue any such questions on appeal. It is from the small proportion of cases that are tried that a constitutional question may emerge.

Constitutional issues in criminal cases may involve either process or substance, although the procedural question is far more common. In these cases, it is almost always the defendant who raises a question on appeal following a conviction. Under certain circumstances, however, the government may press an issue to a higher court. A wide range of procedural questions may be raised by convicted defendants; most stem from alleged errors made as the case progressed through the criminal justice system. Such procedural errors are not inherent in criminal cases, but may originate in specific cases at one of the many steps in the process. Some specific examples follow.

We begin with a case that eventually produces a self-incrimination issue for the Supreme Court. A person is lawfully taken into custody for a serious crime involving assaultive conduct. The police have cause to make the arrest, and their behavior conforms to established rules governing arrest. To this point, there is no constitutional issue because no procedural error has occurred. Nor is there a substantive issue, because making assaultive conduct a crime is certainly a legitimate exercise of governmental authority; thus, the accused cannot seriously challenge the law itself as being unconstitutional. If the arrest was lawful, a search incident to the arrest is permissible to allow officers to protect against the accused accessing a weapon or destroying evidence. In this illustration, no search or seizure problem exists, because law enforcement agents all behaved properly as the accused was taken into custody. At the time of arrest, the police are required to convey the *Miranda* warnings to the accused. This involves informing the accused of the right to silence, that any statements may be used against him or her in court, and that he or she is entitled to consult with counsel, with such counsel to be appointed by the state in the event of indigence. The person in this example is informed of his or her rights, so no appeals issues exists there either.

Upon getting the accused to the police station, but before the person has talked with counsel, the police pose several questions. The person answers some of them, but then requests to consult an attorney. The questions continue nonetheless, and eventually incriminating statements are made by the accused. May these incriminating statements be admitted into evidence? If the prosecutor does not attempt to introduce the statements as evidence, there is no problem, of course. No injury to the defendant has resulted from the questioning. On the other hand, if the prosecutor seeks to use the statements, the judge allows it, and the person is convicted, an appeal focusing on the interrogation could ensue. An appeal based on the events described here could only come from a case where someone suffered direct injury from the questioned action of government. Conviction constitutes such injury. (Incidentally, under current standards the police cannot continue questioning in the absence of the accused's lawyer.)

The case above focuses on a procedural error in the police interrogation of a person in custody. The error in this instance occurred before the case ever entered the court system. *Gideon v. Wainwright* (372 U.S. 335: 1963), a landmark assistance of counsel case, highlights a problem that occurs further into the criminal process. Clarence Gideon was arrested and charged with the felony of breaking and entering for the purpose of committing larceny. This was a state prosecution in a state court for violation of state law. There was no claim that Gideon's arrest was improper or that an unlawful search occurred. Neither was there a claim that Gideon was subjected to an unlawful interrogation. To this point there is no problem of procedure that provides a federal constitutional issue sufficient to be reviewed by the U.S. Supreme Court. The state simply entered the case into the criminal courts of Florida, where it waited its turn for trial. The problem occurred when the case reached the trial stage. Gideon requested appointment of a lawyer to aid him at trial because he was without economic means to retain a lawyer on his own. The trial judge refused on the basis that neither the federal Constitution nor state law required it. As a result of the trial judge's ruling, Gideon had to defend himself against the charges. He was convicted and sentenced to prison. He appealed, and his case was eventually reviewed by the Supreme Court. When the Supreme Court agreed to hear the case, the only question before it was whether a state court could fairly try a felony defendant if he or she was unable to afford a lawyer.

The double jeopardy prohibition prevents the state from appealing an acquittal in a criminal case. An acquittal is a fact judgment that the prosecution did not establish the defendant's guilt beyond a reasonable doubt. The prosecution does not have the right to keep bringing that question to trial. The government can appeal from an adverse ruling on a legal judgment, however, which is distinct from a fact judgment. If a trial judge, for example, excludes a piece of evidence the prosecution wishes to use, the prosecution can appeal that ruling. Such an appeal may ultimately reach a state court of last resort or even the U.S. Supreme Court. A more common occasion for a government-initiated appeal is found in cases where a convicted defendant is successful on appeal. If the ruling comes from other than the U.S. Supreme Court, the state is free to pursue further review of the underlying law issue.

Consider the case of Thomas Tucker, who was interrogated by police after he had been read his rights. The reading of rights had been incomplete, however. Tucker sought relief on the grounds that as a consequence of the defective reading, he had involuntarily incriminated himself. The prosecution had not tried to use all of Tucker's statements, but only the disclosure in which Tucker had identified a person he thought would give him an alibi. The person would not confirm Tucker's whereabouts and eventually became a prosecution witness. Tucker prevailed on a *habeas corpus* motion in the lower federal courts, but the state subsequently petitioned for review by the Supreme Court in an attempt to preserve the conviction based in part on the testimony of the witness Tucker had identified. This constitutional question involving custodial interrogation reached the Supreme Court because the government sought to appeal from an intermediate-level court. The Supreme Court reversed the lower federal court ruling in Tucker's case and permitted testimony from the witness on the grounds that Tucker had not been coerced into making the disclosure.

Substantive appeals in criminal cases are quite rare because there is generally little doubt that the government can legitimately regulate or prohibit such conduct as burglary, assault, arson, or murder. A challenge of a state's arson law as an unreasonable exercise of governmental power, for example, has no chance of succeeding. A prosecution for the crime of distributing obscene material, on the other hand, might raise substantive questions about whether the underlying obscenity law violates the First Amendment. The flag-burning cases of the late 1980s and early 1990s had similar First Amendment connections. The state case, *Texas v. Johnson* (491 U.S. 397: 1989), serves as an example. The state of Texas made it a crime to desecrate the U.S. flag, and Gregory Johnson burned a flag as part of a protest against the policies of the Reagan administration. Johnson's defense was not that he had not broken the law. He had done so consciously, with the specific intention of putting himself in a position to challenge the law. The trial court's task was relatively easy, because a law undisputedly had been broken. But the trial was merely the first step to an appeal. The case contained no claim on the common procedural questions usually raised in criminal cases. Rather, Johnson claimed that his burning of a flag was an act of symbolic expression and was therefore protected by the First Amendment. The essential question Johnson put before the Court was whether a state could criminalize his action; the Supreme Court eventually ruled in Johnson's favor on this point.

Civil challenges to government policies are a little different. Here the initiative rests exclusively with an individual or group who suffered injury by some governmental policy or practice. Obviously, the governmental action had to be taken prior to any legal action, but it is wholly up to a plaintiff to seek relief from the courts. Civil cases containing constitutional questions tend to be public rather than private because a previous government action usually prompts the litigation. A civil case contains an asserted claim by a litigant who is called a plaintiff. The legal action is commenced to obtain court-ordered relief. Though a number of different remedies may be sought in civil cases, actions concerning constitutional questions usually involve a claim that the government has in some way violated a right protected by law. Through the lawsuit, a government policy or practice is challenged as unlawful. The remedy sought by the challenging party is most often the elimination or modification of the particular policy or practice.

Courts with appropriate jurisdiction entertain only those cases with justiciable questions, which means the dispute must be appropriate for judicial resolution. Justiciability depends on whether the case stems from real conflict between two parties rather than from a situation that raises only abstract issues. A justiciable issue satisfies all the requirements of standing. Standing means that the plaintiff bringing suit must have suffered some direct injury, and the injury must relate to a right protected under the Constitution or under statute. A person must have standing to initiate a legal action. This means that suits cannot be brought by a third party or by someone indirectly related to the legal injury. Further, each suit must specify the remedy being sought from the court. The burden rests with the plaintiff to define what relief the court might order. Standing also contains a time dimension in that a court must find a suit ripe, which means that all other avenues of possible relief have been exhausted. Similarly, a case will not be entertained by a court if events have made pursuit of the original remedy inappropriate or impossible. Judicial power extends only to bona fide disputes. Federal courts are unable to respond to hypothetical or friendly suits, and they cannot render advisory opinions. The standing requirement also applies to state courts, although some state courts may issue advisory opinions. Justiciability differs from jurisdiction in that the latter focuses on whether a court has the power to act. Justiciability presumes that the power to act exists but focuses on whether to do so is an appropriate exercise of judicial power. Justiciability requirements are an outgrowth of the separation of powers concept. Courts possess substantial discretion in determining whether an issue is justiciable but will generally proceed with caution before taking action. Such an approach serves to heighten the impact of judicial action in those cases where justiciability clearly exists.

The first example of a civil action is *Lemon v. Kurtzman* (403 U.S. 602: 1971). In this case, a state had authorized reimbursement to nonpublic schools for costs of teachers' salaries, textbooks, and other instructional materials in specified secular subjects. Reimbursement was limited to courses with exact counterparts in the public school curriculum and was explicitly prohibited for any course that contained "any subject matter expressing religious teaching or the morals or forms of worship of any sect." The law was challenged by groups of resident taxpayers and parents of children attending the public schools in the state on the grounds that it violated the First Amendment prohibition on establishment of religion. The action was commenced at the trial court level before a three-judge U.S. district court. No crime or punishment was involved; the citizens brought suit simply to discontinue implementation of the law through a finding that the law was unconstitutional. The trial court dismissed the suit, and appeal to the Supreme Court followed. The plaintiffs eventually succeeded in having the policy struck down.

The second example also involves the First Amendment and was decided by the Court just two days after *Lemon*. The free press case of *New York Times v. United States* (403 U.S. 713: 1971) was actually one of two cases; the other involved the *Washington Post*. Together they are known as the Pentagon Papers cases. The *Times* and the *Post* had come into possession of copies of a classified Defense Department study entitled "History of U.S. Decision-Making Process on Vietnam Policy." The Nixon administration wanted to prevent publication of the documents and sought restraining orders (injunctions) against the two newspapers; the newspapers contested the injunctions. The issue that eventually came before the Supreme Court was whether the federal government could impose a prior restraint on newspapers. A prior restraint is the most severe threat to the press in that it is direct censorship. The trial court had ruled for the *Times,* but the intermediate appeals court reversed that ruling. The newspaper then challenged the legitimacy of the restraint on its publication of the documents. Notwithstanding the asserted national security aspects, the Supreme Court decided against the government.

A challenged policy need not involve the executive branch of the federal government. A school principal, for example, may be the official agent of government instead. Consider the censorship case of *Hazelwood School District v. Kuhlmeier* (484 U.S. 260: 1988). A school newspaper, produced by a journalism class, was regularly published and distributed to the student body. The school principal reviewed all page proofs prior to publication of each issue. The principal objected to two specific articles, one on teenage pregnancy and the other on divorce, and ordered that the pages on which the two articles appeared be withheld from the paper. Former staff members of the newspaper brought legal action in a trial court, claiming the action of the principal constituted unlawful prior restraint. In this case, the challenge was unsuccessful.

The final example is a Fourteenth Amendment equal protection case that involves the medical school admission practices of a state university. The school admitted 100 students annually. To assure minority representation in the medical school class, 16 places were set aside for minority applicants. Allan Bakke, a white male, was denied admission although his credentials were better than those of some of the minority applicants admitted under the affirmative action policy. Consequently, Bakke initiated a suit in a state court, seeking injunctive and declaratory relief. First, he wanted the university enjoined from implementing the policy, which would make it possible to order his admission. He also wanted the court to declare the race-conscious quota policy to be unconstitutional. The trial court refused to order Bakke's admission, but ruled against the university on the broader issues. The state supreme court affirmed the lower court, but also ordered Bakke's admission. The university sought review from the U.S. Supreme Court. The Court agreed that Bakke should be admitted and that the race-based quota system violated the equal protection clause of the Fourteenth Amendment. The university was allowed to continue its attempt to establish diversity within the medical school class, but it could not use quotas as a means of doing so.

Several general propositions are reflected in these examples. First, even landmark cases do not originate at the Supreme Court level. Rather, both civil and criminal cases enter the court system as disputes of fact in federal or state trial courts. Second, criminal cases are initiated by the government and tend not to contain constitutional or policy questions at the outset. If such a question develops, it is likely to involve an alleged procedural error that occurred as police investigated or the courts adjudicated. Seldom does a criminal case involve substantive challenges to criminal law. Finally, cases that contain a constitutional question from the outset are typically cases where a lawsuit is brought for the specific purpose of challenging a particular government policy or practice.

The decisions that most authoritatively define constitutional rights come from the U.S. Supreme Court. The Supreme Court is at least two levels above the trial court where the case enters the judicial system. Moving cases through the appellate courts to the Supreme Court is both time-consuming and costly. Many of the suits involving individual rights that progress through these courts are supported by interest groups. Interest groups tend to be viewed as more active in legislative and executive arenas, but over the last half century, groups have increasingly sought to pursue their objectives in courts as well. This has been especially true of groups that do not possess sufficient political influence to effectively protect or advance the interests of their memberships through the other two branches. Interest groups attempt to use the courts in several ways to impact individual rights policy.

One strategy involves the use of the test case. A test case contains those elements that make it an appropriate vehicle through which to place a policy question before the courts. Groups often initiate test cases themselves or use one or more members to serve as named parties in a suit. If a group does not initiate the suit itself, it may find a case already in progress through which to pursue its policy objectives. When an interest group supports a test case, it may underwrite the financial costs necessary to carry on the case. The group may also provide lawyers with specialized expertise in the particular area of law to serve as counsel. Interest groups also attempt to influence the thinking of appellate courts through the submission of *amicus curiae* briefs. An *amicus curiae,* literally meaning "friend of the court," is not an actual party to an action. An *amicus* is an interested third party who attempts to provide the court with information or arguments that may not have been offered by the actual parties. As long as the parties to a controversy have no objections, *amicus* briefs can be filed at virtually any stage of the legal process, but they are usually submitted with cases under review by appellate courts. *Amicus* participation typically occurs in cases with substantial public policy ramifications. Since the case format primarily focuses on the contesting parties, *amicus* arguments attempt to focus on the broader implications of the particular case.

The trial stage is as far as most cases go. Once the fact dispute is resolved, the case ends and the parties accept the outcome. For some cases, however, the trial process is merely the first step. As described in the previous discussion of organizational structure, if an appeal is pursued, a case typically goes from the trial court having original jurisdiction to the appellate court structurally located just above that trial court. If the case was heard by a state trial court, an appeal would go to the first-level appellate court in the state system. Whether this would involve one or two levels depends on the state in which the trial was held. In larger states with a two-level appellate structure, appeal would occur in an intermediate-level court. In small states with only one appellate level, the court would be the court of last resort. A U.S. court of appeals would be the first step in the federal appellate process.

U.S. Supreme Court Review

Virtually all the cases that come before the U.S. Supreme Court are seeking review of a ruling by a U.S. court of appeals or a state supreme court. Cases can get to the Supreme Court in essentially one of two ways. The first is by writ of appeal, a route established by federal statute. A very narrow range of issues can approach the Court this way. At one time, appeal review was automatically granted to qualified parties, reflecting a congressional belief that the Court should not possess much discretion over its docket. Among the kinds of cases that could be reviewed as a matter of statutory mandate were appeals from state court decisions where a state law was upheld against a federal constitutional challenge. It also used to be the case that the Court could be accessed by writ of error. Under the writ of error process, cases could be brought to the Court by asserting that a legal error had been made by a lower court.

The Supreme Court was given substantial direction over granting the writ of appeal in 1928, when the Congress gave the justices authority to determine whether the issue contained in any case otherwise satisfying writ of appeal conditions also raised a "substantial federal question." If the Court determined a "substantial" question was not present, it could then withhold the writ, which previously would have been granted automatically. Congress again modified the rules for the writ of appeal in 1988, confining it to certain cases coming from three-judge U.S. district courts. Prior to 1928, more than 80 percent of the Supreme Court's docket was writ of appeal cases. Once the Court obtained discretion to decide which of these cases were important enough to review, the number of cases coming to the Court on writ of appeal decreased substantially. Presently, less than 10 percent of the cases the Court decides come to it on writ of appeal.

The second route to the Supreme Court is through the writ of certiorari. This approach to the Court was established by Congress in the Everts Act of 1891, which established the certiorari power that gave the Court complete discretion over much of its caseload. Through certiorari the Court could decline to hear certain cases if a given number of justices felt the cases were not sufficiently important. The writ is granted when at least four of the nine justices of the U.S. Supreme Court agree that a particular case should be reviewed. Since the late 1920s, the proportion of certiorari petitions granted review by the Court has never exceeded 22 percent. More often, the Court grants certiorari in fewer than 1 case in 20. Although the writ is granted in a small proportion of cases, in excess of 90 percent of the Court's cases presently come by certiorari.

The certiorari power is the Supreme Court's principal means of keeping current, and it has become an effective administrative mechanism. A chief justice, as the chief administrative officer of the Court, can similarly impact access to the Court by taking charge of the certiorari process—prescreening cases and creating lists of those cases that should be discussed further and those that should not be reviewed. This prescreening process provides the basis for the Court's case selection. The chief justice can also direct the Court's attention to those cases that he or she thinks raise the most important policy questions. Chief justices prepare lists of cases that summarily deny certiorari; about 75 percent of the cases seeking certiorari are dismissed in this way. The remainder make a "discuss" list, which means the cases will come before the entire membership of the Court. While most of these cases also are not granted review, the cases on the discuss list are voted on individually to determine whether they are to be reviewed. The certiorari process allows the Court to establish an agenda of policy priorities and to choose the cases through which it wishes to address those priorities. Refusal to grant certiorari leaves a case as it stood coming out of the lower court.

The Decisional Process

The process by which the Court decides which cases to review is not complex. The chief justice prepares a list of cases to be discussed by the Court as a whole. This list is relatively short and represents the chief justice's best estimate of those cases worthy of consideration. A small number of cases are added by the other justices. Each justice, with the extensive assistance of his or her law clerks, has screened the cases petitioning for review. As a result, each justice has a good idea of which cases raise the most substantial questions. Unless a justice requests that a case be discussed by the Court as a whole, the petitions other than those on the chief justice's "discuss" list are summarily rejected. Generally, there is consensus on which cases should be selected for review.

The conference is the place where all important business is conducted, and it is used at several stages in the decisional process. The conference is considered by many to be the core of the Court's decisional process. In conferences, the justices engage in intensive discussions that yield decisions on which cases are to be reviewed and, subsequently, decided. The conference discussion shapes not only voting alignments but also the substance of the majority opinion in each case. Conference sessions occupy the better part of two workdays per week during the period the Court hears oral arguments, and they are closed to everyone but the justices. The conferences held early in the Court's annual term are where the cases to be reviewed are selected. At this point, pre-term conferences have already disposed of many of the accumulated petitions. For a case to be selected, a minimum of four justices must agree the case warrants review. The conference method is also used in almost the same way by virtually all courts of last resort with discretionary jurisdiction.

It is difficult to know precisely why any particular case is selected or rejected, as the justices do not explain these judgments. Yet, some discernible patterns do emerge. Certainly, some cases are chosen because they deal with particularly important questions that have significance beyond the outcome between the contesting parties. One characteristic of an important case may be that it contains an issue not previously addressed by the Court. Another factor that underscores the importance of a particular case might be that lower court rulings on the issue are unclear or in conflict. Clearly one of the Court's main functions is to resolve inconsistencies in constitutional interpretation coming from lower courts. Issues that have resulted in conflicting judgments from lower courts present situations where the Court often feels compelled to establish uniformity.

The Court receives information about a case from several sources. The petitions that are filed are supported by documentation that provides some information about the case and the particular legal issue. This information is important, because the justices decide which cases to review based on the material provided with the petitions. Once the Court has agreed to review a case, written briefs on the merits of the issue are filed. A brief is a document submitted on behalf of each of the parties. The brief attempts to represent all the applicable legal materials such as constitutional or statutory provisions and precedents. More important, the brief offers arguments in an effort to persuade the Court to rule in favor of one party over the other. The brief is a vehicle of advocacy. In addition to briefs submitted by the parties themselves, *amicus curiae* briefs are often submitted by third parties such as interest groups. There is some evidence to suggest that an indication of forthcoming *amicus* briefs from certain interest groups or from the federal government underscores the importance of a particular case and enhances the possibility that the case will be selected for review.

Once a case has been selected for review, it is scheduled for oral argument. Oral arguments occur after the written briefs have been filed. The oral argument is a very short presentation, usually 30 to 60 minutes, and is made before the full membership of the Court. Although limited in length, the oral argument represents each party's last chance to advance their position. The oral argument process is highly interactive because the justices frequently pose questions to the attorneys representing each party. The justices are already familiar with the issue and have probably heard most of the arguments before; their questions are designed to clarify a particular point or to go beyond the arguments contained in the written briefs. For justices who are undecided on a case, the oral argument period can be the critical step in the decisional process.

The conference process is used again when the justices consider a case following the oral arguments. The chief justice speaks first, with each associate justice following in turn (in order of seniority). The Court can do one of three things with a particular case. First, it may determine that the case was mistakenly selected for review (review improvidently granted) and dismiss the case. The result here is as though the case had not been selected for review in the first place. Second, the Court may decide to resolve the case by summary judgment. This option means the decision will not have much policy significance; summary judgments typically are not accompanied by a lengthy opinion. Third, the Court may choose to decide the case on its merits and write a full accompanying opinion. Assignment of the opinion by the chief justice occurs after a nonbinding vote that provides a preliminary indication of how the Court will align itself on the issue. The justice assigned to draft the majority opinion must come from the winning side of any split vote. The chief justice may assign himself or herself this responsibility as long as he or she votes with the majority.

Each justice ultimately decides how to vote based on his or her response to the legal arguments advanced by the parties and to the arguments made by other justices in conference. Voting decisions are also affected by the views of each justice concerning the meaning of particular constitutional provisions. Each justice comes to the Court with well-developed opinions on these matters. Each justice will, for example, have a pretty clear idea of how far the First Amendment's free speech protection should extend. When a free speech case comes before the Court, these views come into play. Equally intelligent and well-trained lawyers often have differing views on constitutional provisions, so it is not uncommon for the Court to lack consensus in some cases, a split vote being the result. Each justice's vote on a case becomes final only when he or she actually agrees to or rejects the written opinion offered on behalf of the majority position. The discussion begun in conference continues after the opinion assignment has been made and a draft opinion has circulated; votes may be altered throughout this period. Ultimately a decision and accompanying majority and minority opinions emerge.

THE DECISION

The Supreme Court's decision does two things. It resolves the specific dispute between the two parties, and it also addresses any constitutional or policy question that underlies the case. In many ways, the latter function is more important, but first a word about the former.

Cases reaching the Supreme Court already have been before lower courts, so one party already is in the position of winner. The Supreme Court's options are to uphold the lower court ruling or to modify or reverse it. If the Supreme Court finds the previous decision to be correct on the merits of the case, it affirms the lower court ruling. Remember that the court hearing the case immediately before the Supreme Court was itself an appeals court, so the ruling under review focuses on some procedural or substantive policy issue and not on the fact judgment. If the Court upholds the existing ruling, the losing party from the lower court—the party who pursued review by the Supreme Court—remains the losing party. If this party is a criminal defendant, his or her conviction is upheld because the appeals issue was not considered valid. If, on the other hand, the Court decides the previous ruling is incorrect, it may reverse the lower court. Another term for setting aside a lower court ruling is *vacate*. The Court also has the intermediate option of modifying a lower court ruling, which is a partial or limited reversal.

When a decision is reversed or modified, the case is often remanded, or sent back, to the lower court for reconsideration consistent with the terms of the Supreme Court's decision. This is done because the effect of reversing or vacating is to set aside the outcome of the trial process on legal rather than factual grounds. The original factual question, such as a criminal defendant's guilt, is not addressed by the Supreme Court; thus, the case must be sent back for reconsideration of the factual issue. For example, assume a criminal defendant has been convicted of burglary. One of the pieces of evidence offered by the prosecution was an item stolen from someone's home. However, that item was found in the closet of the defendant's home during a search conducted without a warrant. The defense objected to the introduction of the evidence at the trial, but the trial judge allowed the jury to see the evidence. A conviction followed. On review of the case, the defense was able to convince the Supreme Court that the evidence had been discovered in an illegal search and that it should have been suppressed at the trial. It is impossible, however, for the Supreme Court to calculate what effect the evidence had on the original jury's decision to convict, so the Court must remand the case for a new trial to determine whether the defendant is guilty. The prosecution is permitted in the new trial to do everything it did during the first trial except introduce the item that was ruled inadmissible on appeal.

More important than the decision declaring a winner in a case is the Supreme Court's accompanying opinion, which serves several purposes. First, the opinion may contain specific directions for any reconsideration undertaken by a lower court on remand. Such instructions might offer standards by which reconsideration is to take place. Any direction of this kind will provide guidance to lower courts as they handle similar cases in the future. Second, the opinion represents the Court's rationale for its decision. Finally, it is the opinion that speaks to the broader constitutional or policy questions and establishes clarified principles that become controlling precedent in later cases.

There are several kinds of opinions. The most important is the majority opinion, or opinion of the court. The majority opinion includes the rationale for the Court's conclusion on a question of law. It also defines the scope and reach of the decision. The legal basis for the opinion, called the *ratio decidendi,* is the central proposition that resolves a constitutional question— the irreducible core of the decision. The *ratio decidendi* is distinguished from *obiter dicta,* which are statements in a court opinion on matters that are not essential to the resolution of the law question before the court. It is the *ratio decidendi* that establishes the value of a decision as a legal precedent. Because *obiter dicta* generally go beyond what is necessary to resolve a point of law, they have no precedent value.

The majority opinion is written by a member of the court who votes with the majority side. Assignment of the majority opinion to an individual member of the court occurs at conference. On the U.S. Supreme Court, the chief justice assigns the opinion provided he or she, too, is a member of the majority. If the chief justice is not among the majority, the opinion is assigned by the most senior associate justice on the majority side. The assigned justice drafts an initial version of the opinion, trying to integrate the views of all those among the majority. The opinion is then circulated, discussed, and probably redrafted several times. This rewriting is aimed at developing or holding a consensus on the reasons for a particular decision. While a decision can be made by a majority even if the majority fragments on the reasons, the Court's decisions are much more authoritative if a consensus can be maintained on the reasons as well. Achieving such unanimity is an objective throughout this process. If the written majority opinion cannot accommodate all views, individual opinions may also be written. A member of the majority wishing to express an individual view may issue a concurring opinion, while a justice that disagrees with the majority may issue a dissenting opinion. Occasionally, no opinion is supported by the majority; in such a case the designated opinion of the Court is a plurality opinion. In this case, the justice assigned the task of writing the majority opinion still writes the opinion, but it becomes a plurality statement of the rationale behind the Court's decision.

The Supreme Court may use a *per curiam* opinion instead of a full majority opinion. A *per curiam* opinion is an unsigned statement issued to briefly summarize a ruling without extensively developing the Court's reasoning. *Per curiam* opinions are generally used for cases that undergo abbreviated review, which means the case is reviewed on its merits but without oral argument. These are usually not the major decisions of the Supreme Court. Rather, they are cases in which the issues may be less complicated than those in cases receiving the "full treatment"; thus, a brief opinion summarily representing the decision is sufficient. Occasionally, however, *per curiam* opinions are found in important cases, such as *Furman v. Georgia* (408 U.S. 238: 1972). In this case, the Supreme Court struck down the capital sentencing process used in Georgia, and a brief *per curiam* opinion described the decision. Individual justices then entered lengthy concurring or dissenting opinions. While a majority agreed that the Georgia process was constitutionally defective, no majority existed on a rationale. Thus, the *per curiam* opinion was used to provide the ruling on the point of law, the only point on which the majority could agree.

As mentioned earlier, individual justices may choose to depart from a majority opinion in one of two ways. One way is to issue a concurring opinion, which reflects agreement on the outcome but differs regarding rationale. Concurring opinions may vary widely in the extent to which they depart from the majority opinion. In some instances, the difference may be quite narrow. A justice may wish to mention an additional reason for arriving at the outcome or may want to place emphasis a little differently across several supporting points. On the other hand, a justice may disagree on virtually all the reasons underlying the majority position. In this instance, the justice may be among the majority "in result only," and the concurring opinion would depart extensively from the majority opinion.

A concurring opinion is optional. It is issued by justices on an individual case basis when they wish to express different reasons for arriving at the same decision as the rest of the majority. The role of the concurring opinion can be seen in the *Furman* case mentioned previously. The majority of the Court decided Georgia's practice of assigning total discretion to juries in death penalty cases was unconstitutional, and the ruling was given in a brief *per curiam* opinion. Justice Potter Stewart concurred in this result and, in his concurring opinion, emphasized the arbitrariness of giving jurors no guidance on how to arrive at the death penalty decision. Justice Byron White also found the Georgia process defective, but because it was too infrequently used by juries. Justice William Douglas found fault with the racially discriminatory impact of the policy's application. Finally, the joint concurring opinion by justices William Brennan and Thurgood Marshall asserted that capital punishment was unconstitutional in any form. It is evident from this case that concurring opinions may represent a broad array of viewpoints—the only common ground is agreement on the ruling.

Justices often disagree not only with the language of the majority opinion, but with the ruling itself as well. Justices on the losing, or minority, side of a split decision usually issue a dissenting opinion, which is essentially a minority report. A dissenting opinion may represent the views of as few as one justice or as many as four. A dissenting opinion does not have precedent value as such in that it cannot authoritatively define a point of law. As a result, justices who write dissenting opinions have greater freedom regarding the arguments they advance. Since dissensions need not attend to finely focused legal points as majority opinions must, they often are sweeping in scope and contain powerful language. It also is possible to dissent "in part." If the Court reviews a case containing multiple issues, a justice may agree with the majority position on some points but not all of them. In such a case, the justice's dissenting opinion would address only those one or two points of disagreement. In addition to representing a justice's disagreement with the majority, a dissenting opinion has two other purposes. First, a dissenter may try to limit the impact of a ruling. The dissenting opinion may invite Congress or a state legislature to modify the ruling if it is based on construction of a statute. A dissension may otherwise indicate ways to interpret the ruling narrowly, which can affect the way a lower court applies the ruling. Second, a dissenting opinion can encourage future appeals on the same question. Occasionally, a dissenting position in one case becomes the majority position when the issue is reviewed some time later.

Once all the opinions have been written and the alignment of the justices is finalized, the ruling is announced in open court. Though opinions may be read in their entirety in open court, they are usually summarized. The timing of an announcement rests with the Court, but most decisions are announced in May and June as the Court nears the conclusion of its term.

IMPLEMENTATION

Implementation of judicial decisions involves giving effect to what a court decides. Losing parties in most cases tend to obey decisions voluntarily. The party who needs to take or stop an action as a result of a court decision usually does so on his or her own. Compliance is not automatic, however.

The nature of the implementation process differs between trial and appellate courts. Decisions of trial courts are generally implemented voluntarily or through executive branch action. A criminal sentence, for example, is usually implemented by corrections authorities. Similarly, decisions about search and seizure standards are implemented by state and local police departments. Judgments in civil actions are generally implemented voluntarily as well, but threat of judicial contempt may be used to deter thoughts of noncompliance. The courts also depend on external support for implementation of civil judgments, which typically comes from administrative agencies of the government. The kind of agency support needed for implementation is a function of the content of the decision. If the decision involves classroom practices in public schools, for example, the implementing agency is the local school district and its trustees.

Compliance is obviously not obtained from a losing party because of agreement with the decision. Rather, the party complies because the decision is "the law" and the court has the authority to make such a judgment. Compliance may also occur because sanctions will be imposed without it. Conversely, noncompliance may result if no sanction is forthcoming in the absence of compliance. The likelihood of noncompliance also increases if the court is not perceived as the appropriate source for the decision. Failure to comply with court rulings on school prayer, for example, is attributable in part to school board member perceptions that secular courts are not a legitimate authority in matters of religion and prayer. In addition, compliance often depends on the clarity of a court's decision. The courts must effectively communicate what needs to be done to achieve compliance. Compliance also depends on how lower courts apply the ruling to particular cases. Lower courts can demand full compliance or can circumvent it by making limiting interpretations of what is required. The latter often is a distinct possibility because appellate decisions are normally remanded to lower courts for implementation.

The legislative and executive branches possess powers that directly affect the implementation process. For example, if legislative bodies are dissatisfied with the way courts interpret or apply statutes, judicial decisions can be reversed by enactment of a "clarifying" statute. Legislatures and executives can also affect the implementation process by taking sides on controversial questions. This, in turn, can influence the behavior of key implementors at the state and local levels. Resistance may be encouraged by actions that oppose court decisions. The executive and legislative branches also may or may not provide necessary support to bring about implementation. For example, Congress made it clear that financial support would not be forthcoming if the Supreme Court allowed President Harry Truman to retain operating control of the privately owned steel mills in 1952. On the other hand, presidential support has often been decisive in securing implementation. For example, President Dwight Eisenhower ordered federal troops to Little Rock, Arkansas, to compel compliance with court orders requiring desegregation of the Little Rock public schools.

REFERENCES

Abraham, Henry J., *The Judiciary: The Supreme Court in the Governmental Process,* 8th edition (Boston: William C. Brown, Publishers, 1991).

Baum, Lawrence, *American Courts: Process and Policy,* 2d edition (Boston: Houghton Mifflin, 1990).

———, *The Supreme Court,* 3d edition (Washington, DC: Congressional Quarterly Press, 1989).

Carp, Robert A., and Ronald Stidham, *Judicial Process in America* (Washington, DC: Congressional Quarterly Press, 1990).

Louthan, William C., *The United States Supreme Court: Lawmaking in the Third Branch of Government* (Englewood Cliffs, NJ: Prentice Hall, 1991).

O'Brien, David M., *Storm Center: The Supreme Court in American Politics* (New York: W. W. Norton and Company, 1990).

Wasby, Stephen L., *The Supreme Court in the Federal Judicial System,* 3d edition (Chicago: Nelson-Hall Publishers, 1988).

Juveniles and the Constitution

T he Constitution was written for people of all ages. It applies to all citizens in that it categorically prohibits government from using its power arbitrarily. At the same time, certain population groups, particularly the young, may be treated differently by the government under certain circumstances. The objective of this chapter is to examine some of the constitutional questions concerning juveniles that have come before the U.S. Supreme Court. Confining the discussion to only those issues is a substantial limitation, one that requires some elaboration.

Government has a special role regarding children that provides the basis for the *parens patriae* concept. As a result, children are frequently the subjects of law. The body of law dealing most directly with children is found at the state rather than the federal level. This is true because under the U.S. constitutional system the states are given the primary authority to protect the public health, safety, and welfare. This means a state can enact laws that establish limits on what children may legally do or requirements for what must be done in situations involving children. Many of the laws that have been enacted address the ability of minors to make choices. Children are generally viewed as being unable to choose for themselves about such things as whether they receive medical treatment, go to school, enter into contractual obligations, or transfer property. Until a young person reaches the age of 18 (or possibly 21), or is otherwise deemed self-sufficient (emancipated), many of these kinds of decisions are made for the young person by his or her parents. In some instances, even parental choice is superseded by rules set by the state. The state may choose, for example, to impose special requirements on the situations in which young people may be employed. Similarly, states may wish to establish certain regulations that may apply only to children,

47

such as truancy or curfew laws. So long as these regulations are not arbitrary or do not suffer from a flaw like vagueness, federal constitutional questions are not likely to arise. As a result, court decisions discussed in this chapter do not directly address many of the matters mentioned above.

One area affected by Supreme Court rulings has been the juvenile justice system. Juvenile justice has a distinctive history and unique characteristics. The organization and jurisdiction of the juvenile courts is described here, and the judicial processes regarding delinquency are compared with the adult criminal process. The legal rights that apply to the juvenile justice process are featured. The focus of the chapter then changes to state laws designed to foster the development of children or to protect them from some kind of harm. Several issues relating to the educational environment are examined. Other policy areas in which states have acted to protect the special vulnerabilities of young people—pornography, consumption of alcohol, personal privacy, and abortion—also are discussed.

Juvenile Justice System

The juvenile justice system as we know it did not exist in the mid-nineteenth century. Generally speaking, youths who engaged in minor misconduct were placed in modest local institutions. Juveniles who committed more serious crimes were subjected to the same penalties as adults. Often, these punishments were severe. It was out of this situation that the present juvenile justice system began to evolve. Several elements are particularly relevant to an overview of the transformation.

The first was the rapid growth of urban populations. Large numbers of youths required attention not only because they were uneducated and destitute, but also as part of a strategy to curb potential delinquency. The sheer volume of children overwhelmed existing private efforts, and it became obvious that government involvement in a wide range of youth-focused activities was required. The second factor was the emergence of state-supported institutions for young people. A number of states also enacted laws that empowered courts to place youths in such facilities. Though these institutions were often harsh, state initiatives of this kind attracted great support. Closely related was the development of the *parens patriae* concept discussed earlier. When this concept was extended to institutional programs, the state possessed the virtual equivalent of parental control. Finally, states began to go beyond providing mere refuge programs and started to create other kinds of specialized institutions such as reform schools.

Those seeking to respond to the various needs of young people had made some gains in the second half of the nineteenth century, but major problems remained unsolved. It was thought that the establishment of a separate juvenile court authority might be the answer. With its Juvenile Court Act in 1899, Illinois created the first real juvenile court in the nation. All but three states did the same within less than two decades. The objective of these initiatives was to create a separate authority for delinquent youth. Under this court, juveniles could be separated from adults and placed in individual treatment programs in hopes of stemming or preventing delinquent conduct. The underlying principle of these courts was that juveniles, because of their age, should not be held accountable for conduct in the same way as an adult. Similarly, it was believed that juveniles should not be punished as adult offenders. Rather, individualized development and rehabilitative treatment ought to be provided. Finally, the system through which juveniles are processed must reflect a paternalistic and nonadversarial approach. Reflecting these principles, special juvenile courts eventually were established in every state.

Juvenile court jurisdiction was derived directly from the child's status as a minor. It was not based on the nature of the criminal violation. Neglected and otherwise dependent children fall within juvenile court jurisdiction as well. Prior to the 1960s, the influence of *parens patriae* produced a juvenile court system that was highly informal. Juveniles possessed virtually none of the constitutional protections available to adults. Attorneys were not required, and evidentiary rules were greatly relaxed in juvenile proceedings. This informality was challenged on a number of occasions, but to little effect. Cases were largely decided on due process grounds with the supreme court or other appellate courts at the state level refusing to set forth specific guidelines for juvenile courts.

This situation changed rather dramatically in the mid-1960s as the Warren Court imposed a number of constitutional requirements on juvenile proceedings. Three cases form the foundation of these changes. The first is *Kent v. United States* (383 U.S. 541: 1966), which involved the waiver of jurisdiction by a juvenile court to allow transfer of a juvenile's case to adult court. The juvenile court judge had transferred the case without making any findings in a formal proceeding and offered no reasons in support of the transfer decision. The Supreme Court imposed several specific procedural requirements on the transfer process including a hearing, representation by counsel, and access to all records and reports on the juvenile germane to the waiver. The juvenile court's behavior in *Kent* prompted the Court to say:

We agree with the Court of Appeals that the statute contemplates that the Juvenile Court should have considerable latitude within which to determine whether it should retain jurisdiction over a child or—subject to the statutory delimitation—should waive jurisdiction. But this latitude is not complete. At the outset, it assumes procedural regularity sufficient in the particular circumstance to satisfy the basic requirements of due process and fairness as well as compliance with the statutory requirement of a "full investigation." It does not confer upon the Juvenile Court a license for arbitrary procedure.... The State is *parens patriae* rather than prosecuting attorney and judge. But the admonition to function in a "parental" relationship is not an adequate invitation to procedural arbitrariness.... While there can be no doubt of the original laudable purpose of juvenile courts, studies and critiques in recent years raise serious questions as to whether actual performance measures well enough against theoretical purpose to make tolerable the immunity of the process from the reach of constitutional guarantees applicable to adults.

This paragraph fully embraces the changed view of the Supreme Court with respect to formalizing the activities of juvenile courts, but *Kent* was limited to a relatively small number of cases: those involving waiver or transfer to adult courts. The more comprehensive pronouncement came a year after *Kent* in *In re Gault* (387 U.S. 1: 1967).

Gerald Gault, age 15, was found to have made a lewd telephone call and was committed to the state industrial school as a delinquent. He faced the possibility of having to remain there until he was 21 years of age. For an adult the maximum punishment for such an offense would have been a $50 fine or confinement for not more than 60 days. Gault's parents appealed the outcome, claiming that (1) they had been given inadequate notice of the charges, (2) the complainant had not testified, (3) they had not been offered counsel, (4) Gerald had not been warned that any statements he made could be used against him, (5) no records had been made of the hearing, and (6) Arizona law permitted no appeal in a juvenile proceeding. With only Justice Potter Stewart dissenting, the Supreme Court ruled in favor of Gault.

The majority, through the opinion written by Justice Abe Fortas, recognized that juvenile and adult proceedings had been intentionally different up to that point. Fortas declared, however, that the juvenile process could no longer remain outside the reach of basic constitutional standards. He suggested that the essential difference between Gault's case and an adult criminal case is that safeguards available to adults were discarded for the juvenile. Although some benefits had derived from handling juveniles differently (more informally), there was consensus on the Supreme Court that some procedural protections had to be added. Justice Fortas said, "Under our Constitution, the condition of being a boy does not justify a kangaroo court." The holding in *Gault* required that delinquency proceedings that may lead to detention must provide juveniles with access to counsel (with appointed counsel in the instance of indigence), with adequate notification of charges and a right to confront witnesses, and with the privilege against self-incrimination. The Court repeated its position from *Kent* that proceedings "must measure up to the essentials of due process and fair treatment."

The third case of this group of decisions was *In re Winship* (397 U.S. 358: 1970). In *Winship*, the Court considered whether juvenile courts could continue to use the civil standard of preponderance of evidence to determine delinquency. According to the old civil standard provided by state law, Samuel Winship was found to have stolen money. On appeal, a six-justice majority of the Court ruled that proving guilt beyond a reasonable doubt is an essential element of due process. Consequently, the reasonable doubt standard must be used at the adjudicatory stage of any proceeding in which a juvenile is charged with an act that would constitute a crime if committed by an adult. Justice William Brennan argued that a criminal defendant would be at a "severe disadvantage" if guilt was allowed to be determined on the strength of the "same evidence as would suffice in a civil case." The reasonable doubt standard emphasizes the "necessity of reaching a subjective state of certitude of the facts." As for the need to extend the standard to juvenile proceedings, Brennan said that "civil labels and good intentions do not themselves obviate the need for criminal due process standards in juvenile courts." It was asserted that these more rigorous evidentiary standards would not interfere with confidentiality, informality, flexibility, and the speed with which juvenile proceedings occur. They would not compel states to "abandon or displace any of the substantive benefits of the juvenile justice process." Soon after *Winship*, the Court applied the reasonable doubt standard retroactively to all cases still in the appellate process. The Court said in *Ivan V. v. City of New York* (407 U.S. 203: 1972) that the reasonable doubt standard provides "concrete substance" for the presumption of innocence. Due process requires that no person shall lose his or her liberty "unless the government has borne the burden of . . . convincing the fact finder of his [the accused's] guilt." To that end, the Court asserted that the reasonable doubt standard is "indispensable" and must be given "complete retroactive effect."

Winship gave the Supreme Court an opportunity to use the due process clause of the Fourteenth Amendment as a means to establish fairness standards beyond those expressly contained in the Bill of Rights. The case profoundly affected juvenile as well as adult criminal proceedings. Whereas the reasonable doubt standard previously was only presumed to apply to adults, *Winship* specifically joined the reasonable doubt standard and the concept of due process for juveniles as well. *Winship*, following soon after *Gault*, moved juvenile processes further from the status of civil proceedings and placed them alongside adult criminal trials. Though exact equivalence was not created, a relative parity was achieved by the rulings in *Kent, Gault,* and *Winship*. Juvenile authorities were now expected to treat delinquency in a manner consistent with the requirements of due process. The informality that marked juvenile processes before *Kent* and *Gault* was clearly a thing of the past after *Winship*. The post-*Gault* juvenile process has several steps, each of which is summarily described below. The constitutional rights that apply to each step of the juvenile justice process are woven into this discussion.

Juvenile courts have jurisdiction over persons based on their age and their actions. State legislatures establish the maximum age for juvenile status, which is commonly 18. The juvenile courts have jurisdiction over crimes committed by youths under the age of 18. Criminal conduct by a juvenile is called delinquency. Juvenile courts also have jurisdiction over status offenses, which are acts for which adults are not prosecuted because they stem directly from a person's status as a juvenile. A juvenile, for example, can commit the offenses of truancy or unmanageability. The status offense issue is complicated and is exclusively handled by state law through statutes defining supervisory responsibilities of juvenile authorities.

Juvenile Process: Police Investigations

For most youths, contact with the juvenile justice system begins with the police. A juvenile who commits a crime is subject to police investigation and possible arrest. As is the case with adults, police possess substantial discretion in making the decision to arrest. In the case of juveniles, police must decide whether to merely warn the young person, to release him or her to a parent or guardian, or to refer the matter to juvenile authorities. Cases involving serious misconduct, especially crimes against persons, are typically referred to juvenile authorities. Less serious incidents are seldom referred, or they are diverted to nonjudicial community agencies. As a rule, the rights of juveniles and adults are generally comparable with respect to police contacts. Constitutional protections apply to investigative activities such as searches, seizures, and custodial interrogations.

A legal arrest requires probable cause, which means an officer must have evidence from which to conclude that a crime occurred and that a particular person was involved. The law is exactly the same in this respect for adults and juveniles. Probable cause is a level of evidence that produces conclusions more solid than those based on only suspicion, but it is not equivalent to certainty. Police do have more extensive authority and greater discretion with juveniles because of the existence of status offenses.

The Fourth Amendment protection against unreasonable searches and seizures applies to juveniles. Evidence that is obtained in an unreasonable fashion may be excluded just as in adult proceedings. Indeed, the procedure for doing so is identical—defense counsel files a pre-trial motion to suppress the evidence. This motion requires the judge to determine the adequacy of the search, seizure, or interrogation.

Chapter 5 discusses in detail the protections afforded by the Fourth Amendment. In general, the Fourth Amendment describes the process by which arrest and search warrants may be obtained. Several significant exceptions to the warrant requirement make it possible for an officer to proceed without actually possessing a warrant. Warrantless actions are legally recognized and occur routinely. Automobiles, for example, may be searched with probable cause in the absence of a warrant. So, too, police may search a person whenever he or she voluntarily allows them to. The warrant exceptions described in the warrantless search discussion in chapter 5 apply to juveniles.

Unique ground rules exist concerning searches on school grounds. If probable cause can be established, a student, his or her locker, and his or her personal belongings may be searched. The more difficult questions relate to situations in which probable cause does not exist and the power of school officials, as distinct from police, to enforce school rules is the central issue. Historically, school authorities have been given substantial latitude to protect the general safety and well-being of the school under provisions of state law. In part, this is a product of the *in loco parentis* concept, which allows school officials to act in the place of the parent. This concept includes disciplinary actions. A second rationale hinges on ownership. In many states, courts have concluded that a locker belongs to the school district, not to the student. Thus, control and access rest with the school. Finally, a number of state court decisions distinguish between school officials and police. The effect of these cases is that school authorities are not required to obtain warrants. The reasoning is that a school official is essentially a private citizen and therefore someone who is not accountable to the same search restrictions as official agents of law enforcement. Even in the absence of a warrant, a search conducted by a private citizen is much less likely to be found unreasonable.

The U.S. Supreme Court recently addressed some of these issues in the case of *New Jersey v. T. L. O.* (469 U.S. 325: 1985). The case began when a teacher observed two girls smoking in a school restroom. Though not a crime, smoking did violate a school rule. One of the girls (T. L. O.), age 14, was called to the office of the assistant principal to be asked some questions. Her purse was opened in the course of the inquiry. In the purse were found cigarettes and evidence that the girl dealt small quantities of marijuana. The girl confessed to dealing marijuana at the school following discovery of the evidence in her purse. She was eventually adjudicated as delinquent largely on the basis of the evidence developed from the search of the purse. The Court essentially took a middle ground position in *T. L. O.* The state, on the one hand, had asserted that the Fourth Amendment simply did not apply to school searches. On the other hand, T. L. O. argued that school authorities must strictly observe warrant guidelines.

The Court characterized the state's contention that students have no need to bring personal property into school as not "well anchored in reality." Accordingly, students have a substantial privacy interest to protect from unreasonable intrusions by school authorities. Against this interest is the "substantial interest" of teachers and administrators in "maintaining discipline in the classroom and on school grounds." The Court said the task of maintaining order in schools is extremely difficult because it is often aggravated by the problems of drug use and violence. Thus, "close supervision" of schoolchildren is required as well as enforcement of rules against "conduct that would be perfectly permissible if undertaken by an adult," such as smoking. The school setting, said the Court, requires "some easing of the restrictions to which searches by public authorities are ordinarily subject." The Court called the warrant requirement "unsuited to the school environment" and said it would "unduly interfere with the maintenance of the swift and informal disciplinary procedures needed in the schools." The Court concluded that the school setting also requires a modification of the "level of suspicion of illicit activity needed to justify a search." The Court then recognized the legality of school searches based on suspicion that, "although 'reasonable,' do not rise to the level of probable cause." Thus, the Court lowered the threshold needed to trigger a legal school search, thereby making searches in schools presumptively reasonable.

CUSTODIAL INTERROGATION

Once a juvenile is detained, parents or guardians are typically contacted. Prior to the mid-1960s, authorities could question a juvenile even in the absence of a parent/guardian or a lawyer. The Warren Court dramatically altered the scope of self-incrimination protection with a series of significant decisions, the most important of which was *Miranda v. Arizona* (384 U.S. 436: 1966). *Miranda* directly addressed the rights of the accused during custodial interrogation, an "inherently stressful" and "coercive" setting for a suspect. *Miranda* required police to read to the accused the specific rights about self-incrimination and assistance of counsel and to make a reasonable attempt to determine whether the accused understood those rights. Soon after *Miranda,* the Court extended self-incrimination protections, including those addressed in *Miranda,* to juveniles with the ruling in the previously described *Gault* case.

In virtually all situations, juveniles have access to the guidance of a parent/ guardian or attorney (or both). So long as police make a reasonable effort to comply with *Miranda,* a juvenile is considered sufficiently advised. *California v. Prysock* (453 U.S. 355: 1981) is informative regarding this situation. Randall Prysock was arrested in connection with a murder and advised of his rights. He was again read his rights in the presence of his parents, whereupon he decided to answer questions. He later tried unsuccessfully to have his answers suppressed and was eventually convicted of the murder as well as other charges. Prysock appealed the decision, asserting that although he was generally advised of his rights, he was not explicitly advised of his right to have counsel appointed at no cost prior to questioning. The contention was that his rights had not been fully conveyed. The Supreme Court disagreed, saying that neither *Miranda* nor cases decided after "suggested any desirable rigidity in the form of required warnings." On the contrary, *Miranda* itself "indicated that no talismanic incantation was required to satisfy its strictures." Either the *Miranda* format or a "fully effective equivalent" was sufficient. Based on a consideration of all the circumstances in this case, the Court concluded that authorities had effectively conveyed to Prysock his rights.

Prysock points out the most difficult custodial interrogation problem with respect to juveniles: the failure to utilize the warnings. The central question is the waiver of rights and whether juveniles can make a free and knowing waiver of constitutional protections. The Court has generally said they can so long as the "totality of circumstances" in each case shows that the waiver is reasonable. Some states are more demanding and do not permit a waiver unless made in the presence of a parent/guardian or counsel.

Rights of juveniles during interrogation are also governed by *Fare v. Michael C.* (442 U.S. 23: 1979). In this case, a juvenile was arrested on suspicion of murder and fully advised of his rights prior to questioning. At the outset of questioning, the juvenile, who had a lengthy juvenile record and was on probation, asked to see his probation officer. This request was denied. He then agreed to submit to questions in the absence of a lawyer. His responses were incriminating. After he was charged in juvenile court, the juvenile sought to suppress the statements, arguing that the request for his probation officer was the equivalent of requesting a lawyer and amounted to invoking his right to remain silent. The juvenile court refused to suppress the incriminating statements, concluding that Michael C. had waived his rights associated with *Miranda.* The Supreme Court saw the case the same way.

The Court rejected the contention that the request for the probation officer had the same effect as a request for an attorney. *Miranda* was based on the perception that the lawyer "occupies a critical position in our legal system because of his unique ability to protect the Fifth Amendment rights of a client undergoing custodial interrogation." A probation officer is simply not in the "same posture to either the accused or the system of justice as a whole." The Court also pointed out that the probation officer is not in the same position as the attorney to provide the kind of help the juvenile needs. The probation officer is an "employee of the state which seeks to prosecute the alleged offender." Notwithstanding the obligation owed a juvenile under his or her supervision, the probation officer is generally "duty bound to report wrong-doing by the juvenile when it comes to his attention, even if by communication from the juvenile himself." The probation officer is not able to offer the "type of independent advice an accused would expect from a lawyer retained or assigned to assist him during questioning." As a result, the Court concluded that the juvenile had voluntarily and knowingly waived his *Miranda* rights in this case.

IDENTIFICATION PROCEDURES

Beyond interrogation, other investigatory techniques commonly used by police brush against constitutional protections. Identification of suspects by witnesses is a principal one. The body of rulings that has evolved on this subject is treated in more detail in the discussion of self-incrimination in chapter 6. Adults are generally protected from "unnecessarily suggestive" identification procedures. Witnesses may not be shown lineups, for example, that point to the suspect or be shown a single photograph as opposed to an array from which to choose. The single most protective device is the defense counsel, who may be present during these identification procedures. The rights that exist for adults generally also apply to juveniles. The juvenile is clearly entitled to presence of counsel. If this does not occur and no valid waiver has been made, the pre-trial identification cannot be used.

JUVENILE COURT INTAKE

Police options with a juvenile include release, referral to a nonjudicial agency, or citation and referral to juvenile authorities. The juvenile court conducts its own screening of the juveniles referred to it. In some cases, petitions are filed and an adjudicatory hearing is eventually held. If the child is to be adjudicated, the issue facing the juvenile court is the pre-trial status of the juvenile. In most states, cases are carefully screened by juvenile authorities to determine whether the juvenile is to be released to a parent or guardian or detained in some shelter facility pending adjudication of the case. A formal hearing must be held if the juvenile authorities wish to detain the suspect.

A detention hearing is conducted at the outset of the process before the juvenile spends much time in a shelter. At these hearings, the juvenile is entitled to assistance of counsel and other procedural safeguards such as the protection from self-incrimination. Though the criteria used to make the detention decision vary somewhat from state to state, they typically include protection of the juvenile, the risk the juvenile poses to the community, and the likelihood that the juvenile will appear at subsequent proceedings if released. In a number of states, probable cause that the juvenile committed the crime must be established before detention can occur.

If the determination is made to detain a juvenile, pre-adjudication release may still be available on bail status, at least in some jurisdictions. At this time, there is no interpretation of the federal Constitution establishing a juvenile's right to bail, although some states have adopted such a policy as a matter of state law. The Court upheld the use of preventive detention for juveniles in the case of *Schall v. Martin* (467 U.S. 253: 1984). Preventive detention is a policy that allows a state to keep a person in custody because he or she poses a risk to the community. Those who support preventive detention argue that it keeps the detainee from engaging in additional criminal conduct or threatening the victim of the original crime. In *Schall,* the Court found New York State's juvenile preventive detention law to be constitutional. Under the law, juveniles could be detained if it could be shown that there was "serious risk" of the juvenile committing more crime if released. The Court acknowledged that the state has a legitimate and compelling interest in protecting the community from crime irrespective of the age of the potential perpetrator. Indeed, the crime fighting interest may be accentuated in the case of juveniles given the high rate of juvenile recidivism. In addition, the Court noted the state's "*parens patriae* interest" in protecting the juvenile from the consequences of his or her criminal conduct. Finally, the Court found that the New York law contained the required procedural safeguards and strictly limited detention time through an expedited adjudicatory process for de-tained juveniles.

One of the most important options that exists for both law enforcement agencies and the juvenile courts is to route particular cases out of the court system. This is commonly called diversion. Diversion programs, widely available to adults as well as juveniles, channel offenders into alternate programs prior to formal charging. When a person is diverted, her or she is not actually screened out of the criminal process, but is given the incentive of deferred prosecution to participate in some particular activity. If the alternative program is successfully completed, prosecution does not occur. On the other hand, if a person does not wish to enter into a program or fails to perform satisfactorily once in a program, it is likely that he or she will be prosecuted as though no diversion option existed. Diversion programs are usually quite attractive to offenders because successful completion of the alternative activity eliminates any record of the offense.

Diversion programs may be either police-based or court-based. In the former, juveniles are not processed through to the juvenile courts at all, as the judgment to divert rests with the police. Court-based diversion is more extensive and may involve both community agencies outside the court structure as well as some units structurally attached to the juvenile courts. In either case, juveniles who qualify for diversion are typically status or first offenders. Diversion also attempts to capitalize on the presence of community alternatives, many of which exist for substance abuse problems; thus, many juveniles who are diverted are drug or alcohol dependent.

Adjudication

If a juvenile is not diverted, his or her case proceeds to adjudication. One of three things can occur at the adjudicatory stage. The juvenile can be transferred to adult court, can admit to the conduct alleged in the petition, or can deny the charge and have the matter formally adjudicated by the juvenile court.

Transfer of juveniles to adult court occurs only in extraordinary cases. The decision to transfer has major implications for the juvenile. Since the *Kent* decision, there are specific requirements for the conduct of waiver or transfer proceedings. At minimum, a transfer cannot be made without a formal hearing. Further, the juvenile is entitled to representation by counsel, and sufficient notice must be given both to parents and to counsel before the hearing transpires. Finally, the juvenile judge must put on the record the reasons for approving the transfer.

Those who are critical of transferring juveniles believe that being convicted at a young age in adult court is likely to condemn the juvenile to lifelong deficiencies in education and employment opportunities. Proponents of transfer argue that a few juveniles are beyond the rehabilitative capabilities of the juvenile courts and that these juveniles must be punished like adult offenders. Almost every state permits transfer of juveniles to adult courts and establishes guidelines for doing so under statute. Few jurisdictions allow transfer of a juvenile under the age of 14, and many restrict waiver to juveniles age 15 or older. Some states also establish other criteria as threshold conditions for transfer. Among the most common are seriousness of the alleged offense, prior record as a juvenile, and the likelihood that the rehabilitation treatment available to the juvenile court will succeed.

The Court examined another dimension of the waiver process in the case of *Breed v. Jones* (421 U.S. 519: 1975). The case involved a 17-year-old who was adjudicated in a juvenile court but later transferred to adult court for prosecution because he was "unfit for treatment as a juvenile." Gary Steven Jones appealed his subsequent adult conviction claiming he had already been "in jeopardy" in his juvenile proceeding and that initiation of charges against him in the adult court was foreclosed by the Fifth Amendment prohibition against double jeopardy. The Supreme Court agreed with Jones; the ruling rested primarily on the Court's perception of jeopardy. The Court said it was "simply too late in the day" to think that a juvenile is "not put in jeopardy at a proceeding whose object is to determine whether he has committed acts that violate criminal law," a proceeding "whose potential consequences include both the stigma inherent in such a determination and the deprivation of liberty for many years." So, according to the Court, despite attempts to make juvenile judicial proceedings different from adult trials, the juvenile process resembles the adult process closely enough to create jeopardy.

The Court also rejected the contention that the prosecution of Jones as an adult was merely a continuation of the prosecution begun at the juvenile level. Though the Court agreed the case "had not yet reached its conclusion" in the juvenile proceeding in that no sentence had been assigned, it determined that the failure to sentence Jones had not in any way limited Jones's risk or jeopardy. Putting Jones "at risk" was viewed as the decisive aspect of jeopardy. The juvenile court, "as the trier of facts, began to hear evidence," and at that point Jones's jeopardy began. If the juvenile authorities wished to preserve flexibility in terms of treatment or sentencing options, those matters should have been considered prior to commencing proceedings in the juvenile court. If a defendant cannot be suitably treated as a delinquent, the Court urged that transfer occur prior to adjudicatory hearings.

A juvenile can also admit to the charge(s) contained in a petition, which is known as agreeing to a finding. If a juvenile wishes to take this course, the court must be satisfied that the juvenile understands the right to a fair hearing and that the admission of guilt is wholly voluntary. In most respects, the rules governing juvenile admissions parallel those established for adults in plea bargaining cases such as *Boykin v. Alabama* (395 U.S. 238: 1969). Plea bargaining as such occurs less often with juveniles than with adults. Rather, when juveniles admit guilt, it is typically to the original charge contained in the petition, so the arrangement lacks the exchange character of plea agreements entered by adults.

If a juvenile neither is diverted nor admits guilt, the case remains with the juvenile court and undergoes a formal fact-finding or adjudicatory process. At an adjudicatory hearing, a juvenile judge hears evidence in support of the charges contained in the delinquency petition. Because of Supreme Court rulings such as *Gault,* this hearing is highly formal and has virtually all the procedural protections afforded adult defendants at trial. Included are the right to assistance of counsel, the right to confront adverse witnesses, the right to put forward motions to suppress evidence, and protection from compulsory self-incrimination. Since *Winship,* charges against a juvenile must also be proven beyond a reasonable doubt. The adjudication process ends when the court enters a judgment on the fact questions contained in the case.

Some legal questions regarding juvenile adjudication have not yet been resolved by the Supreme Court. In some jurisdictions, for example, rules of evidence used at the adjudicatory stage are not identical to those applied to adult trials. Often, juvenile proceedings are not public. There are also a few areas where the Court has chosen not to make adult and juvenile processes identical, the most important being the jury trial. The Supreme Court ruled in *McKeiver v. Pennsylvania* (403 U.S. 528: 1971) that juveniles are not entitled to trial by jury. Below we examine more closely the Court's thinking in *McKeiver.*

Decisions such as *Gault* brought substantial changes to the juvenile justice system. However, the Court later said in *McKeiver* that these changes did not mean that every right assured an accused adult would automatically be extended to juveniles. In some instances, said the Court, adult protections would not produce desirable results in the juvenile process. Jury trials was one such instance in the Court's view. A majority of the Court in *McKeiver* saw value in retaining some of the traditional differences between adult and juvenile processes and in maintaining a selective approach on extending constitutional protections.

The Court was trying to "strike a judicious balance" between "procedural orderliness" and the more informal approach of juvenile courts. The majority did not wish to transform juvenile proceedings into a "fully adversarial process" by making access to a jury a required element. Such a policy might diminish the "idealistic prospect of an intimate, informal protective proceeding." Further, the Court felt that the use of a jury would not improve the fact-finding function of juvenile courts. Rather, it might "provide an attrition of the juvenile court's assumed ability to function in a unique manner." Use of the jury would also bring into juvenile courts the "traditional delays, the formality, and the clamor of the adversary system and, possibly, the public trial." The Court said that if such formality is "superimposed" on the juvenile system, there is "little need for its separate existence."

With *McKeiver,* the Burger Court established that the changes in juvenile rights brought by decisions such as *Gault* and *Winship* would not remove all distinctions between adult and juvenile proceedings. *McKeiver* preserved the thrust of the rationale that created separate juvenile courts in the first place. The Burger Court was not unsympathetic to the basic tightening and formalizing of procedural requirements in the juvenile justice system, however; it would later extend juvenile rights to cases involving double jeopardy protection (*Breed v. Jones*). At the same time, *McKeiver* said that juvenile proceedings were not quite a fully adversarial process needing all the constitutional guarantees of adult proceedings. The Court did suggest that state legislatures may opt for jury trials or that state appellate courts may require them through interpretation of state constitutions. Thus, juvenile processes were not to be regarded as full-blown criminal proceedings, although states were free to structure juvenile proceedings more tightly if they wished.

The adjudication process ends when the juvenile court makes a finding on the delinquency petition. If the state cannot show delinquency by proving the allegations beyond a reasonable doubt, the case is over. If, on the other hand, delinquency is demonstrated, the court must conclude the case by imposing some form of disposition on the juvenile. In most jurisdictions, this requires a separate step usually called a dispositional hearing. Disposition is determined by the nature of the offense, the juvenile's prior record, and home situation. The first two of these factors are heavily utilized when determining adult sentences. Far more disposition options exist for the juvenile than for the adult. Though the range is wide, all options relate in some way to the rehabilitative objectives of the juvenile court.

Some post disposition legal questions have developed with respect to juveniles. The Supreme Court has not chosen to review these issues as yet, which leaves the states great discretion under state law. Most jurisdictions provide for appeals from adjudication of delinquency, but the ground rules vary substantially. It is also possible to transfer juveniles to adult institutions such as mental health or penal facilities. In the instance of mental health transfers, the decision rests on whether the juvenile might receive services not otherwise available. Transfer to an adult penal facility occurs if the juvenile cannot be sufficiently controlled in the juvenile institution. In both situations, a hearing with such safeguards as assistance of counsel is usually required. Finally, juveniles may be placed on some kind of after-care program like probation or parole. If revocation of this status is subsequently sought by authorities, the juvenile receives essentially the same due process protections as an adult, which include representation by counsel and a formal revocation hearing.

Generally speaking, adult and juvenile processes are similar. Police investigations and constraints upon them are certainly comparable. Both adults and juveniles are entitled to hearings on a variety of key matters including pre-trial detention and motions seeking to suppress incriminating evidence. Both processes also feature fact-finding at a formal trial or adjudicatory stage. Finally, the cases of both juveniles and adults are concluded by the imposition of treatment or sentencing as a consequence of guilt being admitted or proven. Appellate review is available to both adults and juveniles.

Despite recent Supreme Court decisions drawing the adult and juvenile processes into closer parallel, some differences of significance still exist. The juvenile courts remain an organizational entity separate from the adult courts in most states. Notwithstanding the imposition of many constitutional safeguards, the juvenile process retains its original purpose of treating and rehabilitating delinquent youths in a nonadversarial fashion. In other words, juvenile courts retain at least some of the civil character they possessed prior to *Gault* and other decisions, and somewhat greater informality still exists in the juvenile justice system. Juvenile court jurisdiction is determined principally by the criterion of age and not on the seriousness of the alleged offense. Juvenile courts are required to provide neither open trials nor juries. In contrast, adult trials must be public and defendants in adult courts may have a jury trial on demand. Juveniles are also protected from the release of identifying information to the media. Further, a juvenile record remains confidential and can be sealed when the juvenile is no longer a minor. Adults enjoy none of these advantages. Parents or guardians play a significant role in what happens to a juvenile, especially in terms of pre-trial detention and disposition. Certainly no adult counterpart exists to release into the custody of a parent or guardian. Finally, juveniles have a right to rehabilitative treatment in disposition. A juvenile court is precluded from sentencing juveniles to institutions reserved for adults, and subsequent transfers to such facilities require a formal hearing. Transfers of adults from one prison to another can be done administratively. The death penalty for a juvenile who was 16 or younger at the time a capital offense was committed is also categorically impermissible.

Juveniles and the Educational Process

Much of the Supreme Court's recent activity has focused on procedural rights in the delinquency process. Far many more children attend school than appear in the juvenile justice system, however. Historically, states have retained almost absolute authority to govern their own educational processes, but some interesting constitutional questions developed regarding the public school context during the 1970s and 1980s. The issues of compulsory school attendance, school discipline, and self-expression rights on school grounds have been among the most important. Some other issues affecting the classroom are addressed in other places in this book. Religious activities in the public schools and the extent to which the state may direct "aid" to nonpublic schools, for example, are discussed in chapter 4. The schools have also been a primary battleground in the effort to end racial discrimination. Discussion of some of the most important decisions concerning this issue can be found in chapter 9.

COMPULSORY ATTENDANCE

Compulsory attendance laws require children to attend school until a specified age, most commonly 16. Such laws exist in every state and were generally enacted to reflect the priority the state assigns to educating children. Virtually all challenges to such laws have failed to persuade courts that requiring education is an unreasonable exercise of power. Indeed, the state possesses "paramount" responsibility for education. Violators of compulsory attendance laws can be referred to juvenile authorities for legal action.

A legal challenge to compulsory education on religious grounds did succeed in 1972. In the case of *Wisconsin v. Yoder* (406 U.S. 205: 1972), the Supreme Court created a free exercise exception to the compulsory attendance law of Wisconsin. Jonas Yoder, the parent of children subject to the law, did not challenge the law as discriminatory against religion. Neither did Yoder challenge the state's interest in providing for the education of young people. Yoder was a member of the Old Order Amish who had sent his children to school through the eighth grade but refused to keep the children in school to age 16 as required by law. He argued that attendance of Amish children beyond the eighth grade was contrary to their religious beliefs and way of life. It was contended that attending high school might endanger the children's salvation. More important, it might threaten the ongoing existence of the sect by exposing Amish children to worldly influences that would draw them away from their beliefs.

The Court found for the Amish in this case. Though it acknowledged the state's legitimate and profound responsibility for education, the Court held that even a fundamental function like education was not "totally free from the balancing process when it impinges on other fundamental rights and interests." In this instance, the "impact of the compulsory attendance law on the practice of the Amish religion is not only severe, but inescapable." This impact is not confined to "grave interference with important Amish religious tenets" but also brings the "very real threat of undermining the Amish community and religious practices as it [*sic*] exists today." The effective choice left for the Amish was to "abandon belief and be assimilated into society or be forced to migrate to some other and more tolerant region." The Court attempted to restrict the effect of the ruling by emphasizing that the Amish were disputing only one or possibly two years of high school–level education, which provides training that would be of little value in the agrarian Amish community.

One interesting sidebar to *Yoder* involved who determines whether the Amish child is to leave the public schools: the parent or the student. Though there was no reason to address that question in *Yoder* (the litigation was brought by the parent only), the Court did say that the case involved

> the fundamental interest of parents, as contrasted with that of the State, to guide the religious future and education of their children. The history and culture of western civilization reflect a strong tradition of parental concern for the nurture and upbringing of their children. This primary role of parents in the upbringing of their children is now established beyond debate as an enduring American tradition.

The Court deferred to parental rights here because it is the parents who are

> subject to prosecution here for failure to cause their children to attend school, and it is their right of free exercise, not that of their children that must determine Wisconsin's power to impose criminal penalties on the parent. That State has at no point tried this case on the theory that respondents were preventing their children from attending school against their expressed desires, and indeed the record is to the contrary. The State's position from the outset has been that it is empowered to apply its compulsory attendance law to Amish parents in the same manner as other parents—that is, without regard to the wishes of the child. That is the claim we reject today.

SCHOOL DISCIPLINE

The matter of discipline in the public schools presents some interesting questions. Under the *in loco parentis* doctrine, school authorities historically assumed something like parental rights and were generally allowed to discipline students. More recently the concept of parent delegation has been replaced by the view—more consonant with compulsory education laws— that the state itself may take disciplinary measures as is reasonably necessary for the proper education of the child and the maintenance of order in school operations. At the same time, the Supreme Court has imposed some modest due process requirements on discipline such that some protection exists from excessive and arbitrary punishment in schools.

The Court addressed the issue of corporal punishment in the case of *Ingraham v. Wright* (430 U.S. 651: 1977). Two students in a Florida junior high school were subjected to disciplinary paddling; each sustained injuries and brought suit in federal court. They contended that corporal punishment violated the Eighth Amendment prohibition on cruel and unusual punishment. They also argued that the due process clause of the Fourteenth Amendment entitled them to prior notice and a hearing before the punishment. The Court ruled against the students on both issues. Before addressing the two specific contentions, the Court said that generally at common law, a "single principle" has governed the use of corporal punishment since before the American Revolution: "Teachers may impose reasonable but not excessive force to discipline a child."

The Court rejected the Eighth Amendment arguments, ruling that the amendment was designed to "protect those convicted of crimes" and refusing to extend these provisions to public schools. The prisoner and the school student "stand in wholly different circumstances," and the student has "little need" for such protection. Though attendance "may not always be voluntary, the public school remains an open institution." This provides sufficient protection in itself.

> Except perhaps when very young, the child is not physically restrained from leaving school during school hours; and at the end of the school day, the child is invariably free to return home. Even while at school, the child brings with him the support of family and friends and is rarely apart from teachers and other pupils who may witness and protest any instances of mistreatment.

The openness of the public school and its supervision by the community afford significant safeguards against the kinds of abuses from which the Eighth Amendment protects the prisoner.... As long as the schools are open to public scrutiny, there is no reason to believe that the common law constraints will not effectively remedy and deter excesses such as those alleged in this case.

The Court also saw other sanctions as sufficient protections against deprivation of due process. School authorities are "unlikely to inflict corporal punishment unnecessarily or excessively when a possible consequence for doing so is the institution of civil or criminal proceedings against them." As a result, the Court was quite reluctant to impose notice and hearing requirements to further safeguard due process in the case of corporal punishment.

Contrary to its position on corporal punishment, however, the Court viewed a hearing as a more critical ingredient in the process that might lead to suspension or expulsion. The leading case regarding this topic is *Goss v. Lopez* (419 U.S. 565: 1975). A group of students filed suit against school officials challenging a state law that permitted a principal to suspend a student for misconduct for up to ten days without a hearing. The Court ruled that a state may not authorize suspension for misconduct without processes that satisfy due process requirements. The due process clause forbids "arbitrary deprivations of liberty." In this case, suspensions were authorized on misconduct charges that, if sustained and recorded, "could seriously damage the students' standing with their fellow pupils and their teachers." This could also "interfere with later opportunities for higher education and employment." The Court said this unilateral action authorized by the state "immediately collides with the requirements of the Constitution." The Court concluded by saying:

> The Due Process Clause will not shield him from suspensions properly imposed, but it disserves both his interest and the interest of the State if his suspension is in fact unwarranted. The concern would be mostly academic if the disciplinary process were a totally accurate, unerring process, never mistaken and never unfair. Unfortunately, that is not the case, and no one suggests that it is. Disciplinarians, although proceeding in utmost good faith, frequently act on the reports and advice of others, and the controlling facts and the nature of the conduct under challenge are often disputed. The risk of error is not at all trivial, and it should be guarded against if that may be done without prohibitive cost or interference with the educational process.

Goss requires suspension hearings, although such rights as assistance of counsel and confrontation of accusers are not specifically required as a condition of the hearing.

If due process rights apply to the suspension situation, they clearly apply to expulsions. The Court has heard only one recent case on expulsion, but it involved a federal suit against board members and administrators of a school district for damages. The plaintiffs claimed that their federal constitutional rights to due process were violated by their expulsions. In deciding the case of *Wood v. Strickland* (420 U.S. 308: 1975), the Court made two very interesting observations. First, it said the role of the federal courts is not to "set aside decisions of school administrators which the court may view as lacking a basis in wisdom or compassion." The U.S. system of public education, the Court went on, "relies necessarily upon the discretion and judgment of school administrators and school board members." Damage actions were not intended "to be the vehicle for federal court correction of errors in the exercise of that discretion which do not rise to the level of violations of specific constitutional guarantees." At the same time, the Court did say that school officials are not immune from liability if they "knew or reasonably should have known" that an action taken "within the sphere of official responsibility would violate the constitutional rights of the students affected" or if the action was taken "with the malicious intention to cause a deprivation of such right or injury to the student."

According to Court rulings, students do possess First Amendment expression rights in the schools, but the protections are conditional. Of the many kinds of expression, three are considered here. The first is expression that is passive in character, such as wearing armbands or political buttons or badges. This kind of expression is generally permitted. The principal case on this issue is *Tinker v. Des Moines* (393 U.S. 503: 1969). In this case, students were suspended for wearing black armbands in protest of the war in Vietnam. The Court said that "young people do not shed their constitutional rights at the schoolhouse door." Unless authorities can show that expressive conduct will "materially interfere" with the operation of the school, such conduct cannot be restricted. In this instance, the expression was "silent," "passive," and "unaccompanied by any disorder or disturbance."

Expression that has an active component is more prone to regulation. Such expression includes the uttering of words at a gathering or demonstration. Restrictions on active conduct are permitted because, unlike the wearing of armbands in *Tinker,* it may cause "interference" with school operations and the capacity of the school to maintain order and discipline. Schools have been permitted to take preventive action for such things as demonstrations and sit-ins and have also been permitted to discipline students involved in such activities. In these situations, the courts take a balancing approach in which the expression interests are weighed against the interests of those students not participating and wishing to have their educational rights protected.

Schools are also permitted broad discretion in monitoring student publications. This discretion goes far enough to allow censorship if school officials judge particular content to be objectionable. The definitive Court decision is *Hazelwood School District v. Kuhlmeier* (484 U.S. 260: 1988). Several former staff members of a high school newspaper brought suit claiming the school district had violated their expression rights by deleting articles from a particular issue of the paper. The articles described a student pregnancy experience and the effect on students of parental divorce. The paper was produced by a journalism class as part of the school curriculum, and the principal reviewed all page proofs prior to publication. The principal objected to the article on pregnancy as inappropriate for some of the younger students at the school. The article on divorce was found objectionable because it identified one of the parties by name. In addition, the article discussed abusive parental conduct without giving the parent an opportunity to respond. The principal ordered the pages on which the two articles appeared withheld from the paper even though these same pages contained other, unobjectionable material.

The Court ruled that no First Amendment violation had occurred in this case. Though it acknowledged that students retain constitutional rights in school, the Court said the rights of students in public schools are not "automatically coextensive with the rights of adults in other settings." Rather, these rights must be applied in light of the "special characteristics of the school environment." A school "need not tolerate" student speech that is "inconsistent" with the "basic educational mission, even though the government could not censor similar speech outside the school." The Court rejected the assertion that the paper was a forum for public expression, saying that school facilities are public forums only if they are open for "indiscriminate use" by the "general public" or a portion of the general public. On the other hand, if facilities have been "reserved for other intended purposes," no public forum exists and school authorities may impose "reasonable restrictions."

In this case, the school district merely adhered to its policy that publication of the newspaper was part of the educational process and therefore an activity subject to the control of the school staff. Since there was no intent to open the paper to "indiscriminate use" by the student body or even by the newspaper's student staff, the Court ruled that the school officials were entitled to reasonably regulate the paper's content. Educators may exercise control over certain expression to assure that participants "learn whatever lessons the activity is designed to teach," that readers or listeners are not exposed to material that is "inappropriate for their level of maturity," and that the positions taken are not "erroneously attributed to the school." Educators, said the Court, do not violate the First Amendment by "exercising editorial control over the style and content of student speech in school-sponsored expressive activities" so long as their actions are "reasonably related to legitimate pedagogical concerns."

The Child Protection System

Parents possess great discretion to rear their children free of governmental scrutiny. This has historically included judgments on general care, discipline, and choices of what children see, read, and believe. During the 1970s and 1980s, the problems of parental abuse and neglect prompted reconsideration of the state's proper role with respect to the family. A child protection system has evolved that is designed to formally respond to situations in which children are victimized by parents. A brief description of that system is given below, followed by an examination of several cases that concern the criminal prosecution of those, parents and others, who victimize children.

If a parent abuses or neglects a child, he or she may be prosecuted like anyone who injures a child. In most states, however, parents are processed in courts having jurisdiction over juveniles under specific child abuse statutes. The objectives driving prosecutions are, first, to protect the child and, second, to sanction the abusive parent(s). Statutes set forth the particular processes to be used in abuse cases. The typical approach is through a specialized protective service agency. These agencies, often located within large state social service departments, must investigate and then file formal petitions in juvenile court charging abuse or neglect.

Once a petition is filed, the parents are formally notified of the charges. Parents accused of abuse are entitled to counsel, just as are adults accused of any other crime. Often, however, the juvenile court is required under state law to appoint counsel for the child as well, given that the parental and child interests are adversarial in cases of this kind. The child's attorney is commonly called a guardian *ad litem*. The parents may admit to the charges contained in the petition, in which case the court enters a consent decree and schedules the case for disposition. If the charges are denied, the case proceeds toward trial or adjudication. A formal conference typically occurs before the adjudication where evidence issues are resolved and the evidence itself is reviewed. Many of those who initially deny guilt alter their positions at this conference, and a consent decree is entered as though charges had been admitted from the outset. The few cases that remain must be tried.

The critical part of the process involves disposition. As with criminal sentencing, disposition is a discrete step. Recommendations from the state agency are presented and reviewed, and a formal disposition is ultimately entered and regularly monitored. Several options are available for disposition. The most common is temporary removal of the child from the home to a foster care home. The effectiveness of such temporary intervention continues to be the subject of substantial debate. The court also possesses authority to permanently terminate parental status. Obviously an extreme option, this is reserved for the most severe cases. Interruption of parental rights, either permanent or temporary, is essentially a matter of state law. Cases involving this issue do not frequently go before the U.S. Supreme Court. There are, however, two Supreme Court cases that do address this question.

Both cases involved procedural rights in proceedings to terminate parental status. In *Lassiter v. Department of Social Services* (452 U.S. 18: 1981), the Court ruled that refusal to appoint counsel for an indigent parent contesting termination of her status did not violate due process protections. Abby Lassiter's son was judged to be neglected and was temporarily removed from her custody. She was subsequently convicted of second degree murder and sentenced to a lengthy prison term (25 to 40 years). The social service agency to which custody had been temporarily transferred petitioned to permanently end parental rights. Lassiter did not retain counsel, nor was one appointed. Her parental status was terminated, and she appealed claiming her indigency entitled her to appointment of a lawyer. Essentially the Court rejected her claim on the ground that an indigent is entitled to court-appointed counsel only when he or she "may be deprived of his [or her] physical liberty." If physical liberty is not involved, then the court should weigh three factors: the private interest, the state's interest, and the risk that procedures used will lead to an erroneous decision in making the due process judgment. Upon considering these factors in Lassiter's case, the Court concluded that no due process violation had occurred when the judge did not appoint counsel. The termination petition contained no charges on which criminal charges could be based; further, no "specially troublesome" points of law were involved. In the Court's view, counsel would not have "made a determinative difference" for Lassiter.

The Court applied the same three-prong test in *Santosky v. Kramer* (455 U.S. 745: 1982), a case that focused on a minimum standard of proof in parental termination proceedings. Prior to this decision, termination judgments could be made on a preponderance of the evidence. The Court began by acknowledging the extensive parental interest involved. When the state "moves to destroy weakened family bonds, it must provide the parents with fundamentally fair procedures." The Court said the three factors weighed unevenly in these kinds of cases. The private or parental interest is "commanding," whereas the countervailing governmental interest is "comparatively slight." The risk of error from using a "preponderance standard is substantial." Termination proceedings have a "striking asymmetry" in the resources the parent and the state can bring to the litigation. The state's capacity to "assemble its case almost inevitably dwarfs the parents' ability to mount a defense"; therefore, an "elevated" standard of proof to a level of "clear and convincing" would reduce some of the risk of erroneous decision. "Increasing the burden of proof is done to impress the factfinder with the importance of the decision and thereby perhaps to reduce the chances that inappropriate termination will be ordered." The Court then considered the state's two interests in a termination proceeding: a *"parens patriae"* interest in protecting the child's welfare and an interest in reducing the costs of such proceedings. The Court concluded that a standard of proof "more strict than preponderance of the evidence is consistent with both interests."

Three other cases are relevant here although they do not specifically involve permanent termination. They focus instead on custody issues. In *Palmore v. Sidoti* (466 U.S. 429: 1984), the Court ruled that a natural mother cannot lose custody of a child by remarriage to a person of a different race. Custody of a three-year-old was awarded to the mother following the divorce of two caucasians. The mother subsequently cohabited with and later married a noncaucasian. A state court then awarded custody to the father on the grounds that the child's interests were better served than if she remained in a racially mixed household. On appeal, the Supreme Court unanimously reversed the decision. The Court acknowledged that a state court judgment on custody "is not ordinarily a likely candidate for review" but said that such review had been undertaken in this case because important federal concerns arise from the "Constitution's commitment to eradicating discrimination based on race." The Court said it would "ignore reality" to suggest that racial and ethnic prejudices do not exist. There is a "risk" that a child living with a step-parent of another race "may be subject to a variety of pressures and stresses not present if the child were living with parents of the same racial or ethnic origin." However, according to the Court, the issue is whether the "reality of private biases" and the possible harm they may cause are "permissible considerations" for removing a child from his or her natural mother; "we have little difficulty in concluding that they are not." The Constitution cannot "control such prejudices, but neither can it tolerate them." The "effects of racial prejudice, however real, cannot justify a racial classification removing an infant from the custody of its natural mother found to be an appropriate person to have such custody."

Lehr v. Robertson (463 U.S. 248: 1983) examined whether an unmarried father, lacking any legal or other relationships with a child, has any parental rights. Jonathan Lehr fathered an out-of-wedlock child. The mother eventually married another man who subsequently became the adoptive father of the child. Lehr sought to have the adoption set aside on the grounds that he did not receive notice of the adoption. The Court ruled he was not entitled to notice. He would have been notified had he done any one of a number of things, the most minimal of which was to enter his name in the putative fathers registry, but he did none of those things. The Court said that when an unwed father "demonstrates a full commitment to the responsibilities of parenthood" by participating in the "rearing of his child," his interest "acquires substantial protection under the due process clause." But the "mere existence of a biological link does not merit equivalent constitutional protection."

The third case examines civil liability of a protective service agency for failure to take custody of a child from an abusive parent. Joshua DeShaney was physically abused on a regular basis by his natural father. The Winnebago County Department of Social Services (DSS) received numerous complaints about the abuse and made some effort to protect the child. DSS took no steps to remove Joshua from his father's custody, however. A final beating of Joshua, age four at the time of the incident, left the child permanently brain damaged and profoundly retarded. Action was brought under Title 42, Section 1983 of the U.S. Code against DSS by Joshua and his mother for failure to protect him from his father's abusive conduct. It was asserted that DSS's failure to remove the boy from his father's custody deprived Joshua of his physical safety as protected by the substantive component of the due process clause of the Fourteenth Amendment. A federal district court granted summary judgment for DSS and was affirmed by the court of appeals. In *DeShaney v. Winnebago County Department of Social Services* (489 U.S. 189: 1989), the Supreme Court ruled six to three that the agency did not violate Joshua's rights under due process.

The due process clause does not require the state to protect the "life, liberty, and property of its citizens against invasion by private actors." The clause is intended to limit the state's power to act, not to be a "guarantee of certain minimal levels of safety and security." It forbids deprivation of life, liberty, or property by the state but cannot be expanded to impose an "affirmative obligation on the state to ensure that those interests do not come to harm by other means." The argument presented on behalf of Joshua contended that, even if there was no due process obligation to act to protect the general public, the state had a particular duty in Joshua's case because of a "special relationship" of DSS to the client in this instance. DSS was aware that Joshua "faced a special danger of abuse," and caseworkers had specifically indicated an intention to "protect him against that danger." Having "actually undertaken" to protect Joshua from his father, the state "acquired an affirmative 'duty' " through the due process clause to "do so in a reasonably competent fashion." The Court rejected these contentions, however. The state, said the Court, assumes responsibility for a person's "safety and general well-being" only when it formally takes custody of a person and holds him or her against his or her will. The affirmative duty to protect arises "not from a State's knowledge of an individual's predicament or from its expressions of intent to help him, but from the limitation which it has imposed on his freedom to act on his own behalf." The injury suffered by Joshua in this case occurred while he was in the custody of his father, "who was in no sense a state actor." While the state may have been aware of the "dangers that Joshua faced in the free world," the State "played no part in their creation," nor did it "do anything to render him any more vulnerable to them." That the state once took temporary custody does not alter the analysis. When DSS returned Joshua to his father, it "placed him in no worse position than that in which he would have been had it not acted at all." The state, concluded the Court, does not "become permanent guarantor of an individual's safety by once having offered him shelter."

A final set of cases concerns the issue of special protections afforded juveniles when they are themselves victims of criminal behavior and need to appear as witnesses in the trials of the accused. In *Globe Newspaper Company v. Superior Court* (457 U.S. 596: 1982), the Supreme Court ruled that a state could not close trials to the public and the press in all situations when a minor victim of a sex crime testifies. The state interests asserted in support of this approach were that the policy protects minor victims from further trauma and encourages such victims to come forward and testify truthfully. The Court dismissed the latter of these arguments because it did not agree that closure actually increase the likelihood that other victims would come forward. Safeguarding the psychological well-being of the minor, however, was seen as "compelling." But as compelling as it is, it "does not justify a mandatory closure rule." The Court saw the law as not being "narrowly tailored" to accommodate the asserted state interest. Determination on a case-by-case basis of whether closure is necessary to protect the welfare of a minor witness was clearly preferred by the Court.

Fair trial questions were also raised in *Pennsylvania v. Ritchie* (480 U.S. 39: 1987) and *Kentucky v. Stincer* (482 U.S. 730: 1987). George Ritchie was prosecuted for sex offenses against his minor daughter. He sought some records from a state agency in an attempt to develop a defense, but state law limited access to the records to protect the minor's confidentiality. The Court required at least limited access for Ritchie to ensure discovery of evidence that might clear him. In *Stincer*, the question was the defendant's presence at a hearing to determine the competency of child victims to testify in a molestation case. The Court did not require presence, with the view that if the children were found competent, they would be subject to full cross-examination at the trial. The only issue at the hearing was the witnesses' competency, and the Court concluded that Stincer's presence would not have ensured a more reliable determination on that question.

Finally, there is the question of whether a state can seek to insulate child victims from a defendant when they testify. Under Iowa law, a screen was placed between the defendant and the witnesses. The screen blocked the witnesses' view of the defendant, but the defendant could see and hear the witnesses through the screen. The Court, in *Coy v. Iowa* (487 U.S. 1012: 1988), disallowed the procedure as a violation of the defendant's confrontation rights. The right to confront guarantees a defendant a "face-to-face" meeting with his or her accusers. The face-to-face confrontation ensures the "integrity of the fact-finding process." Such a confrontation may "unfortunately upset the truthful rape victim or abused child," said the Court, but it may also "undo the false accuser, or reveal the child to be coached by a malevolent adult." Constitutional protections simply "have costs." Iowa had argued that the confrontation interest was "outweighed by the necessity of protecting victims of sexual abuse." It further argued that such necessity was established by the statute, which created a "legislative presumption of trauma." The Court ruled that this was not enough. Something more than the "generalized finding" underlying the law is required when an exception to a constitutional protection is not "firmly rooted in our jurisprudence." Since the state made no "individual findings" that the witnesses in this case "needed special protection," use of the screen could not be justified by any exception to the defendant's confrontation rights.

The Court subsequently modified *Coy* in *Maryland v. Craig* (111 L. Ed. 2d 666: 1990). It ruled that states could protect child abuse victims by allowing them to testify on closed-circuit television. Justice Sandra Day O'Connor wrote for a five-justice majority that neither *Coy* nor any other previous ruling established that a defendant has an absolute right to a face-to-face meeting with witnesses. The justices argued that although the confrontation clause "reflects a preference for face-to-face confrontation at trial, . . . we cannot say that such confrontation is an indispensable element of the Sixth Amendment guarantee." The central concern of the clause is to "ensure the reliability of evidence . . . by subjecting it to rigorous testing in the context of an adversary proceeding." Maryland's procedure of using closed-circuit television does prevent the child witness from seeing the defendant, but it "preserves all the other elements of the confrontation right." The Court said that use of the television procedure, "where necessary to further an important state interest, does not impinge upon the truth-seeking or symbolic purposes of the confrontation clause." The critical inquiry in *Craig,* then, became whether use of the television procedure is needed to further an important state interest. The Court concluded that protection of minor victims of sex crimes from "further trauma and embarrassment is a compelling" state interest. The Court also determined that the interest in the "physical and psychological well-being of child abuse victims may be sufficiently important to outweigh, at least in some cases, a defendant's right to face his or her accusers in court."

Several Other Constitutional Issues

The juvenile justice, educational, and child protection systems were each designed exclusively for children. Each represents an approach to child development, rehabilitation, or the physical well-being of minors that depends on a separate and extensive network of facilities and programs. In some other areas public policy treats juveniles differently from adults, but without the elaborate institutional structure. Several of these policy areas have prompted some interesting suits involving constitutional issues. In some cases the Constitution has been interpreted to permit differential treatment, whereas in others it has not. This chapter concludes with an examination of four of the more intriguing policy areas.

PROTECTION OF A JUVENILE'S IDENTITY

Juveniles generally enjoy greater protection from disclosure of identity and records than adults. Juvenile proceedings are usually closed to the public, and the names of juvenile defendants are not released to the media. Similarly, juvenile records are generally closed and cannot be easily accessed. None of these policies has a counterpart in the adult system. All of these practices are designed to insulate juveniles from the possible harsh and stigmatizing effects of publicity. Of course, juveniles would be subject to short-term discomfort and embarrassment with disclosure, but more important, it is generally believed that disclosure would be counterproductive to the more fundamental rehabilitative mission of the juvenile courts. Every state has at least some confidentiality protections. Legal challenges have been infrequent because the substantial interest these measures are designed to protect is readily recognized. Nonetheless, the Supreme Court has had to examine disclosure protections when those regulations have collided with the rights of others. Three cases exemplify some of the constitutional limits on a juvenile's protection from disclosure of identity.

The first case involves the juvenile as a witness for the prosecution in the trial of an adult. The defense wished to develop on cross-examination that the witness had a juvenile record and was on probation at the time he was to testify. The objective of such cross-examination was to introduce the possibility of bias stemming from the probationary status: that the witness was predisposed to make an identification either in an effort to cooperate or because he perceived pressure on him to identify the defendant. State law, however, protected the anonymity of juvenile offenders. Based on that law, the trial judge issued a protective order preventing any reference to the juvenile record of the witness.

On review, the Supreme Court ruled in *Davis v. Alaska* (425 U.S. 308: 1974) that disclosure of the record was necessary for the defense to fully utilize its constitutional right to cross-examine. The state offered the traditional rationale for anonymity, arguing that exposure of a juvenile record "would likely cause impairment" of the rehabilitative goals of juvenile correctional procedures. Such exposure might "encourage" additional delinquent acts or cause the juvenile to lose employment opportunities or to "otherwise suffer unnecessarily for his youthful transgression." The Court agreed that the state had cause to attempt to protect the juvenile but asserted that this interest is "outweighed" by the criminal defendant's right to "probe into the influence of possible bias on the testimony of a criminal identification witness." The state's policy interest in protecting the confidentiality of a juvenile record, concluded the Court, cannot "require the yielding of so vital a constitutional right as the effective cross-examination for bias of a witness." Had the state wished to protect the witness from exposure, it could have tried to make its case without him. The state cannot, "consistent with the right of confrontation," require the defendant to "bear the full burden of vindicating the State's interest in the secrecy of juvenile records."

According to the precedents set in two different cases, the general policy of protecting juvenile identity must also yield to free press interests. The first case is *Oklahoma Publishing Company v. District Court* (430 U.S. 308: 1977). The press had published stories about and a photograph of an 11-year-old charged with second-degree murder. The information reported in the stories and the photograph had been obtained by reporters present at the juvenile's detention hearing. The district court then entered a pre-trial order enjoining the media from publishing or broadcasting any information about the case. The order was challenged as an unconstitutional prior restraint. The Supreme Court ruled in this case—as it had a year earlier in *Nebraska Press Association v. Stuart* (427 U.S. 539: 1976)—that the press cannot be kept from publication of "widely disseminated information obtained at court proceedings which were in fact open to the public." The Court noted that the press were present at the hearing "with the full knowledge" of the judge, the prosecutor, and defense counsel. No objection was made to their presence and nothing suggests that the reporters "acquired the information unlawfully or even with the State's implicit approval." Under these circumstances, the Court found that the order violated the free press protection of the media.

The second case, *Smith v. Daily Mail Publishing Company* (443 U.S. 97: 1979), was slightly different. In this instance a state law made it a crime for a newspaper to publish without juvenile court approval the name of any minor charged as a juvenile offender. The *Daily Mail* identified by name a 14-year-old charged with killing another juvenile. Upon review, the Supreme Court ruled that the press cannot be punished for "truthful publication" of an "alleged delinquent's name lawfully obtained by a newspaper." In this case, the newspaper learned of the shooting through its routine monitoring of the police band and sent reporters and photographers to the scene. The state attempted to justify the statute by asserting that the anonymity of the offender would advance rehabilitation, whereas publication may "encourage further antisocial conduct and also may cause the juvenile to lose future employment or suffer other consequences for this single event." The Court ruled that the press right "must prevail" over the state's interest in protecting juveniles. The "magnitude" of the state's interest was not sufficient, in the Court's view, to "justify application of a criminal penalty" to the newspapers. The Court also said no evidence existed to demonstrate that criminal penalties are necessary to "protect the confidentiality of juvenile proceedings." Every state provides in some way for confidentiality, and yet only five impose criminal penalties for disclosure. Consequently, the Court asserted that although every state has a similar interest in protecting juvenile offenders, "all but a handful have found other ways of accomplishing the objective."

OBSCENITY

The regulation of obscenity for adult consumption has been a very troublesome issue for the Supreme Court. Attempts to protect minors from obscene materials, on the other hand, has proven much less difficult. Generally the Court has been deferential to such initiatives. One decision from the Warren Court and a second from the Burger Court are representative.

New York State enacted a law prohibiting the sale of obscene materials to minors under 17 years of age. The Supreme Court reviewed the statute in *Ginsberg v. New York* (390 U.S. 629: 1968). The law was challenged on the ground that the First Amendment secures to every citizen the opportunity to "read or see material concerned with sex" and that this right "cannot be made to depend on whether the citizen is an adult or a minor." The Court concluded that the statute did not deprive minors of a secured constitutional right. The power of the state to "control the conduct of children reaches beyond the scope of its authority over adults." The well-being of children is clearly within the power of the state to regulate, and the Court found it rational for the legislature to view minors' exposure to obscene material as harmful. The Court said the New York legislature "could properly conclude" that parents and others, such as teachers, who have "primary responsibility for children's well-being are entitled to the support of laws designed to aid discharge of this responsibility." The Court also noted that the law did not proscribe parental options. The law expressly recognized the parental role in "assessing sex-related material harmful to minors." Furthermore, the prohibition against sales to minors "does not bar parents who so desire from purchasing the magazines for their children."

The Burger Court case, *New York v. Ferber* (458 U.S. 747: 1982), involved a New York State law that prohibits knowing promotion of sexual performances by children under the age of 16 and distribution of materials depicting such performances. In essence, the law was designed to regulate the production and distribution of "kiddie" pornography. The objective of this law was slightly different from that of the law reviewed in *Ginsberg*. In *Ginsberg*, the focus was on the minor as the potential consumer of obscene material. The law under review in *Ferber* attempted to deter sexual exploitation of minors. The Supreme Court unanimously upheld the latter law against a First Amendment challenge.

The Court was persuaded that the states are "entitled to greater leeway in the regulation of pornographic depictions of children" for several reasons. The state's interest in safeguarding the well-being of minors is "compelling." Historically, legislation promoting the "physical and emotional well-being of youth" has been upheld even when the laws "have operated in the sensitive area of constitutionally protected rights." The Court asserted that the prevention of sexual exploitation and abuse of children constitutes a "governmental objective of surpassing importance." Neither was the Court willing to "second-guess" the legislature's judgment on this matter. That legislative judgment, as well as the "judgment found in the relevant literature," is that the use of children as "subjects of pornographic materials is harmful to the physiological, emotional and mental health of the child." Second, the Court concluded that distribution of juvenile pornography is "intrinsically related to the sexual abuse of children." The materials become a "permanent record" of the participation of minors, a harm "exacerbated by circulation." In addition, the Court saw closing the "distribution network" as key to controlling the production of material which requires the "sexual exploitation of children." Finally, the Court said the value of allowing "live performances and photographic reproductions of children engaged in lewd sexual conduct is exceedingly modest." The Court considered it "unlikely" that visual depictions of children performing sexual acts "would often constitute an important and necessary part of a literary performance or scientific or educational work."

Finally, the Court ruled in *Osborne v. Ohio* (109 L. Ed. 2d 98: 1990) that states can outlaw the private possession of pornographic materials featuring minors. Crucial to the decision was the Court's choosing *Ferber* rather than *Stanley v. Georgia* (394 U.S. 557: 1969) as the controlling precedent. In *Stanley* the Court had ruled that a state could not prohibit private possession by adults of obscene materials. The law struck down in *Stanley* had been aimed at preventing the "poison[ing of] the minds" of those who looked at such material. In *Osborne,* the state did not "rely on a paternalistic interest in [Clyde] Osborne's mind." Rather, Ohio enacted the law in an attempt to "protect the victims of child pornography; it hopes to destroy a market for the exploitive use of children." The Ohio legislature made the judgment that using children as subjects in pornographic materials is "harmful to the physiological, emotional, and mental health of the child." That judgment, said the Court, "easily passes muster" under the First Amendment. Furthermore, it is "surely reasonable" for Ohio to conclude that it will "decrease the production of child pornography if it penalizes those who possess and view the product, thereby decreasing demand." Given the importance of Ohio's interest in protecting the child victims, the justices said, "we cannot fault Ohio for attempting to stamp out this vice at all levels in the distribution chain." Osborne also challenged the Ohio law as overbroad. The Court rejected this contention as well, finding that the state supreme court had interpreted the law in such a way as to sufficiently focus or confine the materials that could be reached under the regulation.

DRINKING

The Twenty-first Amendment repealed national prohibition and gave the states virtually exclusive authority to regulate production, transport, and sale of liquor. Every state enacted laws defining minimum drinking ages and other laws criminalizing certain conduct while under the influence of liquor. Driving-related offenses constitute a significant portion of these laws. Under terms of the federal Constitution, it is highly doubtful that Congress could enact a law directly reaching these subjects. Given the substantial attention directed to the matter of drinking and driving, however, Congress sought to encourage states to take further action by passing a law in 1984 that allowed withholding a certain percentage of federal highway funds from those states that did not set or revise their minimum drinking age to age 21. The statute was enacted based on the broad spending power Congress is given by Article I of the Constitution.

South Dakota, one of the states with a drinking age below 21 (it was 19), challenged the law, but the Supreme Court upheld the statute in the case of *South Dakota v. Dole* (483 U.S. 203: 1987). The Court ruled that the federal law did not actually set a minimum drinking age and that states retained the prerogative to that "not merely in theory but in fact." Rather, what Congress did was to offer "mild encouragement" to the states to adopt "higher minimum drinking ages than they would otherwise choose." The spending power of Congress can be used to set conditions for federal funds so long as the conditions do not otherwise violate constitutional restrictions. The incentives used here were seen by the Court as a "valid use of the spending power," particularly when viewed in the context that deterring drinking and driving by young people is "directly related to . . . safe interstate travel," one of the "main purposes" for which federal highway money is spent.

Another drinking age regulation that generated constitutional questions was involved in *Craig v. Boren* (429 U.S. 190: 1976). Oklahoma had a statute that prohibited the sale of 3.2 percent beer to males under the age of 21 and to females under the age of 18. The statute was challenged on equal protection grounds as gender discrimination, and the Supreme Court agreed with the challenge. Notwithstanding the Twenty-first Amendment, which gives states authority to regulate alcohol at their discretion, equal protection standards are still applicable in these situations. The law was aimed at "enhancement of traffic safety," clearly an "important function" of state government. The challengers provided statistical data, however, that showed little difference between males and females as measured by arrests for violations such as driving under the influence. The Court said classification by gender must serve important governmental objectives and be substantially related to reaching those objectives. Based on the marginal statistical differences, the law simply did not sufficiently further safety objectives to warrant different treatment based on gender.

The states also have substantial authority to enforce their laws governing driving while intoxicated. These laws do not isolate juveniles specifically but often apply to juveniles more frequently, as reflected by data on driving violations by age group. Two cases are particularly germane to the issue of constitutional rights in the drunk driving situation. The first is *Schmerber v. California* (384 U.S. 757: 1966), which explored whether or not the privilege against self-incrimination extends to defendant-derived evidence of a noncommunicated nature. The privilege clearly covers communicated testimony. *Schmerber* involved a driving-while-intoxicated conviction in which critical evidence against the defendant came in the form of blood test results. The blood sample upon which the tests were performed was taken over Armando Schmerber's objection. Schmerber challenged the conviction on search, self-incrimination, assistance of counsel, and general due process grounds.

A five-justice majority rejected all of Schmerber's contentions. The majority held that taking the blood sample "constituted compulsion for the purposes of the privilege," but the critical question in *Schmerber* was whether the blood sample actually required Schmerber to be a "witness against himself." The Court concluded that the scope of the self-incrimination protection did not extend far enough to reach this situation. The privilege applied only to forcing evidence against the accused "from his own mouth": the testimonial evidence of words from the accused. By contrast, the majority likened the blood sample to fingerprints and other means of identification. The justices said that making a subject provide "real or physical evidence does not violate" the privilege against self-incrimination. The Court asserted that in Schmerber's case, "not even a shadow of testimonial compulsion upon or enforced communication by the accused was involved either in extraction or in chemical analysis." Schmerber's "testimonial capacities were in no way implicated." In the majority's view Schmerber, "except as a donor, was irrelevant to the results of the test."

Schmerber is the definitive ruling on blood samples and self-incrimination. *Schmerber* held that blood samples, because they are not words, are not covered by the privilege against self-incrimination. As long as the sample is not taken in a manner that "shocks the conscience," analysis of that sample is admissible evidence. The Court has also permitted states to admit into evidence a person's refusal to submit to a blood-alcohol test. South Dakota, for example, allows a person suspected of driving while intoxicated to refuse a blood-alcohol test. Refusal, however, can bring two significant costs. First, the person's driver's license may be revoked on the basis of refusing to submit to the test. Second, the refusal can be used as evidence in a subsequent trial on the driving-while-intoxicated charge. The Court upheld these provisions in *South Dakota v. Neville* (453 U.S. 553: 1983).

The Court formally recognized the problem of drunk driving as "compelling" enough to provide states with substantial latitude to regulate: The "carnage caused by drunk drivers is well documented." South Dakota's "implied consent" law is part of its program to deter drinkers from driving. Rather than having officers administer a blood-alcohol test against a person's will, South Dakota offers suspects the choice to refuse. To discourage people from making that choice, the state incorporated the disincentives of license revocation and use of the refusal as evidence against the suspect. The "values behind the Fifth Amendment are not hindered" where the state offers this choice. The test is so "safe, painless and commonplace" that the state could "legitimately compel the suspect, against his will, to accede to the test." Given that the offer of taking the test is "clearly legitimate," the action "becomes no less legitimate when the State offers a second option of refusing the test, with the attendant penalties for making that choice."

ABORTION AND CONTRACEPTION

A number of issues have arisen in the last decade and a half that involve juveniles' right to privacy. The problem of substance abuse is illustrative. A number of states permit juveniles to seek help without parental consent as a precondition. The rationale, of course, is that requiring prior parental consent might discourage the minor from seeking assistance or have other counterproductive consequences. Certainly as troublesome have been the issues of abortion and contraception. Many states have adopted different policies for adults and minors on these matters, several of which have been challenged on constitutional grounds.

The Supreme Court ruled in *Roe v. Wade* (410 U.S. 113: 1973) that states could not prohibit abortions, at least in the first two trimesters of pregnancy. *Roe,* of course, was a highly controversial ruling, and many states attempted to soften its impact by imposing restrictions on the right to abortion. Among these restrictions were some that specifically targeted minors. Missouri, for example, required that where the pregnant minor was unmarried and under 18 years of age, submission of written consent from a parent or guardian was required before the abortion could be performed. The law did not require parental consent where a physician certified that the abortion was necessary to preserve the life of the mother. The Court struck down this requirement in *Planned Parenthood of Central Missouri v. Danforth* (428 U.S. 52: 1976).

Missouri sought to justify the statute by arguing that certain decisions are "outside the scope of a minor's ability to act in [her] own best interest or in the interest of the public." Missouri pointed to laws specifically proscribing minors such as those limiting sale of alcohol, firearms, and certain types of literature. The Supreme Court, however, objected to the blanket character of the consent requirement. The Court concluded that the state does not possess in every minor-pregnancy situation the "constitutional authority to give a third party an absolute, and possibly arbitrary, veto over the decision of the physician and his patient to terminate the patient's pregnancy, regardless of the reason for withholding the consent." Even the suggested state interest of safeguarding the family and parental authority was not viewed as sufficient to justify the consent requirement. Any interest the parent may have in the termination of the minor daughter's pregnancy is "no more weighty than the right of privacy of the competent minor mature enough to have become pregnant."

As strongly worded as the *Danforth* opinion was, it was not the last word. As states began to modify their restrictions, the Court began to soften its objections. In *H. L. v. Matheson* (450 U.S. 398: 1981), for example, the Court reviewed a Utah law that required physicians to notify parents of minors upon whom abortions are to be performed. The Court ruled that this notification requirement did not violate a minor's privacy rights. There can be "little doubt," said the Court, that the law promotes a permissible end by "encouraging an unmarried pregnant minor to seek the help and advice of her parents" in making the abortion decision. The Utah law differed from the Missouri statute in the key respect that it did not convey veto power to the parents on the abortion decision. That the notice requirement may "inhibit" some minors from seeking abortions was not seen as reason enough to invalidate the law. The law "does not compel a state to fine-tune its statute so as to encourage or facilitate abortions." To the contrary, state action "encouraging child birth" is also "rationally related to the legitimate governmental objective of protecting potential life."

Soon after *Matheson,* the Court struck down a blanket consent requirement for minors under the age of 15 in *City of Akron v. Akron Center for Reproductive Health* (462 U.S. 416: 1983). In *City of Akron,* the Court said a state's interest in protecting immature minors "will sustain a requirement of a consent substitute, either parental or judicial." At the same time, the state must provide an "alternative procedure whereby a pregnant minor may demonstrate that she is sufficiently mature to make the abortion decision herself, or that, despite her immaturity, an abortion would be in her best interests." The Court used this judicial alternative condition as the decisive factor when it reviewed and upheld the consent provisions of a Missouri law in *Planned Parenthood Association of Kansas City v. Ashcroft* (462 U.S. 476: 1983).

Following *Webster v. Reproductive Health Services* (492 U.S. 490: 1989), the Court examined a number of state restrictions on abortion. *Hodgson v. Minnesota* (111 L. Ed. 2d 344: 1990) and *Ohio v. Akron Center for Reproductive Services* (111 L. Ed. 2d 405: 1990) reviewed parental notification statutes in Minnesota and Ohio. The Minnesota statute had two key parts. First, the state required notification of both biological parents when a minor daughter sought an abortion. In a five to four decision, the Court struck down this requirement. The statute contained contingency language that if a court enjoined enforcement of the notification requirement, the statute would be amended automatically to provide a judicial bypass as an alternative to parental notification. This alternative allowed a minor to petition a court for permission to obtain an abortion without notifying her parents. The Court upheld this alternative, again by a five to four vote. Justice Sandra Day O'Connor provided the decisive vote in both instances. She joined Justices Thurgood Marshall, William Brennan, Harry Blackmun, and John Paul Stevens in striking down the statute that did not provide judicial bypass. She was joined by Chief Justice William Rehnquist and Justices Anthony Kennedy, Byron White, and Antonin Scalia in upholding the alternative.

The Ohio statute required notification of only one parent. It also contained judicial bypass language, but the Court upheld the one-parent notice requirement on its own by a six to three vote, with Justice Stevens joining the five justices who had upheld the Minnesota judicial alternative. The defect with the Minnesota statute, which did not have the judicial bypass provisions, arose from the fact that only about half of Minnesota's minors resided with both biological parents. Justice Stevens spoke of the "particularly harmful effects" of the two-parent notification requirement on "both the minor and custodial parent when parents were divorced or separated." In addition, the Court concluded that the requirement "does not reasonably further any legitimate state interest." The principal justification for notification is that it "supports the authority of a parent who is presumed to act in the minor's best interest and thereby assures that the minor's decision to terminate her pregnancy is knowing, intelligent, and deliberate." To the extent "such an interest is legitimate," it could be "fully served" by the notification of one parent, who can then seek counsel from the other parent or anyone else. The state has no legitimate interest in questioning the one parent's judgment on whether to seek wider counsel. The Court concluded that the two-parent requirement actually "disserves" any state interest in protecting a minor in "dysfunctional families." Two-parent notice in such situations is "positively harmful to the minor and her family." As in cases involving judicial hearings as an alternative to securing parental consent for an abortion, the Court found the bypass alternative constitutionally sufficient for notification as well. The judicial bypass feature allows a minor to demonstrate she is fully capable of making the abortion decision. The Court decided the Ohio case without actually ruling on whether the judicial bypass provision is necessary in the one-parent notice situation. Rather, the justices upheld the one-parent notification requirement as a "rational way" for a state to assist a pregnant minor who is considering abortion. "It would deny all dignity to the family," wrote Justice Kennedy, "to say that the State cannot take this reasonable step . . . to ensure that, in most cases, a young woman will receive guidance and understanding from a parent." In the Court's view, Ohio's requirement did not impose an "undue, or otherwise unconstitutional, burden on a minor seeking an abortion."

The Court responded less positively to state restrictions on the promotion and sale of contraceptives. In *Carey v. Population Services International* (431 U.S. 678: 1977), for example, the Burger Court struck down a New York State law that made it a crime to sell contraceptives to minors under the age of 16 and to advertise (or display) contraceptives. New York argued that the statute was a reasonable regulation of the "morality of minors," in the furtherance of the state's policy against promiscuous sexual intercourse among the young. In deciding this case, the Court returned to the parental consent issue for abortions. The Court had ruled in *Danforth* that the state could not categorically require parental consent for a minor to terminate a pregnancy. The constitutionality of a "blanket prohibition on the distribution of contraceptives to minors is a fortiori [with stronger reason] foreclosed." The state's interest in protecting the well-being of the pregnant minor and potential life are "more clearly implicated by the abortion decision than by the decision to use a nonhazardous contraceptive."

Six years later the Court dealt with a federal law prohibiting the mailing of unsolicited advertisements for contraceptives in *Bolger v. Youngs Drug Products Corporation* (463 U.S. 60: 1983). The law did not proscribe the receipt of advertising by minors as such. Offered in justification of the ban were two arguments, one of which focused specifically on minors. The first argument was that the law protects recipients from "offensive" mailed materials. The second justification was that the regulation "aids parents' efforts to control the manner in which their children become informed about sensitive and important subjects such as birth control." The Court dismissed the first of these arguments as carrying "little weight." Where protected communication is involved, as was the case here, the fact that it may be "offensive to some does not justify its suppression." The Court found the second argument more substantial. The justices ruled the law deficient, however, as a "means of effectuating" the "parental aid" interest. Parents "already exercise substantial control over information that enters their mailboxes." Parents must also "cope with the multitude of external stimuli that color their children's perception of sensitive subjects." Under these circumstances, the ban would only assist those parents who wish to keep such mailings from their children and are "otherwise unable to do so." This "marginal degree" of protection is achieved by "purging all mailboxes of unsolicited material that is entirely suitable to adults." Such a restriction greatly overreaches the scope of governmental authority, and the government simply may not reduce adults to "reading only what is fit for children." Further, the Court found the ban defective because it "denies to parents truthful information bearing on their ability to discuss birth control and to make informed decisions in this area."

The First Amendment

T he First Amendment, which was added to the Constitution in 1791, protects personal belief and opinion as well as action that stems from them. Its provisions address four basic freedoms, which its authors deemed imperative to free people functioning within a democratic political system. Those freedoms are (1) freedom of religion, (2) freedom of speech, (3) freedom of press, and (4) the dual right to assemble peaceably and to petition the government. Freedom of religion is protected by two provisions, one of which prohibits the government from establishing religion and one that ensures the free exercise of religion. By implication, a right of association also flows from the First Amendment.

It has typically been the position of the Supreme Court that a balance is required between First Amendment freedoms and the powers of a government to govern effectively. Some leading jurists have argued that the First Amendment protects individual rights absolutely, even the action components. That view has never been held by a majority of justices sitting on the Supreme Court at one time. Rather, the Court has engaged in balancing First Amendment rights with the requirements of public order. The Court occasionally has even removed certain conduct from First Amendment protection. In a sense, the primary function of the Court in this instance is drawing lines between protected and unprotected activity. The cases reviewed in this chapter were selected to represent the Court's line-drawing efforts.

Overview

The First Amendment was conceived as a constraint on the power of the central government. With the exception of the Alien and Sedition Acts of

1798, Congress enacted little legislation that was challenged on First Amendment grounds until World War I. Thereafter, the Court became involved in a series of decisions that extended the various components of the First Amendment to the state level through the Fourteenth Amendment. Movement toward connecting the First Amendment to state law was evident in *Meyer v. Nebraska* (262 U.S. 390: 1923), in which the Court struck down a state statute prohibiting the teaching of German to any pre-ninth-grade student in either public or private school. In this case, the Court held that the term *liberty* in the Fourteenth Amendment included, among other things, the right to "acquire useful knowledge" and engage in "common occupations of life," such as teaching. The Court said the Nebraska statute arbitrarily and unreasonably interfered with that liberty to the degree that due process protections of the Fourteenth Amendment had been violated.

The free exercise clause prevents the government from interfering with religious practices and absolutely protects a person's right to believe. The line-drawing problem exists when some kind of conduct is required in addition to belief. As Justice Felix Frankfurter observed in the first of the compulsory flag salute cases, conscientious scruples are insufficient to relieve an individual from "obedience to general law not aimed at the promotion or restriction of religious belief." Thus, a law that has a legitimate secular purpose may impinge on an individual's ability to act out his or her religious beliefs. More recently the Court has required that regulations that interfere with religious practices can only do so in the absence of an alternate method of accomplishing the legitimate secular objective.

The free exercise of religion clause was extended to the state level in *Cantwell v. Connecticut* (310 U.S. 296: 1940), with the Court saying the Fourteenth Amendment has "rendered legislatures of the states as incompetent as Congress to enact such laws." The remaining element of the First Amendment, the establishment clause, was made applicable to the states in *Everson v. Board of Education* (330 U.S. 1: 1947). The Court held that the clause must be extended to the state level because it "reflected in the minds of early Americans a vivid mental picture of conditions and practices which they fervently wished to stamp out to preserve liberty for themselves and their posterity." The result of these decisions is that the safeguards residing within the First Amendment stand against unreasonable actions by both national and state government in circumscribing personal belief and opinion.

The establishment clause was included because the drafters remembered the colonial experience with European state churches. At minimum the clause prohibits government from showing favoritism to a particular church or sect. The Supreme Court, however, has construed the prohibitions more broadly in an attempt to create standards by which it can distinguish the church and state involvements that are forbidden and those that are not. For a policy to withstand the limitations imposed by the clause, a legislative enactment must have a secular purpose, it must have a primary effect that neither advances nor inhibits religion, and it must not excessively entangle church and state authorities. The neutral position to be occupied by the church applies both to spiritual practices such as devotional exercises and to the allocation of public monies for the benefit of religion.

The Court did not have occasion to consider the free speech clause until World War I. In one of the early free speech cases, *Schenck v. United States* (249 U.S. 47: 1919), the Court held that the First Amendment would not protect a person who falsely shouted "Fire!" in a crowded theatre and thus caused a panic. The authors of the First Amendment, however, were not as concerned with an utterance such as "Fire!" as they were with normal political and social expression. The problems of interpretation for the Court have come largely because the right of expression requires that there be a receiver of speech; there must be communication. Even if the participants in the communication exchange are of limited numbers, circumstances might arise in which governmental intervention is appropriate. The key is determining when that intervention might be justified. The interests of those wishing to express themselves must be weighed against the public interest. That complex balancing process has given rise to a typology of expression that distinguishes speech that requires no additional conduct, speech that does require additional conduct, and speech that occurs through symbolism. The Court has fashioned various standards by which it can separate protected from unprotected communication within each of these categories.

The free speech protection was formally extended to the state level in *Gitlow v. New York* (268 U.S. 652: 1925), with the Court holding that the freedom of expression was "among the fundamental personal rights and 'liberties' protected by the Fourteenth Amendment from impairment by the states." Six years later, in *Near v. Minnesota* (283 U.S. 697: 1931), the Court said that it is "no longer open to doubt that the liberty of the press . . . is within the liberty safeguarded by the due process clause of the Fourteenth Amendment from invasion by state action." The right of assembly was incorporated in *DeJonge v. Oregon* (299 U.S. 353: 1937). The Court referred to the right of "peaceable assembly" as a right as "equally fundamental" as those of free speech and press. It is a right that "cannot be denied without violating those fundamental principles of liberty and justice which lie at the base of all civil and political institutions—principles which the Fourteenth Amendment embodies in the general terms of its due process clause."

The fundamental freedom of the press is also included within the First Amendment. The framers of the Bill of Rights believed liberty could not be maintained without a free press, which was a check on government. If the press is truly free, it can criticize all branches of the government, public employees, and, particularly, public policy. The doctrine of free press means the press must be free from government control and able to print what it desires without fear of censorship or prior restraint. There are many related issues the framers did not anticipate, however. Because radio and television were nonexistent in the late eighteenth century, the framers did not anticipate the power and reach of electronic news media. Interference with the rights of those accused of crimes and jeopardizing the fairness of their trials could not occur in 1791 by prejudicial broadcasts over the airwaves. Neither were certain questions of obscenity and commercial speech perceived as major threats at the beginning of U.S. constitutional history.

The enunciated right of peaceful assembly contains elements of expression found in both the right of free speech and the right of association. In recent years assembly rights have been associated with the civil rights movements of the 1960s, with anti–Vietnam War demonstrations in the late 1960s and early 1970s, and with other political protests. Once again the Court has had to balance the right to peaceful assembly against the protection of other rights, including private property rights and state property rights. Assembly cases usually involve marching, picketing, demonstrating, petition gathering, or similar activities. Though free speech may be protected, associated conduct may be subject to regulation. Not only is government interested in protecting property rights, but it is also interested in maintaining public order. The essential rule is that government may regulate the time, place, and manner in which expression may occur through assembly so long as those regulations do not affect the content of the messages expressed through such action.

Free Exercise of Religion

THE FLAG SALUTE CASES AND SECULAR REGULATION

The free exercise clause restricts Congress and state legislatures from passing any law that inhibits religious exercise. The clause also prevents government from compelling worship or belief and from making any right or privilege contingent on religious belief. This presents the problem of differentiating between beliefs and actions that might flow from those beliefs. Though freedom of belief is an absolute right, associated conduct may be regulated. Most government enactments are of wide scope and are not aimed at any particular religious group. Indeed, cases arising under the free exercise clause typically involve conflicts between laws that serve a general secular purpose on one hand and the religious exercise interests of individuals on the other. Religion may not be used to exempt a person from compliance with secular law designed to safeguard, for example, the public health and safety or public order. The Supreme Court said in *Reynolds v. United States* (98 U.S. 244: 1878), the Mormon polygamy case, that "to permit professed doctrines of religious beliefs to prevail over the law of the land would permit every citizen to become a law unto himself." A classic illustration of the secular regulation approach to interpretation of the free exercise clause is found in the two compulsory flag salute cases. Both cases raised the question of whether public school students could be compelled, under threat of expulsion and fine, to salute the flag. The children involved in both cases were Jehovah's Witnesses who refused to participate because to have done so would have violated their religious beliefs.

In the first case, *Minersville School District v. Gobitis* (310 U.S. 586: 1940), the Court held that religious protections do not preclude legislation of a general secular nature so long as the legislation does not take aim at a particular sect. The secular interest being promoted by flag ceremonies was held as preeminent because what it sought was cohesion and national unity, an interest "inferior to none." Accordingly, Justice Felix Frankfurter wrote in the majority opinion that even "conscientious scruples" cannot relieve an individual from "obedience to general law." From this perspective, had the Court ruled for the Jehovah's Witnesses, it would have given religion preferential treatment; it would have given exception based exclusively on the religious values of the Witnesses. In the second case, *West Virginia State Board of Education v. Barnette* (319 U.S. 624: 1943), the Court came at the problem differently. A six-justice majority resolved the issue on broader expression grounds. As an expression issue, the Witnesses' behavior could be evaluated using standards established for free speech cases. The Court concluded that the children's nonparticipation was a form of speech that did not create a danger. Neither did their refusal to salute the flag "interfere with or deny rights of others to do so."

Barnette departed from the heavily criticized *Gobitis,* but it did so without either dismantling the secular regulation doctrine or encouraging religious preference. The Court opted instead to view free exercise interests as largely contained within expression protections. The compulsory flag salute was offensive because it dealt with matters of belief and opinion, a transgression the First Amendment cannot tolerate regardless of religion. Because the state could not require any child to salute the flag, the Court avoided carving out an exception for Jehovah's Witnesses. The implications of the broader basis for decision can readily be seen by comparing the outcomes in *Barnette* and

Gobitis, decisions rendered less than three years apart. *Gobitis* was an example of the secular regulation approach in its purest form. That doctrine emerged from *Barnette* as a much less applicable justification for state policy initiatives prevailing over religious expression.

RELIGION AND TAXES

Taxation and tax exemptions may raise either free exercise or establishment questions. Two tax cases, decided almost 50 years apart, develop the free exercise issue. In *Murdock v. Pennsylvania* (319 U.S. 105: 1943) the Court invalidated a license tax as an impermissible restriction on evangelism. Under terms of the secular regulation doctrine, individuals cannot be exempted on religious grounds from compliance with laws that pursue legitimate secular purposes and do not single out particular religious believers. *Murdock* departs from that rule. The case involved a municipal license tax that was imposed on all persons selling or canvassing door-to-door. The tax was challenged by Jehovah's Witnesses as an infringement on their ability to freely exercise their religious beliefs. The Supreme Court found for the Witnesses, saying that distribution of religious tracts is "an age old form of missionary evangelism." Such distribution is "as evangelical as the revival meeting" and is a form of religious activity as protected as "worship in the churches and preaching from the pulpit." That monies are obtained through distribution of literature does not transform evangelism into a commercial enterprise. Besides the evangelical character of the Witnesses' solicitation, the Court noted the financial realities of surviving as a sect and exempted missionary evangelism from taxation on those grounds. Though an income tax might be collected from a member of the clergy, it is "quite another thing to exact a tax from him for the privilege of delivering a sermon."

Murdock was a departure from earlier free exercise cases that had said that freedom of religious expression was not absolute and that religious beliefs could not exempt an individual from the demands of general purpose secular regulations. The Court upheld compulsory smallpox vaccinations over religious objection in *Jacobson v. Massachusetts* (197 U.S. 11: 1905), for example, and it allowed the outlawing of polygamy despite the adverse consequences of the regulation for Mormons in *Reynolds. Murdock,* however, suggested that injury created by a secular regulation may be too great. In this case, the license tax was imposed on the religious exercise of evangelism, a protected practice. The ruling was that certain regulations, despite their secular purpose and nondiscriminatory administration, simply cannot be applied in some situations.

The second case, *Jimmy Swaggart Ministries v. Board of Equalization*

(107 L. Ed. 2d 796: 1990), upheld a state sales and use tax imposed on a religious organization's sale of religious materials. The law also levied a 6 percent tax on in-state sales and a 6 percent use tax on materials purchased outside the state. The Board of Equalization advised Jimmy Swaggart Ministries that it needed to pay accumulated taxes on articles sold at its "evangelical crusades" dating back several years. The tax was challenged by Swaggart Ministries as a violation of both religion clauses, but a unanimous Supreme Court disagreed. Swaggart Ministries based its free exercise clause challenge squarely on *Murdock*. The Court, however, did not see the two taxes as identical. The flat license tax in *Murdock* operated as a "prior restraint on the exercise of religious liberty," which was different from the function of the sales tax in the *Swaggart Ministries* case. The license taxes in *Murdock* acted as a "precondition" to free exercise of religion. The California tax, in contrast, is not a tax on the right to "disseminate religious information, ideas, or beliefs per se." Rather, the tax is on the "privilege of making retail sales of tangible personal property." The tax is owed regardless of the motivation of the sale; the sale of a Bible by a religious organization is treated like the sale of a Bible by a bookstore. Justice Sandra Day O'Connor did write in the majority opinion that a "more onerous tax rate, even if generally applicable, might effectively choke off an adherent's religious practices." She asserted, however, that "we face no such situation in this case" and that the tax as imposed by California simply did not create a "constitutionally significant burden."

SUNDAY CLOSING LAWS

The secular regulation doctrine was considered further in four cases challenging state and local laws prohibiting commercial activity on Sunday. Two of the four cases, called the *Sunday Closing Cases* collectively, were decided essentially on establishment and equal protection grounds. The regulations in these two cases, *McGowan v. Maryland* (366 U.S. 420: 1961) and *Two Guys from Harrison-Allentown, Inc. v. McGinley* (366 U.S. 582: 1961), were upheld by a vote of eight to one. In the other two cases, *Gallagher v. Crown Kosher Super Market* (366 U.S. 617: 1961) and *Braunfeld v. Brown* (366 U.S. 599: 1961), the petitioners, both Orthodox Jews, added free exercise claims to the establishment and equal protection challenges. They maintained that mandatory Sunday closure placed them at a disadvantage because they must also close on Saturdays due to their religious doctrine. Only three members of the Court found the Sunday closing regulations defective on the free exercise issue, however.

The Court said the commercial regulations were legitimate secular restrictions. The purpose of the laws was simply the designation of a uniform day of rest. The Court held that while the regulation may impose some free exercise burden on the litigants, they were not denied the opportunity for free exercise. They merely had to forgo a day's work. Free exercise only made the practice of their religious beliefs more expensive. The free exercise protection cannot, except in rare circumstances, be used to strike down legislation that "imposes only an indirect burden on the exercise of religion." The clause does not require that legislators enact no law "regulating conduct that may in some way result in the economic disadvantage of some religious sects and not to others because of the special practices of the various religions." After assessing the competing interests, the Court concluded that the burden borne by those whose Sabbath day is Saturday was indirect. If the state had required Saturday work, the burden would have been direct and therefore prohibited. What the state did instead, however, was deny all businesses the opportunity to be open on Sunday, even if they were closed on Saturdays for religious reasons. The Court's use of the direct-indirect burden approach clearly suggested that at least certain kinds of secular regulations would require exemptions if they survived First Amendment scrutiny at all. The Court offered one important qualification, however: A state may enact a general law that has the purpose of advancing the state's secular goals and that may impose an indirect burden on religious observance. But this course is allowable only if the state cannot "accomplish its purpose by means which do not impose such a burden." Thus, the Court fashioned an alternative means factor in evaluating general secular regulations against free exercise challenges. This placed an affirmative obligation on the state to show the lack of alternatives that could accomplish the secular goal without imposing a burden on religious exercise.

UNEMPLOYMENT COMPENSATION

The impact in the changes to secular regulation doctrine became evident less than three years later in the unemployment compensation case of *Sherbert v. Verner* (374 U.S. 398: 1963). Adell Sherbert was a Seventh-Day Adventist who was discharged from her job because she would not work on Saturday. Saturday is the Sabbath Day for Seventh-Day Adventists. Failing to find other employment because of her "conscientious scruples not to take Saturday work," Sherbert filed for unemployment compensation benefits under provisions of South Carolina law. The law required that any claimant is ineligible for benefits if he or she has failed, without good cause, to accept suitable work when offered. Through appropriate administrative proceedings, Sherbert's unwillingness to work on Saturday was determined to disqualify her from benefits. On appeal, the Supreme Court held for Sherbert in a seven to two decision.

The Court ruled that Sherbert was too greatly burdened in this case. She was forced to choose between "following the precepts of her religion and forfeiting benefits," or "abandoning one of the precepts of her religion in order to accept work." Facing such a choice "puts the same kind of burden upon the free exercise of religion as would a fine imposed against appellant for her Sunday worship." The Court failed to find that protection of the unemployment compensation fund from fraudulent claims by unscrupulous claimants feigning religious objections to Saturday work was a sufficiently compelling state interest. Even if the fund were threatened by spurious claims, South Carolina would need to demonstrate that no alternative forms of regulation would combat such abuses. In allowing the religion-based exemption for Sherbert, the Court created the possibility of differential treatment for those seeking unemployment benefits for refusal to work on Saturdays. The Court suggested, however, that such classification was not establishment of religion. Rather, the decision "reflects nothing more than the governmental obligation of neutrality in the face of religious differences." The holding requires only that "South Carolina may not constitutionally apply the eligibility provisions so as to constrain a worker to abandon his religious convictions."

Sherbert was something of a replay of the free exercise issues seen in the *Sunday Closing Cases*. Sherbert was subjected to economic hardship, like the merchants in the *Sunday Closing Cases,* but the burden in the *Sunday Closing Cases* was indirect. In *Sherbert* the Court found the burden to be impermissibly heavy. Even incidental burdens could be justified only by demonstrating a compelling state interest, which is far more demanding than merely showing secular purpose. Coupled with the alternate means requirement carried over from the *Sunday Closing Cases, Sherbert* substantially expanded the protection afforded by the free exercise clause. At the same time, the broadened protection for free exercise produces serious establishment problems.

These same problems were present in *Thomas v. Review Board of the Indiana Employment Security Division* (450 U.S. 707: 1981). Eddie Thomas was denied unemployment compensation after voluntarily quitting his job for religious reasons. The Court held the denial of benefits to be a violation of Thomas's free exercise rights. The Court was even more emphatic than in *Sherbert,* saying, "Where the state conditions receipt of an important benefit upon conduct proscribed by religious faith, or where it denies such a benefit because of conduct mandated by religious belief," a believer is unduly pressured, and a burden upon religion exists. Though the compulsion may be indirect, the infringement upon free exercise is nonetheless substantial. The Court subsequently took a step back from *Thomas* and *Sherbert* in *Estate of Thornton v. Caldor, Inc.* (472 U.S. 703: 1985), invalidating on establishment grounds a state law that gave an employee the absolute right to refuse to work on his or her Sabbath. The Court said that the statute had the primary effect of establishing religion in that it required religious concerns automatically to control all secular interests in the workplace.

The Court soon returned to the *Thomas* position in *Hobbie v. Unemployment Appeals Commission of Florida* (480 U.S. 136: 1987). Paula Hobbie had been employed some two and one-half years before undergoing the religious conversion that produced the employment conflict. Florida attempted to distinguish Hobbie's situation from *Sherbert* and *Thomas* by arguing that she was the agent of change herself and was responsible for the consequences of the conflict between her job and her religious beliefs, as her conversion came subsequent to her employment. The Court rejected this position by saying that Florida had asked the Court "to single out the religious convert for different, less favorable treatment than that given an individual whose adherence to his or her faith precedes employment." The timing of Hobbie's conversion was characterized as immaterial to the issue of burdens on free exercise. The Court said the First Amendment protects the free exercise rights of those who "adopt religious beliefs or convert from one faith to another after they are hired."

Until *Hobbie,* in all the cases involving denial of unemployment compensation benefits to persons who refused to work because of religious beliefs, the claimants had been members of established religious sects. In *Frazee v. Department of Employment Security* (103 L. Ed. 2d 914: 1989), the Court considered the case of a claimant who was not a member of an established sect. Neither did the claimant's refusal to work rest on a tenet or teaching of an established religious body. The Court ruled that none of the previous decisions required formal membership in an established sect. In addition, the prior cases had not required a tenet of faith that specifically "forbade the work the claimants refused to perform." Rather, said the Court, the previous cases "rested on the fact that each of the claimants had a sincere belief that religion required him or her to refrain from the work in question." Membership in an organized religion, especially one with a specific teaching forbidding Sunday work, "undoubtedly" would "simplify the problem of identifying sincerely held religious beliefs," but the Court rejected the notion that to claim free exercise protection "one must be responding to the commands of a particular religious organization."

In a related unemployment compensation matter, *Unemployment Division v. Smith* (108 L. Ed. 2d 876: 1990), the Court ruled that a state could withhold benefits from employees terminated from their jobs for use of peyote, a controlled hallucinogen. The state had refused to pay benefits because use of peyote was a crime in the state, and termination for its use made the employees ineligible for benefits. The employees had used the peyote in the rituals of the Native American Church and sought religious exemption. The Court ruled that while the state legislature could have established such an exemption, the free exercise clause did not require it. "We have never held," wrote Justice Antonin Scalia for the majority, "that an individual's religious beliefs excuse him from compliance with an otherwise valid law prohibiting conduct that the State is free to regulate."

CONSCIENTIOUS OBJECTION

As we have seen, religion-based exceptions to secular regulations require a balancing of free exercise and establishment protections. None of these balancing situations has been more delicate than those involving conscientious objection to military service. This issue is examined through *Gillette v. United States* (401 U.S. 437: 1971). In this case, the Court held that religion-based objection to a particular war, as distinct from wars generally, does not entitle a person to exemption from the military draft. *Gillette* focused on the specific language of the Selective Service Act, particularly that part of the act that exempted registrants who are "conscientiously opposed to participation in war in any form."

Guy Porter Gillette had attempted to limit his objection to participation in the war in Vietnam, but the Supreme Court, with only Justice William Douglas dissenting, held that he was not entitled to such a free exercise exemption. The Court also determined that Congress could provide exemptions to the draft for those having religion-based objections to war generally without violating establishment prohibitions. While conscription of those with "conscientious scruples" against all wars would violate the free exercise protection, there are governmental interests of "sufficient kind and weight" to justify drafting people who object to particular wars. The Court ruled that the draft laws were not "designed to interfere with any religious ritual or practice, and do not work a penalty against any theological position." In addition, the burdens imposed are incidental when compared to the substantial government interest in creating and administering an equitable exemption policy. The Court also noted the interest of the government in "procuring the manpower necessary for military purposes." These interests permit what Gillette alleged to be an interference with his free exercise rights.

Gillette also raised establishment claims. Primarily, he argued that allowing exemption only to those with objection to all wars discriminated against faiths that distinguish between personal participation in "just" as opposed to "unjust" wars. The Court held that congressional objectives in requiring objection to all wars were neutral, secular, and did not reflect a religious preference. The Court focused on the need for the exemption to have a neutral basis. Because a virtually "limitless variety of beliefs are subsumable under the rubric 'objection to a particular war,' " the difficulties of operating a fair and uniform conscription system would be substantial. Sorting through the various claims creates a great "potential for state involvement in determining the character of persons' beliefs and affiliations, thus 'entangling government in difficult classifications of what is or is not religious,' or what is or is not conscientious." Though the Court acknowledged that some discretion exists under any process that takes individual differences into account, it held that establishment problems would be even greater if conscientious objection of indeterminate scope were involved.

Gillette is, to date, the only case that singled out a particular war for religion-based conscientious objection to a U.S. draft law. The Selective Service and Training Act of 1940 provided that conscientious objector status did not require affiliation with a religious sect. The claim of exemption required only theistic religious beliefs and training, and not a "merely personal moral code." The Court addressed this language in *United States v. Seeger* (380 U.S. 163: 1965), ruling that a conscientious objector claimant need not declare a belief in a "Supreme Being" as long as the claimant had beliefs that served in the place of an orthodox belief in God. The term *Supreme Being* was said to mean a broader view of something to which everything else is subordinate. In *Welsh v. United States* (398 U.S. 333: 1970), the Court required exemption for a claimant without the basis of his or her objections resting on religious training or belief as long as the claimant genuinely believed in pacifism. A selective conscientious objector such as Gillette, on the other hand, created problems of implementation so wrought with establishment defects as to outweigh the free exercise interest served by the exemption.

The Vietnam War prompted many of the challenges to the draft law, but the end of that war did not end Supreme Court consideration of the issue. *Rostker v. Goldberg* (453 U.S. 57: 1981) upheld a 1980 presidential proclamation issued pursuant to the Military Selective Service Act requiring every male citizen and resident alien to register for potential conscription. In *Selective Service System v. Minnesota Public Interest Research Group* (468 U.S. 841: 1984), the Court permitted denial of federal student aid to persons failing to register for selective service, saying the policy had been aimed at securing compliance rather than seeking punishment of nonregistrants. The policy had been challenged on bill of attainder, self-incrimination, and equal protection grounds. In *Wayte v. United States* (470 U.S. 598: 1985), the Court allowed the temporary use of a passive enforcement of the selective service registration law whereby initial prosecutions were undertaken only against those nonregistrants who publicized their own resistance to the policy or were reported by others to be in violation. The Court said such an approach would be impermissible only if discriminatory motive and effect could be shown.

COMPULSORY EDUCATION

This final section focuses on free exercise interests as against the state's role in seeing to it that young people are educated. Wisconsin required that all young people in the state attend school through the age of 16, which is the same requirement found in virtually every state. The requirement was challenged in *Wisconsin v. Yoder* (406 U.S. 205: 1971). Jonas Yoder and other members of the Old Order Amish and the Conservative Amish Mennonite Church challenged the law as it applied to their school-age children. Yoder did not contest the attendance law as discriminatory against religion, nor was the legitimacy of the state's interest in advancing education challenged as such. Yoder had sent his children to public schools through the eighth grade, but he refused to keep his children in school until age 16 as required by law. He argued that high-school attendance of Amish children was contrary to his religious beliefs and the Amish ways of life. He contended that it would endanger his children's salvation and might threaten the ongoing existence of the sect by exposing Amish children to unwanted worldly influences that would draw them away from their beliefs.

The Court unanimously found for Yoder. The Court acknowledged the state's paramount responsibility for education but held that even a fundamental function such as education was not "totally free from the balancing process when it impinges on other fundamental rights and interests." In this instance, the impact of the compulsory education law on the practice of the Amish religion was not only "severe," but also "inescapable." The impact was not confined to "grave interference" with important Amish religious beliefs, but also brought the very real threat of "undermining" the Amish community and religious practice as it exists presently. The choice left the Amish was to "abandon belief and be assimilated into society or be forced to migrate to some other and more tolerant region." The Court viewed this choice as too burdensome. The Court did attempt to confine the decision by emphasizing that the Amish were disputing only one or possibly two years of high school–level education, training that would be of little value in the agrarian Amish community. Further, the Court noted the noble character of the Amish, specifically mentioning such characteristics as their self-reliance, their peaceful and law-abiding lifestyle, and their unique history. The Amish history and tradition were crucial in connecting their religious beliefs to their unusual way of life, which, in turn, created a unique free exercise injury when the compulsory attendance law was enforced against them.

Yoder illustrates the extent to which secular regulation has been modified by the Court since the early 1960s. Wisconsin's compulsory education law was clearly a statute of general application with nothing to suggest ill intent with respect to religion or any religious group. The substantial interest a state has in education is unquestioned. Yet, when that interest was weighed against the Amish interest in free exercise, the state's interest was deemed subordinate. The main consequence of *Yoder* is seen in the expansion of free exercise protection at the expense of establishment protection. Chief Justice Warren Burger's opinion unmistakably assigns preference to the religious motives of the Amish. At one point, the chief justice even differentiated between the Amish and Henry Thoreau. If the Amish had asserted their claims because of their "subjective evaluation and rejection of contemporary values" in a Thoreau-like manner, those claims would not rest on a religious basis. The key establishment problem comes from the chief justice's next sentence: "Thoreau's choice was philosophical and personal rather than religious, and such beliefs do not give rise to the demands of the Religion Clause."

Yoder expands on the reasoning first seen in *Sherbert v. Verner* and requires that any exemption from a policy enacted in pursuit of a substantial state interest must be religion-based. As a result, *Yoder* reflects the inevitability of free exercise and establishment conflict when exemptions are created for certain religious groups. Two footnotes to the discussion of *Yoder* need to be considered. First, had the Amish not obtained exemption from the Wisconsin law, and had they kept their children from school anyway, they would have violated the state truancy law. Truancy is an unjustified absence from school, and violators are prosecuted under the authority of the juvenile courts. In most truancy situations, the parents as well as the children are subject to possible penalty. Second, if Amish children are exempt from compulsory attendance beyond the eighth grade, who decides whether a student actually leaves school, the parent or the student? The Court was not required to address this question directly in *Yoder* because the litigation was brought by the parents. At the same time, the Court made it clear that such a decision rests exclusively with the parents of minor children. Therefore, if a ninth-grade Amish student's parents chose to withdraw him or her from school, they could do so even if the student wished to remain.

Establishment of Religion

The other provision of the First Amendment affecting religion is the establishment clause. The narrowest interpretation of the clause would hold that no official or state church can be established in the United States and that no particular religion can be preferred by government action. The most stringent application of the clause would produce an absolute separation of church and state. The Supreme Court has historically steered a course that approaches but does not reach the latter position. *Everson v. Board of Education* (330 U.S. 1: 1947) provided key definitions on the issue as well as a linkage of the establishment prohibition to the states. *Everson* said the clause erected a "wall of separation" between church and state that precluded government from aiding all religions or preferring one religion over another. Government could neither aid religion in preference to nonreligion nor participate in the affairs of any religious organization. A closely related position is defined as the concept of governmental neutrality toward religion. The neutrality position does not prohibit all interaction of church and state, but only forbids governmental policies that aid or handicap religion. Another interpretation of the clause accommodates certain governmental linkages to religion. This position was termed "benevolent neutrality" by Chief Justice Burger in *Walz v. Tax Commission of New York City* (397 U.S. 664: 1970). More on the *Walz* case follows below.

The establishment clause has been interpreted in recent years to mean that government should not be prevented from providing benefits to people simply because they have religious beliefs. According to this view, government services such as fire protection should not constitute an establishment of religion. Current establishment cases are generally evaluated using three criteria. This three-pronged standard was discussed at length by the Court in *Lemon v. Kurtzman* (403 U.S. 602: 1971) and is sometimes called the "*Lemon*" test. First, government policy must have a secular purpose. The prayer and Bible-reading exercises struck down by the Court in the early 1960s were seen as having spiritual rather than secular purposes. Second, no enactment can have as its principal or primary effect the advancing or inhibiting of religion. Third, no policy may create an excessively entangling relationship between government and religion. The entanglement criterion was especially important in some of the school aid cases because the Court felt government would be placed in a continuous monitoring relationship with religious institutions. The Supreme Court has also developed a concept known as "child benefit" for establishment challenges of various educational aid programs. Under the child benefit approach, textbooks distributed to nonpublic school students are seen as benefitting individual students rather than institutional religion. These criteria will be developed further in the establishment sections that follow.

TAX EXEMPTIONS

Walz v. Tax Commission of New York City (397 U.S. 664: 1970) addressed the question of whether tax exemptions for religious property are compatible with the establishment clause. The exemption authorized by state law included real or personal property "used exclusively" for religious, educational, or charitable purposes and owned by nonprofit agencies created to pursue such purposes. Frederick Walz, a property owner and taxpayer, contended that the exemption indirectly compelled him to support financially religious organizations owning exempted properties. The Supreme Court upheld the exemption over the dissent of Justice William Douglas. Chief Justice Burger asserted for the majority that the First Amendment "will not tolerate either governmentally established religion or governmental interference with religion." As long as those pro-scribed acts are avoided, "there is room for play in a benevolent neutrality which will permit religious exercise to exist without sponsorship and without interfer-ence." Evaluation of policies using the religion clauses rests on "whether particular acts in question are intended to establish or interfere with religious beliefs and practices or have the effect of doing so." The legislative purpose served here is legitimate, Burger wrote. Historically, common exemptions recognize the "beneficial and stabilizing influences" of the nonprofit groups exempted from taxation. The policy also responds to the "latent danger inherent in the imposition of property taxes." What New York is doing is "simply sparing the exercise of religion from the burden of property taxation levied on private profit institutions." On considering primary effect, the Court introduced the entanglement criterion, which would become a decisive factor in many subse-quent establishment cases. The chief justice argued that government involve-ment with religion existed with or without the exemption. Indeed, "elimination of the exemption would tend to expand the involvement of government by giving rise to tax valuation of church property, tax liens, tax foreclosures, and the direct confrontations and conflicts that follow in the train of those legal processes." Though some indirect economic benefits and some involvements result from granting the exemption, they are lesser involvements than collecting the property tax.

Walz provided the Supreme Court a comparatively easy way to handle the establishment issue associated with taxation. Unlike direct aid programs, tax exemption has a long history, and that history created a presumption for the practice. Though benefits may be conveyed at least indirectly to religion, such tax exemptions were quite distinct from grant programs. The exemptions were also different politically in that they did not generate the divisive debate often associated with direct grant programs. *Walz* was viewed as a strongly accommodationist decision. The specific reference to the "benevolent neutrality" was seen as a signal that the state may assume something other than a strictly neutral position regarding religion. The new "excessive entanglement" test, though not critical to the outcome of *Walz* itself, was to become the principal criterion in many subsequent establishment cases. Indeed, when the Burger Court invalidated practices on establishment grounds, it often did so on the basis of excessive church-state entanglement.

More recently, the tax exemption issue reappeared in an establishment case decided by the Rehnquist Court. In *Texas Monthly, Inc. v. Bullock* (103 L. Ed. 2d 1: 1989), the Court considered a state sales and use tax exemption for religious publications. The law exempted periodicals published or distributed by a "religious faith" that consisted entirely of writings either "promulgating the teachings of the faith" or "sacred to a religious faith." The exemption was challenged by the publisher of a "general interest" periodical not entitled to the exemption. The Court struck down the exemption essentially because it had no secular purpose. When exemptions are granted, they must fall to a "wide array of nonsectarian groups as well as religious organizations." That did not occur in this situation. Rather, the exemption was confined exclusively to religious publications, which gave it insufficient "breadth" to serve a secular objective.

RELIGION AND SCHOOLS

The establishment issues arising out of the educational context have been numerous and troublesome. Among the most troublesome have been those cases involving religious exercises or content in the public schools. We start with school prayer and the case of *Engel v. Vitale* (370 U.S. 421: 1962). The spiritual exercise at issue in *Engel* was a prayer composed by a public body, the New York State Board of Regents. The regents, an agency with broad supervisory authority over the public schools, recommended to school districts that the school day begin with a specific prayer, although no student was compelled to join in the recitation. The prayer was:

> Almighty God, we acknowledge our dependence on Thee, and we beg Thy blessings upon us, our parents, our teachers, and our Country.

The Supreme Court ruled that by using its public school system to encourage recitation of the regents' prayer, New York State had adopted a practice "wholly inconsistent" with the establishment clause of the First Amendment.

Justice Hugo Black wrote for a six-justice majority that the establishment clause must "at least mean that in this country it is no part of the business of government to compose official prayers for any group of the American people to recite as part of a religious program carried on by government." The exercise, said the Court, "officially establishes" the religious beliefs embodied in the Regents' prayer. That the prayer was not overtly denominational or that participation was voluntary could not save the prayer from the fatal establishment defect that its purpose was not wholly secular. The establishment prohibitions go beyond just keeping governmental power and influence from coercing religious minorities to conform to prevailing, officially approved religion. The clause, wrote Justice Black, rests on the belief that a union of government and religion "tends to destroy government and degrade religion." The Court emphasized that its decision did not indicate a hostility toward religion or prayer. The problem was the state's role in writing and designating the prayer for use as a spiritual exercise. It is not antireligious, concluded the Court, to say that governmental entities should stay out of the business of writing or sanctioning prayers. Rather, that function should be "left to the people themselves."

Engel took a decidedly different direction from earlier cases such as *Everson. Everson* tolerated some interaction of church and state so long as that interaction was essentially "neutral." Under this view, religious practitioners might constitutionally benefit from general, secular-purpose enactments. *Engel,* however, held that strict separation is required when governmental interaction involves actual spiritual exercises. As might be expected, *Engel* prompted a wave of criticism. The Court held firm, however, and in the following year struck down other school exercises in *School District of Abington Township v. Schempp* and *Murray v. Curlett* (374 U.S. 203: 1963). At issue in these cases were legislative enactments that designated recitation of the Lord's Prayer and the reading of Bible passages as spiritual activities to begin each school day. As in *Engel,* the Court found the states' involvement with such practices to be offensive to establishment prohibitions. The Court said in *Abington* that the principle of separation of church and state was based on a recognition of the teachings of history, which showed that powerful sects or groups might bring about a fusion of governmental and religious institutions. The other possibility that the establishment clause prohibited would be to convert a dependence of one upon the other to the end that official support of government would be "placed behind the tenets of one or of all orthodoxies."

In the case of *Wallace v. Jaffree* (472 U.S. 38: 1985), the Court struck down an Alabama law authorizing a moment of silence to be used for meditation or voluntary prayer in public schools. Justice John Paul Stevens wrote that the First Amendment "embraces the right to select any religious faith or none at all." This conclusion is based not only from protection of the interest of freedom of conscience, but also from the view that religious beliefs "worthy of respect are the product of free and voluntary choice by the faithful." Justice Stevens then applied the three-pronged establishment test set out in *Lemon v. Kurtzman* (402 U.S. 602: 1971) to Alabama's moment of silence law. The first of the three prongs requires that a statute have a secular purpose. In this case, the legislative record provided an unambiguous answer that the intent of the law was not secular. The bill's sponsor had said, on the record, that the law was an effort to "return voluntary school prayer" to the public schools of Alabama. The Court also looked at earlier versions of the law and saw that the words "or voluntary prayer" had been added to the sentence calling for a moment of silence. Addition of these words indicated to the Court that Alabama had intended to "characterize prayer as a favored practice." Such an endorsement was not consistent with the principle that government must pursue a course of complete neutrality toward religion.

Another school issue that has been before the Supreme Court is the teaching of evolution versus or alongside creationism. The most recent case is *Edwards v. Aguillard* (482 U.S. 578: 1987), in which the Court struck down a state "creation science" law. The Louisiana legislature enacted the Balanced Treatment for Creation-Science and Evolution-Science in Public School Instruction Act, which prohibited the teaching of the theory of evolution in public schools unless accompanied by instruction in the theory of creation science. No school was required to teach evolution or creation science, but if either theory was taught, the other had to be taught as well. The stated purpose of the law was to protect academic freedom. In the majority opinion, Justice William Brennan first outlined the general parameters of the Court's inquiry. Determination of whether challenged legislation comports with the establishment clause is based on the now familiar three-prong *Lemon* test. Under this standard, the legislature must have enacted the law for a secular purpose, and the law's principal or primary effect may neither advance nor inhibit religion. The Court concluded that the Balanced Treatment Act failed the secular purpose test. Though it noted that the stated purpose of the law was the protection of academic freedom, the Court said it was clear from the legislative history of the law and comments from the law's sponsor that the act was not truly designed to further that goal. Under the act, teachers "once free to teach any and all facets of this subject are now unable to do so." In addition, the act fails to ensure instruction in creation science. The Court concluded that the act, rather than protecting academic freedom, had the "distinctly different purpose of discrediting evolution by counter-balancing its teaching at every turn with the teaching of creation science."

Justice Brennan wrote that the Court "need not be blind to the legislature's preeminent religious purpose," which was "to advance the religious viewpoint that a supernatural being created humankind." The act's legislative history documented the fact that the proposed change in the science curriculum was done to "provide persuasive advantage to a particular religious doctrine that rejects the factual basis of evolution in its entirety." As a result, the Court concluded that the primary purpose of the act was to endorse particular religious doctrine through the use of symbolic and financial support of government and that it therefore violated the establishment clause. Brennan observed that the Court has been particularly vigilant in monitoring the establishment clause in elementary and secondary schools. "Families," he wrote, "entrust public schools with the education of their children, but condition their trust on the understanding that the classroom will not purposely be used to advance religious views." This vigilance is necessary because students at these levels are impressionable and because their attendance is involuntary.

The creationism question was preceded in the Court by the matter of released-time religious instruction. The case of *Zorach v. Clauson* (343 U.S. 306: 1952) upheld such instructional programs so long as they took place off public school premises. The Court found the released time approach to be satisfactory because the program involved neither religious instruction in public school classrooms nor the expenditure of public funds. The Court did not view the establishment clause as requiring that in "every and all respects there shall be a separation of Church and State." To hold otherwise, state and religion would be "aliens to each other—hostile, suspicious, and even unfriendly."

The Court returned to the matter of using public school facilities in *Board of Education of the Westside Community Schools v. Mergens* (110 L. Ed. 2d 191: 1990). *Mergens* upheld provisions of the Equal Access Act of 1984 that require public secondary schools receiving federal educational funds to allow political or religious student groups to meet on school premises provided other noncurriculum-related groups do so. Under the act, a school is not required to permit any student group beyond those related to the curriculum to use facilities. If at least one group unrelated to the school curriculum has access, however, the school becomes a "limited open forum," and religious or political groups must be able to access facilities as well.

The Court first determined that the school district allowed noncurriculum-related groups to meet. The school district had a formal policy recognizing that student clubs are a "vital part of the education program." About 30 student clubs met on a voluntary basis on school premises at the time Bridget Mergens sought access for a Christian Bible club. As a result, the act's equal access obligations were triggered. The question then became whether the act violated the establishment clause. It was argued that if a school district permitted religious groups to access school facilities, it would constitute an official recognition or endorsement of religion. The Court disagreed. The Court applied the three-pronged *Lemon* test and extended the "logic" of *Widmar v. Vincent* (454 U.S. 263: 1981), which allowed access of facilities at state universities, to the high school setting. Congress's reason for enacting the law challenged in *Widmar v. Vincent* was to "prevent discrimination against religious and other types of speech." Such a purpose, wrote Justice Sandra Day O'Connor, "is undeniably secular." Neither did access to facilities advance religion. There is a "crucial difference between *government* speech endorsing religion . . . and *private* speech endorsing religion." The Court concluded that high school students were "mature enough and likely to understand that a school does not endorse religion or support student speech that it merely permits on a nondiscriminatory basis." The proposition, Justice O'Connor continued, that "schools do not endorse everything they fail to censor is not complicated." Indeed, Congress specifically rejected the contention that high school students are "likely to confuse an equal access policy with state sponsorship of religion." Furthermore, the act limits participation of school officials at meetings of student religious organizations and requires that meetings occur during noninstructional time. As a result, the act "avoids the problems of 'the students' emulation of teachers as role models' and 'mandatory attendance requirements.' "

The Court acknowledged that the possibility of student peer pressure remained. The majority concluded, however, that a school can "make clear" that permitting a religious club to use facilities is not an endorsement of the club members' views. To the extent a school makes its objectives clear, students will "reasonably understand that the school's official recognition of the club evinces neutrality toward, rather than endorsement of, religious speech." In addition, the district recognized a "broad spectrum" of organizations and invited the formation of more clubs. This "counteract[s] any possible message of official endorsement of or a preference for religion or a particular belief." Last, the Court found little risk of "excessive entanglement" in this situation. Although the act permits assignment of a school staff member to meetings for "custodial purposes," such oversight of a student-initiated religious group is "merely to ensure order and good behavior." This does not "impermissibly entangle government in the day-to-day surveillance or administration of religious activities."

"AID" TO NONPUBLIC SCHOOLS

The first of the establishment cases that came to the Supreme Court claiming impermissible "aid" to religious schools was *Everson v. Board of Education* (330 U.S. 1: 1947). In *Everson,* the Court upheld reimbursement of costs of transporting nonpublic school students. At issue was a New Jersey statute that authorized local school districts to contract for the transportation of children to and from school. The Ewing Township Board of Education, acting upon the statute, authorized reimbursements to parents for the costs of transporting their children to nonpublic schools including parochial schools. These church schools gave their students, in addition to secular education, regular religious instruction conforming to the religious tenets and modes of worship of the specific faith. The Court upheld the reimbursement program in a five to four decision.

The Court first explored the nature of the establishment prohibition and concluded, as had Thomas Jefferson, that the clause was intended to erect a "wall of separation" between church and state. But the wall did not require the state to make it "far more difficult" for church schools. The clause requires the state to be "neutral" in its relations with groups of religious believers and nonbelievers; it does not "require the state to be their adversary." The Court said the reimbursements were not an aid to religion, but rather an attempt to protect the well-being of schoolchildren generally. Providing safe transportation is like "general governmental services" such as police and fire protection and sewer and water service. Cutting off these kinds of services, which are "separable and indisputably marked off from the religious function," would handicap religion unnecessarily. Crucial to the Court's decision was the proposition that institutional religion was not the recipient of any aid. Rather, services (or reimbursement for services in this case) were extended directly to students and their parents. The transportation program "does no more than provide a general program to help parents get their children, regardless of their religion, safely and expeditiously to and from accredited schools." This concept became known as the "child benefit" theory or doctrine, and it has been invoked frequently to place certain aid programs outside the coverage of the establishment clause. Justice Robert Jackson, in a dissenting opinion, responded to the child benefit approach by saying the "prohibition against establishment of religion cannot be circumvented by a subsidy, bonus, or reimbursement of expense to individuals receiving religious instruction and indoctrination." Justice Wiley Rutledge, also in a dissenting opinion, observed that religious content is the reason parents send their children to religious schools. He viewed transportation as an essential component in delivering that religious content.

Everson was one of the Court's first direct considerations of the establishment clause. In addition to placing state initiatives like this one within the reach of the clause, *Everson* is especially important in that the Court took an essentially accommodationist position. Despite the urging that the wall between church and state be kept "high and impregnable," the Court said the actions of the state should not be adversarial to religion. The child benefit concept was invented to buttress the Court's view of neutrality through the holding that the establishment clause does not prevent religious institutions from indirectly benefitting from programs that are themselves neutral with regard to religion. The child benefit approach also has been used in more recent school aid cases such as *Board of Education v. Allen* (392 U.S. 236: 1968). In *Allen* a New York State program to loan textbooks to nonpublic school students was upheld. The Court concluded that the program's purpose was the "furtherance of the educational opportunities available to the young" and that the law "merely makes available to all children the benefits of a general program to lend school books free of charge." The only books available for loan were books that were found to be suitable for use in public school and were confined to secular content. With comparable limitations, textbook lending practices have consistently been upheld in such cases as *Meek v. Pittenger* (421 U.S. 349: 1975) and *Wolman v. Walter* (433 U.S. 229: 1977).

Salary supplements for nonpublic schoolteachers are another matter. The case of *Lemon v. Kurtzman* (403 U.S. 602: 1971) involved a Pennsylvania law that authorized reimbursement to nonpublic schools for expenditures for "teachers, textbooks, and instructional materials." The reimbursement was limited to courses completely equivalent to those presented in the curricula of the public schools. A school seeking reimbursement needed to identify the separate costs of the eligible "secular educational service." The contested statute specifically prohibited reimbursement for any course that contained subject matter "expressing religious teaching, or the morals or forms of worship of any sect." The Supreme Court struck down the law in a unanimous decision on the ground that the statute fostered an "excessive entanglement with religion."

In assessing the entanglement question, the Court indicated that it must "examine the character and purposes of the institutions which are benefitted, the nature of the aid the State provides, and the resulting relationship between the government and the religious authority." The main problem in this instance was the "ideological character" of teachers. The Court could not "ignore the dangers that a teacher under religious control and discipline poses to the separation of the religious from the purely secular aspects of pre-college education." Although parochial teachers may not intentionally violate the First Amendment, a "dedicated religious person," teaching in a school controlled by his or her faith and operated to "inculcate its tents," will inevitably experience difficulty in remaining religiously neutral. If a state is to make reimbursements available, it must be certain that subsidized teachers do not inculcate religion. The comprehensive and continuing surveillance required to maintain that limitation itself becomes an establishment because the protective contacts will involve "excessive and enduring entanglement" between church and state. Ongoing inspection of school records is a relationship "pregnant with dangers of excessive government direction in church schools." Finally, the Court found entanglement of a different character created by the "divisive political potential of state programs." Continuation of such state assistance would "entail considerable political activity." Though political debate is normally a "healthy manifestation of our democratic system . . . political division along religious lines was one of the principal evils" the First Amendment was intended to prevent.

Lemon reflected the decisive role of the entanglement criterion in the currently used three-prong establishment test. The Burger Court's reliance on that criterion never diminished. With *Lemon,* the Court also emphasized the distinction between pre-college levels of education and higher education. Religious indoctrination is only an incidental purpose of education at the college level, whereas educational objectives at the lower levels have a "substantial religious character." *Lemon* underscored the Court's view that programs at the elementary and secondary levels are much less susceptible to entanglement problems. *Lemon* also cast serious doubt on purchase-of-service programs. Monitoring personnel, especially teachers, would be an ongoing obligation that would inevitably lead to entangling relationships between church and state. Transportation and books, on the other hand, have no content to be evaluated or are subject to only a one-time review. Service items are much more difficult to fit into child benefit coverage than are books or transportation.

Lemon involved an insoluble entanglement problem. Religion obviously would be advanced in violation of the purpose and effects criteria without the monitoring of the teachers. At the same time, the maintenance of the monitoring system produced the establishment defect through excessive entanglement. The Court reaffirmed the *Lemon* ruling in two shared time cases in 1985. In *Grand Rapids School District v. Ball* (473 U.S. 373: 1985) and *Aguilar v. Felton* (473 U.S. 402: 1985), the Court struck down programs in public schools that sent teachers into nonpublic schools to provide remedial instruction. These programs were seen as advancing religion and fostering an excessively entangled relationship between government and religion. The Court said that state-paid teachers, "influenced by the pervasively sectarian nature of the religious schools in which they work," may subtly or overtly indoctrinate students with particular religious views at public expense. The symbolic union of church and state inherent in the provision of secular, state-provided instruction in religious school buildings "threatens to convey a message of state support for religion."

The primary effect criterion was the undoing of a New York State initiative that provided both maintenance grants to nonpublic schools and tuition reimbursement and tax deductions for parents of nonpublic school students in *Committee for Public Education and Religious Liberty v. Nyquist* (413 U.S. 756: 1963). The maintenance program provided grants for upkeep and repair of facilities and equipment to qualifying schools in low-income urban areas. The Court ruled that the program advanced religion in that it "subsidized directly" the religious activities of sectarian schools. A state may not erect buildings in which religious activities are to take place. Similarly, it may not "maintain such buildings or renovate them when they fall into disrepair."

The tuition reimbursement and tax deduction initiatives were defective for other reasons as well. Reimbursement for nonpublic school tuition was available to parents with annual incomes of less than $5,000. The tax deductions for nonpublic school tuition costs could be claimed by parents who exceeded the reimbursement income standard. The central question in the two programs was whether or not use of the parents as conduits met the primary effect test. The Court concluded that both the reimbursements and the tax deductions were incentives. The establishment problem was that the programs provided encouragement to send children to nonpublic schools. More recently, in *Mueller v. Allen* (463 U.S. 388: 1983), the Court upheld a Minnesota statute that gave parents a state income tax deduction for all educational costs of elementary- and secondary-level children. Deductions applied to expenses for public as well as private schools, even though most benefits fall to parents of private school students. In a five to four decision, the Court ruled the Minnesota plan "vitally different" from the plan in *Nyquist*. The Minnesota plan contained several tax deductions, including the one for educational costs, and was said to gain secular character from its breadth. It also channeled "whatever assistance it may provide to parochial schools through individual parents."

Another group of cases raises different kinds of establishment issues. Illustrative is *Wolman v. Walter* (433 U.S. 229: 1977). This case concerned a package of six financial aid programs for nonpublic elementary and secondary schools. *Wolman* tested a statute providing aid to private schools in the form of textbooks, standardized testing services, diagnostic and therapeutic services, instructional materials and equipment, and field trip services. All disbursements authorized under the law had equivalent expenditure categories for public schools. The amount of the aid for any category was limited by the amount of per-pupil expenditures for public school students. By varying majorities, the Court upheld four programs and invalidated two others. The two invalidated were those that provided instructional materials and field trips. Only Justices Potter Stewart and Harry Blackmun were in the majority on all six components of the decision. *Wolman* did not significantly change establishment doctrine, but it does provide a further example of how the Court has used the three-pronged purpose, primary effect, and entanglement criteria in school aid cases.

Most of the assistance in question was sufficiently proscribed to satisfy establishment concerns. The textbooks, for example, were lent upon pupil request, and the students' choices were confined to texts approved for use in the public schools. The Court upheld the testing, diagnostic (speech, hearing, and psychological), and therapeutic services because (1) no nonpublic school personnel delivered the services; (2) the services were obtained off public school grounds, i.e., in neutral locations; (3) none of the services advanced ideology; and (4) little need existed to monitor the activities. These components of the aid package passed the three-pronged test with majorities ranging from eight to one to six to three. The instructional materials and field trip services did not fare as well. The Court found that because of the sectarian mission of the nonpublic school, "aid to the educational function of such schools necessarily results in aid to the sectarian school enterprise as a whole." Despite the limitation of materials to those "incapable of diversion to religious use," these materials "inescapably had the primary effect of providing direct and substantial advancement of the sectarian enterprise." Loaning the materials to the pupil rather than to the nonpublic school directly only "exalts form over substance" and cannot alter the judgment that advancement of religion is a primary effect. The field trips were found defective because the nonpublic schools control timing and, within a certain range, the "frequency and destinations" of the trips. The trips become an "integral part of the educational experience, and where the teacher works within and for a sectarian institution, an unacceptable risk of fostering religion is an inevitable byproduct."

The Court was more willing to allow interaction of church and state in the educational sphere when institutions of higher education were involved. The best example of this is the case of *Tilton v. Richardson* (403 U.S. 672: 1971). *Tilton* upheld Title I of the Higher Education Facilities Act of 1963. The act provided construction grants to church-related colleges and universities for buildings and facilities "used exclusively for secular educational purposes." It also prohibited use of funds for any project that may be used for "sectarian instruction, religious worship, or the programs of a divinity school." Applicants for funds were to "provide assurances that these restrictions will be respected," and enforcement was to be accomplished by government onsite inspections. The act had a provision through which the government would retain a 20-year interest in the financed facilities, enabling the government to recover at least a portion of the grant if the facility were to be used for other than secular purposes. The Court, in the majority opinion written by Chief Justice Burger, found the act to have a "legitimate secular objective entirely appropriate for government action" without having the effect of advancing religion. The 20-year limit on governmental interest in preserving the exclusively secular character of building uses was voided, however. The Court found it "cannot be assumed that a substantial structure has no value after that period and hence the unrestricted use of a valuable property is in effect a contribution of some value to a religious body."

Key to upholding the act otherwise was the Court's opinion that "excessive entanglement did not characterize the relationship between government and church under the Act." The Court cited three factors that diminished the extent and the potential danger of the entanglement. First, institutions of higher learning are significantly different from elementary and secondary schools. Because "religious indoctrination is not a substantial purpose or activity of these church-related colleges and universities, there is less likelihood than in primary or secondary schools that religion will permeate the area of secular education." Second, the aid provided through the building grants is of a "non-ideological character," and the resulting need to monitor buildings would be less than monitoring teachers. Third, entanglement is lessened because the aid comes in the form of a "one-time, single purpose construction grant." There are "no continuing financial relationships or dependencies." The inspections that do occur to monitor use of funds create only minimal contact. These factors also substantially lessen the potential for diverse religious fragmentation in the political arena. Justices William Douglas, Hugo Black, William Brennan, and Thurgood Marshall dissented from the decision. They argued that the act would produce excessive entanglement and that the restrictions cited in the act were insufficient. The dissenters pointed out that even if the specific buildings funded under the grant were used only for secular purposes, religious institutions were aided by being able to use monies freed by the receipt of the federal grant for religious purposes. *Tilton* had two substantial impacts on establishment standards. First, the entanglement criterion introduced the year before in *Walz v. Tax Commission of New York City* (397 U.S. 664: 1970) was decisive in *Tilton*. It marked the first application of the standard in a school aid case. Second, Chief Justice Burger developed the distinction between higher education and the elementary-secondary levels of education as a key element in determining the degree to which entanglement existed. Because the aid in this case was for buildings rather than for instruction and because the buildings were for students beyond the secondary level, an impermissible, excessive entanglement did not exist.

RELIGIOUS DISPLAYS ON PUBLIC PROPERTY

The schools were the principal establishment battleground through the 1960s and 1970s. More recently, establishment questions have been raised concerning displays with religious content located on public property. A very helpful discussion came in *Allegheny County v. American Civil Liberties Union* (106 L. Ed. 2d 472: 1989), which involved two displays. The first was a display of a crèche on the main inside staircase of the Allegheny County Courthouse. The scene was accompanied by a banner that read "Glory to God in the Highest." The crèche was donated by a Roman Catholic group, a fact indicated on a sign attached to the display. The second display consisted of an 18-foot Chanukah menorah placed next to a Christmas tree and a sign saluting liberty on the steps of the Pittsburgh City Hall. The menorah was owned by a Jewish group, but was stored and placed on display by the city. The American Civil Liberties Union (ACLU) and several local residents sought to permanently enjoin both displays on establishment clause grounds. In a five to four decision, the Court ruled that the crèche display impermissibly advanced religion, but by a six to three vote the justices allowed display of the menorah, the Christmas tree, and the sign.

Concerning the crèche display, Justice Harry Blackmun wrote on behalf of justices William Brennan, Thurgood Marshall, John Paul Stevens, and Sandra Day O'Connor. He began by asserting that the "essential principle" of the establishment prohibition is that government does not "take a position on questions of religious belief." Government's use of symbolism becomes unconstitutional if it "has the effect of endorsing religious beliefs." The effect of the government's use of symbolism, Blackmun continued, "depends upon its context." In ruling on the crèche and menorah displays, the task of the Court is to determine whether, in their "particular physical settings," either has the effect of "endorsing or disapproving religious beliefs." The crèche used "words as well as the picture of the nativity scene to make its religious meaning unmistakably clear." In addition, there was nothing in the context of the courthouse display that "detracts from the crèche's religious message." Allegheny County, wrote Blackmun, sent an "unmistakable message that it supports and promotes the Christian praise to God that is the crèche's religious message." While government may celebrate Christmas "in some manner," it may not do so in a way that "endorses Christian doctrine." Allegheny County "transgressed that line" in this instance. Justice Anthony Kennedy issued a dissenting opinion on the crèche decision. His opinion was also signed by Chief Justice William Rehnquist, Justice Byron White, and Justice Antonin Scalia. Kennedy viewed the striking down of the crèche display as reflecting "unjustified hostility toward religion." He regarded displays of the crèche and the menorah as comparable and equally permissible. The dissenters charged the majority with creating an orthodoxy of secularism. "Obsessive, implacable resistance to all but the most carefully scripted and secularized forms of accommodation requires this Court to act as a censor, issuing national decrees as to what is orthodox and what is not." Kennedy objected to government being limited to acknowledging only a Christmas "in which references to religion have been held to a minimum." Such a policy "lends assistance to an Orwellian rewriting of history."

The menorah display brought both a different result and a different alignment of justices. In this ruling the crèche dissenters (Kennedy, Rehnquist, White, and Scalia) joined Blackmun and O'Connor in the majority opinion, which held that no establishment defect existed. While the menorah is a religious symbol, its "message is not exclusively religious." Like Christmas, the menorah has "secular dimensions" as well. As a result, the menorah display presented a "closer constitutional question." Again, overall setting was the key. At city hall, the menorah stood "next to a Christmas tree and a sign saluting liberty." This display was not an endorsement of religion, but "simply a recognition of cultural diversity." Thus, for establishment clause purposes, the city's "overall display" must be seen as conveying a "secular recognition of different traditions for celebrating the winter holiday season." Justices Brennan, Marshall, and Stevens dissented from the part of the decision allowing display of the menorah. They saw no difference in the religious messages sent by the two displays.

Allegheny County was not the Court's first experience with religious displays. In *Lynch v. Donnelly* (460 U.S. 668: 1984) a municipality had included a crèche in its Christmas celebration display. When the crèche was challenged as a violation of the establishment clause, the justices ruled in favor of the display in a five to four decision, asserting that the Court had consistently rejected a "rigid, absolutist view" of the clause throughout its history. Furthermore, the decision suggested that it was not completely accurate to speak of a wall of separation dividing church and state. "Our society cannot have segments or institutions which exist in a vacuum or in total isolation from all other parts, much less from government." The Court maintained that history shows unbroken acknowledgment of the role of religion in U.S. life and that the crèche scene merely depicted the historical origins of Christmas. If the crèche scene benefitted religion at all, it was only in an "indirect, remote, and incidental fashion." The Court concluded that the city's motives for including the crèche were secular, that religion was not impermissibly advanced, and that an excessive entanglement of religion and government was not created. Allegheny County departed from Lynch largely in its emphasis on the overall display setting and the extent to which religious messages were integrated with the secular.

Free Speech

The free speech clause of the First Amendment was designed to provide comprehensive protection for expression. The clause states in absolute-sounding terms that Congress cannot make any law that abridges the freedom of speech. The protection afforded by the clause was extended to the state level through the due process clause of the Fourteenth Amendment, although that did not happen until 1925. Despite the absolute language of the clause, it does not convey unlimited protection for expression. Rather, certain categories of expression can be regulated and others are not protected at all. As a result, it has become necessary to establish standards by which regulations can be evaluated.

The free speech clause protects "pure" speech more than any other form of expression. Pure speech is communication that has no additional action element. For pure speech to be legitimately restricted, it must somehow endanger the public interest. If pure speech advocates unlawful acts, for example, and involves a substantial and immediate danger of a kind the government is empowered to prevent, the expression loses its protection. Advocacy of abstractions is typically not seen as having a sufficiently close connection to action. As a result, this kind of expression is virtually unrestricted. A more restrictive position might result from use of a balancing standard such as the "bad tendency" test, which allows regulation if there is a chance that substantive evil will occur as a result of the expression. Such an approach weighs the expression interest against societal danger in an effort to determine whether restriction of speech is warranted in a particular case.

Once speech has gone beyond its pure form and requires some supporting action, the additional action becomes the possible object of regulation even though the content expression deserves protection. This is called "speech plus," which may take such forms as picketing or demonstrating. Such situations draw not only on the free speech clause, but on the First Amendment right of assembly as well. These kinds of expression may be subject to time, place, and manner regulations provided the restrictions are evenhandedly applied and are content neutral. Symbolic expression, which is gestures that are substituted for words, is recognized as having some character of expression. Symbolic expression may be regulated only if the surrogate action is itself unlawful or subject to regulation. These concepts will become clearer in the following review of some situations in which they have been applied.

Expression offered in stressful times often presses the limits of constitutional protection. Consider the case that established the "clear and present danger" test, S*chenck v. United States* (249 U.S. 47: 1919). At issue was the constraint on speech imposed by the Espionage Act of 1917, which made it a crime to interfere with recruitment of persons into the armed forces. Charles Schenck was convicted of conspiracy to obstruct the draft by printing and distributing materials that urged draft-eligible men to resist conscription. The Court unanimously upheld his conviction. Justice Oliver Wendell Holmes wrote the opinion, in which he asserted that the right of expression was not absolute. Like other acts, expression is conditional and has boundaries set by the circumstances in which it is undertaken. Even the most "stringent protection of free speech would not protect a man in falsely shouting fire in a theatre and causing a panic."

Having established a situational context for evaluating expression, Justice Holmes then described a standard by which expression could be assessed. The standard became known as "clear and present danger." The issue in every case involving expression is whether or not the words are used in such circumstances and are of such a nature as to "create a clear and present danger that they will bring about the substantive evil that Congress has a right to protect [against]." If speech is linked closely enough to illegal action, it is speech that can be restricted. As Justice Holmes put it, "it is a question of proximity and degree." Schenck's expression was intended to have an effect on persons subject to the draft, a point conceded by Schenck himself. In a time of peace, this expression would not have been sufficiently dangerous to warrant prosecution. But because Schenck's words were disseminated while the nation was at war, they had quite a different effect. The clear and present danger test allowed certain speech to be regulated so long as the government could show that the expression endangered legitimate governmental functions and societal interests. The test also required that the danger be shown to be significant and immediate.

Schenck provided a basis by which to examine certain free expression issues, and several cases immediately following *Schenck* gave the Court an opportunity to refine further the clear and present danger standard. In *Frohwerk v. United States* (249 U.S. 204: 1919), a unanimous Court upheld the conviction of the author of several newspaper articles that were highly critical of U.S. involvement in World War I. The Court felt the language of the articles was comparable to Schenck's leaflets. The Court also upheld the conspiracy conviction of Eugene Debs for a speech critical of the war efforts in *Debs v. United States* (249 U.S. 211: 1919). The speech focused on socialism, including "its growth and a prophecy of its success." The Court did not object to the content, but made it clear that if the "manifest intent" of a speech encourages those hearing it to obstruct the recruiting service, the "immunity of the general theme may not be enough to protect the speech." In cases involving the Sedition Act of 1918, however, justices Holmes and Louis Brandeis dissented from the rest of the Court. In *Abrams v. United States* (250 U.S. 616: 1919), the Court upheld Jacob Abrams's conviction for distributing materials critical of the U.S. government's commitment of forces to Russia in the wake of the Russian Revolution. Holmes and Brandeis argued that neither sufficient danger nor appropriate proximity had been demonstrated. Only "present danger of immediate evil" warrants limitation of expression, they wrote, not the "surreptitious publishing of a silly leaflet by an unknown man."

May the government regulate expression before it creates a clear danger of immediate evil? The clear and present danger framework was modified in *Gitlow v. New York* (268 U.S. 652: 1925) to allow such intervention. The state statute under review in *Gitlow* allowed suppression of speech that might tend to produce substantive evil. To examine this question, the Court first had to determine whether the free speech language of the First Amendment extended to the states. The Court ruled that it did, and consequently states became subject to the same expression limitations as those applied to the federal government. Notwithstanding the extension of the free speech clause to the state level, the Court ruled against Benjamin Gitlow on the expression issue contained in the case.

Gitlow, a member of the Left Wing Section of the Socialist Party, was convicted under provisions of New York State's criminal anarchy statutes for his advocacy of the "overthrow of the government by force, violence, or unlawful means." The criminal advocacy was demonstrated in two publications entitled "The Left Wing Manifesto" and "The Revolutionary Age." The Court ruled that the law did not deprive Gitlow of his "liberty of expression," nor did it "penalize the utterance or publication of abstract doctrine or academic discussion having no quality of incitement to any concrete action." Rather, the statute aimed at language "advocating, advising, or teaching the overthrow of organized government by unlawful means." The Court felt the statute was properly focused on advocacy of action directed toward the accomplishment of the illegal purpose, overthrow of the government. The Court held that the police power of the state is appropriately used to "punish those who abuse freedom of expression by utterances inimical to the public welfare." As for the point at which the state may intervene, the Court argued that the state cannot reasonably be required to measure the danger from every such utterance in the "nice balance of a jeweler's scale." A state cannot be said to have acted unreasonably when it seeks to "extinguish the spark without waiting until it has enkindled the flame or blazed into the conflagration." A state may, in the exercise of its judgment, "suppress the threatened danger in its incipiency."

Gitlow had the practical effect of permitting legislatures to restrict expression if it could lead to unlawful ends. The consequences need not be immediate. *Gitlow* permits dousing the spark before it develops into a fire, also referred to as killing the serpent in the egg. This case reflected as well the Court's generally deferential position toward legislative judgments. The Court explicitly asserted that legislation of this kind would be presumed constitutional. As a result, those who challenge such laws would have to demonstrate the excesses of any regulation. In the years following *Gitlow,* however, the Court began to suggest that it would be more demanding of the government in cases involving the First Amendment. Unlike laws involving economic regulation, for example, legislation touching First Amendment protections would be viewed with suspicion because the Constitution affords these freedoms a "preferred position." This view had its origin in a footnote written by Justice Harlan F. Stone in *United States v. Carolene Products Company* (304 U.S. 144: 1938). This footnote was frequently cited in the 1940s, especially in labor picketing and free exercise of religion situations. An intermediate position between the preferred position theory and the *Gitlow* "bad tendency" doctrine began to evolve after World War II with the balancing test adopted by the Court in *Dennis v. United States* (341 U.S. 494: 1951).

The *Dennis* decision upheld portions of the Alien Registration Act of 1940, better known as the Smith Act. The act was the first federal attempt to restrict expression and association since the Alien and Sedition Acts of 1798. *Dennis* focused particularly on the sections of the act that prohibited advocating forceful overthrow of the government and organizing groups to that end. Eugene Dennis was a leader of the Communist Party of the United States. The criminal charges brought against him and others were confined to illegal advocacy and conspiracy. The Court upheld the Smith Act in *Dennis* by a six to two decision. The Vinson Court had the option of developing a rationale along the lines of *Gitlow* that would have permitted the government to declare that advocating governmental overthrow was unprotected expression. Alternatively, it could have chosen to utilize the clear and present danger test to determine whether sufficient threat existed to warrant restriction. The Court opted for the latter approach, but Chief Justice Fred Vinson reshaped the clear and present danger test in doing so. He wrote that the severity of the threat involved was more important than the immediacy or probability of the danger. Regarding immediacy he reasoned, "Obviously the words of the test cannot mean that before the Government may act, it must wait until the putsch is about to be executed, the plans have been laid, and the signal is awaited." Not only is government response allowed in such a situation, it is required if the government is "aware that a group aiming at its overthrow is attempting to indoctrinate its members and to commit them to a course whereby they will strike when the leaders feels the circumstances permit."

The likelihood of the threat succeeding is not required either. Any attempt to overthrow the government by force, even though doomed from the outset, is a "sufficient evil for Congress to prevent it." The Court adopted a sliding scale concept of clear and present danger, as fashioned by Judge Learned Hand when the court of appeals reviewed the case. Judge Hand's formulation required that courts "ask whether the gravity of the evil, discounted by its improbability, justifies such invasion of free speech as is necessary to avoid the danger." Applying Judge Hand's standard, the Supreme Court found the conspiracy to advocate forceful overthrow sufficient to bring sanctions against Dennis. Justices Hugo Black and William Douglas dissented, arguing that the decision "watered down" the First Amendment so that it amounted to "little more than an admonition to Congress." The amendment interpreted in that way, they felt, is not likely to protect anything but "safe or orthodox views which rarely need its protection."

Dennis cleared the way for a number of conspiracy prosecutions under the Smith Act between 1951 and 1957. Several produced convictions, which, in turn, prompted further appeals to the Supreme Court. In *Yates v. United States* (354 U.S. 298: 1957), the Court severely limited the capacity of the Smith Act to reach political "conspiracies." The Court did not explicitly overrule *Dennis,* but it said the *Dennis* distinction between advocacy of illegal acts and abstract doctrinal advocacy had been ignored by the trial courts subsequent to *Dennis.* Whether or not *Dennis* had really made this distinction is debatable, but the key result of *Yates* was that the government was now required to demonstrate specific illegal acts by party members to convict under the Smith Act. Mere party membership itself was insufficient. This clarification weakened the impact of *Dennis.* Four years later, however, the Court upheld the section of the Smith Act that made it a crime to be a member of a group advocating forcible overthrow, in *Scales v. United States* (367 U.S. 203: 1961). In *Scales,* the Court did require evidence comparable to that required in *Yates,* saying, for example, that to obtain a conviction under the membership clause, a person's membership had to be both knowing and active, and that the person had to have shown "specific intent to bring about violent overthrow" of the government. The evidentiary requirements established in *Yates* and *Scales* greatly diminished the likelihood of successful prosecutions under the Smith Act, and none have been initiated since the 1960s.

SYMBOLIC EXPRESSION

Symbolic speech, which is the use of action or gesture as a substitute for words, is generally protected by the First Amendment because of its expressive character. It may be restricted, however, if the substituted action warrants regulation. The dimensions of symbolic expression are examined through two cases.

The first is *Tinker v. Des Moines Independent School District* (393 U.S. 503: 1969), which involved three Iowa public school students who were suspended from school for wearing black armbands to protest the U.S. government's policy in Vietnam. The students brought suit to prevent the school district from enforcing its regulation against the wearing of armbands, and the Supreme Court ruled that the armbands could be worn. The Court found the "silent, passive expression of opinion, unaccompanied by any disorder or disturbance" to be closely akin to free speech. Though the wearing of armbands was a symbolic action rather than speech as such, the conduct was protected. In a case such as this, the state may not prohibit an expression of opinion without proving that the regulation is necessary to avoid interference with school discipline or the rights of others. The Court also found the ban defective in that it singled out the symbol representing opposition to the Vietnam War while ignoring other political symbols. This meant enforcement of the regulation was not content neutral.

The *Tinker* decision had its origins in *Stromberg v. California* (283 U.S. 359: 1937), in which the Court struck down a California statute outlawing display of a red flag because the flag symbolized "opposition to organized government." The Court felt that if such symbolic expression could be restricted, more general political debate would be seriously jeopardized. The Court has also had occasion to review similar cases involving symbolic use of the U.S. flag. Although the Court has recognized the government's authority to punish certain improper conduct regarding the flag, the justices have generally permitted symbolic uses of the flag. In *Smith v. Goguen* (415 U.S. 566: 1974), for example, the Court reversed a conviction for the "contemptuous" conduct of a person who had sewn a small flag to the seat of his pants.

In *United States v. O'Brien* (391 U.S. 367: 1968), the Court upheld a conviction for the burning of a draft card in protest of the Vietnam War. The Court recognized that David Paul O'Brien's gesture was communicative, but it ruled that the government's interest in protecting the recruitment of persons for military service prevailed when the competing interests were balanced. In a rather unsupportive statement about symbolic speech, Chief Justice Earl Warren said that the Court could not take the position that an "apparently limitless variety of conduct can be labelled 'speech' whenever the person engaging in the conduct intends thereby to express an idea." More typically, the Court has supported litigants claiming protection for symbolic expression.

The most recent examples of people using U.S. flags in an attempt to express themselves symbolically involve desecration of the flag. In *Texas v. Johnson* (491 U.S. 397: 1989), the Supreme Court upheld the right of persons to express their political views through the burning of the U.S. flag. Gregory Johnson was part of a group that gathered in Dallas to demonstrate at the 1984 Republican National Convention. The group marched through downtown Dallas to city hall, where Johnson set fire to a flag. He was arrested and subsequently convicted for violation of the Texas law prohibiting flag desecration. On appeal, the Supreme Court voted five to four to strike down the law. Reagan Court appointees Scalia and Kennedy joined justices Brennan, Marshall, and Blackmun in the majority, with Justice Brennan writing the majority opinion. Texas defended its conviction of Johnson by claiming an interest in preserving the flag as a "symbol of national unity." In response, Brennan pointed to prior decisions "recognizing the communicative nature of conduct relating to flags" and wrote that although government generally has a "freer hand in restricting expressive conduct" than it does with the written or spoken word, it may not "proscribe particular conduct because it has expressive elements." Preservation of the flag as a symbol, on the other hand, relates to "suppression of expression." If there is a "bedrock principle underlying the First Amendment," argued Brennan, it is that government may not "prohibit expression of an idea simply because society finds the idea itself offensive or disagreeable." Prior cases have not recognized an exception where the flag is involved, nor have they allowed government to "insure that a symbol be used to express only one view of that symbol or its referents." To allow government to "designate symbols to be used to communicate only a limited set of messages would be to enter territory having no discernable or defensible boundaries."

Johnson presented a line-drawing problem. The question, wrote Brennan, is how the Court should determine where symbols are "sufficiently special" to qualify for this special protection. Judges would be forced, he believed, to consult their own "political preferences, and impose them on the citizenry, in the very way the First Amendment forbids us to do." The First Amendment does not so protect other "sacred concepts" from "going unquestioned in the market place of ideas. . . . [Therefore,] we decline . . . to create for the flag an exception to the joust of principles protected by the First Amendment." Brennan concluded by saying that the decision strengthens the flag's "deservedly cherished place in our community" and reflects the conviction that "our toleration of criticisms such as Johnson's is a sign and source of our strength." The way, he wrote, to "preserve the flag's special role" is not to punish those who "feel differently about these matters." Rather, it is to "persuade them that they are wrong." We do not "consecrate the flag by punishing its desecration, for in doing so we dilute the freedom that this cherished emblem represents." The dissenters argued the unique position of the flag "as the symbol of our nation"—a position, wrote Chief Justice Rehnquist, that warrants a "governmental prohibition against flag burning."

Texas v. Johnson was among the more controversial decisions in recent years. It was not the first case involving symbolic use of the U.S. flag, however. The Court has recognized the government's authority to punish certain improper conduct regarding the flag but has generally permitted the symbolic uses. *Street v. New York* (394 U.S. 576: 1969), for example, struck down a state law prohibiting flag mutilation. This case involved a flag burning, but the Court focused on the overbroad character of the restriction. In the 1974 case of *Spence v. Washington* (418 U.S. 405: 1974), the Court ruled that superimposing a peace symbol on the flag and flying it upside down was protected. These decisions notwithstanding, symbolic expression is subject to regulation. The line is drawn by examining the action or conduct through which the message is conveyed. If the conduct is illegal, it is subject to regulation along with the associated expression.

Following the Court's decision in *Texas v. Johnson,* Congress enacted the Flag Protection Act of 1989. The act made it a crime to "knowingly mutilate, deface, physically defile, burn, maintain on the floor or ground, or trample upon any flag of the United States." When the federal law was passed, flags were burned in a number of political demonstrations. *United States v. Eichman* and *United States v. Haggerty* (110 L. Ed. 2d 287: 1990) arose out of prosecution for flag-burning incidents in Seattle and Washington, D.C., respectively. The cases were combined for review by the Supreme Court. The Court held that the federal law, like the state law in *Johnson,* violated the free speech protection of the First Amendment. Justice Brennan spoke for the same five-justice majority found in the Texas case, and his opinion was a substantial reiteration of the *Johnson* rationale. Although the government conceded that flag burning is "expressive conduct," it sought to have the Court declare flag burning a kind of expression that falls outside the full protection of the First Amendment. This, said Brennan, "we decline to do." When the federal law was drafted, an effort had been made to avoid regulating conduct based on the content of the expressive message, as this was the key defect in the Texas law. However, Brennan said that although the Flag Protection Act "contains no explicit content-based limitation on the scope of prohibited conduct, it is nevertheless clear that the Government's asserted interest is related to the suppression of free expression, and is concerned with the content of such expression." The government's interest in "protecting the physical integrity of a privately owned flag" is based on the "perceived need to preserve the flag's status as a symbol of our nation and certain national ideals."

The destruction of a flag by itself, however, does not "diminish or otherwise affect the symbol." Rather, the government's desire to "preserve the flag as a symbol for certain national ideals is implicated only when a person's treatment of the flag communicates a message to others that is inconsistent with those ideals." The "precise language" of the act "confirms" Congress's intent regarding the "communicative impact of flag destruction." Each of the terms chosen to define the criminal conduct "unmistakably connotes disrespectful treatment of the flag and suggests a focus on those acts likely to damage the flag's symbolic value." Allowing the government to prohibit flag burning when it endangers the flag's symbolic role would permit the state to "prescribe what shall be orthodoxy by saying that one may burn the flag to convey one's attitude toward it . . . only if one does not endanger the flag's representation of nationhood and national unity." Though Congress sought to couch the federal law in "broader terms" than the Texas law overturned in *Johnson*, the act "still suffers from the same fundamental flaw: it suppresses expression out of concern for its likely communicative impact." Following the Court's ruling in *Haggerty* and *Eichman*, the Congress considered a constitutional amendment that would have permitted prosecution of flag burning notwithstanding First Amendment protection of symbolic expression. The proposed amendment was defeated in the House of Representatives on June 21, 1990. Renewal of efforts to elevate the flag to constitutionally protected status will likely be a function of the congressional election politics.

OFFENSIVE SPEECH

Offensive speech is expression that is objectionable and distasteful to a listener because it contains obnoxious language. Offensive speech is, however, often a form of pure speech in that no supporting conduct is required. As a result, the Supreme Court has held that offensive speech is generally protected expression. Offensive speech standards are influenced by the fact that words are often chosen as much for their emotional as their cognitive value. Some offensive speech is not protected, as in the case of obscenity, libel, and "fighting words." Fighting words are inherently insulting or likely to incite a breach of the peace. Indeed, attempts to punish offensive speech typically take the form of prosecution for breach of peace. Expression found to be offensive is not protected by the First Amendment because it is of such slight communicative value as to be outweighed by the public interest in maintaining order.

Illustrative of the way the Court handles the issue of offensive speech is *Cohen v. California* (403 U.S. 15: 1971). Paul Cohen was arrested in the Los Angeles County Courthouse for wearing a jacket upon which were emblazoned the words "Fuck the Draft." At his trial Cohen testified the jacket was his means of stating his intense feelings about the draft and U.S. involvement in Vietnam. Cohen was convicted of violating a statute prohibiting "malicious and willful disturbing of the peace" by conduct that is "offensive." On appeal, the Supreme Court invalidated the statute in a five to four decision. The Court ruled that in this instance the words were the issue rather than the conduct, and therefore that it was "speech" that was prohibited by the statute. Moreover, the majority held that the California law was vague, that the words were not personally directed at anyone, and that a state cannot excise offensive epithets by functioning as a guardian of public morality. Justice John Harlan, writing for the majority, said the First Amendment is "designed and intended to remove government restraints from the arena of public discussion." A consequence of such freedom "may often appear to be only verbal tumult, discord, and even offensive utterance," but that is the price of freedom. "We cannot lose sight of the fact that, in what otherwise might seem a trifling and annoying instance of individual distasteful abuse of a privilege, fundamental societal values are truly implicated."

The majority was also troubled by the "inherently boundless" nature of what California was attempting through the statute. "Surely the State has no right to cleanse the public debate to the point where it is grammatically palatable to the most squeamish among us." Finally, Justice Harlan pointed out that language serves a dual communicative function. It not only conveys ideas capable of relatively precise and detailed explication, but it also conveys otherwise inexpressible emotions as well. Words are often chosen as much for their emotive as their cognitive force. Harlan concluded, "We cannot sanction the view that the Constitution, while solicitous of the cognitive content of individual speech, has little or no regard for that emotive function which, practically speaking, may often be the more important element of the overall message sought to be communicated." Chief Justice Burger and Justices Blackmun, Black, and White dissented and said Cohen's "absurd and immature antic" was essentially regulatable conduct.

Cohen involved an attempt to punish offensive speech. Such attempts typically take the form of prosecution for breach of the peace. In *Chaplinsky v. New Hampshire* (315 U.S. 568: 1942), the Court held that some speech, notably that that is obscene, libelous, or insulting, is not protected by the First Amendment. These types of speech are of such slight value that any benefit derived from them is clearly outweighed by the social interest in order and morality. In *Terminello v. Chicago* (337 U.S. 1: 1949), the Court reversed a breach of the peace conviction of a highly provocative speaker, holding that a municipal ordinance was inappropriately applied to limit speech that "invites dispute." Two years later, however, the Court upheld the disorderly conduct conviction of a street-corner speaker in *Feiner v. New York* (340 U.S. 315: 1951). The Court said that when "clear and present danger of riot, disorder, interference with traffic upon the public street, or other immediate threat to public safety, peace, or order appears, the power of the State to prevent or punish is obvious."

OVERBREADTH DOCTRINE

The overbreadth doctrine requires that enactments proscribing certain activity must not touch constitutionally protected conduct. Overbreadth refers to any statute that fails to adequately distinguish between those activities that may be regulated and those that cannot. The way in which the doctrine is applied can be seen in the case of *Village of Schaumburg v. Citizens for a Better Environment* (444 U.S. 620: 1980). In this case, the Supreme Court examined a local ordinance that prohibited door-to-door solicitations for contributions by organizations that use less than 75 percent of their receipts for charitable purposes. A charitable purpose excluded such items as salaries, overhead, solicitation costs, and other administrative expenses. An environmental group was denied permission to solicit because it could not demonstrate compliance with the 75 percent requirement, and the organization sued on First Amendment grounds.

The Court struck down the ordinance over the single dissent of Justice Rehnquist. The Court's primary objection was the overbreadth of the ordinance. The justices noted that a class of organizations existed to which the 75 percent rule could not constitutionally be applied. These were organizations "whose primary purpose is not to provide money or services to the poor, the needy, or other worthy objects of charity, but to gather and disseminate information about and advocate positions on matters of public concern." The costs of research, advocacy, or public education typically exceed 25 percent of the funds raised, and the Court felt that lumping together all organizations failing to meet the 75 percent standard imposed a direct and substantial limitation on protected activity. Though the village interest in preventing fraud may generally be legitimate, the means to accomplish that end must use more precise measures to separate one kind from the other.

The overbreadth doctrine is an important device in certain First Amendment cases because it requires that regulations distinguish sufficiently between lawful and unlawful expression or behavior. In *Coates v. Cincinnati* (402 U.S. 611: 1971), the Court struck down a city ordinance that prohibited three or more persons from assembling on public sidewalks and conducting themselves in such a way as to "annoy any police officer or other persons who should happen to pass by." The Court found that the ordinance "makes a crime out of what under the Constitution cannot be a crime" and that it was impermissibly vague. It conveyed no standard of conduct and "men of common intelligence must necessarily guess at its meaning." Although the overbreadth and vagueness doctrines have often been invoked to invalidate enactments, as in *Schaumburg* and *Coates,* some ordinances survive such challenges. In *Grayned v. Rockford* (408 U.S. 104: 1972), for example, the Court upheld an antinoise ordinance that prohibits disturbances in the proximity of schools in session. The specific school context separated the restriction from the typically vague and general breach of the peace ordinance; consequently, the enactment was seen as a reasonable time, place, and manner restriction. It was narrowly tailored to further the compelling interest of Rockford, Illinois, in having undisrupted school sessions, and it was not impermissibly overbroad.

SPEECH PLUS

"Speech plus" refers to expression that requires additional action or conduct, including such forms of expression as picketing, marching, demonstrating, and sit-ins. These situations raise difficult First Amendment questions because the action dimension may take the normally protected speech out of bounds. Many speech-plus cases are grounded in the right to assemble, a right explicitly provided in the First Amendment. This right to assemble includes the right to protest government policies as well as to advocate particular, even distasteful views. However, although the people have a right to peaceably assemble, the government may legitimately act to preserve order. These two interests may collide, and the right of assembly does not provide absolute protection. In the words of Justice Black, the right of assembly does not include expression "whenever and wherever one pleases." The government can impose regulations on the time, place, and manner of assembly, provided that substantial interests, such as preventing threats to public order, can be shown. Time, place, and manner restrictions must be evenhandedly applied and must be wholly unrelated to the content of the expression involved. As in other matters involving free expression, restrictions on the right to assemble are suspect.

These elements are exemplified by several right-of-assembly cases. The first is *Adderley v. Florida* (385 U.S. 39: 1966). *Adderley* held that demonstrators may be barred from assembly on the grounds of a county jail. Harriett Louise Adderley and a number of others were convicted of trespassing for gathering at a county jail to protest both the arrest of several students the day before and local policies of racial segregation at the jail itself. When the demonstrators would not leave the jail grounds as requested, they were warned of possible arrest for trespassing. Adderley and others remained on the premises, were arrested, and subsequently were tried and convicted. The Court upheld the conviction in a five to four decision that focused on whether or not the trespass convictions deprived the demonstrators of their freedom of speech.

In the majority opinion written by Justice Black, the Court concluded that "nothing in the Constitution of the United States prevented Florida from even-handed enforcement of its general trespass statute against those refusing to obey the sheriff's order to remove themselves from what amounted to the curtilage of the jailhouse." The fact that the jail was a public building did not automatically entitle the protesters to demonstrate there. The state, no less than a private owner of property, has power to preserve the property under its control for its lawfully dedicated use. The security purpose to which the jail was dedicated outweighed the expression interests of the protesters. The justices felt that to find for Adderley would be to endorse "the assumption that people who want to propagandize protests or views have a constitutional right to do so whenever and wherever they please." The Court categorically rejected that premise and concluded its opinion by saying that the Constitution does not forbid a state from controlling the use of its own property for its own lawful nondiscriminatory purposes.

Adderley involved speech plus—conduct beyond oral expression itself—and the additional conduct is subject to regulation at a cost to expression. In *Cox v. Louisiana* (379 U.S. 536: 1965), the Court upheld a state statute that prohibited picketing near a courthouse and said a state could legitimately insulate its judicial proceedings from demonstrations. Although restrictions were said to be warranted in *Adderley* and *Cox,* breach-of-the-peace convictions of persons demonstrating on the grounds of a state capitol were reversed in *Edwards v. South Carolina* (372 U.S. 229: 1963). Similarly, a peaceful sit-in at a library was protected in *Brown v. Louisiana* (383 U.S. 131: 1966). More recently, the Court struck down an ordinance that prohibited picketing in the proximity of school buildings when classes were in session in *Chicago Police Department v. Mosley* (408 U.S. 92: 1972). The ordinance was invalidated largely because it excepted labor picketing from the ban. The Court did suggest the city had a legitimate interest in preventing school disruption, however. Time, place, and manner restrictions have generally been recognized by the Court, provided that significant governmental interests can be demonstrated. In *City Council of Los Angeles v. Taxpayers for Vincent* (466 U.S. 789: 1984), the Court ruled that a municipality could ban the posting of political campaign signs on utility poles. The ban was seen to be content neutral and directed toward a legitimate aesthetic interest. The purpose of the regulation was "unrelated to the suppression of ideas" and interfered with expression only to the extent necessary to eliminate visual clutter. The Court noted that the ban on posting signs did not impinge on any alternative modes of communication.

A city's authority to regulate concerts held in a municipal park was before the Court in *Ward v. Rock Against Racism* (105 L. Ed. 2d 661: 1989). An association called Rock Against Racism (RAR) had sponsored annual concerts at a bandshell in New York City's Central Park. The city received many complaints about the excessive noise associated with RAR concerts but had experienced similar problems with other bandshell events as well. The complaints were typically about substandard equipment and technicians unskilled at mixing sound. In response to these problems, the city issued a set of use guidelines governing all bandshell concerts. Among other things, it was specified that the city would furnish the amplification equipment and employ an experienced sound technician to operate it. RAR sought a declaratory judgment against the guidelines as an interference with their First Amendment expression rights. The Supreme Court ruled the guidelines to be a valid place and manner regulation and recognized that government is not permitted to adopt a regulation of speech because of "disagreement with the message it conveys." In this instance, the city had two objectives in instituting the guidelines: controlling noise and ensuring sound quality. Neither of these purposes, concluded the Court, had anything to do with content.

In *PruneYard Shopping Center v. Robins* (447 U.S. 74: 1980), the Court declared that demonstrators may access privately owned shopping malls to circulate and distribute political pamphlets. *PruneYard* involved a group of high school students who sought to express their opposition to a UN resolution against Zionism. They set up a table near the central courtyard of the shopping center, began distributing pamphlets, and asked patrons of the shopping center to sign a petition. The students were orderly and no objection to their presence was registered by any shopping center customer. However, the students were informed by a shopping center security guard that their activity was in violation of mall policy, which prohibited all such conduct. The group subsequently filed suit and sought access to the center through a restraining order. The California Supreme Court held that the state constitution entitled the students access to the mall, and the U.S. Supreme Court upheld the state court in a unanimous decision.

The crucial issue for the Supreme Court was whether state-protected rights of expression infringed upon the property rights of PruneYard's owners. Citing the state court, Justice Rehnquist said that a "handful of additional orderly persons soliciting signatures and distributing handbills do not interfere with normal business operations." In the Court's view, the students did not "markedly dilute" the owner's property rights. Two other arguments also were developed in support of the state court decision. First, PruneYard, "by choice of its owner," is not limited to the "personal use" of the owners. Rather, PruneYard is a business establishment that is "open to the public." Any views expressed by mall patrons "thus will not likely be identified with those of the owner." Second, PruneYard and any of its shop owners could easily disclaim any connection to the expression of the demonstrators. They could explain that the "persons are communicating their own messages by virtue of state law."

The final issue involves attempts to restrict assembly before it occurs. The case of *Carroll v. President and Commissioners of Princess Anne* (393 U.S. 175: 1968) speaks to the manner by which court restraining orders may be sought to prevent persons from demonstrating in some way. Such injunctions are frequently, but not always, used in situations in which permits or licenses to march or demonstrate have been denied. Joseph Carroll, a member of a white supremacist organization known as the National States Rights Party, participated in a rally at which aggressive and militant racist and antisemitic speeches were made. At the conclusion of the speeches, it was announced that the rally would be resumed the next night. Local government officials obtained a restraining order in the meantime in an ex parte proceeding. The injunction restrained Carroll and others from holding public meetings for ten days. The Supreme Court struck down the order in a unanimous judgment. The Court's primary objection was to the ex parte procedure, in which the order was issued without notice to Carroll and without effort to invite or permit the other party's participation in the proceedings. The Court recognized that ex parte orders may be appropriate in some situations, "but there is no place within the area of basic freedoms guaranteed by the First Amendment for such orders." Absence of an adversary proceeding deprives a trial court of the facts necessary to make a judgment and provides "insufficient assurance of the balanced analysis and careful considerations which are essential in the area of First Amendment adjudication." The same absence of information makes it more difficult to construct an order in the "narrowest and least stifling terms."

Carroll established procedural guidelines through which court orders might be obtained against demonstrators. The permit-injunction approach had often been used against civil rights demonstrators. In *Walker v. Birming-*

ham (388 U.S. 307: 1967), the Court upheld an injunction issued following the denial of a parade permit. Wyatt Tee Walker, Dr. Martin Luther King, Jr., and others involved in the proposed parade disobeyed the injunction without seeking appellate review of either the injunction or the permit denial that had led to the court order. A five-justice majority found the potentially persuasive objections to the Birmingham permit system to be subordinate to the demonstrators' failure to obey the court order.

Permits are a satisfactory approach so long as they are confined to reasonable time, place, and manner limitations. Permit or license requirements that are not content neutral or that allow too much discretion to permit-granting public officials are unacceptable. A more recent injunction episode involved attempts by Skokie, Illinois, to prevent an assembly of the National Socialist Party of America, a self-proclaimed Nazi organization. More than half of Skokie's residents were Jewish, and a sizeable number of these Jews were survivors of German concentration camps. Prior to the assembly, an injunction was secured from a state court enjoining the party from a uniformed march, display of swastikas, and distribution of materials that might "promote hatred against persons of the Jewish faith or ancestry." The Illinois Supreme Court refused to stay implementation of the injunction. The U.S. Supreme Court, however, reversed denial of the stay in *National Socialist Party v. Skokie* (432 U.S. 43: 1977). The Court held that the injunction deprived the party of its right to demonstrate for the period until an appellate review could occur. That period was estimated to be a year or more. The Court said that if a "State seeks to impose a restraint of this kind, it must provide strict procedural safeguards including appellate review. Absent such review, the State must instead allow the stay." The party never assembled in Skokie, choosing instead to hold a rally in a Chicago park.

Right of Association

The right of association permits people to act together to advance a mutual interest or achieve a common objective. The right of association is not expressly protected by the First Amendment, but rather is derived from safeguards for expression and assembly contained in the amendment. Association is an effective means of achieving political and social goals. Given the fundamental role of associational activity, government is obligated to ensure that interference with such activity does not occur. At the same time, association may still be regulated. The most troublesome association cases have involved statutory attempts to either proscribe subversive organizations or regulate the electoral process. The basic character of associational freedom was examined by the Warren Court in *NAACP v. Alabama* (357 U.S. 449: 1958). This case involved an attempt by Alabama to compel disclosure of the National Association for the Advancement of Colored People (NAACP) membership list as a means of inhibiting the activities of the organization. The association refused to disclose the list and was sanctioned, but the Supreme Court unanimously reversed the sanction.

This case provided the foundation of the concept of the constitutional right of association. In its opinion the Court first had to resolve the matter of standing. Alabama argued that the NAACP could not assert constitutional rights of its members, which was a pivotal issue in the case. The Court found the NAACP relationship with its individual members to be close enough to "permit it to act as their representative." Indeed, the Court said the NAACP is the "appropriate party to assert these rights, because it and its members are in every practical sense identical." The Court then addressed the infringement of protected freedoms threatened by the compulsory disclosure. It recognized that "effective advocacy," particularly of controversial issues, is "undeniably enhanced by group association." The compelled disclosure was viewed as adversely affecting the ability of the NAACP and its members to pursue their "collective effort to foster beliefs which they admittedly have a right to advocate." The Court saw disclosure as having adverse consequences in two ways. First, the NAACP itself would likely suffer diminished financial support and fewer membership applications. Second, disclosure of the identity of members might prompt "economic reprisal, loss of employment, threat of physical coercion, and other manifestations of public hostility." The Court found that Alabama had not shown a "controlling justification for the deterrent effect on the free enjoyment of the right to associate which disclosure of membership lists is likely to have."

In a case not directly involving the disclosure issue, the NAACP was able to affirm another dimension of associational freedom, in *NAACP v. Button* (371 U.S. 415: 1963). *Button* upheld the NAACP's strategy of representing membership interests through litigation. Many states had enacted antisolicitation laws prohibiting the "stirring up" of lawsuits. In the case of the NAACP, the Court recognized such activity as a means for achieving lawful objectives and as a form of political expression. Indeed, for such a group, "association for litigation may be the most effective form of political association." Litigation seeking vindication of constitutional rights is a different matter from "avaricious use of the legal process purely for personal gain."

A decade after *NAACP v. Alabama,* the Court ruled in *Keyishian v. Board of Regents* (385 U.S. 589: 1967) that more than "mere membership" in organizations had to be demonstrated before the imposition of restrictions on associational rights. *Keyishian* examined New York State statutory provisions known collectively as the Feinberg law, which authorized the Board of Regents to monitor organizational memberships of state employees. The board was required by state law to generate a list of subversive organizations, and membership in any one of those organizations was prima facie evidence for disqualification from public employment, including appointments to academic positions. Although the person being terminated could have a hearing, the hearing could not address the classification of the organization as subversive. Harry Keyishian and several other faculty members in the state university system were dismissed because of their membership in the Communist Party. On review of this case, the Supreme Court struck down the Feinberg law in a five to four decision. The majority rejected the premise that "public employment, including academic employment, may be conditioned upon the surrender of constitutional rights which could not be abridged by direct government action" and found "mere membership" to be an insufficient basis for exclusion. "Legislation which sanctions membership unaccompanied by specific intent to further the unlawful goals of the organization or which is not active membership violates constitutional limitations." The Court also said the statutes suffered from overbreadth. The regulations "seek to bar employment both for association which legitimately may be proscribed and for association which may not be sanctioned." The flaw of their overbroad sweep was as fatal as the flaw of vagueness.

The Rehnquist Court has spoken to the issue of associational freedom on several occasions. Two of these cases were brought by labor unions. Section 109 of the Omnibus Budget Reconciliation Act of 1981 provided that the household of a striking worker could not become eligible for food stamps unless eligibility was established prior to the strike. These provisions were upheld by the Court in *Lyng v. International Union, United Automobile, Aerospace and Agricultural Implement Workers of America* (485 U.S. 360: 1988). The law was challenged on the ground that it interfered with the right of strikers to associate with their families, unions, and fellow union members. It was further contended that the provisions violated the strikers' right of expression about union affairs free of governmental coercion. The Court said the statute did not "directly or substantially interfere" with either family living arrangements or the right of workers to associate with each other. Indeed, the Court said, it is "exceedingly unlikely" that relatives would choose to live apart simply to increase food stamp allotments because the additional costs would exceed the "incremental value of the additional stamps." Neither did the law "prevent" or "burden" workers' ability to "associate together in unions to promote their lawful objectives." Any impact that might exist here results from the government's refusal to extend benefits to those with diminished income. In *Communications Workers of America v. Beck* (487 U.S. 735: 1988), the Court ruled that unions cannot compel nonmembers to pay "agency fees" if those fees are used for political or other purposes that are not directly related to collective bargaining. Prior to this decision, unions were free to use such agency fees for non-collective bargaining activities. A number of nonmember employees challenged the Communication Workers of America (CWA) use of agency fees to, for example, support endorsed political candidates, organize employees at other companies, and conduct various lobbying activities. They contended that use of fees for such purposes violated the CWA's "duty of fair representation." The issue in this case was whether the minimum support or "financial core" required under closed shop provisions includes the obligation to "support union activities beyond those germane to collective bargaining, contract administration, and grievance adjustment." The Court ruled that it does not.

ASSOCIATION AND THE ELECTORAL PROCESS

The most recent cases affecting associational rights have come from attempts to protect the integrity of the electoral process. A critically important case is *Buckley v. Valeo* (424 U.S. 11: 1976). This case examined the constitutionality of the Federal Election Campaign Act of 1974. *Buckley* evaluated the act against various First Amendment challenges, including the possibility that regulation of the electoral process impinges upon individual and group expression. The act, passed in the wake of Watergate, sought to protect the electoral process by (1) limiting political campaign contributions, (2) establishing ceilings on several categories of campaign expenditures, (3) requiring extensive and regular disclosure of campaign contributors and expenditures, (4) providing public financing for presidential campaigns, and (5) creating a Federal Election Commission to administer the act. Suit was filed by a diverse collection of individuals and groups that included U.S. Senator James Buckley, the Eugene McCarthy presidential campaign, the Libertarian Party, the American Conservative Union, and the New York Civil Liberties Union. By differing majorities, the Court upheld those portions of the act that provided for campaign contribution limits, disclosure, public financing, and the Federal Election Commission.

The section imposing limits on expenditures was invalidated. The Court said the act's contribution and expenditure ceiling "reduces the quantity of expression because virtually every means of communicating ideas in today's society requires the expenditure of money." The Court distinguished, however, between limits on contributions and limits on those things for which the contributions might be spent. Although the latter represents substantial

restraint on the quantity and diversity of political speech, limits on contributions involve "little direct restraint." The contributor's freedom to discuss
candidates and issues is not infringed in any way. Even though contributions
may underwrite some costs of conveying a campaign's views, the contributions must be transformed into political expression by persons other than the
contributor. The Court acknowledged a legitimate governmental interest in
protecting the "integrity of our system of representative democracy" from
quid pro quo arrangements that might arise from financial contributions.
Expenditure limits, on the other hand, severely burden one's ability to speak
one's mind and engage in vigorous advocacy. In addition, the First Amendment cannot be used to equalize political influence. "The concept that
government may restrict the speech of some elements of our society in order
to enhance the relative voice of others is wholly foreign to the First
Amendment." By striking the expenditure limits, the Court allowed unlimited use of personal wealth or expenditures made on behalf of campaigns
separate from the actual campaign organization of a candidate. On the matter
of disclosure, the Court agreed that the requirement might deter some
contributions but viewed it as a "least restrictive means of curbing the evils
of campaign ignorance and corruption."

The Court extended the *Buckley* reasoning in *Federal Election Commission v. National Conservative Political Action Committee* (470 U.S. 480:
1985), saying the Federal Election Campaign Act could not limit political
action committees (PACs) to an expenditure of $1,000 for promoting
candidacies of publicly funded presidential aspirants. Such an expenditure
limit was found to impermissibly infringe on First Amendment speech and
associational rights. The Federal Election Campaign Act came under further
review in *Federal Election Commission v. Massachusetts Citizens for Life*
(479 U.S. 238: 1986). Under challenge was the section prohibiting corporations from using general funds to make expenditures related to an election to
any public office. Massachusetts Citizens for Life (MCFL), a nonprofit,
nonstock corporation, was formed to promote pro-life causes. MCFL used its
general treasury to prepare and distribute a special election edition of its
newsletter that categorized all candidates for state and federal offices in
terms of their support for or opposition to MCFL's views. The Supreme
Court ruled unanimously that the special edition of the newsletter fell within
the scope of the prohibition of the law but that the provision created
unacceptable First Amendment violations for corporations such as MCFL.
Most of the rationale supporting regulations of this kind stems from the
special characteristics of the corporate structure. The "integrity of the
marketplace of political ideas" must be protected from the "corrosive
influence of corporate wealth." Direct corporate spending "raises the

prospect that resources amassed in the economic marketplace may be used to provide an unfair advantage in the political marketplace." The availability of resources may make a corporation a "formidable political presence, even though the power of the corporation may be no reflection of the power of its ideas." The Court held that such groups as MCFL simply do not pose that danger of corruption. MCFL was formed for the express purpose of promoting political ideas, and its activities cannot be considered as business activities. This ensures that its political resources reflect political support. Because the group sells no shares, persons affiliated with MCFL will have no economic disincentive for disassociating if they disagree with its political activity.

The Court upheld, however, the power of the federal and state governments to regulate the campaign expenditures of business corporations in *Austin v. Michigan Chamber of Commerce* (108 L. Ed. 2d 652: 1990). The Michigan Campaign Finance Act prohibited corporations from using general treasury funds for independent expenditures for state political candidates. Rather, corporations were required to use funds specifically segregated for political purposes. The state regulation did allow business corporations to establish political action committees to make such independent expenditures. The Michigan Chamber of Commerce wished to use general treasury funds on behalf of a specific candidate for state office, and it sought to enjoin enforcement of the restriction. The Supreme Court ruled that the regulation did not violate the First Amendment. The Court found that protecting the electoral process from the "corrosive and distorting effects of immense aggregations of wealth" was a sufficiently compelling interest to justify the regulation.

The Court disagreed with the chamber's claim that, like MCFL, it, too, was a nonprofit ideological corporation. MCFL was formed for the "express purpose of promoting political ideas, and cannot engage in business activities." Its "narrow political focus" ensured that its political resources "reflect its political support." The chamber, on the other hand, had "more varied purposes." Second, MCFL had no shareholders or similarly affiliated members. Although the chamber lacked shareholders as such, many of its members may be "reluctant to withdraw as members if they disagree with the Chamber's political expression, because they wish to benefit from the Chamber's nonpolitical programs and to establish contacts with other members of the business community." Third, MCFL was "independen[t] from the influence of business corporations." Indeed, it was on this basis that the Court found the chamber to differ "most greatly from the Massachusetts organization." Further, because MCFL did not accept contributions from corporations, it could not serve as a "conduit for the type of direct spending that creates a threat to the political marketplace." In "striking" contrast, the chamber's members are largely business corporations, whose "political contributions and expenditures can be constitutionally regulated by the State." Business corporations therefore could "circumvent the Act's restrictions by funneling money through the Chamber's general treasury."

Rules that govern the actual election process raise slightly different associational questions. Consider *Tashjian v. Republican Party of Connecticut* (479 U.S. 208: 1986). Under a state law enacted in 1955, Connecticut required that voters in a party primary be registered members of that party. In an effort to broaden its own electoral base, the Republican Party of Connecticut changed its rules of participation in primaries for federal and state offices. Possessing insufficient strength to amend state law, the Republican Party brought suit in federal court asserting that enforcement of the law substantially burdened the First Amendment right of association. In a five to four decision, the Supreme Court ruled for the party. The party's First Amendment interest was clearly evident to the Court. The freedom to engage in voluntary association is an inseparable aspect of the liberty embraced by freedom of speech. The freedom of association includes partisan political organization and the right to associate with the party of one's choice. Accordingly, the party's attempt to broaden its base is conduct "undeniably central to the exercise of the right to association." The statute in this case limits whom the party may invite to participate in the basic function of selecting the party's candidates. The law thus limits the party's "associational opportunities at the crucial juncture at which the appeal to common principle may be translated into concerted actions, and hence to political power in the community." The state claimed the administration of primaries under the party rule would cost too much. Even if it is assumed that the state was accurate in its projections, the Court said, the possibility of future cost increases in administering the election policy is not a sufficient basis in this case for interfering with the party's associational rights. Connecticut also contended that its law protected the integrity of the two-party system and the responsibility of party government. Here the Court refused to consider the wisdom of open versus closed primaries and was unwilling to let the state substitute its own judgment for that of the party, even if the latter's course of conduct might be harmful to its own interests.

The Court has generally steered clear of intervention in partisan political processes. In *O'Brien v. Brown* (409 U.S. 1: 1972), for example, the Court invoked the political question doctrine when it held that federal courts did not possess the authority to interject themselves into the deliberative processes of a presidential nominating convention. A decade later the Court ruled in

Democratic Party v. LaFollette (450 U.S. 351: 1981) that a state could not require national party convention delegates to support the candidacy of the winner of the state's presidential primary. Notwithstanding this generally noninterventionist tendency, the Court has found state interest to be compelling in some restrictions on the electoral process. In *Rosario v. Rockefeller* (410 U.S. 752: 1973), the Court upheld a requirement that voters register in a party at least 30 days prior to a general election in order to participate in the next primary. Similarly, the Court upheld a California law that denied ballot access to independents who had been registered party members within 17 months prior to an election (*Storer v. Brown*, 415 U.S. 724: 1974). Both of these cases were explicitly distinguished from Connecticut's law in *Tashjian*. Justice Marshall said the regulations upheld in *Rosario* and *Storer* were designed to protect parties from the "disorganizing effect of independent candidacies launched by unsuccessful putative nominees." The action in *Tashjian* was undertaken to protect the disruption of the political parties from without and not to prevent parties from taking internal steps affecting their own process for the selection of candidates. Marshall was careful to point out, however, that *Tashjian* should not be read as blanket support for open primaries or as an indication that no state regulation of primary voting qualifications could be sustained. In a footnote, Marshall said that party rules seeking to open primaries to anyone would pose a set of considerations different from those involved in *Tashjian*.

Keeping partisan practices at arm's length has not restrained the Court from the partisan arena altogether. The Burger Court's rulings on political appointments are good examples. In *Elrod v. Burns* (427 U.S. 347: 1976), the Court held that an incoming county official could not fire department employees because they belonged to the other party. *Branti v. Finkel* (445 U.S. 507: 1980) involved assistant public defenders. The rationale shared by these two cases was that firings based on party affiliation penalized political thought. The thinking in these cases was substantially broadened by the Rehnquist Court in *Rutan v. Republican Party of Illinois* (111 L. Ed. 2d 52: 1990). In *Rutan,* the Court ruled that hiring decisions for public positions could not be based on party affiliation. Justice Brennan, writing for a five-justice majority, said political victors are entitled to "only those spoils that may be constitutionally obtained." Unless party affiliation is an "appropriate requirement" for a position, the First Amendment precludes use of party affiliation in hiring, promotion, recall, and transfer decisions. Employees who do "not compromise their beliefs" stand to lose in a variety of ways. For example, an employee may lose "increases in pay or job satisfaction attendant to promotion." These are "significant penalties . . . imposed for the exercise of rights guaranteed by the First Amendment." Denial of a state job on the basis of partisan affiliation was similarly seen as severly punitive. State jobs are "valuable," and the inability to secure one "is a serious privation." Unless use of patronage is "narrowly tailored" to further a "vital" governmental interest, it encroaches on the First Amendment. Illinois asserted that patronage both produces a more effective workforce and protects political parties. The Court disagreed. Justice Brennan said that government can secure "effective" employees by sanctioning workers whose work is "deficient." Party affiliation is not a proxy for deficient performance as such. Neither is the democratic process furthered by patronage. Parties are "nurtured by other, less intrusive and equally effective methods." To the contrary, patronage "decidedly impairs the elective process by discouraging free political expression by public employees."

The related question of ballot access was considered in *Munro v. Socialist Workers Party* (479 U.S. 189: 1986). Washington State established a two-step process for minor party candidates seeking to get on the general election ballot. Any such candidate must first secure the convention nomination of his or her party; as the nominee, the candidate would appear on the primary election ballot. To access the general election ballot, the candidate needed to receive at least 1 percent of all votes cast for that office in the primary election. Candidate Dean Peoples was placed on the primary election ballot as the nominee of the Socialist Workers Party but received only 596 of the 681,690 votes cast in the primary, or .09 percent. Accordingly, his name was not placed on the general election ballot. Action was brought in federal court by Peoples, the party, and two registered voters claiming abridgment of rights secured by the First Amendment. In a seven to two decision, the Supreme Court upheld the restrictions on ballot access. In reviewing the restrictions of this type, Justice White said it is clear that states may condition access to the general election ballot by minor party or independent candidates upon a showing of a modicum of support among the potential voters for the office.

When states attempt to justify access restrictions, there is no requirement of a "particularized showing of the existence of voter confusion, ballot overcrowding, or the presence of frivolous candidates prior to the imposition of reasonable restrictions." To require actual proof of these conditions would invariably lead to lengthy disputes over the sufficiency of the evidence offered by a state in support of the restriction. In this case, the Court concluded that Washington State had created no impediment to voting in primary elections. Candidates and members of any organization, regardless of size or duration of existence, were viewed as wholly free to associate, to proselytize, to speak, to write, and to organize campaigns for any school of thought they wish. States do not have a constitutional imperative to reduce voter apathy or assist unpopular candidates to enhance their chances of gaining access to the general election ballot. All Washington did was require a candidate to demonstrate a significant modicum of voter support, a condition the state was entitled to impose. The dissenters felt the state had impermissibly preempted participation by minor parties and allowed them to be "excised from the electoral process before they have fulfilled their central role in our democratic political tradition: to channel dissent into that process in a constructive fashion."

The ballot access issue examined in *Munro* is not new. For years the Court refrained from engaging in direct supervision of state electoral processes. That policy began to change with the Warren Court's decision to address the issue of legislative apportionment. Regulations that made it difficult for new or minor parties to get on the ballot began to be scrutinized more carefully. In *Williams v. Rhodes* (393 U.S. 23: 1968), for example, the Court voided an Ohio statute that required new parties to file a substantial number of petition signatures to access the ballot. Established parties were exempt from the requirement, and the Court ruled that the policy unfairly burdened new parties. Similarly, the Court struck down an early filing date for candidates other than those nominated by the two major parties in *Anderson v. Celebrezze* (460 U.S. 780: 1983). But as Justice White said in *Munro,* some cases decided during this same period established with unmistakable clarity that states may, as a manifestation of their interest in preserving the integrity of the election process, require candidates to make a preliminary showing of support to qualify for ballot access. In *Jenness v. Fortsen* (403 U.S. 431: 1971), for example, the Court sustained a Georgia requirement that independent and minor party candidates submit petitions signed by at least 5 percent of those eligible to vote in the election for the office involved. Likewise, the Court upheld a state requirement in *American Party of Texas v. White* (415 U.S. 767: 1974) that minor party candidates demonstrate support through signatures of voters numbering at least 1 percent of the total votes cast in the most recent gubernatorial election. Such cases as *Jenness, White,* and *Munro* clearly indicate that the Court will permit states significant latitude in restricting ballot access as long as access conditions are not excessive.

Freedom of the Press

The free press clause of the First Amendment prohibits both Congress and the states from enacting any law abridging the freedom of the press. First and foremost, this protects the press from prior or previous restraint. A prior restraint is a restriction on publication before it takes place or before published material can be circulated. Such restraint typically occurs through licensure or censorship procedures. The First Amendment prohibits such regulation because of the gravity of the threat it imposes on expression. Exceptions to the prohibition on prior restraint may be justified if publication threatens national security, incites overthrow of the government, is obscene, or seriously interferes with the private rights of other persons. The free press clause also protects the information gathering function of the press, although an absolute right of access and confidentiality does not exist. Freedom of the press occasionally collides with the fair trial interests of criminal defendants. Some limitations may therefore be imposed on the press to minimize prejudicial pre-trial publicity. The press cannot be barred from criminal trials, however, and it cannot be restrained from reporting what is observed there except in extraordinary circumstances. The broadcast media are permitted to cover criminal proceedings provided they do so with no adverse consequences to the accused. Several forms of published expression remain unprotected by the First Amendment. Obscenity, for example, has consistently been held to be subject to government regulation. Another area outside free press clause protection is libel, which is printed material that falsely and maliciously defames a person. Despite its unprotected character, libel has been narrowly defined, especially where public officials are involved, because it is believed that debate on controversial public issues should not be inhibited by threats of libel actions.

PRIOR RESTRAINT

The basic dimensions of the prior restraint doctrine were established in *Near v. Minnesota* (283 U.S. 697: 1931). Tag Near published a weekly newspaper that contained vicious attacks on public officials in Minneapolis. Near was subsequently enjoined from publication under provisions of a state law that authorized the abatement of any "malicious, scandalous and defamatory newspaper, magazine or periodical" as a "public nuisance." The Court found the law to be unconstitutional in a five to four decision. In this ruling, the Court first determined that the liberty of the press and of speech is within the liberty safeguarded by the Due Process Clause of the Fourteenth Amendment from invasion by state action. In other words, *Near* was the case through which the Supreme Court extended the free press provisions of the First Amendment to the states. As a consequence of that judgment, the Court was able to examine the Minnesota law itself. The Court found the statute defective in that it was "not aimed at the redress of individual or private wrongs." Rather, it was aimed at distribution of material "for the protection of the public welfare." Although prosecution might legitimately be brought against such publications, the state had insufficient interest to warrant a prior restraint.

Chief Justice Hughes, speaking for the majority, argued that the "object of the statute is not punishment, in the ordinary sense, but suppression." The suppression is "accomplished by enjoining publication, and that restraint is the object and effect of the statute." In short, the objectives and the means embodied in the statute were the essence of censorship. The Court also pointed out that the statute too seriously limited what might be said about public officials. References to public corruption and malfeasance or neglect of duty create a public scandal by their very nature. Under the statute, such references were subject to regulation. The Court said that "the recognition of authority to impose previous restraint upon publication in order to protect the community against the circulation of charges of misconduct, and especially of official misconduct, necessarily would carry with it the admission of the authority of the censor against which the constitutional barrier was erected." Disallowing the prior restraint was paramount. Although charges of official misconduct may create highly uncomfortable situations, the theory of the constitutional guarantee is that "even a more serious public evil would be caused by authority to prevent publication."

Near v. Minnesota provided the baseline for consideration of prior restraints. *Near* held that such restraint is heavily suspect but is possibly justifiable in the instance of threats to national security, obscenity, incitements to governmental overthrow or other violence, or interference with private interests as in criminal trials. The prior restraint exceptions set forth in *Near* have remained largely undisturbed. Using the standards from *Near,* the Court struck down a "gag order" intended to safeguard jury selection in a criminal trial in *Nebraska Press Association v. Stuart* (427 U.S. 539: 1976). The Court also freed the publication of the Pentagon Papers in *New York Times v. United States* and *United States v. Washington Post* (403 U.S. 713: 1971).

One of the *Near* exceptions to the prior restraint doctrine involved national security. The *Pentagon Papers Cases* examined the national security exception more closely. The *New York Times* and the *Washington Post* had come into possession of Defense Department documents detailing the history of U.S. involvement in the Vietnam War. After a failure to prevent publication by direct request to the newspapers, injunctions against the two papers were sought by the Nixon administration in federal court to stop publication of the documents on national security grounds. An injunction was obtained from a federal court against the *Times,* but the government failed in another court with its case against the *Post.* On appeal, the Supreme Court determined that injunctive restraint against either paper was unwarranted, in a six to three decision. In a brief *per curiam* opinion, the Court said there was a "heavy presumption" against prior restraint and that the "heavy burden" had not been carried by the government in these cases. Each member of the Court entered an individual opinion.

Justices Black and Douglas both categorically rejected prior restraint. Justice Black said that "every moment's continuance of the injunction against these newspapers amounts to a flagrant, indefensible and continuing violation of the First Amendment." Justice Black emphasized the essential function of a free press. It is to "serve the governed, not the governors." The government's power to censor the press, he continued, "was abolished so that the press would remain forever free to censure the Government." Of all the press functions, paramount is its duty to prevent any part of the government from "deceiving the people and sending them off to distant lands to die of foreign fevers and foreign shot and shell." Justice Brennan allowed that prior restraint might be constitutional in the most extreme circumstance but found no such circumstance present in these cases. The other members of the majority—Justices Stewart, White, and Marshall—focused on the absence of statutory authority for federal courts to issue injunctions such as those sought by the government. Indeed, Congress had directly rejected enacting such an option. Justices White and Stewart, however, did indicate concern that national security had been compromised. They suggested that the criminal process could be utilized against the newspapers instead of seeking to enjoin publication. The Supreme Court's decision in the *Pentagon Papers Cases* had been expected to provide a definitive statement on when prior restraint might constitutionally be imposed, but the decision did not produce such a ruling. Rather, the decision hinged on the fairly narrow issue of whether the government had sufficiently demonstrated that immediate and irreparable harm would result from publication of the documents. Although the *Times* prevailed, the Court's inability to find consensus on a rationale minimized the future importance of this case.

A different kind of prior restraint issue was raised in *Hazelwood School District v. Kuhlmeier* (484 U.S. 260: 1988). In *Hazelwood,* the Court upheld broad authority of school officials to monitor student publications. Indeed, the Court held that this authority goes so far as to allow censorship of content thought to be objectionable by school officials. Former staff members of a high school newspaper brought suit claiming Hazelwood School District violated their First Amendment rights by deleting articles from a particular issue of the newspaper. The articles described student pregnancy experiences and the effect on students of parental divorce. The newspaper was produced by a journalism class as a part of the high school curriculum. The procedure established by the school district was that the principal would review all page proofs prior to publication. In this case, the principal objected to the article on pregnancy as inappropriate for some of the school's younger students. The article on divorce was found objectionable because it actually identified a parent by name and included accusations of abusive conduct. The principal ordered the pages on which the two articles appeared to be withheld from the paper even though these pages contained other, unobjectionable material. In a five to three decision, the Court ruled that there was no First Amendment violation.

Although it acknowledged that students do not " 'shed their constitutional rights to freedom of speech or expression at the schoolhouse gate,' " the Court said the rights of students in public schools are not automatically equivalent to the rights of adults in other settings. Rather, they must be applied in light of the "special characteristics of the school environment." A school "need not tolerate" student speech that is "inconsistent" with its "basic educational mission, even though the government could not censor similar speech outside the school." The Court rejected the assertion that the paper was a forum for public expression. School facilities are public forums only if they are open for "indiscriminate use" by the "general public" or a portion of the general public. On the other hand, if facilities have been "reserved for other intended purposes," no public forum exists and school authorities may impose reasonable restrictions. In this case, the school district merely adhered to its policy that publication of the newspaper was part of the educational process and an activity subject to the control of the school staff. As there was no intent to open the paper to "indiscriminate use" by the student body or even the newspaper's student staff, the Court ruled that the school officials were entitled to reasonably regulate the paper's content. Educators may exercise greater control over certain expression to assure that partici- pants "learn whatever lessons the activity is designed to teach," that readers or listeners are not exposed to material that may be "inappropriate for their level of maturity," and that the positions taken are not "erroneously attributed to the school." Educators, said the Court, do not violate the First Amendment by "exercising editorial control over the style and content of student speech in school-sponsored expressive activities" so long as their actions are "reasonably related to legitimate pedagogical concerns."

Another prior restraint issue was examined in *Florida Star v. B. J. F.* (491 U.S. 524: 1989). Florida law prohibited publication of identifying informa- tion about the victim of a sex crime, and as a result the newspaper had been ordered to pay damages for publishing a victim's name although the name had been lawfully obtained from police records. The information had been included in a police report left in a law enforcement agency press room. Access to the room or documents located there was not restricted. The police report in which B. J. F. was identified had been discovered by a reporter-trainee who copied the entire report. The information was subsequently published in a story appearing in the *Florida Star*. B. J. F. filed and won a suit against the newspaper claiming negligent violation of the statute. The Supreme Court disagreed in a six to three decision. The Court chose not to establish the broad principle that damages for encroachment on privacy rights could never prevail over truthful publication. Instead, the Court resolved the issue on "limited principles" that "sweep no more broadly" than the "appropriate context" of this particular case. The Court drew heavily on *Smith v. Daily Mail Publishing Company* (443 U.S. 97: 1979), which said that if a newspaper "lawfully obtains truthful information" it may not be punished for publication of that information "absent a need to further a state interest of the highest order." In this case, the newspaper had accurately reported information lawfully obtained from a government agency. The Court saw "ample" and "less drastic means" open to the state to safeguard information than limiting publication. Although the Court acknowledged that protecting the privacy of sexual assault victims was "highly significant," the justices believed that imposing liability under these circumstances is "too precipitous a means" of protecting those interests. The Court went on to make two other points with respect to application of the *Daily Mail* principle. First, the press ought not be punished for publishing information that is otherwise publicly available as such punishment is "unlikely to advance" the interest of victim anonymity the state seeks to protect. Second, the Court indicated that punishment of truthful publication in this situation may result in press "timidity and self-censorship."

PRESS PRIVILEGE

A privilege is a benefit possessed by a person or a class that gives advantage. The press has long claimed that the First Amendment confers privilege with respect to several press functions, among them the confidentiality of news sources. The question of source confidentiality was considered in *Branzburg v. Hayes* (408 U.S. 665: 1972). The Court rejected in *Branzburg* the argument that newspersons possess a privileged relationship with their sources. After having published reports about drug use and manufacture, John Hayes was subpoenaed to appear before a state grand jury and identify those persons he had seen using and making illegal narcotics. Hayes refused to testify and was cited for contempt. In a five to four decision, the Court decided that the First Amendment does not "invalidate every incidental burdening of the press that may result from the enforcement of civil or criminal statutes of general applicability." In balancing the interests of protecting the criminal process and the news gathering function of the press, the Court held that the former must prevail. The possible burden on the press was not seen as sufficient to treat newspersons differently from any other citizen subpoenaed to testify in a criminal proceeding. Journalists must respond to relevant questions put to them in the course of a valid grand jury investigation or criminal trial. Though the justices acknowledged some burden on the press in this case, they felt the fact that the burden could not compare to a prior restraint, a tax, a penalty on content, or a compulsion to publish. To the contrary, the Court suggested that any burdensome impact on the press would be limited. "Only where news sources themselves are implicated in crime or possess information relevant to the grand jury's task need they or the reporter be concerned about grand jury subpoenas." Furthermore, the Court argued that abuse or harassment of the press would be subject to judicial scrutiny and possible intervention.

Branzburg v. Hayes said that the privilege of source confidentiality was not required by the First Amendment. A number of states disagreed and have enacted shield laws designed to protect the confidentiality of sources. No such legislation exists at the federal level, although the *Branzburg* decision did prompt introduction of such proposals. The Burger Court also rejected other claims of press privilege regarding the gathering of information. In *Saxbe v. Washington Post Company* (417 U.S. 843: 1974), the Court upheld federal prison regulations that prohibited press interviews with individual inmates. The Court said the Constitution does not impose upon the government the "affirmative duty to make available to journalists sources of information not available to members of the public generally." Four years later, in *Houchins v. KQED* (438 U.S. 1: 1978), the Court upheld a refusal to allow media access to a county jail that had been the site of a prisoner's suicide and other alleged violent incidents, as well as having been charged with inhumane conditions. The majority felt the case involved a "special privilege of access" such as that denied in *Saxbe*. This is a "right which is not essential to guarantee the freedom to communicate or publish."

THE PRESS AND CRIMINAL PROCEEDINGS

Constitutional protections may sometimes collide with each other. Consider the First Amendment press protection on the one hand and the criminal defendant's right to a fair trial on the other. The collision of these two protections was clearly evident in the case of *Sheppard v. Maxwell* (384 U.S. 333: 1966). *Sheppard* considered whether pervasive pre-trial publicity, most of which was highly adverse to the defendant, deprived him of the fair trial guaranteed him under the Sixth Amendment. The media was not restrained in any way in this case and every stage of *Sheppard* was subjected to intensive coverage—from inquest through indictment to the trial itself. The coverage given Sam Sheppard was generally hostile. Among other things, jurors were subjected to continuous publicity about principals in the case. Sheppard was eventually convicted of the murder of his wife, but the Supreme Court reversed the conviction. The Court focused its discussion on the failures of the trial judge to provide Sheppard with the "judicial serenity and calm to which he was entitled." Specifically, the trial judge should have used stricter rules governing media use of the courtroom, better insulated the jury and witnesses from the media, limited the flow of information to the media from key people in the case, and admonished the media to monitor the accuracy of their reports. The Court found the failure to properly insulate the jury the most glaring error. Several jurors admitted hearing media broadcasts about the case after their selection as jurors. The Court said Sheppard's trial turned into an avoidable "carnival" and deprived Sheppard of a fair trial.

The press has always been able to affect the impartiality of a criminal trial, but technical developments in the broadcast media have increased that capacity dramatically. Virtually an entire community can be reached with information that may have a prejudicial effect on a particular case. The *Sheppard* case represents such prejudicial effects at their extreme, and the result was that the Court did not require Sheppard to identify any actual prejudice to him. The totality of circumstances raised the possibility of prejudice, which was sufficient to grant Sheppard a retrial. Even with the excesses that occurred in *Sheppard,* the Supreme Court resisted imposing restrictions on the press for First Amendment reasons. Instead the Court focused on the trial judge as the key figure in ensuring a fair trial. It talked about the option of delaying a trial until adverse publicity had subsided or of changing the venue (location) of a case. The Court emphasized how the voir dire examination could have been used to determine whether prejudicial publicity existed. It suggested sequestering or isolating juries in particularly visible cases. The Court's caution in addressing press behavior prompted initiatives elsewhere. The industry itself, through meetings with representatives of trial courts, has fashioned principles for media coverage of criminal cases.

A follow-up decision to *Sheppard, Murphy v. Florida* (421 U.S. 589: 1975), provided more clarity on the question of when information reported by the media becomes prejudicial. The Court said prospective jurors need not be "totally ignorant" of a case. Rather, they need only be able to "reach a verdict based on the evidence presented in the court." The thrust of *Murphy* was reiterated in *Patton v. Yount* (467 U.S. 1025: 1984), in which the defendant challenged the jury selection process for a retrial following his successful appeal. Though extensive publicity had attended the first trial, the

Court felt that the four-year period between trials had greatly reduced "any presumption of prejudice" that existed at the time of the initial trial. The Court said that when the matter of prejudice was examined, the relevant question was not whether the community remembered the case, but whether the jurors had such fixed opinions that they could not judge impartially. Press treatment of a case, especially if the media restrain themselves, does not necessarily mean that publicity will be prejudicial. The *Sheppard* case, however, clearly demonstrated the need for safeguards to ensure a fair trial for criminal defendants.

Sheppard placed the responsibility for maintaining a fair trial environment with the trial judge. In the case of *Nebraska Press Association v. Stuart* (427 U.S. 539: 1976), the trial judge restrained the media from publishing or broadcasting accounts of any "implicative" information until after the jury was empaneled. In other words, the judge "gagged" the media. Though the Court noted that the judge had acted out of a legitimate concern for the defendant's fair trial, it unanimously ruled that the gag order was excessive in this case. The Court suggested that truly extraordinary pre-trial publicity must be present to consider an action as severe as prior restraint. Given that a gag order is a prior restraint, the Court said it must carefully review whether the record justified such an extraordinary remedy. Included in such examination are certain factors: the "nature and extent" of the media coverage, alternate measures and their likely impact on mitigating publicity, and the effectiveness of the gag order in preventing damaging and prejudicial publicity. The Court concluded that the record in this instance was not sufficient on the last two factors. Although the Court did not rule out the possibility that a restraining order might be sustained under certain circumstances, the trial judge's gag order was found to be an excessive restriction on the press in this case.

The *Stuart* case dealt with whether the press should be precluded from publishing information it already possesses. This problem is different from that in *Sheppard,* which focused on remedies after prejudicial publicity had been published. *Stuart* looked at the gag order as a means of stemming pre-trial publicity before the fact. Though the *Stuart* ruling stopped short of invalidating the gag rule altogether, the clear thrust was to impose conditions that are virtually impossible to satisfy. It is apparent from *Stuart* that prohibiting the press from reporting what they observe directly in open court is the least favored approach.

Gannett Company v. DePasquale (443 U.S. 368: 1979) posed the question of whether the media could be denied access to a pre-trial suppression hearing. If the press is allowed to observe a judicial proceeding, it will generally be allowed to report what it observed. Because both the defense and prosecution agreed to close the proceeding at issue in *Gannett*, the case really asked whether the public has an independent right to an open pre-trial hearing. In a five to four decision, the Court upheld the closed hearing. The majority reasoned that pre-trial suppression hearings, as distinct from trials, pose "special risks of unfairness." The objective of such hearings is to screen out unreliable or illegally obtained evidence. Pre-trial publicity about such evidence could "influence public opinion" and "inform potential jurors of inculpatory information wholly inadmissible at the actual trial." As for the public's independent right to access, the Court stressed two points. First, public interest in the application of the Sixth Amendment does not create a "constitutional right on the part of the public." The public interest is protected by the participants in the adversary process. Thus, the public has no claim that could displace the defendant's desire to close the proceeding. Second, the common law tradition recognizes the difference between a pre-trial proceeding and the trial itself. "Pretrial proceedings, precisely because of concern for a fair trial, were never characterized by the degree of openness as were actual trials."

The censorship question raised in *Stuart* was not present in *Gannett*, because the media were not prohibited from publishing information they already possessed. Rather than consider infringement of the First Amendment press protection, *Gannett* focused on whether a defendant's interest in closing a pre-trial hearing supersedes the public's interest in an open proceeding. The decision in *Gannett* raised the prospect of all judicial proceedings, even trials, being closed at the initiative of the defense. But the Court subsequently refused to take that step in *Richmond Newspapers, Inc. v. Virginia* (448 U.S. 555: 1980). In the *Richmond Newspapers* case, the defendant's counsel requested that a murder trial be closed to the public. The prosecutor expressed no objection, and the trial judge ordered the courtroom closed. Under Virginia law, the judge had the authority to exclude from a trial anyone whose "presence would impair the conduct of a fair trial." The Supreme Court, however, ruled that the closure order was a violation of the right of access. Chief Justice Burger spoke for the Court and began with a lengthy discussion of the history of open trials. This "unbroken, uncontradicted history, supported by reasons as valid today as in centuries past," forced the Court to conclude that a "presumption of openness inheres in the very nature of a criminal trial under our system of justice." The Court said the open trial serves a therapeutic purpose for the community, especially in the instance of shocking crimes. Open trials offer protection against abusive or arbitrary behavior. They allow criminal processes to "satisfy the appearance of justice." Though access to trials is not specifically provided in the First Amendment, it is implicit in the amendment's guarantees. Without the freedom to attend trials, important aspects of free speech and a free press could be "eviscerated."

The closure order was defective in this case because the trial judge made no specific finding to support such an order. Alternatives to closure were not considered, there was no recognition of any right of the public or the press to attend the trial, and there was no indication that problems with witnesses could not have been handled otherwise. In a concurring opinion, Justice Brennan wrote that "open trials play a fundamental role in furthering the efforts of any judicial system to assure the criminal defendant a fair and accurate adjudication of guilt or innocence." The open trial is also a means by which a society becomes aware that it is governed equitably.

Beyond the issue of access is the question of how extensively the media may cover a criminal trial. The most instructive case on this issue is *Chandler v. Florida* (449 U.S. 560: 1981). The Florida Supreme Court, as part of the Florida Code of Judicial Conduct, fashioned a policy that permitted electronic media and still photographic coverage of trial and appellate proceedings. The policy conveyed authority over all media coverage to the presiding judge. On review, the Supreme Court decided in *Chandler* that, absent a specific showing of prejudice, the Florida policy was constitutional. Chief Justice Burger wrote for a unanimous Court that the level of risk to trials did not justify a categorical ban on coverage. The "mere presence" of the broadcast media does not "inherently" adversely affect the process. The Florida policy permitted trial judges to carefully monitor individual cases and take action necessary to protect the integrity of each. On appeal, the burden was on the defendant to show that his or her case was influenced by the coverage. Because Noel Chandler could demonstrate no specific adverse impacts stemming from the media coverage of his trial, the Court upheld his conviction.

Chandler reflects the Court's deference to the discretion of trial judges in managing problems related to media coverage of criminal trials. As in earlier press cases, the Court left critical assessments of adverse effects of coverage to the presiding judge. *Chandler* also reinforced the swing away from *Gannett* begun in *Richmond Newspapers*. Courtroom coverage by electronic media has the potential to be most problematic in terms of the fair trial standards. Yet in *Chandler* the Court refused to find such coverage inherently violative of due process. *Chandler* also placed the burden of proving prejudice with the defendant. *Gannett* had allowed an accused to simply request closure. Due to the *Chandler* ruling, absent a demonstration of adverse effect, a defendant cannot simply terminate coverage or achieve closure by request alone. *Chandler* clearly invited greater media coverage of criminal cases, and most states have adjusted their policies to enable that to happen.

COMMERCIAL PRESS

Commercial press is expression primarily designed to advertise a product or a service. The commercial press doctrine had its origin in *Valentine v. Chrestensen* (316 U.S. 52: 1942). This ruling essentially placed commercial expression outside the protection of the First Amendment, though more recent decisions have altered this policy. A case that retained the original view, at least in part, is *Pittsburgh Press Company v. Human Relations Commission* (413 U.S. 376: 1973). The Pittsburgh Press Company was found to be in violation of a Human Relations Commission ordinance because it placed help-wanted advertisements in sex-designated columns. The commission ordered the newspaper to end the gender-referenced layout of the advertisements, and the Supreme Court upheld the order.

The Court first determined that the advertisements were commercial speech, not merely because they were advertisements but also because of their commercial content. They were, in fact, "classic examples of commercial speech" because of the proposal of possible employment. They were therefore unlike political advertisements. The Pittsburgh Press Company argued that editorial judgment about where to place an advertisement should be the controlling issue, rather than the advertisement's commercial content. The Court majority answered that a "newspaper's editorial judgments in connection with an advertisement take on the character of the advertisement and, in those cases, the scope of the newspaper's First Amendment protection may be affected by the content of the advertisement." The kind of editorial judgment involved in this case did not strip commercial advertising of its commercial character. Even more crucial was the fact that the commercial activity involved was illegal employment discrimination. In the Court's view advertisements could be forbidden in this instance just as advertisements "proposing the sale of narcotics or soliciting prostitution" could be forbidden. The justices concluded their opinion by ruling that any First Amendment interest that applies to an ordinary commercial proposal is "altogether absent when the commercial activity itself is illegal and the restriction on advertising is incidental to a valid limitation on economic activity."

The commercial speech holding in *Pittsburgh Press Company v. Human Relations Commission* substantially narrowed the *Chrestensen* concept of commercial speech. Following *Pittsburgh Press Company*, the Burger Court narrowed the definition even further. In *Bigelow v. Virginia* (421 U.S. 809: 1975), the Court protected the publication of an advertisement by an organization offering services related to legal abortions in another state. The Court held that the advertisement "conveyed information of potential interest and value to a diverse audience" and was not merely a commercial promotion of services. The next year, in *Virginia State Board of Pharmacy v. Virginia Citizens Consumers Council, Inc.* (425 U.S. 748: 1976), the Court struck down a statute that made advertising of prescription drugs a form of conduct that could lead to a suspension of license. The Court argued that even if the advertiser's interest is purely economic, such speech is not necessarily disqualified from protection. The consumer and society in general have a "strong interest in the free flow of commercial information." Such a free flow is indispensable in a predominantly free enterprise economy that requires many private economic decisions.

BROADCAST REGULATION

The free press protection afforded by the First Amendment clearly covers the medium of print. It also reaches broadcast. The protections do not identically apply, however. Instead, broadcast media are subject to greater regulation than print. The reasons for this were discussed in *Red Lion Broadcasting Company v. Federal Communications Commission* (395 U.S. 367: 1969). This ruling upheld the Federal Communications Commission (FCC) regulation known as the fairness doctrine. Red Lion broadcast a particular program during which the honesty and character of a third party were impugned. The third party demanded free air time for a response, but was refused. The FCC held that Red Lion had failed to satisfy a requirement of equal access, and the Supreme Court unanimously upheld the FCC's position. The Court acknowledged that broadcasting is a medium affected by First Amendment interests, but it emphasized some critical differences from print media. Among these are the limited number of channels available and the incomparably greater reach of the radio signal. Scarcity of access means Congress "unquestionably has the power to grant and deny licenses," a power vested by Congress in the FCC. The license permits broadcasting, but the licensee "has no constitutional right to be the one who holds the license or to monopolize a radio frequency to the exclusion of his fellow citizens." The Court said the First Amendment does not prevent the government from requiring a licensee to share a frequency with others and to "conduct himself [or herself] as a proxy or fiduciary," with obligations to present views that are representative of his or her community and that would otherwise be barred from the airwaves. Government has an obligation to preserve access for divergent views because of the unique character of the broadcast medium. The Court said the people retain their interest in free speech by radio and have a collective right to the medium functioning consistently with the ends and purposes of the First Amendment. It is the "right of the viewers and listeners, not the right of broadcasters, which is paramount." Without regulation through the FCC in the form of such rules as the fairness doctrine, station owners and a few networks would have "unfettered power to make time available only to the highest bidders, to communicate only their own views on public issues, people and candidates, and to permit on the air only those with whom they agreed."

The position of the Court in *Red Lion* was that a balance must be struck between the First Amendment interests of the broadcast medium and the need to regulate governmentally granted channel monopolies. The fairness doctrine at issue in *Red Lion* had not kept the station from expressing its own views. It had only required that reply time be provided when a station carries a broadcast that personally attacks an individual. Print media may not be required to do the same thing, however. In *Miami Herald Publishing Company v. Tornillo* (418 U.S. 241: 1974), the Court overturned a Florida right-to-reply statute that required reply space in a newspaper for any political candidate who was attacked. Such required space was found to be as offensive to the First Amendment as prior restraint. Indeed, it was in effect an affirmative prior restraint in that the newspaper would be compelled to print content it would not have printed otherwise. This kind of law, said the Court, authorizes governmental "intrusion into the function of editors in choosing what material goes into a newspaper."

Similarly, the Court has also held that the airwaves need not become a common carrier with access to any private citizen or group. *Columbia Broadcasting System, Inc. v. Democratic National Committee* (412 U.S. 94: 1973) determined that a broadcaster policy of refusing to sell editorial advertisements was an acceptable practice and not incompatible with the fairness doctrine. The power of Congress to prohibit editorials on stations receiving funds from the Corporation for Public Broadcasting was explored in *FCC v. League of Women Voters* (468 U.S. 364: 1984). While broadcast media may be subject to more regulation than print media, Congress cannot restrict broadcast editorials. Such regulation affects "precisely that form of speech the framers were most anxious to protect." Content-defined discussion of public issues is the purest example of discourse that must be allowed to proceed without regulation. Although the FCC has recently abandoned the fairness doctrine as part if its movement toward deregulation of the broadcast industry, that industry remains subject to greater regulation than print.

OBSCENITY

Obscenity is content that offends accepted standards of decency. Obscenity is not protected expression under the First Amendment because it is "utterly without redeeming social importance or value." Because obscenity falls outside the scope of the First Amendment, a carefully constructed definition is essential to distinguish between protected expression and unprotected obscenity. Central to the identification of obscenity is its appeal to what the Supreme Court has described as "prurient interest." It is material that prompts "lustful thoughts." The Court made its first serious attempt to define obscenity in *Roth v. United States* (354 U.S. 476: 1957).

Samuel Roth had been convicted of violating the federal obscenity statute by using the mail to distribute "obscene, lewd, lascivious, filthy, or indecent" material. The Supreme Court upheld his conviction, and began its ruling by saying that the First Amendment did not protect every utterance. As in the case of libel, the Court said strong historical evidence existed that obscenity also fell outside the scope of protected expression. Obscenity is not protected because it is "utterly without redeeming social importance," a judgment reflected in many obscenity statutes in various states and throughout the world. Because obscenity does not warrant protection, the Court set about fashioning a modern definition. Key to identification of obscenity is its appeal to prurient interests. Treatment of sex per se is "not in itself sufficient reason to deny material the constitutional protection of speech and press."

The Court sought to establish a standard sufficiently proscribed as not to encroach on material legitimately treating sex. The standard chosen was "whether to the average person, applying contemporary community standards, the dominant theme of the material taken as a whole appeals to prurient interest." Using this standard, the Court concluded that the federal statute under consideration in *Roth* did not offend the First Amendment. Justices Black and Douglas dissented, saying "any test which turns on what is offensive to the community's standards is too loose, too capricious, too destructive of freedom of expression to be squared with the First Amendment."

Roth clearly established that obscenity is not protected speech. The more troublesome issue was differentiating protected speech from unprotected obscenity. The leading definition prior to *Roth* had come from an English case, *Queen v. Hicklin* (3 Queen's Bench 360: 1868). Like *Roth,* the *Hicklin* test focused on material that prompted lustful thoughts but allowed material to be judged "merely by the effect of an isolated excerpt upon particularly susceptible persons." Though *Roth* was less restrictive than *Hicklin,* many questions remained. As the Court struggled with these questions, the definition of obscenity became less restrictive but also less clear. The Court finally lost all consensus on standards. In *A Book Named "John Cleland's Memoirs of a Woman of Pleasure" v. Attorney General of Massachusetts* (383 U.S. 413: 1966), the Court described obscenity in terms of "patent offensiveness" and elevated the role of the social value component. Obscenity was still seen as being "utterly without redeeming social value," but the Court placed a severe burden on prosecutors by requiring proof of the utter absence of social value. Furthermore, the Court said that all the elements of the obscenity definition were to be applied independently. The effect of these combined changes was to put all but hardcore pornography outside the reach of regulation because prosecutors could virtually never prove the complete absence of social value, and failure to make such proof could not be cancelled out by presence, even in the extreme, of all the remaining factors.

The only Warren Court case upholding a conviction during this period came in *Ginzburg v. United States* (383 U.S. 463: 1966). Ralph Ginzburg's conviction was affirmed because he commercially exploited the sexual content of the materials he offered for sale. He engaged in pandering. Ginzburg's materials were viewed "against a background of commercial exploitation of erotica solely for the sake of their prurient appeal." In situations in which the "purveyor's sole emphasis is on the sexually provocative aspects of his publications, that fact may be decisive in the determination of obscenity." *Ginzburg* modified *Roth* in that materials may pass the original *Roth* test and yet be found obscene because of improper promotional conduct by the seller. Though the materials themselves may not be obscene in isolation, they can become illicit merchandise through the "sordid business of pandering."

The definition of obscenity remained unclear until 1973, when the Burger Court delivered its ruling in *Miller v. California* (413 U.S. 15: 1973). Marvin Miller had been convicted of distributing obscene material because he had conducted an aggressive book sales campaign by sending unsolicited brochures through the mail. A five-justice majority upheld Miller's conviction and offered a redefinition of the test from *Roth v. United States.* The Court found no fault with *Roth* but said that subsequent decisions had "veered sharply away from the *Roth* concept." Thus, the need existed to restore its original intent. Though many cases had brought about such a need, the major offender in Chief Justice Burger's view was *Memoirs v. Massachusetts,* in which a plurality of the Court produced a "drastically altered test" that required the prosecution to prove a negative. The prosecution had to prove that material was "utterly without redeeming social value—a burden virtually impossible to discharge." In establishing the revised standard, the Burger Court drew heavily from *Roth,* saying that an obscenity statute must be limited to works that, taken as a whole, appeal to the prurient interest in sex or portray sexual conduct in a patently offensive way. The material when taken as a whole must lack serious literary, artistic, political, or scientific value.

The Burger Court specifically handled the social value aspect differently from the manner in which the Warren Court had dealt with it in *Memoirs.* It also proposed some flexibility in applying the social value guidelines to specific cases. The nation is "simply too big and too diverse" for a uniform standard of prurient interest or patently offensive sexual conduct. The Court viewed it as unrealistic to base proceedings around an abstract formulation. To require a state to try a case around evidence of a national community standard would be an exercise in futility. The Court asserted that people in different states vary in their tastes and attitudes, and "this diversity is not to be strangled by the absolutism of imposed uniformity." State obscenity trials can therefore base evaluation of materials on the contemporary community standards of the particular state.

Miller v. California (413 U.S. 15: 1973) represented the first consensus statement on obscenity standards since *Roth* in 1957. *Miller* is significant primarily because the Court's rejection of a national standard prompted diverse approaches to the regulation of obscenity. The Court cautioned that local juries and their application of community standards are still subject to First Amendment boundaries. *Miller* did prompt greater regulation, however, and these regulatory activities have generally been supported by the Court. In *New York v. Ferber* (458 U.S. 747: 1982), for example, the Court unanimously upheld a statute prohibiting "persons from knowingly promoting a sexual performance by a child under the age of 16." The Court said the states are "entitled to greater leeway in the regulation of pornographic depictions of children." Because state-defined morality "bears so heavily and pervasively" on the welfare of children, the balance of compelling interests is clearly struck, and it is permissible to consider these materials as without First Amendment protection.

A 1988 amendment to the Federal Communications Act made it a crime to use a telephone to send an "indecent" as well as an "obscene" message for commercial purposes. Whereas the objective of earlier regulations had been to protect minors from such communications, the 1988 amendment banned "obscene and indecent" communications to any recipient. A challenge to the amendment was considered by the Court in *Sable Communications of California, Inc. v. Federal Communications Commission* (106 L. Ed. 2d 93: 1989). The Supreme Court ruled for Sable Communications with respect to the regulation of "indecent" messages, but upheld the authority of Congress to impose a total ban on "obscene" messages. Obscenity, said the Court, is not protected expression under the First Amendment, and a prohibition on the interstate transmission of obscene commercial messages is permissible. The Court unanimously struck down the regulation of "indecent" content as an overly broad restriction. The amendment was designed to protect minors from the messages, an interest the Court acknowledged to be compelling. The ban, however, denied adult access to messages that are "indecent but not obscene," a policy that "far exceeds that which is necessary to limit the access of minors to such messages." The Court distinguished regulation of "indecent" radio broadcasts from the "dial-it medium" because the latter requires the listener to take "affirmative steps to receive the communications." The government's contention that only a total ban could protect against access by minors was, accordingly, seen as "unpersuasive" by the Court.

As we have seen, government can regulate obscenity by bringing criminal charges against those who produce and distribute such material. But what of basic censorship—preventing allegedly obscene material from reaching the public? *Kingsley Books, Inc. v. Brown* (354 U.S. 436: 1957) considers this question. A section of the New York State Code of Criminal Procedure authorized enforcement officials to invoke injunctive remedies against the sale and distribution of written and printed matter found to be obscene in a judicial proceeding. The law also allowed authorities to obtain an order for the seizure of "condemned publications" if they were not voluntarily surrendered. The law entitled the enjoined persons to have a trial within one day following the issuance of an injunction. Certain items found in Kingsley Books were judged to be obscene, and consequently their further distribution was enjoined and their destruction ordered. Kingsley Books did not challenge the state's authority to prohibit distribution of obscenity. Instead, the appeal focused on the means of regulation including the power to enjoin distribution during the course of litigation. Kingsley Books asserted that such use of the injunctive remedy amounted to an unconstitutional prior restraint. The Supreme Court disagreed in a five to four decision.

In approving the approach, the Court compared it to imposing criminal sanctions on booksellers. Rather than requiring the seller to "dread that the offer for sale of a book may without prior warning subject him to criminal prosecution with the hazard of imprisonment," the section of the code "assures him that such consequences cannot follow unless he ignores a court order specifically directed to him for a prompt and carefully circumscribed determination of the issue of obscenity." The Court concluded that the code "moves after publication" by enjoining from display or sale "particular booklets theretofore published and adjudged to be obscene." When compared with criminal penalties, the "restraint upon [the booksellers] as merchants in obscenity was narrower." The Court saw the restriction imposed here as altogether different from the injunctive restraint found in *Near v. Minnesota*. Unlike those in *Near,* the code provisions in this instance are "concerned solely with obscenity," and they "studiously withhold restraint upon matters not already published and not yet found to be offensive."

In *Freedman v. Maryland* (380 U.S. 51: 1965), the Court upheld film licensure requirements so long as they contained the same procedural safeguards described in *Kingsley Books*. Ronald Freedman violated a Maryland statute requiring a license to exhibit any motion picture when he refused to submit a film to the State Board of Censors prior to showing it. Maryland stipulated that the film would have been licensed had it been submitted. Freedman sought, however, to have movie censorship declared unconstitutional per se. The Court did not do so, but it did unanimously reverse his conviction. The Court said a prior restraint mechanism bears a "heavy presumption against its constitutional validity." Specifically, the "administration of a censorship proceeding puts the initial burden on the exhibitor or distributor." The justices went on to outline procedural safeguards "designed to obviate the dangers of the censorship system" that looked almost exactly like the procedural requirements of *Kingsley Books*. Though *Freedman* did not prohibit the practice of censorship as such, it did establish important process prerequisites. Arbitrary interference with exhibitors was clearly not permissible.

A number of localities have attempted to regulate obscenity through their power of zoning. This approach was upheld in *Young v. American Mini Theatres, Inc.* (427 U.S. 50: 1976). The *Young* ruling approved amendments to Detroit zoning ordinances providing that "adult" theaters be licensed. Even though the First Amendment does not allow total suppression, the Court held that a state may legitimately use the content of mini-theater materials as the basis for placing them in a classification different from other motion pictures. The Court upheld the regulated use classification on the basis of the city's interest in preserving the character of its neighborhoods and the quality of urban life. This interest "must be accorded high respect," and the city must be allowed "a reasonable opportunity to experiment with solutions to an admittedly serious problem." Justices Brennan, Stewart, Marshall, and Blackmun dissented, basing their opinion on the vagueness and content orientation of the ordinance.

Young v. American Mini Theatres, Inc. represented a different approach to the local regulation of "adult" entertainment. The Court has generally supported local regulation provided expression is not completely prohibited and a compelling interest can be demonstrated. Meeting these conditions is not always easy, however. In *Erznoznick v. Jacksonville* (422 U.S. 205: 1975), the Court struck down an ordinance that prohibited the exhibition of films containing nudity if the screen could be seen from a public street. The Court cited the limited privacy interest of persons on the streets, but it also stressed the overly broad sweep of the ordinance. Ten years after *Young*, the Court once again reviewed a local attempt to regulate the location of adult theaters in *City of Renton v. Playtime Theatres, Inc.* (475 U.S. 41: 1986).

Using the same rationale stated in *Young,* the Court upheld a municipality's authority to require dispersal of such establishments. Because the municipal ordinance did not bar adult theaters entirely, it was reviewed as a time, place, and manner regulation. Such regulations are acceptable so long as they serve a substantial interest and do not unreasonably limit avenues of communication. Justice Rehnquist said for the Court that the First Amendment requires only that a local unit refrain from denying individuals a "reasonable opportunity to open and operate an adult theater within the city." He said the city of Renton easily met that requirement in the ordinance under review.

PRIVATE POSSESSION OF OBSCENITY

Regulation of commercial establishments that distribute allegedly obscene materials is one thing. Regulation of privately possessed obscenity is much more troublesome. Two cases focus on this issue. In *Stanley v. Georgia* (394 U.S. 557: 1969), the Court held that a state could not prohibit private possession of obscene materials. Robert Stanley was convicted of possessing obscene films. The films were discovered while federal and state agents searched Stanley's home under authority of a warrant issued in connection with an investigation of Stanley's alleged involvement in bookmaking. The Supreme Court unanimously reversed Stanley's conviction. Stanley's First Amendment claim was based on his "right to read or observe what he pleases—the right to satisfy his intellectual and emotional needs in the privacy of his own home, and the right to be free from state inquiry into the contents of his library."

Although privacy was a key consideration, the Court stressed the First Amendment aspects of *Stanley.* Justifications for regulation of obscenity "do not reach into the privacy of one's own home. If the First Amendment means anything, it means that a State has no business telling a man, sitting alone in his house, what books he may read or what films he may watch. Our whole constitutional heritage rebels at the thought of giving government the power to control men's minds." The interests of the state are insufficient to protect individuals from obscenity in this fashion. "Whatever the power of the State to control public dissemination of ideas inimical to the public morality, it cannot constitutionally premise legislation on the desirability of controlling a person's private thoughts." Neither may the state justify the prohibition of privately held obscene materials as a means of forestalling antisocial conduct. The state "may no more prohibit mere possession of obscenity on the ground that it may lead to anti-social conduct than it may prohibit possession of chemistry books on the ground they may lead to the manufacture of homemade spirits." The Court also rejected the argument that outlawing possession of obscenity is required to allow enforcement of prohibitions against its distribution. The right to read or observe is dominant, and "its restriction may not be justified by the need to ease the administration of otherwise valid criminal laws."

The Burger Court followed *Stanley,* however, by closing off the means of delivering obscene material. *United States v. Reidel* (402 U.S. 351: 1971) held that obscene material was unprotected expression and constitutionally could be excluded from the mail. On the same day, in *United States v. Thirty-Seven Photographs* (402 U.S. 363: 1971), the Court allowed a prohibition on the importation of obscenity from abroad even if it was intended for private use. The following year, in *United States v. 12 200-ft. Reels of Super 8mm. Film* (413 U.S. 123: 1972), the Court allowed seizure of materials coming into the country from Mexico. The justices declared that the right to privately possess obscene materials did not afford a "correlative right to acquire, sell, or import such material even for private use only." The most note-worthy modification of *Stanley* came in *Paris Adult Theatre I v. Staton* (413 U.S. 49: 1973), a companion to *Miller v. California* (413 U.S. 15: 1973). *Paris Adult Theatre I* held that obscene films do not "acquire constitutional immunity from state regulation simply because they are exhibited for consenting adults only." The Court recognized the "legitimate state interests at stake in stemming the tide of commercialized obscenity." It is an interest that includes protecting the "quality of life and the total community environment."

Finally, the Court ruled in *Osborne v. Ohio* (109 L. Ed. 2d 98: 1990) that states can outlaw the private possession of pornographic materials featuring minors. Crucial to the decision was the choice of *New York v. Ferber* (458 U.S. 747: 1982) rather than *Stanley* as the controlling precedent. The law struck down in *Stanley,* however, was intended to prevent "poison[ing] the minds" of those who observed such material. In this case, the state did not "rely on a paternalistic interest in [Clyde] Osborne's mind." Rather, Ohio enacted the law in an attempt to "protect the victims of child pornography; it hopes to destroy a market for the exploitive use of children." The Ohio legislature made the judgment that using children as subjects in pornographic materials is "harmful to the physiological, emotional, and mental health of the child." That judgment, said the Court, "easily passes muster" under the First Amendment. Furthermore, it is "surely reasonable" for Ohio to con-clude that it will "decrease the production of child pornography if it penalizes those who possess and view the product, thereby decreasing demand." Given the importance of Ohio's interest in protecting child victims, "we cannot fault Ohio for attempting to stamp out this vice at all levels in the distribution chain."

LIBEL

Libel is the use of false and malicious material that injures a person's standing or reputation. Libel has consistently been seen as a category of unprotected speech, and relief from libel may be pursued through civil or criminal proceedings. Libel laws may not inhibit debate on public issues, however, even if the debate includes vigorous and unpleasant attacks on the government and/or public officials. Statements must be made in print with reckless disregard of their falsehood and with actual malice before libel occurs. The critical ruling on libel is *New York Times v. Sullivan* (376 U.S. 254: 1964). *Sullivan* held that publications may not be subjected to libel damages for criticism of public officials and their official conduct unless deliberate malice can be shown. *Sullivan* attached stringent conditions to certain kinds of libel actions involving speech attacking public officials.

A state libel action was brought by a police commissioner in an Alabama court against the *New York Times* for its publication of a paid advertisement that charged police mistreatment of black students protesting racial segregation. It was stipulated that the advertisement contained errors of fact. The trial judge found the statements in the advertisement to be libelous and instructed the jury that injury occurred through publication and that damages could be presumed. Substantial damages were awarded by the jury, which found malice on the part of the *Times*. The Supreme Court reversed the judgments in a unanimous decision, holding that libel law must provide free speech safeguards. To allow unrestricted libel actions "would discourage newspapers from carrying 'editorial advertisements' of this type, and so might shut off an important outlet for the promulgation of information and ideas." Such laws would shackle the First Amendment in its attempt to secure the widest possible dissemination of information from diverse and antagonistic sources. Even the factual errors did not jeopardize the advertisement's protected status. The protection of the advertisement, clearly an "expression of grievance and protest on one of the major public issues of our time," is not contingent on the "truth, popularity, or social utility of the ideas and beliefs which are offered." Mistakes or errors of fact are inevitable in free debate and must be protected if freedom of expression is to have the "breathing space" it needs. Neither does injury to the reputation of a public official justify limiting expression. "Criticism of their official conduct does not lose its constitutional protection merely because it is effective criticism and hence diminishes their official reputations." Any rule "compelling the critic of official conduct to guarantee the truth of all his factual assertions—and to do so on pain of libel judgments virtually unlimited in amount—leads to a comparable self-censorship." Such a rule severely dampens the vigor and limits the variety of public debate. The Court did allow for recovery of damages where it can be proved that statements were made with actual malice, which means they were made with knowledge that they were false or with reckless disregard of whether they were false or not.

The Court has historically included libel in the category of unprotected speech. *Sullivan* provided the Court with an opportunity to refine that classification. Libel laws cannot inhibit debate on public issues even if such debate includes strong and unpleasant attacks on the government and its officials. *Sullivan* did hold that public officials could protect themselves through libel actions in situations in which false statements were made with reckless disregard of their untruthfulness. But the *Sullivan* decision approaches an almost unconditional free press position relative to public officials. The Court soon extended *Sullivan* to criminal libel prosecutions in *Garrison v. Louisiana* (369 U.S. 64: 1964).

Sullivan protected publications from libel suits where critical comment had been made about government officials. Soon thereafter the category of the government official was enlarged to include "public figures," which includes private citizens who are in the midst of public events or persons who attract wide public attention. In *Rosenbloom v. Metromedia, Inc.* (403 U.S. 29: 1971), the Court went so far as to require reckless falsity in all actions, whether the plaintiff was a public official, a public figure, or a private individual. *Gertz v. Robert Welch, Inc.* (418 U.S. 323: 1974) held that an individual did not become a public figure simply because the public was interested in a particular event with which he or she was associated. Similarly, the Court ruled in *Hutchinson v. Proxmire* (443 U.S. 111: 1979) that a federally funded researcher's receipt of a U.S. senator's award for wasting public funds did not establish him as a public figure simply because he responded to the award in the media.

Sullivan established the requirement that actual malice be demonstrated in libel actions brought by public officials. The Court ruled in *Herbert v. Lando* (441 U.S. 153: 1979) that a plaintiff in a libel action is entitled to inquire into the editorial processes of the defendant. Anthony Herbert was a retired army officer who had served extended tours in Vietnam. He received widespread media attention when he accused his superior officers of covering up reports of atrocities and other war crimes. Some three years after Herbert's disclosures, Herbert and his charges were discussed on the CBS program *60 Minutes*. Barry Lando produced and edited the program and also published an article on Herbert in the *Atlantic Monthly*. Herbert's suit alleged that the television program and the article "falsely and maliciously portrayed him as a liar and a person who made war crimes charges to explain his relief from command." Herbert conceded that he was a "public figure" and that he had to carry the burden of proof required under *Sullivan* for someone of that status.

Herbert tried to meet this burden of proof by attempting to obtain testimony from the defendant, Lando. Lando refused, claiming that the First Amendment protected against "inquiry into the state of mind of those who edit, produce, or publish, and into the editorial process." The Court disagreed and held that the First Amendment does not restrict the sources from which a plaintiff can obtain evidence. Indeed, it is "essential to proving liability that plaintiffs focus on the conduct and state of mind of the defendants." If demonstration of liability is potentially possible, the "thoughts and editorial processes of the alleged defamer would be open to examination." Such examination includes being able to inquire directly from the defendants whether they knew or had reason to suspect that their damaging publication was in error. The editorial privilege sought by Lando, the Court ruled, would constitute a substantial interference with the ability of a defamation plaintiff to establish the ingredients of malice.

Finally, the Court held in *Hustler Magazine v. Falwell* (485 U.S. 46: 1988) that a public figure cannot be awarded damages for the "intentional infliction of emotional distress" caused by the publication of a parody. This was a particularly interesting case because it involved two parties about whom many people held strong opinions: *Hustler Magazine* and its publisher, Larry Flynt, and the Reverend Jerry Falwell, leader of the Moral Majority. Campari Liqueur conducted an advertising campaign in which celebrities discussed their first experiences with the liqueur as their "first times." *Hustler* published an advertisement parody, so labeled in small print at the bottom of the page, in which Falwell was represented as recalling his "first time" as a drunken and incestuous affair with his mother in an outhouse. Falwell brought suit against *Hustler* in U.S. district court claiming that publication of the parody entitled him to damages for libel, invasion of privacy, and intentional infliction of emotional distress. The court directed a verdict for *Hustler* on the invasion of privacy issue. As later characterized by the court of appeals, the jury found that the parody could not reasonably be understood as representing actual facts, and it ruled for the magazine on the libel claim. The jury did, however, award Falwell damages on the emotional distress claim. The court of appeals affirmed the decision, saying that when the libel standard of actual malice is applied in a tort action for emotional distress, knowing or reckless falsity need not be demonstrated. The court of appeals further held that even if the ad parody was constitutionally protected opinion, the only relevant factor was whether the publication was sufficiently outrageous to constitute the intentional infliction of emotional distress.

The Supreme Court unanimously reversed the court of appeals (with

Justice Kennedy not participating). The opinion of the Court was offered by Chief Justice Rehnquist. The case, he said, presented the Court with a "novel" First Amendment question: whether or not a public figure may recover damages for "emotional harm" caused by publication of material "offensive to him, and doubtless gross and repugnant in the eyes of most." Falwell was asking the Court to find that a state's interest in protecting public figures from emotional distress is "sufficient to deny First Amendment protection to speech that is patently offensive and is intended to inflict emotional injury even when that speech could not reasonably been interpreted as stating actual facts about the public figure involved." This, said Rehnquist, "we decline to do." The sort of "robust" political debate encouraged by the First Amendment will necessarily produce expression that is "critical" of public figures who are "intimately involved in the resolution of important public issues." Such criticism will not always be "reasoned or moderate," and public figures will be subjected to "vehement, caustic, and sometimes unpleasantly sharp attacks." Only defamatory falsehoods uttered with knowledge that they are false or with "reckless disregard" for the truth provide a public figure with an opportunity to hold a speaker liable for damage to reputation. False statements uttered without actual malice may have little or no value, but they are "inevitable in free debate." Legal rules imposing stricter liability would have a "chilling effect" on expression and would not give freedoms of expression the "breathing space" they require.

Rehnquist characterized Falwell's arguments as urging a different standard because the state is trying to prevent severe emotional distress to people subjected to offensive publication. In Falwell's view, said Rehnquist, so long as the utterance was "intended to inflict emotional distress, was outrageous, and did in fact inflict serious emotional distress," it is of "no constitutional import" whether the statement was fact or opinion or whether it was true or false. The Court rejected this contention. In response, Rehnquist said that although the law does not regard the intent to inflict emotional distress as one that should "receive much solicitude," many things done with motives that are "less than admirable are protected by the First Amendment." Accordingly, though bad motives may be deemed as controlling issues for purposes of liability in other areas of the law, the First Amendment prohibits such a result in the "area of public debate about public figures." Were the court to hold otherwise, said Rehnquist, there can be "little doubt" that political cartoonists and satirists "would be subject to damage awards without any showing that their work falsely defamed its subject." Rehnquist examined the history of political cartoons and caricatures and concluded that despite their "sometimes caustic nature . . . , graphic depictions and satirical cartoons have played a prominent role in public and political debate." From a historical perspective, it is "clear that our political discourse would have been considerably poorer without them."

Rehnquist then rejected Falwell's contention that the *Hustler* parody was "so outrageous as to distinguish it from more traditional political cartoons." Rehnquist acknowledged that the *Hustler* caricature of Falwell was "at best a distant cousin" of the traditional political cartoon. If it were possible, he said, to lay down a "principled standard" to separate them, "public discourse would probably suffer little or no harm." Rehnquist doubted, however, that such a standard existed and "was certain" that the "pejorative description 'outrageous' does not supply one." "Outrageousness," in the field of political and social discourse, has "an inherent subjectiveness" that would allow a jury to "impose liability on the basis of the jurors' tastes or views, or perhaps on the basis of their dislike of a particular expression." Rehnquist concluded the Court's opinion by saying that public figures may not recover damages for the tort of intentional infliction of emotional distress without showing that the publication "contains a false statement of fact which was made with 'actual malice.' " This conclusion, said Rehnquist, "reflects our considered judgment that such a standard is necessary to give adequate 'breathing space' to freedoms protected by the First Amendment."

The Court's decision in *Hustler Magazine v. Falwell* was important for two reasons. First, the decision indicates that the Court is not interested in making it easier for public figures to collect damages when they are subjected to criticism and satire. On the contrary, the decision ought to discourage plaintiffs who feel offended by media treatment from resorting to litigation as a means of recovery. Second, the decision dispelled speculation that the Court was on the verge of abandoning the "actual malice" rule established in *Sullivan.* The *Sullivan* rule has served as the basis for publications defending themselves in libel actions. During the 1980s, the Court seemed to be in doubt as to whether the *Sullivan* rule provided public figures with enough room to protect themselves. The Court's decision in the *Hustler* case was squarely founded on *Sullivan,* and it seems apparent that the Court is satisfied, at least for now, with the *Sullivan* rule serving as the basis for limiting libel actions against the media. For the quarter century since *Sullivan,* statements of opinion, as opposed to statements of "fact," have enjoyed virtual protection from libel actions. In addition to *Sullivan,* further support for a privilege for "comment" can be found in *Gertz v. Robert Welch, Inc.,* in which the Court said that, under the First Amendment, "there is no such thing as a false idea. However pernicious an opinion may seem, we depend for its correction not on the conscience of judges and juries, but on the competition of other ideas."

The Fourth Amendment

T he Fourth Amendment safeguards U.S. citizens from unreasonable searches and seizures by government officials. The amendment was included in the Bill of Rights as the direct result of the British use of writs of assistance in the American Colonies. These general warrants allowed for arbitrary searches and seizures of persons and property. They proliferated in the years immediately preceding the American Revolution, when they were issued to seize contraband smuggled into the colonies in violation of acts of Parliament that imposed duties and tariffs on imports. The framers of the Bill of Rights insisted on specific language to ensure that probable cause existed to issue a warrant. The amendment required that name, place, and things sought be identified. Further, the warrant must issue from a neutral magistrate who would be a disinterested third party between the individual citizen and the law enforcement officer seeking the warrant. However, the Fourth Amendment only extended to the federal government in early U.S. history.

The Fourth Amendment established an absolute right against threat of unreasonable intrusion by agents and officials of the newly formed U.S. government. The demand for the Fourth Amendment, as well as the other Bill of Rights amendments, came largely from the state constitutional ratifying conventions. The delegates to the Maryland convention, for example, said that the adoption of the Fourth Amendment was necessary because "a free people" must be provided a constitutional check effective to "safeguard our citizens" against the issuance of general warrants. In making their arguments, many of the states relied heavily on the views of Sir William Blackstone expressed in his *Commentaries,* in which he argued that general warrants were illegal.

The Fourth Amendment protects citizens from unreasonable intrusions by the government. Any search, of course, constitutes a governmental intrusion. The idea is to balance the interests of personal privacy on the one hand and the legitimate governmental interest in effective law enforcement on the other. The principal means of limiting government's power was the warrant process. A warrant is an order issued by a court authorizing the arrest of someone or the search of a specified location and thereby allowing an official government intrusion into personal privacy.

The warrant process has several components. A request for a warrant must establish probable cause that the person to be arrested is linked to a criminal act or that the location to be searched is likely to contain particular seizable items. A warrant can only be obtained from the appropriate authority, a judicial officer. Finally, the warrant must describe in relative detail the person to be arrested or the items to be sought in a search. Each of these components is examined at greater length below.

Probable Cause

The first element necessary to securing an arrest or search warrant is probable cause, which is a level of evidence required to convince a neutral third party, a judge or magistrate, to issue a warrant. The level of evidence needed for probable cause is not as substantial as that required to prove guilt. Probable cause does, however, require a sufficient level of certainty as to separate a bona fide criminal suspect from the public in general. This is sometimes called making a "prima facie" case. Prima facie means "at first sight" and refers to a case or claim that may be sufficient without further support or evaluation.

Probable cause relates to reasonable inferences rather than technical judgments based on rigid requirements. The considerations that go into establishing probable cause were clearly described by the Court in *Draper v. United States* (358 U.S. 307: 1959). James Draper was arrested in Chicago by a federal agent who neither knew Draper nor had seen him commit any criminal offense. The agent had been told by a "previously reliable" informant that Draper was engaged in narcotics distribution and that Draper would be arriving in Chicago by train. The arrest occurred at the railroad station, where the officer recognized Draper from the physical description provided by the informant. A search conducted incident to the arrest yielded heroin. Draper was subsequently convicted on narcotics charges, with the heroin used as evidence at his trial. With only Justice William Douglas dissenting, the Supreme Court upheld the search.

The critical question for the Court was whether the apprehending officer had probable cause to make the arrest. The Court emphasized that the evidence needed to satisfy the probable cause standard is quite different from that needed to prove guilt. The Court said, "We deal with probabilities," which are "not technical . . . [but] are the factual and practical considerations of everyday life on which reasonable and prudent men, not legal technicians, act." The arresting officer had found the informant to be reliable in the past, and the officer "would have been derelict in his duties" had he not pursued the information. The Court suggested that a standard of probable cause exists where sufficient reasonably trustworthy information is known to authorities to "warrant a man of reasonable caution in the belief that an offense has been or is being committed." Thus, the arresting officer had probable cause in this case. As a result, the arrest of Draper was valid, and the search of his person incident to the arrest produced admissible evidence.

Allowable arrest and search incident to arrest, without a warrant, depend upon whether or not the arresting officer had cause to act. An officer is entitled to consider such information as is available, even if it is hearsay, in determining whether he or she has probable cause within the parameters of the Fourth Amendment. *Draper* provides the perspective that although an arrest or search is a governmental intrusion upon personal privacy, and although a warrant can authorize the intrusion, a warrantless arrest and search are legally permitted if probable cause exists. *Draper* establishes that probable cause is not drawn from technical or rigid legal requirements. Rather, it comes from reasonably drawn inferences based on objective evidence. It is clear that probable cause does not require support conclusive of guilt. Instead, it is based upon probabilities. These probabilities must be sufficiently high in the judgment of the magistrate as to focus tightly enough on a person or a place to justify an authorized invasion of privacy. The probable cause standard can be met by evidence such as direct observation of criminal acts by a law enforcement officer or indirect observation by citizens or informants, physical evidence, or accounts of crimes by witnesses. The *Draper* test requires a non-neutral police officer to exercise the same judgment as a neutral judicial officer.

Informants and Probable Cause

Intriguing probable cause issues can arise through the use of informants, as shown in *Draper*. An informant is someone who provides information to authorities about criminal violations. Information from informants can be used to further an investigation and may be offered to support an attempt to establish probable cause in the warrant process. Because the information obtained from an informant is typically represented by another person through an affidavit, it is hearsay information. Hearsay may be used if the informant is reliable, the information is credible, and some corroborative evidence exists to support the substance of the informant's data. Additional supportive evidence may be required when the informant is unnamed or anonymous.

A helpful and recent case on the matter of informants and probable cause is *Massachusetts v. Upton* (466 U.S. 727: 1984). In *Upton,* the Court held that the totality of circumstances standard is appropriate in determining probable cause for a warrant based on information provided by an informant. *Upton* represents the Burger Court's reformulation of policy relative to the use of informant information in the warrant process. George Upton was convicted of several offenses in a trial in which evidence obtained through a search based on informant information was admitted. The Massachusetts Supreme Court reversed Upton's conviction, ruling that the affidavit supporting the warrant that authorized the search was defective. The affidavit did not establish probable cause based on the two-prong test established by the Warren Court in *Aguilar v. Texas* (378 U.S. 108: 1964). Massachusetts appealed the reversal, and the U.S. Supreme Court upheld the initial conviction in a seven to two decision.

The Court said the probable cause requirement could be adequately maintained through a "totality of circumstances" approach. The two-prong test required first that affidavits submitted in support of warrants establish the means by which the informant came to know the information, the so-called basis of knowledge prong. The other requirement was that the affidavit establish either the general veracity of the informant or the specific reliability of his or her information in the particular case. The Court chose to move away from both requirements in *Upton.* The Burger Court rejected the two-prong test as "hypertechnical" and "divorced from the 'factual and practical considerations of everyday life on which reasonable and prudent men, not legal technicians, act.' " The Court said it was wiser to abandon the two-prong test and replace it with a totality of circumstances approach more in keeping with the practical, common-sense decisions demanded of judicial officers granting warrants. The totality analysis permits necessary flexibility rather than encouraging "an excessively technical dissection" of informant tips. The previous standard allowed undue attention to isolated or independent issues. The new approach, a "more deferential standard of review," permits the magistrate to put together pieces of evidence in a more general way to support his or her decision to issue a warrant. *Upton* represents the abandonment of the Court's stricter standards regarding informant information existing since the mid-1960s.

Subsequent to the establishment of the two-prong test in *Aguilar,* the Court said in *United States v. Harris* (403 U.S. 573: 1971) that hearsay may be used when seeking a warrant. This modified previous decisions by ruling that information about the reputation of the person to be searched could be used to support the warrant request. In addition, the *Harris* decision held that the previous receipt of reliable information was not required to demonstrate an informant's reliability. This ruling reinterpreted *Aguilar* by assigning weight to a suspect's reputation and by deferring to the experience and knowledge of police officers in assessing the credibility of information from informants. The modification of *Aguilar* standards was continued in *Illinois v. Gates* (462 U.S. 213: 1983), in which the Court rejected the two-prong test for the first time. The *Aguilar* elements of informant veracity, reliability, and basis of knowledge remain considerations for magistrates issuing warrants, but the totality of circumstances approach of *Gates* and *Upton* is said by the Court to be more flexible and "will better achieve the accommodations of public and private interests that the Fourth Amendment requires." *Gates* and *Upton* constitute a major policy shift regarding informants and probable cause; consequently, law enforcement officers now possess greater operating latitude in establishing probable cause through the use of informants.

One of the key issues in stop-and-frisk situations also involves how much information is needed to establish reasonable suspicion. The question in *Alabama v. White* (110 L. Ed. 2d 301: 1990) was whether or not an anonymous tip, uncorroborated by evidence of criminality, can provide the basis for a stop-and-frisk. The Court ruled that an anonymous tip, if sufficiently supported by independent evidence, could provide reasonable suspicion. Like probable cause, reasonable suspicion is "dependent upon both the content of information possessed by the police and its degree of reliability." In *White*, police were able to corroborate significant aspects of the informer's tip, which, in turn, imparted a degree of reliability to the other allegations. In addition, the tip contained a "range of details" related not only to "easily obtained facts and conditions existing at the time of the tip," but also to "future actions of third parties ordinarily not easily predicted." This information of future conduct "demonstrated inside information" and a "special familiarity" with the suspect's activities. Such familiarity made it reasonable for police to believe that a person "with access to such information is likely to also have access to reliable information about the individual's illegal activities."

Neutral Magistrate

The second element of the warrant process involves the neutral judicial officer. The judge or magistrate has the authority to issue warrants based on probable cause. He or she possesses sufficient training and qualifications to assess evidence presented by law enforcement officials and make warrant judgments accordingly. The need for placing the probable cause determination in the hands of an official with no interest in the outcome of the case is evident from the case of *Coolidge v. New Hampshire* (403 U.S. 443: 1971). During an investigation of Edward Coolidge, some evidence was obtained from his home without a search warrant. After his arrest, following warrantless seizure of guns and other evidence, a warrant to search Coolidge's automobile was obtained by the state. The arrest and search warrants, however, had been issued by the state attorney general acting as a justice of the peace, a practice permitted under state law. Prior to issuing the warrants, however, the attorney general had supervised the police investigation of the case, and he subsequently served as chief prosecutor at Coolidge's trial. The Supreme Court concluded that the warrants issued by the attorney general were irreparably flawed. The Court said the Fourth Amendment offers protection by requiring that inferences from evidence "are drawn by neutral and detached magistrates instead of being judged by the officer engaged in the often competitive enterprise of ferreting out crime." The Court felt that executive branch officials must be categorically disqualified from making warrant judgments because "prosecutors and police simply cannot be asked to maintain the requisite neutrality with regard to their own investigation." Since the attorney general could not be regarded as the "neutral and detached magistrate required by the Constitution, the search stands on no firmer ground than if there had been no warrant at all." The message of *Coolidge* was that the appropriate authorizing party must have no direct interest in the search. Officials within the judicial branch are typically viewed as the neutral party most appropriately vested with the power to issue warrants. The basic constitutional rule is that searches conducted outside the judicial process without prior approval by a judge or magistrate are unreasonable under the Fourth Amendment.

The required neutrality can disappear if the magistrate issuing the warrant stands to gain financially. In *Connally v. Georgia* (429 U.S. 245: 1977), the Court struck down a Georgia statute that allowed warrants to be issued by unsalaried justices of the peace who collected a fee only when a warrant was authorized. A judge may compromise neutrality by participating in the execution of the warrant as well. In *Lo-Ji Sales, Inc. v. New York* (442 U.S. 319: 1979), a judge issued an open-ended warrant for seizure of allegedly obscene materials. He accompanied the police in the execution of the warrant and listed on the warrant additional seized items that he determined to be obscene. The Court unanimously condemned the practice because the judge "undertook to telescope the process of the application for warrants, the issuance of the warrant, and its execution." Furthermore, the Court said it was "difficult to discern when he was acting as a 'neutral and detached' judicial officer and when he was one with the police and prosecutors in the executive seizure." These cases have determined that judicial officers typically possess the requisite neutrality to issue warrants and that a warrant issued by a nonjudicial official makes the search essentially warrantless.

Warrant Particularity

Finally, the Fourth Amendment requires that warrants be specific. The particularity provisions of the amendment reflected intense feelings held by the authors of the Bill of Rights about invasions of privacy committed under authority of the "general warrant" common in eighteenth-century Britain. The general warrant was a broad license under which virtually unrestricted searches could occur. Warrants obtained in compliance with the Fourth Amendment must make some references to the person who is to be searched. Such reference may be other than an actual name as long as it allows a reasonably reliable identification of the person. The particularity issue was pivotal in the search reviewed by the Supreme Court in *Ybarra v. Illinois* (444 U.S. 85: 1979).

Ventura Ybarra was a customer at a tavern that underwent a warrant-authorized search. The warrant specified the tavern and the bartender as subjects of the search. In executing their duties, officers performed a "cursory weapons search" on all tavern patrons under provision of Illinois law. The officer who frisked Ybarra "felt a cigarette pack with objects in it," but did not remove the packet from Ybarra's pocket. The officer eventually returned to Ybarra, however, removed the packet, and found heroin. Ybarra's motion to suppress this evidence was denied, and he was convicted of possession of a controlled substance. The Supreme Court reversed the conviction in a six to three decision. Illinois attempted to justify the search on two bases. First, the state contended that the initial weapons search was reasonable and that the follow-up search was sufficient as an outgrowth of a reasonable frisk. The Court rejected this argument, saying the "State is unable to articulate any specific fact that would have justified the police officer at the scene in even suspecting that Ybarra was armed and danger-ous." Illinois's second argument was to justify the search as included in the warrant issued for the search of the bar and bartender; that argument was rejected as well. The Court said, "a person's mere propinquity to others independently suspected of criminal activity does not, without more, give rise to probable cause to search that person." It is necessary to focus on an individual to effect a search. The Court concluded that a "search or seizure of a person must be supported by probable cause particularized with respect to that person." The expectations of privacy require the protection of particularity, and this "requirement cannot be undercut or avoided by simply pointing to the fact that coincidentally there exists probable cause to search or seize another or to search the premises where the person may happen to be."

In the absence of any warrant reference to people, an officer must have a reasonable suspicion that a person encountered in a search is armed and dangerous. Such suspicion would permit a weapons frisk. In the *Ybarra* case no reasonable inference of danger was said to exist. The Court did note that the warrant "did not allege that the bar was frequented by persons illegally purchasing drugs." This reference suggests that had it been established at the time the warrant was obtained that patrons were often engaged in related criminal conduct in the tavern, this fact may have had a bearing on determining the sufficiency of the search of Ybarra, even though the search occurred incidental to the execution of a warranted search of the tavern itself. Nonetheless, the clear message of *Ybarra* is the necessity for particularity in warrants.

Stop-and-Frisk

The stop-and-frisk is a limited detention of a suspicious person accompanied by a cursory weapons search. A stop-and-frisk occurs without warrant and is undertaken when probable cause to arrest does not exist. The action is based on an officer's reasonable suspicion that a crime is occurring or is about to occur. A stop-and-frisk is intended to be protective, but is nonetheless "an intrusion upon the sanctity of the person" and therefore is extensively restricted. The definitive ruling on stop-and-frisk is *Terry v. Ohio* (392 U.S. 1: 1968). The major importance of *Terry* is that it distinguishes stops from arrests and frisks from full searches. Under *Terry,* even situations lacking probable cause may be appropriate for the preventive action of a temporary stop and a cursory weapons search. Custodial arrest with a full search may follow if the frisk yields a weapon.

In *Terry,* a police officer of 39 years' service observed two men, later joined by a third, acting "suspiciously." Specifically, the officer felt the men were "casing" a particular store. The officer approached the men, identified himself as a police officer, and requested identification. Upon receiving an unsatisfactory response to his request, the officer frisked the men. John Terry was found to have a gun in his possession and was subsequently charged and convicted for carrying a concealed weapon. The Supreme Court upheld the validity of the stop-and-frisk practice. It was conceded in *Terry* that the officer did not have "probable cause" to search Terry fully; indeed, this is why *Terry* is important. In this case, the Court distinguished between a frisk and a full search. The justices ruled that the officer in *Terry* was entitled to conduct a cursory search for weapons. Such a search is "protective," and although it constitutes an "intrusion upon the sanctity of the person," it is briefer and more limited than a full search. The frisk is justified by the need to discover weapons that may be used to harm the officer or others. Thus, where an officer "observes unusual conduct which leads him reasonably to conclude in light of his experience that criminal activity may be afoot," where he identifies himself as a police officer, and where "nothing in the initial stages of the encounter serves to dispel his reasonable fear for his own or others' safety," he is entitled to conduct a cursory search.

Terry provided law enforcement authorities with the capability of executing preventive actions. Not only did *Terry* allow police to stop a person in situations deemed to be "suspicious," but it also authorized a limited weapons search. Key in *Terry* was observed behavior that would justify the stop. *Terry* does not allow a full search unless the cursory search yields a weapon, which would lead to an actual custodial arrest. In *Sibron v. New York* (392 U.S. 40: 1968), a case decided with *Terry,* the Court disallowed a stop-and-frisk that netted a package of narcotics because the searching officer could not demonstrate sufficient reasonable suspicion for the stop. There was no clear reason to infer that Nelson Sibron was armed at the time of the stop or that he presented a danger to the officer. The Court felt the search of Sibron, as distinct from the frisk of Terry, was a search for evidence and not for weapons. The absence of focused suspicion in *Sibron* was similar to that in *Ybarra*.

The Burger Court expanded upon *Terry* in *Adams v. Williams* (407 U.S. 143: 1972) when it permitted a frisk based upon an informant tip as opposed to an officer's own observations. Five years later, the Court held in *Pennsylvania v. Mimms* (434 U.S. 106: 1977) that an officer could order a lawfully detained driver out of his or her automobile. Once the driver is out, however, the *Terry* standard must still be met. The Court concluded that considerations of an officer's safety justified asking a driver to leave the car, and if cause exists to proceed with a frisk, a pat-down is permissible. *Terry* and the cases that build upon it authorize substantial latitude for a cursory weapons search if observed or reported behavior can focus sufficient suspicion.

Terry was extended again in *Michigan v. Long* (463 U.S. 1032: 1983), in which the Court allowed a protective search of the passenger compartment of a stopped car. The Court ruled that "*Terry* need not be read as restricting the preventive search to the person of the detained suspect." Search of a passenger compartment of a car is permissible so long as the police "possess an articulable and objectively reasonable belief that the suspect is potentially dangerous." Contraband discovered in the course of such a protective search is admissible evidence. The Court used the reasonable suspicion standard of *Terry* to uphold searches by school officials in *New Jersey v. T. L. O.,* a case discussed in detail under "Juvenile Process: Police Investigations" in chapter 3.

A police practice closely related to stop-and-frisk is stopping a pedestrian and asking for identification. In *Brown v. Texas* (443 U.S. 47: 1979), the Court examined a state "stop and identify" law that made it a crime to refuse to report one's name and address upon request by police. Brown was arrested and convicted of violating the statute after being stopped by a police officer who had observed Zachary Brown and another person "walking in opposite directions" in an area of "high incidence of drug traffic." The Supreme Court unanimously set aside the conviction, asserting that a search or seizure "must be based on specific, objective tests." To detain a person for questioning, an officer must "have reasonable suspicion, based on objective facts, that the individual is involved in criminal activity." The officer who stopped Brown could not sufficiently demonstrate "a reasonable suspicion" that Brown was involved in criminal conduct. Nothing in Brown's behavior "was different from the activities of other pedestrians in that neighborhood." Neither the fact that the neighborhood was "frequented by drug users" nor the "understandable desire to assert a police presence" was seen as sufficient to "negate Fourth Amendment guarantees."

Brown is representative of several Burger Court decisions that underscored the reasonable suspicion criterion for stop-and-frisks. The Warren Court found that sufficient cause existed for a stop in *Terry.* But several more recent cases, including *Brown,* provided examples of insufficient cause. In *United States v. Brignoni-Ponce* (422 U.S. 873: 1975), the Court held that vehicle stops to search for illegal aliens were impermissible unless specific cause could be shown. Random stops of vehicles simply on the basis of observed substantial trafficking in aliens was inadequate. More recently, the Court held in *Delaware v. Prouse* (440 U.S. 648: 1979) that police could not randomly stop automobiles to check licenses and registration without some focused suspicion of a violation. To stop a driver an officer must have cause comparable to that required to stop a pedestrian.

Exceptions to the Warrant Requirement

The principal problem associated with searches and arrests stems from police failure to obtain a warrant before taking action. Of course, in numerous occasions the warrant process simply cannot be completed before an arrest or search, but failure to possess a warrant does not necessarily preclude a legally sufficient arrest or search. The circumstances under which the action is taken determine whether the search or arrest is reasonable, and reasonableness is all the Fourth Amendment requires. To understand the protections provided by the Fourth Amendment, it is essential to understand several warrant exceptions. As a rule, warrant exceptions relate in some way to emergency, or exigent, situations. An exigent circumstance creates the need for an exception because the special demands of the situation make normal warrant requirements impractical if not impossible. Exigent circumstance searches include searches of automobiles, for example. The exigency is created by the unforeseeable need to search and the fleeting opportunity to do so because of a vehicle's mobility.

The exigent circumstance doctrine rests on the premise that completing the warrant process is impossible in certain situations where a search or an arrest may be demanded. Authorities bear a heavy burden, however, when attempting to show an urgent need to justify a warrantless arrest or search. If an arrest or search takes place inside a person's residence, it is "presumptively unreasonable" without a warrant. In *Welsh v. Wisconsin* (466 U.S. 740: 1984), the Court held that it would be virtually impossible to demonstrate an exigency for a warrantless home arrest when the underlying offense is minor.

Welsh involved an erratic driving incident reported to authorities by a witness. The driver abandoned the car, but officers learned his address by checking the registration. Without a warrant, they went to Edward Welsh's residence, entered it, and found him in bed. Welsh was arrested and taken to police headquarters, where he refused to take a breath test. The trial court ruled his arrest to be lawful and suspended his license for failure to take the test. The Supreme Court reversed that ruling in a six to three decision. In 1980, the Court had held in *Payton v. New York* (445 U.S. 573: 1980) that a warrantless search of a person's home was prohibited unless both probable cause and exigent circumstances existed. *Welsh* examined one aspect of the question of what constitutes exigent circumstances. The Court said "the physical entry of the home is the chief evil against which the wording of the Fourth Amendment is directed." Accordingly, warrantless searches and arrests that occur inside a home are presumptively unreasonable, and exceptions are few and carefully delineated. The Court's hesitation in allowing exigencies is especially appropriate where the offense for which probable cause exists to arrest is relatively minor. When the government's interest is only to arrest for such an offense, the presumption of unreasonableness is difficult to rebut. Furthermore, the government usually should be able to make such arrests only with a warrant issued by a neutral and detached magistrate. When an officer undertakes to act as his or her own magistrate, he or she ought to be able to point to some real, immediate, and serious consequences if seeking the warrant is postponed.

The nature of the underlying offense is an important factor in evaluating exigent circumstances. Most courts have refused to permit warrantless home arrests for nonfelonious crimes. The warrant exception for exigent circumstances is narrowly drawn to cover real and not contrived emergencies. The exception is thus limited to investigations of serious crime, and misdemeanors are excluded. It is difficult to conceive of a warrantless home arrest that would be reasonable when the underlying offense is minor. In *Welsh,* the only potential emergency claimed was the need to ascertain the petitioner's blood-alcohol level. The state's classification of the first offense for driving while intoxicated as a noncriminal, civil forfeiture offense was viewed as reflective of the state's limited interest in taking the offender into custody. Given the state's minimal interest, the warrantless home arrest could not be upheld simply because evidence of the petitioner's blood-alcohol level might have dissipated while the police obtained a warrant. The matter of how much authority officials possess to enter private homes to make a warrantless arrest has always been troublesome. In the previously mentioned *Payton* case, the Court said that authority to enter a private residence without a warrant was absolutely contingent on the presence of probable cause and an emergency. In *Payton,* the police were attempting to make a routine arrest for a felony-level offense, but the Court held that the arrest was unreasonable. The *Payton* ruling did not attempt to define what constituted sufficiently exigent circumstance to support a warrantless arrest, however. Pursuing a fleeing suspect into a private residence was permissible, but beyond that the contours of judicial policy remained vague. In *Welsh,* the Court attempted to clarify the nature of an emergency. The Court insisted that the state show an urgent need for a warrantless arrest, suggesting that demonstration of an actual exigency may be virtually impossible if the underlying offense is minor. If a state has classified an offense as minor, not even the preservation of evidence produces a sufficiently compelling need for a warrantless arrest.

A related rule is that incriminating statements made following a warrantless arrest in a person's residence are inadmissible. The question in *New York v. Harris* (109 L. Ed. 2d 17: 1990) was whether or not the existence of probable cause and administration of the *Miranda* warnings might overcome the taint of an unlawful arrest. Police had probable cause to believe that Bernard Harris had committed murder. They entered his house without a warrant and advised him of his rights. By police accounts, Harris then confessed to the crime. He was arrested and taken to the police station, where he was again read his rights. He then signed a written confession. The

Supreme Court permitted use of those statements made outside the house despite the defective arrest. *Payton,* said the Court, was intended to "protect the physical integrity of the home." It was not intended to grant suspects "protection from statements made outside their premises where the police have probable cause to arrest the suspect for committing a crime." Presence of probable cause was controlling in this instance. Police had cause to question Harris prior to his arrest; thus, statements made at the police station were not an "exploitation of the illegal entry into his home." Suppressing the station house statement would, in the Court's view, not serve the purpose of *Payton* since evidence stemming from the defective arrest was already inadmissible under *Payton.* In-home statements made following warrantless entry remain inadmissible, so the principal incentive to follow *Payton* remains. Suppression of Harris's station house statements would have only minimal value in deterring *Payton* violations.

Welsh discusses failure to get a warrant in the absence of an exigency. The Court refused to consider an exception for the nonexigent situation. Neither can a warrant issued for one person be extended to reach another. *Steagald v. United States* (451 U.S. 204: 1981) speaks directly to the second issue. Federal agents, possessing an arrest warrant for Ricky Lyons, went to the home of Gary Steagald in search of Lyons. Though the officers failed to find Lyons, they did find evidence that led to Steagald's arrest. The search of Steagald's home that produced the evidence was conducted without a search warrant. On review of the case, the Court disallowed the search. The majority distinguished between arrest and search warrants and concluded that the arrest warrant for Lyons had no bearing on "petitioner's [Steagald's] privacy interest in being free from an unreasonable invasion and search of his home." Given that no exigent circumstance could be shown, Steagald was entitled to judicial determination of probable cause through the warrant process. To hold otherwise would create a "significant potential for abuse." Police, using only an arrest warrant for a particular person, "could search all the homes of that individual's friends and acquaintances."

A valid arrest warrant is a limited authorization entitling officers to search the premises on which the named person is located at the time of arrest. The Court delineated in *Steagald* the interests protected by arrest and search warrants. The former protects an individual from unreasonable seizure. The latter "safeguards an individual's interest in the privacy of his home and possessions." Both *Steagald* and *Payton* reflect the Court's view that privacy interests must be protected through the warrant process and that that process can only be bypassed in the presence of exigent circumstances. Using similar reasoning, the Supreme Court ruled in *Minnesota v. Olson* (109 L. Ed. 2d 85: 1990) that a warrantless arrest of a guest in a friend's residence violates the

Fourth Amendment. The Court found that the guest had an expectation of privacy sufficient to protect him from warrantless arrest. To find that a guest has such an expectation of privacy "merely recognizes the everyday expectations of privacy we all share." Staying overnight in another's home "is a longstanding social custom that serves functions recognized as valuable by society." That the host possesses ultimate control is not incompatible with a guest having a legitimate expectation of privacy. The house guest is there "with the permission of the host, who is willing to share his house and his privacy with his guest." Every guest shares the expectation of privacy "despite the fact that they have no legal interest in the premises and do not have the legal authority to determine who may or may not enter the household." For permissible warrantless entry, there must be probable cause to believe, among other things, that destruction of evidence is imminent, that the suspect will escape, or that danger to the officer(s) or others is likely.

Unlike the arrest in *Welsh,* there is an established exception for the proverbial "hot pursuit" situation. This doctrine allows an officer to arrest a fleeing suspect who has gone beyond the officer's assigned area of authority. Hot pursuit is established both in common law and by statute. Attempts to go after a suspect after an unreasonable interruption, however, are not permitted under the hot pursuit rule. Hot pursuit also permits a warrant exception to allow police officers to chase a fleeing suspect onto private premises. Such a chase constitutes an exigent circumstance that relieves an officer of normal warrant requirements, at least prior to making a search or arrest.

Search Incident to Lawful Arrest

Police are allowed some latitude to search without a warrant those people placed under arrest. The rationale for this warrant exception and the scope of the exception are defined in *Chimel v. California* (395 U.S. 752: 1969). Ted Chimel was arrested at his home. The police proceeded to conduct a warrantless search of Chimel's home including the garage and attic. Certain items were found and admitted into evidence at his trial over his objection. On appeal, however, the Supreme Court reversed Chimel's conviction in a seven to two decision. The majority of the Court, through Justice Potter Stewart, said that officers have two primary interests when making an arrest. The first is to "remove any weapons that [the arrestee] might seek to use in order to resist or effect his escape." Second, the Court allowed that it is "entirely reasonable for the arresting officer to search for and seize any evidence on the arrestee's person in order to prevent its concealment or destruction." The question in *Chimel* is the extent to which an actual search may be conducted toward either or both of these ends. *Chimel* concludes that the area to be searched incident to an arrest is narrowly confined. The Court defined this area as one "within his [the arrestee's] immediate control" and as an area "from within which he might gain possession of a weapon or destructible evidence." Such an area clearly did not extend to an entire residence. The Court also argued that there is "no comparable justification . . . for routinely searching through all the desk drawers or other closed or concealed areas in that room itself." The latter kind of search may only proceed under authority of a search warrant. *Chimel* thus significantly reduced the scope of a permissible search stemming from a valid arrest.

Like many cases before it, *Chimel* recognized the warrant exception that applies when searches are conducted during a lawful arrest. Such searches are justified as a means of protecting the safety of arresting officers and others as well as preventing the destruction of evidence. *Chimel* specifically addressed the extensiveness of a search attending an arrest. In cases prior to *Chimel*, the Court had held that full premises searches could occur. *Chimel*, however, imposed more stringent limits on the area that could reasonably be searched. Whereas prior cases had considered the "control" an arrestee might have over weapons or evidence on the premises, *Chimel* both restricted and replaced these decisions by inserting the qualifier "immediate" on the term *control*. Thus, *Chimel* permitted warrantless searches incident to lawful arrest, but greatly limited their scope. Officers may only search that area from which an arrestee might be able to access a weapon or evidence. If a fuller search of the premises is desired, *Chimel* requires a warrant.

The reasoning from the stop-and-frisk decision in *Terry v. Ohio* (392 U.S. 1: 1968) was extended to protective sweeps in *Maryland v. Buie* (108 L. Ed. 2d 276: 1990). A protective sweep is a "quick and limited search of a premises incident to an arrest." Such a sweep is conducted to protect the safety of police officers or others. The sweep is "narrowly confined to a cursory visual inspection of those places in which a person might be hiding." The Court emphasized that the sweep cannot be a full search of the premises. Rather, it can extend only to those spaces where a person may be found, and it can last no longer than necessary to "dispel the reasonable suspicion of danger." The Court acknowledged that a suspect has an expectation of privacy in the remaining areas of his or her residence, but this did not mean that such rooms were immune from entry. The ingredients to apply the balance struck in *Terry*, said the Court, were "present in this case." In *Terry*, the Court was concerned with the interest of the officers in "taking steps to assure themselves that the persons with whom they were dealing were not armed with or able to gain immediate control of weapons that could unexpectedly and fatally be used against them." The Court saw an "analogous interest" in law enforcement officers taking steps to assure themselves that "the house in which a suspect is being or has just been arrested is not harboring other persons who are dangerous and who could expectedly launch an attack." Furthermore, the Court said that neither a warrant nor probable cause was required for such a protective sweep. The sweep can commence based solely on a "reasonable, articulable suspicion that the house is harboring a person posing a danger to those on the arrest scene."

There are other incident-to-arrest exceptions. *United States v. Edwards* (415 U.S. 800: 1974), for example, considered the issue of how long after a person is taken into custody a search can still take place incident to that arrest. Eugene Edwards was arrested around 11:00 P.M. for attempting to break into a post office. From paint chips found at the scene, investigators had reason to believe Edwards's clothing contained material evidence of the crime. Edwards's clothing was taken from him without a warrant the following morning, some ten hours after his arrest. The clothing did yield paint chips similar to those on the window sill of the post office, and over Edwards's objection, the clothing was admitted into evidence at his trial. Edwards appealed his conviction on the ground that the search had not been incident to his arrest. The Supreme Court disagreed in a five to four decision. The majority, in an opinion written by Justice Byron White, emphasized that seizure of Edwards's clothing would have been permitted at the time Edwards was taken into custody. The delay in this instance occurred because it "was late at night; no substitute clothing was then available for Edwards to wear, and it would certainly have been unreasonable for the police to have stripped respondent of his clothing and left him exposed in his cell through-out the night." Delay until the next morning was a "normal incident" to the custodial arrest, and "reasonable delay" in effecting the seizure "does not change the fact that Edwards was no more imposed upon than he could have been at the time and place of the arrest at the place of detention."

Edwards examined whether the warrant exception permitting a search incident to arrest allows that incidental search to occur the next day. Clearly the search must occur within the same general time period as the arrest. If too much time elapses, or the suspect is fully secured, the necessity for the warrant exception diminishes. The *Edwards* decision provides some flex-ibility. *Edwards* does not require that searches incident to arrest occur immediately following the arrest. The greater the delay, however, the greater the burden to demonstrate continuing necessity. In *Edwards,* the incidental search was not conducted on a location, but upon clothing. The majority of the Court agreed that the actual arrest and the subsequent processing of Edwards had concluded but that the delayed seizure of the clothing could be justified. Certainly an immediate confiscation of Edwards's clothing would have been permitted as incidental to his arrest. That seizure would have occurred but for the late night arrest and the unavailability of substitute clothing; those two factors provided the basis for tolerating the delay. At the same time, Edwards's place of residence could not have been subjected to a warrantless search on the following day.

Edwards focuses on the duration of the incident-to-arrest warrant exception. *Michigan v. Tyler* (436 U.S. 499: 1978), the so-called arson search case, considers how long an exigency exists that permits a warrantless search. A fire began about midnight in a store co-owned by Loren Tyler. Before the fire was fully extinguished, the fire chief made a cursory inspection of the fire scene. Among the things noted at the time were containers of flammable liquid. The police were immediately informed and a fuller investigation commenced. After leaving the scene for several hours, both police and fire officials returned to the unsecured location around 8:00 A.M., more systematically examined the scene, and seized evidence. In the days that followed, additional visits to the scene were made and additional evidence, largely in the form of photographs, was obtained. None of the inspections, either those taking place during the fire itself or those occurring up to 30 days after the fire, was conducted with a warrant or with Tyler's consent. The Supreme Court unanimously ruled that the searches occurring during and immediately after the fire had satisfied the conditions of the exigent circumstance exception. Those occurring more than nine hours after the fire did not satisfy the exigency definition.

The Court rejected the argument that no privacy interests remained, that the badly burned premises had been abandoned, and that searches by officials other than police are not encompassed by the Fourth Amendment. Warrants are the norm, even in this situation, and an official must show more than "the bare fact that a fire has occurred." Even though there is a "vital social objective in ascertaining the cause of the fire, the magistrate can perform the important function of preventing harassment by keeping that invasion to a minimum." However, this search was subject to the exigent circumstance exception. The Court said, "A burning building clearly presents an exigency of sufficient proportions to render a warrantless entry 'reasonable.' " The authorities were properly on the premises and could thus seize evidence in plain view. Justice Stewart argued that "it would defy reason to suppose that a fireman must secure a warrant or consent before entering a burning structure to put out the blaze." And once in the building for this purpose, firefighters may seize evidence of arson that is in plain view.

The exigent circumstance exception is based on the recognition that prior authorization through a warrant may simply be impossible under the conditions. To expect an officer to interrupt the "hot pursuit" of a suspect to obtain a warrant to continue the chase onto private property is generally regarded as unreasonable. Key to proceeding without a warrant is demonstrating a compelling emergency. In *Tyler,* the Court found presence of firefighters on the burning private property to be justified. Once legally on the property, the officers could reasonably investigate the origin of the fire. The investigation was permitted not only because it could be related to the preservation of potential evidence of crime, but also because it was necessary to reduce the likelihood of the fire recurring. Thus, the fire was viewed as an emergency sufficient to allow fire officials to be on the premises legally. The legal presence also allowed warrantless investigation for a reasonable time following the onset of the fire. Those searches that occurred in days following the first, however, were not seen as closely enough connected to the emergency that permitted the initial and legal entry onto the property. Once property can be secured, the exigency ends and no necessity for proceeding without a warrant remains.

The "Plain View" Exception

Police are also permitted to seize contraband that is in "plain view" without a warrant. The nature of the plain view exception is fully revealed in *Washington v. Chrisman* (455 U.S. 1: 1982). Neil Chrisman was stopped by a campus police officer for illegally possessing liquor. The officer asked Chrisman for identification. Chrisman had no identification on him and requested that he be permitted to return to his dormitory room to obtain it. The officer agreed and accompanied him to the residence hall. The officer stood at the open door of Chrisman's room and watched him look for identification. While waiting, the officer noticed what he believed to be marijuana lying "in plain view" on a desk in the room. The officer entered the room, confirmed that the substance was marijuana, and advised Chrisman and his roommate of their rights. The students consented to a broader search of the room, which yielded more marijuana and LSD. The students subsequently sought to have the evidence suppressed on the ground that the officer was not entitled to enter the room and either examine or seize the marijuana and LSD without a warrant. In a six to three decision, the Supreme Court upheld the search.

The plain view doctrine was crucial here. The doctrine "permits a law enforcement officer to seize what clearly is incriminating evidence or contraband when it is discovered in a place where the officer has a right to be." The Court concluded that the officer had properly accompanied Chrisman to his room and that remaining at the doorway was irrelevant to sustaining the warrantless search. The officer had an "unimpeded view of and access to the area's contents and its occupants." The officer's "right to custodial control did not evaporate with his choice to hesitate briefly in the doorway." He had a "right to act as soon as he observed the seeds and the pipe." This is a "classic instance" of incriminating evidence found in plain view when a police officer, for unrelated but entirely legitimate reasons, obtains lawful access to an individual's area of privacy.

Chrisman rested upon the plain view exception to the warrant requirement and drew heavily upon *Harris v. United States* (390 U.S. 234: 1968) and *Coolidge v. New Hampshire* (403 U.S. 443: 1971). *Harris* involved discovery of evidence while securing an impounded car as defined by department regulations. *Harris* held that evidence may be seized that is "in the plain view of an officer who has the right to be in a position to have that view." Controlling in *Harris* was the recognition that the officer had legally opened the door to Harris's car before finding the evidence. The *Harris* decision did not permit warrantless entry of a residence, however, simply because an officer notes contraband through a window. *Coolidge* refined *Harris* by saying that "plain view is never enough to justify the warrantless seizure of evidence." The exigent circumstance alone can provide the basis for the warrantless seizure of evidence in plain view. *Coolidge* also established that plain view discoveries "must be inadvertent." Anticipated discovery cannot be included within plain view and must be handled through a warrant. *Chrisman* reiterates that legal entry by an officer must occur prior to the plain view discovery and seizure. Standing in the doorway of the students' room was a legal crossing of the "constitutionally protected threshold," and thus the seizure of the evidence noticed in plain view was permissible.

A variation on the plain view theme was developed in *United States v. Jacobsen* (466 U.S. 109: 1984). Several bags of white powder were found concealed in a tube by freight company employees as they examined a damaged package. The employees notified authorities, who subjected the powder to tests without a warrant. The substance was confirmed to be cocaine. A warrant was subsequently obtained to search the location to which the package was addressed. The Court said a warrant was not necessary for the chemical test. The original discovery had been made by private citizens, so it was not seen as official conduct subject to Fourth Amendment limitations. The subsequent inspection by law enforcement agents did not materially expand the scope of the search conducted by the freight company personnel. The law enforcement search "impinged no legitimate expectation of privacy." The Court saw the seizure of the bags as appropriate because it was apparent the bags contained contraband. Given what the agents came to know about the package, the Court found the contents to be virtually in plain view and thus seizable. Conducting the test was not seen as compromising a legitimate privacy interest because it merely disclosed whether or not the substance was cocaine.

The plain view situation was also present in *Oliver v. United States* and *Maine v. Thornton* (466 U.S. 170: 1984). The Court said police officers do not need a warrant to search for drugs in "open fields." An open field was not found to be a person, house, or effect entitled to Fourth Amendment protection. No expectation of privacy exists with an open field. Similarly, the Court upheld warrantless aerial observations and aerial photography in two cases decided in 1986. In *California v. Ciraolo* (90 L. Ed. 2d 210: 1986), the Court permitted aerial surveillance of a fenced private backyard. The police suspected that marijuana was being grown on the property. In a five to four decision, the Court said any citizen flying in the airplane over the yard could have seen what a police officer observed. The Fourth Amendment does not require that police officers flying in public airspace must obtain a warrant to observe what is visible to the naked eye.

The Court reconsidered the plain view inadvertence requirement in *Horton v. California* (110 L. Ed. 2d 112: 1990). A warrant was obtained to search Terry Horton's home for evidence related to an armed robbery. Though the supporting affidavit referred to weapons used in commission of the crime, the warrant only authorized a search for the crime's proceeds. The officer who executed the search did not find stolen property, but did seize weapons discovered in plain view during the search. The officer subsequently testified that while he was searching for the stolen property covered by the warrant, he was also "interested in finding other evidence" linking Horton to the offense. His seizure of the weapons was, thus, not inadvertent. As readers may recall, the inadvertence limitation on the plain view warrant exception had been set forth in *Coolidge*. By a seven to two vote, the Court overruled the *Coolidge* inadvertence rationale, finding it flawed in two ways. First, law enforcement standards ought not to "depend upon the subjective state of mind" of an officer. That an officer "is interested" in particular evidence and "expects to find it" during the search "should not invalidate its seizure if the search is confined in area and duration by terms of the warrant." If an officer has a valid warrant to search for one item and merely a suspicion concerning a second item, "we fail to see why that suspicion should immunize the second item from seizure if it is found during a lawful search for the first." Second, the Court was not persuaded that the inadvertence requirement prevented general searches or the conversion of specific warrants into general warrants. That interest, wrote Justice John Paul Stevens, "is already served by the requirement that no warrant issue [*sic*] unless it 'particularly describes the place to be searched and the person or things to be seized.' ... Scrupulous adherence to these requirements," Stevens continued, "serves the interests in limiting the area and duration of the search that the inadvertence requirement inadequately protects." Once those requirements have been met and lawful access has been established, no other Fourth Amendment interest is "furthered by requiring that the discovery of evidence be inadvertent."

Automobile Searches

The automobile creates the most common warrant exception. Since the mid-1920s, the Court has recognized that automobiles necessarily create exigency. *Chambers v. Maroney* (399 U.S. 42: 1970) illustrates how the moving vehicle exception applies. Following an armed robbery, descriptions of the suspected robbers and their car were broadcast. Police stopped a car meeting the description and arrested the occupants. The car was taken to the police station and subsequently searched without warrant. The search produced both weapons used and property taken in the robbery. Following his conviction, Frank Chambers sought *habeas corpus* relief on the ground of unconstitutional search. The Supreme Court unanimously rejected Chambers's claim. The Court cited prior cases that recognized "a necessary difference between a search of a store, dwelling house or other structure ... and a search of a ship, motor boat, wagon or automobile." The Court said the circumstances that furnish probable cause to search a particular auto for particular articles are most often "unforeseeable." Moreover, the opportunity to search is "fleeting, since a car is readily movable." Given this situation, an "immediate search is constitutionally permissible." The Court could have chosen to require immobilization of the car until a warrant could be obtained, but it rejected this course as only a "lesser" intrusion. In the Court's view, no difference existed between "seizing and holding a car before presenting the probable cause issue to a magistrate and ... carrying out an immediate search without a warrant." As long as probable cause exists, either course is permitted. Since Chambers's car was properly under the control of the police, there was "little to choose in terms of practical consequences between an immediate search without a warrant and the car's immobilization until a warrant is obtained."

Chambers provided a current reiteration of the "moving vehicle" exception to the warrant requirement first introduced in 1925 in *Carroll v. United States* (267 U.S. 132: 1925). The moving vehicle doctrine allows a warrantless vehicle search because the mobility of vehicles creates a particular exigency, due to the possibility that the vehicle could be moved out of the jurisdiction. The same standards of probable cause exist, however, as would apply if a warrant could be feasibly sought. The searching officer must be able to support a belief that the vehicle contains seizable materials. *Carroll* thus created a key distinction between vehicles and places of residence. Mobility of the former creates a generally applicable warrant exception. *Chambers* expanded on *Carroll* by allowing the mobility exigency to pertain if the vehicle was first taken to the police station. *Chambers* rejected the need to obtain a warrant once the vehicle had been secured, which broadens the scope of the exception. It is also clear from *Chambers* that the rationale that applies to automobiles extends as well to other movable conveyances such as ships, trucks, planes, and mobile homes.

United States v. Robinson (414 U.S. 218: 1973) considered whether or not a traffic violation may trigger an arrest that then provides the basis for a full search. Willie Robinson was stopped by a police officer who had reason to believe Robinson was driving with a revoked license. Probable cause was satisfied in that the same officer had stopped Robinson only four days earlier and had found Robinson's license to have been revoked. The officer put Robinson under a full-custody arrest and conducted a thorough search. The search yielded a packet containing heroin capsules, and Robinson sought to have the evidence suppressed. The Supreme Court upheld the search in a six to three decision.

The question faced by the Court was whether the full search was justified, as it could not yield any evidence pertaining to the traffic offense. The majority agreed that Robinson had been legally arrested and that a custodial arrest allowed a full search. The Court said this situation was not bound by the limits placed on investigative searches under stop-and-frisk guidelines. The Court asserted that "standards traditionally governing a search incident to lawful arrest are not . . . commuted to the stricter *Terry* standards by the absence of probable fruits or further evidence of the particular crime for which the arrest is made." Further, custodial arrests subject officers to "extended exposure" of danger, more so than the "fleeting contact" of stop-and-frisks; thus, a fuller search than a cursory weapons frisk can be justified. The majority concluded that if the arrest is lawful, authority to search is established, and the full search is "not only an exception to the warrant requirement of the Fourth Amendment, but is also a 'reasonable' search under that Amendment."

Robinson held that a traffic violation may provide the basis for a lawful custodial arrest. The custodial arrest, in turn, permits a full warrantless search of the person and the area within the suspect's "immediate control" incident to that lawful arrest. The primary impact of *Robinson* is found in the breadth of the warrant exception permitted. *Robinson* allowed a full search, not a search confined to discovery of weapons. The Court explicitly distinguished this situation from that of *Terry* and the stricter stop-and-frisk guidelines. The *Robinson* search was not connected to finding evidence related to the offense for which Robinson was under arrest. The search in *Robinson* also differed from incident-to-arrest searches such as that in *Chimel* in that no arrest warrant authorized Robinson's detention. In *Robinson,* the officer had probable cause to believe the driver was driving on a revoked license, a serious offense in the traffic codes of all states. More generally, the traffic stop can provide sufficient cause for a variety of actions. In *New York v. Class* (475 U.S. 106: 1986), for example, the Court ruled that the Fourth Amendment was not violated by an officer's confiscation of a gun found when he was reaching into the car to move papers that obscured the vehicle's registration number. The Court cited three reasons in upholding the action. First, the registration number played an important role in the government's scheme of automobile registration, a clearly legitimate governmental activity. Second, because the number was to be placed in plain view, the motorist had a diminished expectation of privacy. Third, the officer had directly observed the driver commit two traffic violations. The search was limited and sufficiently nonintrusive to be permissible given the lack of substantial expectation of privacy.

Carney v. California (471 U.S. 386: 1985) focused the vehicle exception in the special case of mobile homes. It is clear from cases such as *Chambers v. Maroney* that the exigency created by mobility applies to other movable conveyances such as trucks, ships, and planes. Charles Carney argued that his mobile home was more like a dwelling than a vehicle and thus should not fall within the vehicle warrant exception. The Court disagreed. Though the justices recognized that a mobile home possesses many of the attributes of a home, it is also readily mobile, a characteristic that makes a mobile home comparable to an automobile. In addition, because the mobile home was a vehicle, there were diminished expectations of privacy. Because it was licensed to operate on public streets and highways, it was more subject to regulation and inspection than a residence. Carney also contended that mobile homes should be distinguished from other vehicles because they are capable of functioning as a residence. The Court refused to distinguish worthy from unworthy vehicles because to do so would require applying the vehicle exception depending on vehicle size and the quality of appointments. The Court chose to retain the established basis for applying the exception— ready mobility and the presence of the vehicle in a setting that objectively indicates the vehicle is being used for transportation.

When police arrest a driver, the automobile is routinely impounded by authorities. Several cases have addressed the inventory search that is customary with impoundment. One of the leading cases is *South Dakota v. Opperman* (428 U.S. 364: 1976). Donald Opperman's car was impounded for numerous parking violations. A police officer noted some personal property in the car, and following established inventory practices, inventoried the contents of the car. During the inventory marijuana was discovered in the unlocked glove compartment. Opperman was subsequently prosecuted for possession of marijuana. He sought to have the evidence suppressed, but his motion was denied and he was convicted. The Supreme Court affirmed the conviction in a five to four decision. In addition to the mobility dimension involved with automobiles, the majority stressed that there is a diminished "expectation of privacy with respect to one's automobile" as distinct from "one's home or office." The primary function of automobiles is transportation, and a car "seldom serves as one's residence or as the repository of personal effects." In the course of their "community caretaking functions," police often take automobiles into custody. Impounded cars are normally secured and inventoried to protect the owner's property, to minimize claims against the police for lost or stolen property, and to protect police from potential danger. The majority found the "caretaking procedures" to be an established practice within state law. The search was reasonable because the inventory was "prompted by the presence in plain view of a number of valuables inside the car." *Opperman* never suggested that this "standard procedure, essentially like that followed throughout the country, was a pretext concealing an investigatory police motive."

Opperman broadened permissible seizures under the plain view doctrine by approving the warrantless entry into an impounded car for purposes of conducting a standard inventory. Though the Court limited the *Opperman* holding to the facts of that case, two points stand out in the opinion. First, authorities were allowed to seize criminal evidence from a car that was entered neither with a warrant nor with probable cause to believe that evidence of a crime was located in it. The rationale was the "diminished expectation of privacy" attached to a car and the various needs served by conducting the inventory. Second, the Court suggested such inventories ought not to be evaluated in probable cause terms. In a footnote the Court observed that the "probable cause approach is unhelpful when analysis centers upon the reasonableness of routine administrative caretaking functions." The majority maintained that *Opperman* represented "standard practice" for the police and that there existed no suggestion of any investigatory motive. Had such a motive been shown, the inventory would have been a "subterfuge for criminal investigation" and would not have been permitted.

The Court broadened the scope of impoundment searches permissible without a warrant in *Florida v. Meyers* (466 U.S. 380: 1984). At the time of John Meyers's arrest, his car was searched by authorities and taken to an impoundment lot. Some eight hours later, a second search was conducted without a warrant. The Court upheld the second search because police officers had cause to believe evidence was still located in the car. The Court said the impoundment search was justified on the same grounds as the initial search incident to the arrest.

The Court considered the admissibility of evidence obtained from a closed backpack discovered in a warrantless inventory search in *Colorado v. Bertine* (479 U.S. 367: 1987). Steven Bertine argued that the validity of the backpack search was dependent on the application of probable cause and warrant requirements. The Court disagreed in a seven to two decision and chose to apply the well-defined inventory exception to the warrant requirement. Such inventories serve to protect an owner's property while it is in the custody of the police, as well as to guard the police from danger. These are strong governmental interests, and given the diminished expectation of privacy in an automobile, previous cases have accorded deference to such caretaking processes. In *Bertine* there was no showing that the police had acted in bad faith or for the sole purpose of investigation. They were merely following standardized procedures. Indeed, the Court concluded that reasonable police regulations relating to inventory procedures administered in good faith satisfy the Fourth Amendment even though courts as a matter of hindsight might be able to devise equally reasonable regulations using different inventory techniques.

Bertine considered the search of a closed item discovered during an impound inventory search. The searching of closed containers discovered in stopped vehicles has been a troublesome issue for the Court. The current leading case is *United States v. Ross* (456 U.S. 798: 1982). The holding in *Ross* was that as long as probable cause exists, police authority to perform a warrantless search is coextensive with a magistrate's authority to issue a warrant. Following a tip, police officers found a car in a location specified by the informant. The informant was known to the police and had provided reliable information previously. The driver of the car, Albert Ross, matched the informant's description. The informant had said that drugs were contained in the trunk of the car. On stopping the car and opening the trunk, the police found a closed paper bag. It was opened and heroin discovered. A zippered pouch containing cash was subsequently found as well. Ross sought to have the evidence suppressed, but he was unsuccessful and was convicted. The court of appeals agreed with Ross, holding that the bag and pouch could not be opened in the absence of a warrant, but the Supreme Court upheld the original conviction in a six to three decision.

Justice Stevens traced the history of the automobile warrant exception and reiterated the impracticality of having to secure a warrant where transportation of contraband is involved. He said, however, that relief from securing a warrant does not diminish the probable cause requirement. The only warrantless automobile search permissible is one "supported by probable cause." The probable cause determination must be based on objective facts that could justify the issuance of a warrant by a magistrate. The mere "subjective good faith" of a police officer is insufficient to constitute probable cause. Once the probable cause requirement has been met, the practical consequences of the automobile warrant exception would be largely nullified if the scope of the search could not include containers and packages found inside the vehicle. A warranted search of any premises extends to the entire area in which the object of the search may be found. This rule applies equally to all containers and carries over to the warrantless search of an automobile. Justice Stevens noted that the protection of the Fourth Amendment "varies in different settings." A container in a person's possession at the time of arrest may be searched "even without any specific suspicion concerning its contents." The privacy interests of an individual must give way to the finding of probable cause. Stevens concluded by saying the scope of a warrantless automobile search is not defined by the nature of the container but by "the object of the search and places in which there is probable cause to believe that it may be found."

In *Ross,* the Court allowed the warrantless search of containers found in automobiles, which constitutes a significant change in Court policy in this sensitive area. Prior to *Ross,* the Court held that containers found in cars were protected unless their contents were in plain view, a rule derived from several cases having to do with expectations of privacy attaching to luggage. In *United States v. Chadwick* (433 U.S. 1: 1977), the Court refused to permit the warrantless search of a secured footlocker taken from an automobile trunk. *Chadwick* held that the locked container conveyed a privacy expectation that required warrant protection. In *Arkansas v. Sanders* (442 U.S. 753: 1979), the Court rejected the automobile exception as the basis for a warrantless search of anything, including a suitcase, found in the course of the examination of an automobile. Two years later, in *Robbins v. California* (453 U.S. 420: 1981), the Court held that a closed container found during a lawful automobile search was constitutionally protected to the same extent as are closed items of luggage found anywhere else. *Ross* separated itself from *Chadwick* and overruled *Robbins.* The Court maintained that the *Chadwick* decision did not rest on the automobile exception because the footlocker itself "was the suspected locus of contraband." But not all movable containers are subject to warrantless search after seizure even if they come in contact with an automobile. Thus, the *Ross* decision retained the *Chadwick* holding. *Robbins,* on the other hand, involved cause to search a whole automobile, not just the footlocker. The *Robbins* prohibition on the search of a closed container found in the execution of the lawful search of an automobile was rejected by *Ross*. So long as probable cause exists to search an automobile, the expectation of privacy does not extend to closed containers that might be capable of concealing the object of the search.

Consent Search

Consenting to a search constitutes a waiver of Fourth Amendment protection. The Supreme Court has established that the burden of proving the voluntariness of such consent rests with the prosecution and cannot be inferred from silence. The Supreme Court has not gone so far as to require that persons be informed that they may withhold consent, although a number of states have done so. Assuming that consent is voluntary, a person may limit his or her consent to particular places to be searched and specific items to be searched for. Once granted, consent also may be withdrawn. Even uncoerced consent cannot purge taint stemming from an impermissible action occurring prior to consent. If a person is illegally detained, for example, any subsequent search is flawed.

The matter of voluntariness is controlling in consent searches. In *Schneckloth v. Bustamonte* (412 U.S. 218: 1973), the Court explored what is involved in determining the voluntariness of consenting to a search. A police officer stopped an automobile occupied by six persons including Merle Bustamonte. After requesting identification and establishing that Bustamonte was the brother of the car owner, the officer asked if he could search the interior of the car. When the officer asked whether the trunk opened, Bustamonte took the car keys and opened the trunk. Several stolen checks were found in the trunk and were subsequently entered into evidence at trial. The Supreme Court upheld use of the evidence. Key to the decision was determining whether consent had been voluntary. A six-justice majority said, "two competing concerns must be accommodated in determining the meaning of a 'voluntary' consent—the legitimate need for such searches and the equally important requirement of assuring the absence of coercion." Such problems cannot be "resolved by any infallible touchstone." The Court stressed consideration of the "totality of circumstances" in making judgments in these kinds of cases. On that basis, the Court concluded that consent had been voluntarily given by Bustamonte. The majority rejected the argument that consent must be evaluated in the same way as a waiver of rights pertaining to a fair trial. The majority opted not to require that individuals know of their right to refuse consent in order to establish a voluntary consent.

Bustamonte effectively distinguished between search and self-incrimination situations, holding that an individual need be apprised of legal options only in the instance of self-incrimination. Though the decision still requires that the prosecution bear the burden of proof in showing that consent was voluntarily obtained, *Bustamonte* excludes knowledge of the right to withhold consent as an absolute element of showing voluntary consent. A number of states use the more demanding standard that all persons must be informed that they may opt not to consent to a search. Presuming that consent has been voluntarily obtained, the question remains of how much the consent allows the authorities to search. Consent may be limited to specific places to be searched or specific items to be searched for. If it cannot be shown that an unlimited search has been voluntarily consented to by a suspect, the search ought to be carefully limited. Consent may also be withdrawn, and searches continued after consent is revoked must be otherwise defensible. Even a suspect's consent may be insufficient to uphold a search. The Court held in *Florida v. Royer* (460 U.S. 491: 1983) that if a suspect is detained beyond the permissible bounds of an investigative stop, his consent to a search of his suitcases becomes "tainted by the illegal detention."

A different kind of consent issue involves who may give the permission to search. *United States v. Matlock* (415 U.S. 164: 1974) provides some guidance. *Matlock* considered whether or not a third party may consent to a search. William Matlock was convicted of bank robbery. Part of the evidence used against him was stolen money found during a warrantless search of a bedroom Matlock shared with someone else. Consent for the search yielding the stolen money was obtained from that other person, not from Matlock. The Supreme Court allowed the search. The decisive element in determining the adequacy of a third party consent is joint occupancy or control of the premises subjected to the search. The Court found such joint control present in this case because Matlock had often represented the other person as his wife, the consenting person "harbored no hostility" toward Matlock, and the person admitted cohabitation out of wedlock with Matlock, a criminal offense in the state of search. The majority concluded that she was in a position to give valid consent to the search.

Bustamonte provides basic guidelines for consent searches. If the suspect does not offer consent, however, the question then becomes whether anyone else may legally consent to a search of the suspect's premises. In *Matlock,* the Court focused the "common authority" criterion. If a third party shares common authority over a place or items within a place, that person may properly consent to the search. Generally, common authority would cover consent by a spouse or persons otherwise living together, such as in *Matlock*. Consent in these situations, however, may be limited if certain places or items within the shared premises are "exclusively used" by the nonconsenting other party. Parents may consent to searches of rooms occupied by minor children. Minors, on the other hand, typically may not provide consent to search shared premises, such as the family home. The ability to consent is independent from possessing title to the premises to be searched. Accordingly, a landlord may not provide legal consent to the search of a leased room or rooms, nor may the employee or agent of any landlord consent to a search on behalf of a tenant. This applies even to short-term renters in hotels or motels. *Matlock* permits third-party consent searches only if the third party has common authority over the premises to be searched. The common authority criterion prevails over all others in determining the legality of a third-party consent search.

The question before the Court in *Illinois v. Rodriguez* (111 L. Ed. 2d 148: 1990) was whether a warrantless entry is lawful if based on the consent of a third party whom the police reasonably believe to have common authority over the premises, but who does not in fact possess such authority. The Court upheld the entry essentially on "good faith" grounds. According to the Court, various elements can make the search of a person's home reasonable, one of which is "consent of the person or his cotenant." The essence of Edward Rodriguez's argument was that the Court should categorically disallow consent from persons who are no longer cotenants. The general rule is that factual determinations made by agents of government must be reasonable but not necessarily correct. The Constitution is no more violated in this instance than it is when police enter without a warrant because they reasonably (though erroneously) believe they are in pursuit of a violent felon who is about to escape.

Third Party Searches

An issue closely related to the questions posed in *Matlock* involve third party holders of evidence. In *Matlock,* the third party who consented to the search actually shared the residence that was searched. A different third party situation involves consent to search of a location although the occupant is neither a suspect nor shares the residence with someone who is. Such a situation arose in *Zurcher v. Stanford Daily* (436 U.S. 547: 1978).

A demonstration occurred at the university hospital at Stanford University. During the demonstration a number of persons, including police officers sent to contain the demonstration, were injured. The *Stanford Daily,* a student newspaper, published several articles and photographs of the incident. It was thought that the *Daily* had photographs that could lead to the identification of the demonstrators who had assaulted the officers, and a warrant was issued for the police to search the *Daily* offices. The *Daily* sought a judgment against execution of the warrant. In a five to three decision, the Supreme Court upheld the warrant. The Court rested its decision on several points. First, probable cause for a search warrant relates to evidence sought rather than who might possess it. If the state can show that evidence will probably be found by a search, a warrant is issued and an invasion of privacy is justified. Second, warrants may be issued to search any property. "Nothing on the face of the Amendment suggests that a third party search warrant should not normally issue." That is, a warrant authorizing a third party search is not precluded by the Fourth Amendment. Third, the Court rejected the argument that only the property of those suspected of an offense may be subject to a search. Justice White said it is "untenable to conclude that property may not be searched unless its occupant is reasonably suspected of crime and is subject to arrest." Finally, there was the special issue in this case about the First Amendment interest of the paper. The majority felt that the press interests were sufficiently protected through consideration of the probable cause requirement for the warrant. The "preconditions for a warrant . . . should afford sufficient protection against the harms that are assertedly threatened by warrants for searching newspaper offices."

Zurcher held that no special protection of privacy interests flows from the First Amendment. Adequate protections exist through the rigors of the warrant process itself to safeguard First Amendment rights. If the warrant requirements are carefully applied, a search that might occur under terms of a warrant should not interfere with the press's ability to gather, analyze, and disseminate news. More generally, *Zurcher* permits warrant searches of places neither owned nor occupied by persons actually suspected of criminal conduct. Again, protection from abuse resides in the process through which warrants are obtained. That process requires demonstration of a reasonable expectation that evidence relating to a criminal investigation is located in the place to be searched. Relevant evidence can often be found with third parties, such as evidence for investigations of white-collar crime, which might be located in bank, medical, or insurance records. As computer-dependent record-keeping expands, probabilities increase dramatically that potentially valuable evidence is stored in anonymous third party locations.

The Court was asked in *Zurcher* to prohibit such searches, but the justices found the safeguards afforded by the warrant process to be adequate. Another policy option rejected by the Burger Court in *Zurcher* was the subpoena approach to obtaining evidence from third parties. Because subpoenas do not require a showing of probable cause, they possess the liability of possible indiscriminate use. At the same time, the subpoena technique does allow the third party to better control the search and maintain privacy of other materials on the premises. Justice Stewart, in dissent, was very concerned that freedom of the press was threatened by *Zurcher*. Not only would the newsroom be "disrupted" by a lengthy search, but also the possibility of disclosure of information received from confidential sources would tend to prevent the press from fulfilling "its constitutionally designated function of informing the public."

Drug Screening

The epidemic of drug abuse has generated several constitutional questions, one of which focuses on drug testing as a condition of employment. The Court had occasion to consider this matter in two important cases decided early in 1989: *Skinner v. Railway Labor Executives' Association* (489 U.S. 602: 1989) and *National Treasury Employees Union v. von Raab* (489 U.S. 656: 1989). The Court upheld drug testing programs in both cases, but these endorsements were guarded. Both rested on the special character of the job responsibilities as the determining element for the compulsory drug screening.

In *Skinner*, the Court examined regulations issued by the Federal Railroad Administration (FRA) under authority given the secretary of transportation (Samuel K. Skinner) to adopt industry safety standards. The challenge focused on two particular regulations. The first required blood and urine tests of specified employee groups following major train accidents or incidents. The second regulation authorized administration of breath and urine tests to employees who violate certain safety rules. The court of appeals ruled that the Fourth Amendment requires "particularized suspicion" prior to testing. Particularized suspicion would have required that evidence be shown that a particular employee was taking drugs before any testing could be done. In other words, it would have required a showing of probable cause before testing could be done on any individual. On review of this case, the Supreme Court disagreed.

The Court ruled that the regulations were reasonable under the Fourth Amendment despite the absence of warrant or reasonable suspicion requirements. The Court saw the government interest in regulating conduct of railroad employees as critical. Such employees have "safety-sensitive" responsibilities that bear directly on the traveling public, and this creates a "special needs" interest that "plainly justifies" prohibiting employees from drug or alcohol use while on duty. In addition, these "special needs" create an interest that "goes beyond normal law enforcement" and therefore may justify "departures from" usual probable cause and warrant requirements. The Court held that neither the requirements for warrant nor individualized suspicion were "essential to render the intrusions reasonable." After reviewing the purposes of warrants, the Court concluded that in this context the use of warrants would "do little to further those aims" of keeping intrusions reasonable. The intrusions are "narrowly and specifically defined" and "well known to the covered employees." Furthermore, the warrant requirement would "significantly hinder" and otherwise "frustrate" the purposes of testing, and the time needed to obtain a warrant would result in "destruction of valuable evidence." As for individualized suspicion, the Court saw the testing as posing only "limited threats" to employee privacy expectations. This was especially true because the railroad industry was already subject to "pervasive" safety regulation at both the federal and state levels.

The government interest in testing without individualized suspicion was also seen as compelling because employee impairment may not become noticeable before an accident. Employees subject to testing, said the Court, "discharge duties fraught with such risks of injury to others that even a momentary lapse of attention can have disastrous consequences." Accordingly, regulations that produce effective deterrence are reasonable. The testing under review in *Skinner* was upheld in a seven to two vote.

The ruling in the Customs Service case (*von Raab*) was similar but differed slightly because of the differences in the job responsibilities. The Customs Service required urinalysis testing of employees seeking transfer or promotion to positions directly involved with drug interdiction, positions that required the carrying of firearms, or positions that involved handling "classified" information. The Court ruled five to four that the testing requirements as a condition of promotion or transfer must meet Fourth Amendment standards of reasonableness, but held that the drug screening was reasonable even without warrant or individualized suspicion provisions. The warrant requirement, said the Court, would "divert valuable agency resources" and provide "little or no protection of personal privacy" because the testing purpose is "narrowly and specifically" defined. Moreover, the Court reasoned that affected employees are aware of the testing requirement and the procedures used. The procedures are specifically set forth and are not subject to discretion. As a result, there is no determination to be made by a judicial officer, as "implementation of the process becomes automatic" upon the employee's pursuit of one of the defined positions. In assessing the reasonableness of the process, the Court had to balance the public interest in agent fitness against the individual privacy concerns of the employees. The

Court referred to the Customs Service as "our Nation's first line of defense against one of the greatest problems affecting the health and welfare of our population." Many of the service's employees are "often exposed" to both the criminal element involved with drug smuggling and the controlled substances they attempt to bring into the country. Because of this exposure, the government has a "compelling interest in ensuring that front-line inter-diction personnel are physically fit, and have unimpeachable integrity and judgment." The Court compared this interest with that of searching travelers entering the country and said it was "at least as important."

The Court also said that Customs Service employees who carry firearms or are directly involved in drug interdiction efforts have a "diminished expectation of privacy" with regard to the required urine testing. Unlike private citizens or other government personnel, service employees engaged in interdiction "reasonably should expect effective inquiry into their fitness." The same is true of those carrying firearms. Successful performance of their job responsibilities depends "uniquely on their judgment and dexterity," and these employees cannot reasonably expect to "keep from the Service infor-mation that bears directly on their fitness." Though screening designed to elicit this information "doubtless infringes on some privacy expectations," the Court concluded, "we do not believe these expectations outweigh the Government's interest in safety and the integrity of our borders."

Heightened concern about drugs and alcohol has produced a number of other Fourth Amendment questions. One involves investigatory stops, a technique frequently used to combat drug trafficking. *United States v. Sokolow* (490 U.S. 1: 1989) considered whether reasonable suspicion exists when an individual fits the characteristics of a drug-courier "profile," a composite of factors based on law enforcement experience that correlate with involvement in drug trafficking. Andrew Sokolow was stopped as he entered a taxi at the Honolulu airport. When Sokolow was stopped, Drug Enforcement Administration (DEA) agents knew, among other things, that he had paid more than $2,000 for two round-trip airline tickets from a large roll of $20 bills. He was also traveling under a name that did not match the name under which his telephone number was listed. His original destination had been Miami, a "source" city for illicit drugs. He had stayed in Miami only a short time despite a 20-hour one-way flight. Further, he had appeared nervous throughout the flight and had checked none of his luggage. Warrants were subsequently obtained after a drug-detection dog alerted officers to a shoulder bag Sokolow was carrying. A search of the shoulder bag yielded an amount of cocaine in excess of 1,000 grams. The court of appeals had reversed Sokolow's conviction, saying the stop was impermissible because there was no objective evidence of "ongoing criminal behavior" prior to the stop. The Supreme Court reversed the court of appeals and characterized the lower court's standard as creating "unnecessary difficulty" by drawing an "unnecessarily sharp line between types of evidence." Rather, the Court recognized the value of the "probabilistic" factors from the profile. Though none of these factors was itself proof of illegal conduct, and may even be "quite consistent with innocent travel," when the factors here are "taken together, they amount to reasonable suspicion." The factors observed here have evidentiary value by themselves, and the fact that these factors were listed in the profile does not "detract from their evidentiary significance as seen by a trained agent."

Finally, there is the matter of trying to more effectively combat drunk driving. The Supreme Court upheld the use of so-called sobriety checklanes against Fourth Amendment challenge in *Michigan Department of State Police v. Sitz* (110 L. Ed. 2d 412: 1990). Law enforcement officers briefly stop all drivers at such checkpoints in an attempt to detect signs of intoxication. Every state utilizes some kind of checkpoint method in the current effort to combat drunk driving. Such stops are seizures within the meaning of the Fourth Amendment, and the question in *Sitz* was whether such seizures are reasonable. The question was resolved by weighing the state's interest in preventing drunk driving against the "intrusion" on drivers as individuals. The Court began by focusing on the scope of the problem. "No one can seriously dispute the magnitude of the drunk driving problem or the state's interest in eradicating it." Chief Justice Rehnquist said the statistical data show an annual death toll in excess of 25,000. At the same time, the intrusion on motorists stopped briefly at sobriety checkpoints is "slight." The Court said these stops were similar to highway stops to detect illegal aliens. Stops such as these do not involve "standardless and unconstrained discretion" on the part of law enforcement officers. Empirical data showed that operation of the checkpoints produces arrests for alcohol impairment. Though the checklanes may not be the best means available to enforce drunk driving laws, the approach can reasonably be said to "advance" the state interest in preventing alcohol-impaired driving.

Exclusionary Rule

The exclusionary rule is a court-fashioned rule of evidence that in criminal trials prohibits the use of items gained from an unconstitutional search or seizure. The exclusionary rule was designed to give effect to the Fourth Amendment prohibition against unreasonable searches and seizures. The rule is highly controversial and is not explicitly required by the Fourth Amendment.

The exclusionary rule is justified in many ways. It is seen by some as an indispensable doctrine that supports the personal protections guaranteed by the Fourth Amendment. The rule creates disincentives for police misconduct during evidentiary searches by making the items found in illegal searches inadmissible. Every search case eventually gets to a judgment as to whether the search or seizure was reasonable. If it was not, then the exclusionary rule applies. Others argue that the exclusionary rule protects the integrity of the courts by keeping the judicial process free of illegally seized evidence.

Criticisms of the rule are numerous and substantial, however. Many regard it as excessive because it goes beyond the express language of the Fourth Amendment. The costs of the rule are also seen as too high because it often results in criminal conduct going unpunished. Good evidence obtained in an unreasonable search is disallowed, and criminal defendants are not convicted and possibly not even charged at all. Further, the rule tends to defeat the best test of evidence, which is its reliability. The rule frequently allows suppression of reliable evidence because the means of obtaining it were flawed. In sum, critics of the exclusionary rule argue that instead of sanctioning unacceptable police behavior, the rule rewards criminal defendants. The rule is clearly threatened, as political pressures are mounting to modify it, but the rule survives because detractors have not been able to find an adequate alternative. Several key Court decisions on the exclusionary rule require more detailed discussion.

Since 1961, the Court has had occasion to consider the exclusionary rule quite often. Though the Court has chosen to retain the rule, dissatisfaction with it is apparent. Two patterns are revealed in the Court's recent handling of the problem. First, the rule will not be extended beyond the trial setting. The Burger Court rejected extension of it to grand jury proceedings in *United States v. Calandra* (414 U.S. 338: 1974). The Court also allowed illegally obtained evidence to be used in a civil tax proceeding in *United States v. Janis* (429 U.S. 874: 1976). Second, the Court is willing to limit the coverage of the rule. It allowed otherwise inadmissible evidence to be used, for example, to impeach a defendant's trial testimony in *Oregon v. Hass* (420 U.S. 714: 1975), and it limited *habeas corpus* access to the federal courts in state search cases in *Stone v. Powell* (428 U.S. 465: 1976). In 1984, the Court fashioned a good faith exception to the exclusionary rule in *United States v. Leon* (468 U.S. 897: 1984). The Court said that evidence seized by police in "reasonable, good faith reliance" on a search warrant may be used at trial even if the warrant is later found to be defective.

Application of the exclusionary rule evolved over many years. Until 1914, common law provided that evidence obtained in violation of the Fourth Amendment could still be used in a criminal trial. In *Weeks v. United States*

(232 U.S. 383: 1914), the Court adopted the rule in federal cases, at least for evidence illegally obtained by federal agents. The Court said that the "tendency of those who execute the criminal laws" by means of illegal seizures "should find no sanction in the judgments of courts." If illegal searches can yield admissible evidence, the "protection of the Fourth Amendment declaring [a citizen's] right to be secure against such searches and seizures is of no value and, so far as those so placed are concerned, might as well be stricken from the Constitution."

The Court chose not to extend the rule to the state level, however. As late as 1949, the Court held that the rule was not required at the state level despite the linkage of the provisions of the Fourth Amendment to the state level through the Fourteenth Amendment. The key case on this issue is *Wolf v. Colorado* (338 U.S. 25: 1949). Although the Court ruled in *Wolf* that states must comply with the reasonable search expectations of the Fourth Amendment, it said the "ways of enforcing" such a right raise questions "of a different order." The Court agreed that exclusion of evidence was an "effective way of deterring unreasonable searches" but refused to condemn state reliance on other methods for dealing with due process standards. Though the *Wolf* decision was maintained through the next decade, the Court showed signs of altering its course. In *Elkins v. United States* (364 U.S. 206: 1960), for example, the Court ended the "silver platter" practice. This was a loophole left from *Weeks* that allowed evidence illegally seized by state authorities to be handed "on a silver platter" to federal authorities for use in federal proceedings. Following *Elkins,* full reconsideration of *Wolf* was inevitable, and it came in *Mapp v. Ohio* (367 U.S. 643: 1961).

The police who conducted a warrantless search of Dollree Mapp's residence were looking for evidence of a bombing and for materials associated with gambling. Instead they found "obscene" materials. The materials were confiscated and Mapp was subsequently convicted for their possession. The Supreme Court, in a six to three decision, held that a state was required to exclude illegally gained evidence. In applying the exclusionary rule to the states, the majority argued that the right of privacy was of sufficient priority to warrant the most effective methods of implementation. The means of protecting privacy other than the exclusionary rule were found to be "worthless and futile." The Court felt compelled to "close the only courtroom door remaining open to evidence secured by official lawlessness in flagrant abuse of that basic right." The Court had refused to extend the rule to state proceedings in earlier cases, but in *Mapp* the majority determined that the Fourth Amendment remains an "empty promise unless secured through the exclusionary rule."

Mapp extended the exclusionary rule to state criminal proceedings.

Though the rule is intended to deter police misconduct in the execution of searches and to preserve the integrity of trial courts by insulating them from tainted evidence, it is highly controversial because its utilization has crime control costs. Further, imposition of the rule by the U.S. Supreme Court preempts a policy decision previously retained by the states. Clearly, the *Mapp* ruling had fundamental policy impact. It was an attempt by the Warren Court to establish an effective deterrent to search misconduct. *Mapp* was also intended to locate principal monitoring responsibility for search practices with state trial judges.

The rule remained intact throughout the 1960s although it never lost its controversial character. The Burger Court's response to the exclusionary rule was lukewarm at best, and its disaffection was manifest in two ways. First, when given situations in which the rule might be extended, the Burger Court consistently refused to do so. In *United States v. Calandra* (414 U.S. 338: 1974), the Court held that the exclusionary rule did not apply to grand jury proceedings. It said the rule had "never been interpreted to proscribe the use of illegally seized evidence in all proceedings" and that "extension of the exclusionary rule would seriously impede the grand jury." Similarly, the Court ruled in *United States v. Janis* (428 U.S. 433: 1976) that the exclusionary rule ought not to be extended to evidence in civil proceedings.

Second, the Burger Court was receptive to modification of the rule. Though the Court chose to retain the rule, decisions such as *Stone v. Powell* (428 U.S. 465: 1976) narrowed the impact of such cases as *Mapp*. *Powell* gave the Court the opportunity to limit federal *habeas corpus* jurisdiction as a method by which state prisoners could receive collateral review on search issues. The case diminishes the possibility of federal judges intervening in state cases featuring search issues where those issues have had a "full and fair" review within the state courts. *Powell* thus conveys greater conclusiveness to state determinations about the applicability of the exclusionary rule. An alternative to the exclusionary rule is to bring federal civil action against offending officers. In *Bivens v. Six Unknown Named Agents of the Federal Bureau of Narcotics* (403 U.S. 388: 1971), the Court ruled that allegations of Fourth Amendment violations by federal officers acting "under color of federal law" may be subject to civil suit. Finally, there is the matter of exceptions to the rule. One potentially significant exception involves officer "good faith." The leading ruling on good faith comes in *United States v. Leon* (468 U.S. 857: 1984), which involved an attempt to suppress evidence obtained through a search conducted under warrant. It was determined that the affidavit supporting the application for warrant did not actually establish probable cause. The lower courts ruled that despite the fact that police officers acted in good faith and in accordance with what they felt was a legally sufficient warrant, the evidence had to be suppressed. In a six to three decision, the Supreme Court reversed that ruling.

Justice White defined the issue in *Leon* as whether the exclusionary rule should be modified to allow admission of evidence seized "in reasonable, good faith reliance" on a search warrant that is subsequently held to be defective. White commenced with discussion on the exclusionary rule itself, saying the Fourth Amendment contains no provision "expressly precluding the use of evidence in violation of its commands." The exclusionary rule operates as a judicially created remedy designed to protect Fourth Amendment rights generally rather than as a "personal constitutional right of the person aggrieved." White pointed to the "substantial societal cost" exacted by the rule, and he argued that unbending application of it "impedes the truth-finding functions of judge and jury." An additional objectionable consequence is that some guilty defendants go free or receive reduced sentences through plea bargaining. Indiscriminate application of the rule also generates disrespect for the law and the administration of justice. This is more likely when law enforcement officers have acted in good faith or their transgressions have been minor. For these reasons, recent Court decisions have focused on the remedial objectives of the rule, and the Court has become more inclined to adopt a balancing approach.

White said that application of the rule must continue where a Fourth Amendment violation is substantial and deliberate, but that the rule should be modified to allow use of evidence obtained by officers reasonably relying on a warrant. The police must be sure that affidavits supporting the warrant are not knowingly or recklessly false and that the magistrate issuing the warrant has functioned in a neutral and detached manner. To extend the rule further serves no deterrent function, as the rule is designed to limit police misconduct rather than punish errors of judges and magistrates. It is contrary to the rule's purpose to apply it to diminish objectively reasonable police conduct. Once the warrant has been issued, there is "literally nothing more the policeman can do in seeking to comply with the law." Penalizing the officer for the magistrate's error rather than his or her own "cannot logically contribute to the deterrence of Fourth Amendment violations." In *Leon,* because the officers' reliance on the judge's determination was objectively reasonable, the exclusion of evidence based on their activity was not necessary.

The Court said in *Leon* that the exclusionary rule may be modified to permit use of evidence seized by police officers as long as they reasonably relied on a warrant subsequently found to be defective. *Leon* represents a substantial alteration of the exclusionary rule, but the Court was careful to point out that the "good faith" exception does not apply under all conditions.

The police may not mislead a magistrate or offer knowingly false information in support of an affidavit, for example. Neither may police officers claim good faith when it is clear the magistrate is not neutral. Further, reasonable reliance on a warrant cannot exist where the warrant lacks specificity or is otherwise facially defective.

Electronic Surveillance

Electronic surveillance involves monitoring persons by electronic means and includes telephone wiretaps and a wide variety of mechanisms that permit eavesdropping. Electronic surveillance was not considered to fall under the purview of the Fourth Amendment until the late 1960s because physical entry onto private property had not occurred nor had seizure of tangible items taken place. In the late 1960s the Supreme Court reinterpreted the Fourth Amendment to create a protection for personal privacy, and this reinterpretation extended Fourth Amendment coverage to electronic surveillance. Congress subsequently enacted the Omnibus Crime Control Act of 1968, incorporating certain proscriptions on surveillance fashioned by the Court from its review of Fourth Amendment requirements. The act mandates use of an application procedure to obtain prior approval for electronic surveillance, a process that closely resembles that used in obtaining a warrant.

Electronic surveillance constitutes a substantial threat to personal liberty. Though law enforcement does not attempt electronic surveillance often, modern technology is advanced enough that many sophisticated forms of intrusion yield thorough results. The Supreme Court has not forbidden such surveillance altogether, but its use is now extensively regulated. The various means of executing an authorized surveillance need not be separately approved by judicial officers.

The Court's first critical electronic surveillance decision came in the wiretap case of *Olmstead v. United States* (277 U.S. 438: 1928). Roy Olmstead and a number of others were convicted of conspiracy to violate the Prohibition Act. The convictions were gained largely through evidence obtained by tapping telephone lines. The Court ruled that the Fourth Amendment did not apply to these intercepted conversations because it was intended only for seizures of "material things." The language of the amendment "cannot be extended and expanded to include telephone wires, reaching to the whole world from the defendant's house or office." The Court's conclusion was that the Fourth Amendment is not violated unless there has been an "official search and seizure" of tangible material effects or an "actually physical invasion . . . for the purpose of making a seizure." It was in *Olmstead* that Justice Brandeis urged a broader view of the Fourth Amendment, saying that it was "immaterial" where the connection to the tap was made and that the "intrusion was in aid of law enforcement." The "greatest dangers to liberty," Brandeis said, "lurk in insidious encroachment by men of zeal, well-meaning, but without understanding."

Congress itself prohibited wiretapping by provision of the Communications Act of 1934. The act, however, did not reach other forms of electronic eavesdropping. Neither was the act fully applicable to state law enforcement authorities. A number of eavesdropping cases made their way to the Court between 1934 and the late 1950s but were generally resolved on the basis of the "physical entry–tangible evidence" premises of *Olmstead*. In *Goldman v. United States* (316 U.S. 129: 1942), for example, the Court allowed use of a listening device placed against a wall from an adjacent room because no trespass took place. On the other hand, the Court disallowed use of a microphone on the end of a spike driven through a wall and into a suspect's premises in *Silverman v. United States* (365 U.S. 505: 1961).

Though use of such equipment does not occur frequently, the technology has come to allow invasions of privacy unimagined at the time of *Olmstead*, to say nothing of the time the Fourth Amendment was written. The Warren Court became convinced of the magnitude of the problem, at least potentially, and ultimately took a more adaptive view of the Fourth Amendment. Eventually the *Olmstead* doctrine was reversed by several decisions in the late 1960s. The Court did not go so far as to declare that wiretaps and electronic eavesdropping violate the Fourth Amendment as such, but it did tightly proscribe this kind of evidence gathering. The key case is *Katz v. United States* (389 U.S. 347: 1967).

Charles Katz was convicted on federal gambling charges. The crucial evidence against him was recordings of telephone conversations obtained by the FBI through a microphone installed in a public telephone booth. With only Justice Black dissenting, the Supreme Court held that incriminating recordings could not be used against Katz. The decision said the protection of the Fourth Amendment "protects people, not places." The phone booth itself is not a protected area as such, but rather as Katz entered the phone booth he brought with him an expectation of privacy. What Katz "seeks to preserve as private, even in an area accessible to the public, may be constitutionally protected." Even if he could be seen from outside, he deserved protection from the "uninvited ear," and he should be able to "assume that the words he utters into the mouthpiece will not be broadcast to the world." Thus, expectations of privacy are critical to application of the Fourth Amendment. The Court qualified its decision, however, by adding that the protections of the Fourth Amendment are not absolute.

Electronic surveillance is not foreclosed altogether. The government's surveillance of Katz was flawed because the FBI agents failed to secure prior authorization. Even though the government had probable cause to believe Katz was using the phone for criminal purposes, and despite the limited scope and duration of the surveillance, the Court insisted on advance authorization. If probable cause, appropriate limitations on scope and duration, and prior review are present, invasion of privacy through electronic surveillance techniques is permissible.

Katz and *Berger v. New York* (388 U.S. 41: 1967) reversed *Olmstead* and tightly proscribed this kind of evidence gathering. Electronic surveillance could only be undertaken with prior judicial authorization, and such approval was contingent on a demonstration of probable cause. Further, *Katz* and *Berger* applied relatively stringent standards with respect to scope and duration of authorized surveillance. These standards were subsequently embodied in the Omnibus Crime Control Act of 1968. This statute moved wiretap and electronic surveillance into a different era. In addition, a series of Burger Court decisions provided interpretation of the act that basically prohibited communication interception except under particular conditions. The exceptions are structured around controls such as prior judicial approval and other limitations required in *Katz*. The statute also permitted emergency surveillance without judicial authorization for up to 48 hours in cases involving national security. The Burger Court, however, unanimously found surveillance of domestic political activists under the emergency provisions to be deficient in *United States v. United States District Court* (407 U.S. 297: 1972). The key defect was absence of judicial oversight. Fourth Amendment protections cannot be guaranteed if "domestic security surveillances may be conducted solely within the discretion of the executive branch." Those charged with the investigative and prosecutorial function "should not be the sole judge[s] of when to utilize constitutionally sensitive means in pursuing their tasks."

The Burger Court otherwise upheld provisions of the act and demonstrated a very literal approach to construction of the act's provisions. For example, in *United States v. Giordano* (416 U.S. 505: 1974), the Court had occasion to examine the procedures by which applications for approved interceptions are made. The act requires that applications be signed by the attorney general or a specified designated assistant attorney general, but in this case the applications were signed by an executive assistant. The Court reversed Dominic Giordano's conviction because of the process deviation.

The Court has also considered whether the means of implementing an approved surveillance must also be reviewed in *Dalia v. United States* (441

U.S. 238: 1979). Lawrence Dalia tried to have certain evidence suppressed on the ground that the surveillance equipment used to intercept various conversations was illegally installed. The *Dalia* decision said among other things that covert entry to install surveillance equipment must be explicitly and separately authorized by the judicial authority approving the surveillance request. A five to four majority of partial concurrences held that the covert entry in *Dalia* did not violate the Fourth Amendment, however. The Court rejected the argument that the Fourth Amendment proscribes all covert entries, noting that it is "well established that law officers may constitutionally break and enter to execute a search warrant where such entry is the only means by which the warrant effectively may be executed." Second, the majority rejected the argument that Title III of the Omnibus Crime Control Act itself limited use of covert entry. Need for the surveillance must be demonstrated in accordance with the statute's requirements, but "nowhere in Title III is there any indication that the authority of courts . . . is to be limited to approving those methods of interception that do not require covert entry for installation of intercepting equipment." Finally, the majority rejected the assertion that even if Title III allows covert entry, explicit authorization is required prior to implementation. The Court said such explicit authorization would "promote empty formalism." The Fourth Amendment does not "require that a Title III surveillance order include a specific authorization to enter covertly the premises described in the order." *Dalia* reflects the Court's unwillingness to demand more than the statute explicitly requires. The case suggests that the key element in providing protection from abuse in this sensitive area is prior judicial authorization for the surveillance. Once the surveillance is approved, the means of executing it are beyond judicial supervision. According to *Dalia,* any limitations on implementation must come through legislative initiative.

The Fifth Amendment

T he Fifth Amendment was a U.S. adaptation of elements of the British common law tradition. Its origins were based on particular colonial experiences with such unpleasant devices as the general warrant. The Fifth Amendment includes several separate clauses that are founded on what Sir William Blackstone referred to as "universal maxims." The first clause provides that "No person shall be held to answer for a capital, or otherwise infamous crime, unless on a presentment or indictment of a Grand Jury, except in cases arising in the land or naval forces, or in the militia, when in actual service in time of war or public danger." This language was drawn directly from Blackstone by James Madison. Madison tried with this clause to incorporate the rule from British common law that no case could be prosecuted until a duly sworn grand jury had attested that grounds existed for such prosecution. The exception regarding land or naval forces and the militia was designed to avoid potential conflicts between civilian and military tribunals.

Second is the double jeopardy clause, which states, "Nor shall any person be subject for the same offense to be twice put in jeopardy of life and limb." This clause also comes from Blackstone and is based on the idea that the power and resources of the state shall not be directed against a citizen more than once on the same allegation. At a minimum, re-prosecution requires a person to go through the ordeal of again defending against the charge. At worst, the state could secure a conviction in one of its repeated attempts at prosecution.

Third, the Fifth Amendment says no person shall be "compelled in any criminal case to be witness against himself." The origin of this clause was in the practices of the British Star Chamber Court, where persons even suspected of some offense were interrogated before any formal accusation had been made. The British system of justice at the time produced frequent forced confessions. The authors of the Bill of Rights were determined not to have this kind of justice system.

Fourth, no person shall be "deprived of life, liberty, and property, without due process of law." Alexander Hamilton vigorously argued that insertion of the phrase "due process" would remove any doubt that it was "the process and proceedings of the courts of justice" being addressed in the Constitution. Thus, the courts would interpret the legitimate rights of citizens, not legislative bodies, which would presumably enact legislation to "disfranchise or deprive" citizens of any right. Because of the clause's general thrust and applicability, the Supreme Court historically has been reluctant to give precise definition to this language.

Finally, the clause directs that no private property "be taken for public use, without just compensation." The framers of the Constitution considered property rights to be absolute and paramount. Again, this is based on British common law dating from the Magna Carta.

The Fifth Amendment has been the basis of many Supreme Court decisions. The broad and dramatic interpretations of the due process clause after passage of the Fourteenth Amendment in 1868 make the Fifth Amendment a fundamental element of U.S. constitutional law. The Fifth Amendment's prohibition against self-incrimination has become one of the foremost privileges of citizens of the United States. The fact that the Supreme Court can review on both substantive and procedural due process grounds under the Fifth and Fourteenth amendments gives the Court unparalleled power in modern democratic government. Although due process, in Daniel Webster's words, fundamentally may only provide that a court "hear before it condemns," it has in U.S. practice been elaborated to provide a series of checkpoints for the courts to assure the preservation of a distinctly American tradition: that it is better for the guilty to go free than for one innocent person to be deprived of life, liberty, or property. In the remainder of this chapter, we examine in more detail the evolution of the grand jury, double jeopardy, and self-incrimination protections established through the Fifth Amendment.

Grand Jury

The Fifth Amendment begins by saying that "No person shall be held to answer for a capital, or otherwise infamous crime, unless on a presentment or indictment of a Grand Jury." Excluded from this directive are cases involving persons in the armed forces during "time of war or public danger."

A grand jury is an investigative body that makes accusations rather than determines guilt. The grand jury usually evaluates information brought to it by a prosecutor although it has the capacity to generate information on its own. If it determines that probable cause exists, it returns an indictment against an accused person. The indictment signifies that the grand jury feels a trial on specific charges is warranted. In British law the grand jury had the function of protecting persons from being tried arbitrarily. A U.S. grand jury typically ranges from 12 to 23 persons, with selection occurring under guidelines that require neutral and nondiscriminatory processes. Grand juries operate in secret as a protection to persons who may not be indicted. Witnesses appear before grand juries under subpoena. Failure to provide information desired by a grand jury may result in a witness being cited for contempt. Upon hearing all testimony relating to a particular person, the grand jury determines by simple majority whether to indict or not.

The grand jury, or accusatorial, function is substantially different from the adjudication of guilt. As a result, grand jury proceedings have been freed from the rigorous procedural and evidentiary standards used at trials. A leading case regarding these standards is *Costello v. United States* (350 U.S. 359: 1956). Frank Costello, an organized crime figure, was indicted by a grand jury for tax evasion. He claimed that the grand jury indictments had been based on hearsay evidence and should be dismissed. A unanimous Supreme Court upheld his subsequent conviction. The Court held that no constitutional provision "prescribes the kind of evidence upon which grand juries must act." The work of grand juries was intended not to be "hampered by rigid procedural or evidentiary rules." Citing the history out of which the British grand jury system evolved, the Court noted that grand jurors could "act on their own knowledge and were free to make their presentments or indictments on such information as they deemed satisfactory." The Court also predicted that excessive delays would be produced by challenges to indictments on grounds of inadequacy of evidence. It would mean that a defendant could "insist on a kind of preliminary trial to determine competency and adequacy of evidence before the grand jury." Such a process is not required by the Fifth Amendment. The Court concluded its opinion by reiterating that a preliminary trial "would run counter to the whole history of the grand jury institution, in which laymen conduct their inquiries unfettered by technical rules."

Costello clearly reflects the broad operating latitude the Supreme Court has typically extended to grand juries. *Costello* also reveals the categorical distinction between the charging process and processes designed to adjudicate guilt. Without question, the grand jury can operate more informally. Although the case was decided in 1953, the position taken in *Costello* remains unaltered, and the consequences are apparent in at least three ways. First, *Costello* underscored the investigative function of grand juries and the Court's view that grand juries must be exposed to the widest range of information in performing their accusatorial function. Second, because of the primacy of the investigatory role, *Costello* enhances the influence of the prosecutor in guiding the operations of a grand jury. Third, by embracing substantial informality in grand jury proceedings, *Costello* raises certain questions regarding protection of witnesses' rights, specifically the right against self-incrimination and the right to assistance of counsel.

Though grand juries may function through their own initiative, they are usually guided and sometimes dominated by a prosecutor. The prosecutor determines which witnesses will appear and which evidence will be developed. As a result, prosecutors have virtually complete discretion in grand jury proceedings through control of relevant information. Grand juries usually indict persons whom prosecutors want to be indicted, although grand juries also possess the power to direct indictment of people in the absence of prosecutorial request. A person need not appear before the grand jury to be indicted. Witnesses who do appear usually are not permitted counsel at the proceeding itself, although out-of-room consultation during the proceeding is often permitted. A witness must be advised of his or her rights against self-incrimination, but this warning may be quite general, as can be seen in the case of *United States v. Washington* (431 U.S. 181: 1977).

Gregory Washington was not specifically warned that he might himself be indicted and that his grand jury testimony could be used against him. Nonetheless, the Supreme Court ruled that his grand jury statements were admissible. The majority concluded that the Fifth Amendment does not "preclude a witness from testifying voluntarily in matters which may incriminate him." Unless compulsion can be shown, the Fifth Amendment does not automatically apply because testimony has an incriminating effect. Once Washington had been warned generally that he could remain silent and that statements he made could be used against him, that advice "eliminated any possible compulsion to self-incrimination which may otherwise exist." The Court went on to say, "Even in the presumed psychologically coercive atmosphere of police custodial interrogation, *Miranda* does not require that any additional warnings be simply given because the suspect is a potential defendant." The majority sought to discount Washington's challenge with other distinctions as well. First, the Court felt he had been warned adequately to allow him to know his status as a potential defendant. Given all that transpired, "by the time he testified respondent knew better than anyone else" his status. Second, the majority was not convinced that any additional warnings would have aided Washington.

Washington was one of several cases decided by the Burger Court involving grand jury practices. The philosophy of *Washington* is repeated in each of these cases. In *United States v. Calandra* (414 U.S. 338: 1974), for example, the Court refused to extend the exclusionary rule to grand jury proceedings. Once again the Court spoke of the need to maintain broad investigative powers for grand juries. Extending the exclusionary rule would "seriously impede" grand jury inquiries and "unduly interfere with the effective and expeditious discharge of the grand jury's duties." The policy preferences reflected in *Washington* prevailed because the grand jury function is clearly distinct from guilt adjudication at the trial stage. Because a grand jury is designed to investigate and accuse, the Court decided it can best perform that function by using the widest range of evidence available. That evidence may properly come before a grand jury through procedures that are substantially less formal than those found at the trial stage.

The Fifth Amendment requires grand juries in the federal court system. The requirement has never been extended to the state level, however. In *Hurtado v. California* (110 U.S. 516: 1884) the Supreme Court held that California's use of the information process, instead of the grand jury, did not deny due process. *Hurtado* gave the states the opportunity to determine their own preferred procedure for bringing criminal charges. Thirty-two states have elected to use the grand jury for at least some portion of their criminal code. Only eight states use it for all cases. Decisions subsequent to *Hurtado* have enhanced the investigative powers of grand juries. An alternative to grand jury indictment is the accusatorial process called information. This procedure allows a prosecutor to submit charges and supporting evidence directly to a judge for a determination of sufficiency. If the evidence is adequate, the accused is bound over for trial.

Double Jeopardy

The double jeopardy clause prohibits the government from placing a person in jeopardy more than once for the same offense. The principle underlying this protection was stated very well by Justice Hugo Black in *Green v. United States* (355 U.S. 184: 1957). He said that the state "with all its resources and power should not be allowed to make repeated attempts to convict an individual for an alleged offense, thereby subjecting him to embarrassment, expense and ordeal and compelling him to live in a continuing state of anxiety and insecurity, as well as enhancing the possibility that even though innocent, he may be found guilty."

Several issues have dominated the Court's considerations of double jeopardy. The first is when jeopardy begins. A helpful case on this issue is *Breed v. Jones* (421 U.S. 519: 1975), which involved a juvenile defendant. Gary Jones, age 17, was adjudicated in a juvenile court proceeding but later transferred to adult court for prosecution because he was "unfit for treatment as a juvenile." Jones appealed his adult court conviction claiming he had been "in jeopardy" in his juvenile proceeding and that initiation of charges against him in the adult court was foreclosed by the double jeopardy prohibition. The Supreme Court agreed.

The Court's ruling rested primarily on its perception of jeopardy. The Court said it was "simply too late in the day" to think that a juvenile is "not put in jeopardy at a proceeding whose object is to determine whether he has committed acts that violate criminal law," a proceeding "whose potential consequences include both stigma inherent in such a determination and the deprivation of liberty for many years." This ruling amounted to a substantial change from previous policy. Despite historical attempts to make juvenile proceedings different from the adult process, the juvenile process was now being seen as similar enough to the adult system to create jeopardy. The Court also rejected the contention that the prosecution of Jones as an adult was merely a continuation of the prosecution begun in the juvenile court. Though the Court recognized that the case had not reached conclusion because a suitable sentence had not been found, it also ruled that failure to sentence Jones did not in any way limit Jones's jeopardy. Putting Jones "at risk" was viewed as the decisive aspect of jeopardy. The juvenile court, "as the trier of facts, began to hear evidence," and at that point Jones's jeopardy began.

The decision of when jeopardy begins is a critical determination in that a person must be in jeopardy once before he or she can be protected from a second jeopardy. In the *Jones* case, jeopardy occurred when the juvenile authorities began to hear evidence in the adjudication of Jones. A person is "at risk" for double jeopardy purposes when fact-finding on guilt begins. More specifically, the risk begins at the time a jury is chosen or when a court begins to hear evidence. A judgment on that evidence by a jury or a court need not occur. Immunity from future prosecution on the original charges does not extend to cases in which the defendant initiated a cessation of the trial. Nor does it extend to those cases in which a defendant successfully appeals following a conviction and has the conviction set aside on grounds other than insufficiency of evidence. A case that does not reach the evidentiary stage, stopping at some preliminary point, affords no protection from further prosecution on the same charges. Neither dismissal of charges at a preliminary hearing nor dismissal of an indictment before trial actually commences precludes those same charges from being brought again.

A second critical question is what constitutes the "same" offense. When the Fifth Amendment provision on double jeopardy was authored, there were very few federal crimes, and the government had little opportunity to institute new prosecutions on slightly different charges. Current criminal codes are substantially more complex and overlapping in the crimes that are defined. Criminal codes contain many statutes that focus on slightly different manifestations of essentially the same conduct. The Court has struggled with the issue of "sameness," but little clarity has been achieved. We use *Ashe v. Swenson* (397 U.S. 426: 1970) as representative of the Court's thinking for our discussion of sameness. *Ashe* looked specifically at whether a principle known as collateral estoppel was contained within the double jeopardy protection in state criminal proceedings. Collateral estoppel is a legal principle that prohibits re-litigation of an issue once a valid judgment has been made on that issue. The facts of *Ashe* were that six persons were robbed while they were playing poker. Bob Ashe was charged with armed robbery of each of the six players, i.e., six separate offenses. Ashe was tried for robbing one of the victims and was acquitted. The jury found the evidence "insufficient" to convict. Several weeks later, Ashe was tried for the robbery of another of the victims and was convicted. The Court, however, set aside Ashe's conviction. The justices felt the central issue in dispute in the first trial was the identification of Ashe as one of the several robbers. The jury had resolved that question in the negative. Substituting one victim for another "had no bearing whatever upon the issue of whether the petitioner was one of the robbers." The majority found the fact issue of the two trials to be identical and suggested the "situation is constitutionally no different" from what it would have been had the state attempted to re-prosecute Ashe for the robbery of the first victim. The two offenses were the same.

Ashe addressed the most troublesome double jeopardy question, that of "sameness." The double jeopardy protection prevents a second prosecution only if charges are brought for the same offense. Thus, determination of sameness is fundamental. With a large number of acts defined as crimes, it is likely that multiple prosecutions can arise out of overlapping offenses and single transactions. Prior to *Ashe,* one of two criteria was typically used in handling this problem. The first related to evidence required to convict on particular charges. If the "same evidence" was required for both, the offenses were deemed the same for purposes of double jeopardy. The essence of this test comes from *Blockburger v. United States* (284 U.S. 299: 1932). In *Blockburger,* the Court said that "where the same act or transaction constitutes a violation of two distinct statutory provisions," the standard to be applied to determine whether there are one or two offenses is "whether each provision requires proof of an additional fact which the other does not." If, however, at least one element of each could not be proved with common evidence, the offenses were said to be different. The same evidence approach created limits to the protection afforded against re-prosecution because of the overlapping character of modern criminal codes. The same evidence criterion does, however, preclude re-prosecution for included offenses—offenses that are generally less serious than a connected greater offense but are so tightly related that one cannot convict on the greater charge without necessarily convicting on the lesser charge as well. Second degree murder, for example, is an included offense of first degree murder; they share the common element of victim death, but the greater offense has the added element of premeditation.

The Court returned to the sameness issue in *Grady v. Corbin* (109 L. Ed. 2d 548: 1990). Under the *Blockburger* "sameness" test, two offenses are not the same if they contain at least one different evidentiary element. Thomas Corbin was responsible for an automobile accident in which a person died. Corbin was ticketed at the scene for drunk driving and driving on the wrong side of the road. Shortly thereafter, Corbin pled guilty to those charges. The prosecution failed to inform the trial court that the accident had resulted in a fatality before the court accepted Corbin's plea and imposed sentence. Two months later, Corbin was indicted on several charges stemming from the accident including negligent homicide and third-degree reckless assault. Under the *Blockburger* test, the indictments covered charges that were not the same as those to which Corbin had earlier pled. The Supreme Court said that a subsequent prosecution must do more than "merely survive" *Blockburger* standards, however. The state had admitted in this case that it would attempt to establish the essential elements of the homicide and assault charges on the basis of Corbin's conduct that had led to the earlier convictions. The Court ruled that the state is precluded from establishing an "essential element" of a crime on the basis of the same conduct for which a defendant has been convicted. The Court made it clear this was not a "same evidence" test. Rather, the "critical inquiry is what conduct the State will prove, not the evidence the State will use to prove that conduct." Subsequent prosecutions for homicide and assault could have been pursued in this case if they did not rely on proving the conduct for which Corbin had already been convicted. The Court also pointed out that with "adequate preparation and foresight" on the part of the prosecution, the traffic offenses and the charges from the indictment could have been pursued in a single proceeding, thus "avoiding this double jeopardy question."

The double jeopardy clause does not extend to retrial of defendants who have been successful at the appellate level. If an appeals court finds error sufficient to require reversing the outcome, a case is always returned (remanded) to the jurisdiction from which it came for a decision on retrial.

The decision rests with the prosecutor, who possesses control on charging in any case. The principle that applies in this instance, which is called continuation, views the remanded case as still unfinished. Re-prosecution under the continuation principle is possible because an outcome free of procedural error is still being sought.

The retrial of defendants whose convictions are overturned on appeal has itself generated issues. One involves the concept of "implicit acquittal," an issue present in *Price v. Georgia* (398 U.S. 323: 1970). Implicit acquittal arises when a jury convicts on a lesser included charge. In essence, the jury acquits on the greater charge by convicting on the lesser charge. Earl Price was convicted of manslaughter although the state had charged him with murder. Manslaughter is a less serious form of life-taking than murder. Price appealed his conviction on jury instruction grounds and had the verdict set aside by a Georgia appellate court. Price was then retried, with the indictment again charging him with murder. He was again convicted of manslaughter, but appealed on double jeopardy grounds claiming impermissible jeopardy on the murder charge in the second trial. The Supreme Court agreed with Price. Chief Justice Warren Burger wrote for the majority that the "first verdict, limited as it was to the lesser included offense, required that the retrial be limited to that lesser offense." The chief justice emphasized that the double jeopardy protection "flows inescapably" from a concern about "risk of conviction," and Price was "twice put in jeopardy." Price's jeopardy on the murder charge "ended when the first jury 'was given full opportunity to return a verdict' on that charge and instead reached a verdict on a lesser charge." Burger concluded by suggesting that no effective difference exists between direct or explicit acquittal and one "implied by conviction on a lesser included offense when the jury was given full opportunity to return a verdict on the greater charge."

The exception to the retrial rule applies to cases in which a successful appeal determines that the conviction was based on legally deficient evidence. The "implicit acquittal" principle of *Price* applies at this point. It limits the charge on re-prosecution to no greater than the equivalent of the original conviction. Thus, if a jury opted to convict on a lesser included offense at the initial trial, the retrial is limited to a charge no more serious than the lesser included offense. *Price* sets the limitation on the scope of re-prosecution following a successful appeal.

On a related matter, the Court ruled in *Ohio v. Johnson* (467 U.S. 493: 1984) that the double jeopardy clause did not preclude prosecution for offenses not included in a guilty plea to other charges stemming from the same indictment. Kenneth Johnson was indicted for four offenses. Over the prosecution's objection, he pled guilty to two of the charges at his arraignment. The trial judge dismissed the two remaining charges on the ground that further prosecution would constitute double jeopardy. The Supreme Court reversed this decision, saying that dismissal of the remaining and more serious charges did more than prevent cumulative punishment; it precluded a verdict on the charges. Johnson had not been "exposed to conviction" on the charges to which he did not plead, and the state retained the option to marshal its evidence on these charges. Acceptance of the pleas to lesser offenses does not carry implicit acquittal consequences. The overreaching of government is not involved, so double jeopardy does not apply.

But a new trial is not always required. In *Morris v. Mathews* (475 U.S. 237: 1986), the Court held that modification of a double jeopardy–barred conviction to a lesser included offense that was not barred to double jeopardy was an adequate remedy. James Mathews and another person robbed a bank and fled to a farmhouse. Shots were fired inside the house and Mathews then surrendered. His companion was found dead. The death was ruled a suicide by the coroner, and Mathews was charged only with robbery. He pled guilty to that charge. Subsequently, Mathews admitted killing his companion, and the state indicted him for aggravated murder in connection with the robbery. He was convicted on the aggravated murder charge. An appeals court barred the aggravated murder conviction on double jeopardy grounds and modified the conviction to that of the lesser offense of murder. The Supreme Court said that under such circumstances the burden shifts to the defendant to demonstrate a reasonable probability that he would not have been convicted on the nonbarred offense "absent the presence of the jeopardy-barred offense."

The issue of double jeopardy and the sentencing process arose in *Bullington v. Missouri* (451 U.S. 430: 1981). Also involved in *Bullington* was the implicit acquittal concept discussed above. Robert Bullington had been sentenced to life imprisonment by a jury in the second stage of a bifurcated (two-stage) process in which the determination of guilt was separate from the sentence. Bullington was subsequently granted a new trial for certain procedural reasons. The prosecutor indicated the death penalty would be sought at the second trial. Bullington claimed that double jeopardy barred the death penalty following his conviction at the second trial because a jury had decided against it in the initial sentencing stage. A five-justice majority of the Supreme Court agreed with Bullington.

The majority acknowledged that attempts to extend the double jeopardy clause to sentencing had not previously been successful. The Court found the two-stage death penalty process sufficiently different from other sentencing situations, however. Given this two-stage process, the Court concluded that it was analogous to the guilt adjudication stage of other cases. The process gives sentencing the "hallmarks of the trial on guilt or innocence." Thus, if a jury acquits a defendant on a more extreme penalty option, it forecloses that sentence from being utilized in a retrial. The Court found the implicit acquittal principle to be applicable here just as if Bullington's jury had chosen to convict of a lesser included offense. *Price* confirmed that a person cannot be retried for a more serious charge following a successful appeal. In *North Carolina v. Pearce* (395 U.S. 711: 1969), the Court held that the double jeopardy protection did not prohibit a more severe sentence as such. As a safeguard against vindictive sentence increases, however, *Pearce* required that the more severe sentence be based on new information not available at the initial sentencing. *Bullington* went beyond *Pearce* in extending the double jeopardy coverage and the implicit acquittal principle where juries make sentencing judgments in a two-staged process. Despite *Bullington,* however, the Court has limited the extent to which the double jeopardy protection impinges on sentencing.

A final double jeopardy issue focuses on successive prosecutions by different governmental levels. These situations arise out of criminal conduct that simultaneously violates the law of separate political entities. Though overlap is not extensive, some does exist. The following cases all stem from the zones of overlap. These situations also involve the "sameness" question, but are handled under a principle known as the "dual sovereignty" doctrine. An early dual sovereignty decision came in *United States v. Lanza* (260 U.S. 377: 1922). During the period of prohibition, Vito Lanza was prosecuted and convicted for production and distribution of liquor at both the state and federal levels. The Court permitted the double prosecution, pointing out that "we have here two sovereignties, deriving power from different sources, capable of dealing with the same subject-matter within the same territory." Each sovereign may, said the Court, "without interference by the other, enact laws to secure prohibition" so long as such laws do not otherwise conflict with constitutional limitations. The Court concluded by saying that each governmental level, "in determining what shall be an offense against its peace and dignity, is exercising its own sovereignty, not that of the other."

By the same dual sovereignty rationale, the double jeopardy prohibition does not preclude simultaneous prosecutions in two or more states if the criminal act occurred in more than one state. A recent example is *Heath v. Alabama* (474 U.S. 82: 1985). Larry Heath had contracted for the murder of his wife. She was kidnapped from their Alabama home and killed, and her body was abandoned in Georgia. After pleading guilty to a murder charge in Georgia, Heath sought to bar his indictment on a similar charge in Alabama on the grounds that he had already been in jeopardy in Georgia for the crime. The Court permitted Alabama to prosecute, however. The Court said each state possesses its own "inherent sovereignty" preserved by the Tenth Amendment. Given their distinct sources of power to prosecute, the states are "no less sovereign with respect to each other than they are with respect to the Federal Government." The Court came to the far-reaching conclusion that to deny a state power to enforce its criminal laws because another state "won the race to the courthouse" would be a "shocking and untoward deprivation" of states' rights and the obligations of each to maintain peace and order within their respective boundaries.

The dual sovereignty principle does not apply, however, to state and local levels of government. Successive prosecutions at the state and local levels are not permitted because local units of government are simply subordinate levels of one large state government. In other words, separate sovereignty does not exist between the state and local levels. The operative case in this situation is *Waller v. Florida* (397 U.S. 387: 1970). Joseph Waller was convicted for destruction of city property, an ordinance violation. The state later tried him for theft of the property. The damage to the property had occurred while it was being illegally taken. Waller was convicted of grand larceny in the second proceeding, and he appealed on double jeopardy grounds. The Supreme Court reversed the second conviction and rejected the notion that separate sovereignty between a state and a municipality is analogous to the relationship between the states and the federal government. The Court argued that political subdivisions of states have never been "considered as sovereign entities." Instead, they have been viewed as "subordinate governmental instrumentalities created by the State to assist in carrying out state governmental functions." Though the Constitution permits dual prosecution of an individual for federal and state offenses stemming from the same act, Waller could not be so prosecuted by a municipal and a state government. As applied in that situation, the Court said the "dual sovereignty theory is an anachronism, and the second trial constituted double jeopardy."

Self-Incrimination

The Fifth Amendment provides that no person "shall be compelled in any criminal case to be a witness against himself." No defendant can be compelled to testify against himself or herself at trial. The clause covers testimony at the trial of an accused person or statements made prior to the trial, to law enforcement officials, for example, which may have the effect of implicating the person in a crime. The clause generally requires the prosecution to demonstrate guilt without involuntary assistance from the accused.

The clause was fully recognized in Great Britain by the early eighteenth century and was established in common law by the time the U.S. Constitution was written. As the Supreme Court said in *Murphy v. Waterfront Commission of New York Harbor* (378 U.S. 52: 1964), the clause reflects "many of our fundamental values and most noble aspirations." Those values and aspirations include "our unwillingness to subject those suspected of crime to the cruel trilemma of self-accusation, perjury or contempt." Although the privilege against self-incrimination extends only to criminal prosecutions and does not prevent compelled testimony that may damage a witness's reputation or create adverse economic or social consequences, such a privilege represents a society's preference for an accusatorial rather than an inquisitorial system of criminal justice. In the former, charges are brought by a prosecutor on behalf of the state in a system that is neutral and provides procedural protection for the accused. An inquisitorial system, on the other hand, is not neutral. Rather, it is a process aimed at building a case against the accused. In such a proceeding, even the judge is an active participant in representing the state's interest.

The Supreme Court resisted early attempts to make the self-incrimination clause applicable to the states through the Fourteenth Amendment. In *Twining v. New Jersey* (211 U.S. 78: 1908), the Court concluded that the privilege did not rank "among the fundamental and inalienable rights of mankind," but rather it constituted a "wise and beneficent rule of evidence." The Court said it may be a "just and useful principle of law," but it need not be required at the state level. *Twining* remained until reversed by the Warren Court in *Malloy v. Hogan* (378 U.S. 1: 1964). *Malloy* declared that the "*Twining* view of the privilege has been eroded" and that it was "incongruous" to have different standards dependent upon whether the right was asserted in a state or a federal court. The contemporary significance of the self-incrimination protection was underlined by the Warren Court's decision to extend the privilege to the state level. Decisions that followed *Malloy* extended the privilege to situations other than just the trial. Most important was the Court's decision to apply the protection to custodial interrogations. This decision came in *Miranda v. Arizona* (384 U.S. 436: 1966). *Miranda* required that all detained persons be advised of their constitutional rights prior to interrogation. The importance of *Miranda* is developed in some detail later in this chapter, but *Miranda* did not prohibit use of voluntary confessions. Neither did *Miranda* prohibit the use of improperly obtained statements to impeach a defendant's own trial testimony. The privilege against self-incrimination has also been limited exclusively to communicative or testimonial evidence. Accordingly, it prohibits comment on a defendant's refusal to testify, but the prohibition does not extend to such defendant-derived evidence as blood samples or to involuntary identification procedures such as lineups. The protection of the clause may also be satisfied by granting immunity to a witness, which protects that witness from having compelling testimony used in subsequent prosecution against him or her. We examine each of these aspects of self-incrimination in the following pages.

The privilege certainly means that the state cannot compel a witness to take the stand and disclose damaging information. A witness at the trial of another may invoke the privilege as each question is posed. A defendant's situation is somewhat different in that a defendant claims the privilege simply by not taking the stand at all. If he or she does take the stand, the privilege is regarded as waived with respect to questions about the charged offense. Historically, a number of states have allowed prosecutors to comment on the defendant's choice not to testify. The Court, however, formally ended this practice in *Griffin v. California* (380 U.S. 609: 1965). The Court specifically ruled in *Griffin* that neither judge nor prosecutor could suggest that guilt could be inferred from the accused's decision to not take the stand. An extension to the *Griffin* "no comment" rule was announced in *Carter v. Kentucky* (450 U.S. 288: 1981).

Lonnie Joe Carter requested a specific jury instruction indicating that he was not obligated to testify and that his failure to testify should not prejudice the jury in any way. The trial judge refused the request, and Carter was convicted. The Supreme Court reversed the conviction with only Justice William Rehnquist dissenting. The majority found that the Fifth Amendment does more than simply preclude adverse comment on the defendant's silence. The "defendant must pay no court-imposed price for the exercise of his constitutional privilege not to testify." And that penalty "may be just as severe when there is no adverse comment" and the jury "is left to roam at large with only its untutored instincts to guide it." A defendant is entitled to request special mention of his choice not to testify so as to "remove from the jury's deliberations any influence of unspoken adverse inferences." The Court noted the impact of the jury instruction and concluded that a trial judge "has an affirmative constitutional obligation to use that tool when a defendant seeks its employment." Although those instructions may not prevent jurors from speculating about a defendant's silence, the "unique power of the jury instruction . . . [can] reduce that speculation to a minimum."

Immunity

Immunity is a strategic response by the government to the self-incrimination protection. Immunity prevents a person from involuntarily becoming a witness against himself or herself. The government cannot compel a person to disclose incriminating evidence, but when a witness is granted immunity, he or she cannot be prosecuted based on the compelled testimony. Immunity was first considered by the Supreme Court in the late nineteenth century. In *Counselman v. Hitchcock* (142 U.S. 547: 1892), the Court held that the federal immunity statute was defective in that it left a witness vulnerable to prosecution based on evidence derived from compelled testimony. Four years later, in *Brown v. Walker* (161 U.S. 591: 1896), the Court was asked to determine whether or not immunity could shield a witness beyond the prevention of actual prosecution. The Court decided that disgrace or impairment of reputation, which are possible consequences of involuntary testimony, were outside the coverage of the self-incrimination privilege; therefore, they need not be addressed when granting immunity.

The matter of personal disgrace arose again in the mid-twentieth century during investigations conducted into political subversion and national security. In *Ullmann v. United States* (350 U.S. 422: 1956), the Court upheld provisions of the Immunity Act of 1954 that authorized immunity for testimony in national security cases. *Ullmann* and *Brown* both held that self-incrimination only protects from danger of prosecution, not from the danger of disgrace and the costs stemming from it. Immunity is typically used to obtain evidence from one person leading to the conviction of another. It allows information to develop that is not readily available through other investigative techniques. Because the technique is regularly used, a critical question involves the scope of immunity: how extensive it must be. Certainly, immunity must extend to direct use of the testimony itself, which is known as use immunity, but full immunity must cover more.

Counselman held that a witness must be protected from prosecution based on evidence derived from compelled testimony. This level of immunity is called derived use. Even derived use immunity is limited, however. It does not prevent prosecution of a witness for a crime about which he or she may have involuntarily testified as long as the evidence used in the prosecution was developed wholly apart from the witness's testimony. Transactional immunity is the most inclusive form of immunity. It prevents prosecution for any matter or transaction about which the witness testifies.

In *Kastigar v. United States* (406 U.S. 441: 1972), the Court examined the extent of immunity from prosecution required to satisfy self-incrimination requirements. Charles Kastigar was subpoenaed to testify before a federal grand jury. He was granted derived use immunity, which prohibits direct use of the compelled testimony or any information derived from that testimony. Kastigar argued that the derived use immunity granted was not coextensive with his jeopardy and refused to testify. He was then found to be in civil contempt and jailed. The Court upheld the contempt. Kastigar argued that only transactional immunity would satisfy the protections of the Fifth Amendment. The Court disagreed and found derived use immunity to be "coextensive with the scope of the privilege against self-incrimination." The immunity "need not be broader" than the protection "afforded by the privilege." In the Court's view, the "privilege has never been construed to mean that one who invokes it cannot subsequently be prosecuted." If a subsequent prosecution does occur, the prosecution has the "affirmative duty to prove that the evidence it proposes to use is derived from a legitimate source wholly independent of the compelled testimony." The Court felt this protection was "substantial" and "commensurate with that resulting from invoking the privilege itself."

Kastigar focused on the critical immunity issue of coextensiveness. The immunity granted a witness in exchange for testimony must cover, or be coextensive with, the vulnerability created by compelling the witness to testify. Prior to 1970, witnesses who were compelled to testify were granted transactional immunity. Such immunity insulates a witness from prosecution for any transaction about which the witness is required to testify regardless of how serious a crime is involved or how tangential the crime is to the primary issue under investigation. In 1970 Congress passed the Organized Crime Control Act, which authorized the more limited derived use immunity. This immunity extends only to the testimony itself and any information derived from that testimony. Derived use immunity still allows the witness to be prosecuted subsequent to testifying as long as all the evidence used against him or her is wholly independent of the compelled testimony. The real significance of *Kastigar* is that it established a less rigorous standard of coextensiveness than had existed before. Rather than absolute immunity being required, the *Kastigar* ruling established that derived use or limited immunity sufficiently meets the demands of self-incrimination. Though the testimony itself cannot be used directly or indirectly, compelled testimony may prompt investigation because it makes authorities aware of a witness's guilt. Immunity policy requires consideration of the balance between self-incrimination interests and the interest of public security served by gaining information about criminal activities. *Kastigar* shifts the balance point in favor of public security interests.

Identification Procedures

Police use various methods to assist a witness in recognizing and identifying a suspect. Identification procedures usually involve direct confrontation in a lineup or, if a lineup is not feasible, in a showup, in which typically the suspect is brought into the same room with the witness, who is anticipating the one-on-one confrontation. Identification may also be made from photographs. Such procedures have raised self-incrimination issues that have been reviewed by the Court. Generally these procedures are permissible, as long as they are not unnecessarily suggestive or likely to prompt mistaken identification. There are no specific criteria that must be met in each identification situation. Rather, when the Court reviews identification procedures, it considers the totality of circumstances and, primarily, the reliability of the identification. Reliability rests upon the witness's opportunity to observe the suspect at the time of the offense, the witness's attentiveness at that time, the accuracy of the witness's description of the suspect, and the witness's level of certainty at the time of confrontation with the suspect. Without sufficient reliability, identification testimony may not be used.

Two leading cases serve to illustrate, one based on a victim confrontation and the other involving identification by photograph. Direct confrontation by a witness is frequently used to identify persons suspected of criminal acts. *Neil v. Biggers* (409 U.S. 188: 1972) examined the confrontation process and addressed the principal considerations. Archie Biggers was convicted of rape. The most significant piece of evidence against him was the testimony of the rape victim, who was asked to identify Biggers when two police officers walked him past her. This confrontation, or showup, occurred seven months after the crime. A showup, rather than a lineup, was used for identification purposes because the police could not assemble a sufficient number of other persons resembling Biggers.

The Supreme Court ruled that the showup was adequate and upheld Biggers's conviction. The Court said that in these situations, a defendant must demonstrate that the identification process was "so unnecessarily suggestive and conducive to irreparable mistaken identification" as to deny due process. The primary evil to be prevented is a "very substantial likelihood" of a mistaken identification. A confrontation may be suggestive, but not so suggestive as to make a mistake likely. The showup was suggestive because Biggers was the only person placed before the victim, but it was not judged as overly suggestive because other factors supported the reliability of the victim's identification. The Court noted several criteria that must be used in evaluating the reliability of the identification, including (1) the witness's opportunity to "view the criminal at the time of the crime," (2) the witness's "degree of attention," (3) the accuracy of the witness's "prior description" of the subject, and (4) the "level of certainty demonstrated by the witness" at the confrontation. On the basis of these factors, the Court concluded that even though the showup had been suggestive, the victim's identification had been reliable enough.

Neil v. Biggers provides generally applicable standards by which the reliability of identifications can be assessed. The Supreme Court has never held that requiring a person to be viewed by a witness violates due process rights. It has circumscribed identification processes through such cases as *Biggers,* but the *Biggers* criteria do not always come into play. For example, the confrontation itself may be more than merely unnecessarily suggestive; it may be excessively suggestive. In *Foster v. California* (394 U.S. 440: 1969), the Court reviewed a lineup that contained only one person dressed in the manner described by a witness, only one person approximating the physical description provided by the witness, and only one person appearing in a second lineup who had appeared in an earlier lineup. A confrontation such as this makes positive "identifications virtually inevitable." This kind of confrontation is categorically prohibited. If the confrontation is not judged to be overly suggestive, the reliability of the identification is evaluated further using the *Biggers* criteria. The Court has also determined that confrontations that occur after indictment are a sufficiently critical stage in the criminal process that a suspect is entitled to assistance of counsel at that point.

Manson v. Brathwaite (432 U.S. 98: 1977) involved a photographic identification also challenged as excessively suggestive as well as unnecessary. An undercover police officer purchased heroin from a person in a lighted apartment hallway. The transaction took several minutes, during which time the officer was in close physical proximity to the seller. After the transaction, the officer described the seller to another officer. Based on the physical description, the second officer concluded the seller was Nowell Brathwaite and gave a single photograph of Brathwaite to the first officer. The first officer examined the photograph and positively identified Brathwaite as the seller. The photograph and the officer's identification were received as evidence at Brathwaite's trial. Brathwaite was convicted, and the Supreme Court upheld the conviction.

The crucial question for the Court was whether the reliability of the identification outweighed the procedural problems with it. The procedures used in this case were both suggestive and unnecessary. Only one photograph had been supplied to the undercover officer, and no exigent circumstances were present that required immediate identification. Thus, there were two policy options before the Burger Court in this case. The first was to adopt a firm rule precluding the use of evidence stemming from suggestive or unnecessary identification procedures with no consideration of the reliability of the identification. The other was to evaluate the reliability of each identification based on the "totality of the circumstances." The Court chose the latter course. The Court concluded that while an absolute prohibition might best deter police misconduct, such a rule "goes too far since its application automatically and peremptorily, and without consideration of alleviating factors, keeps evidence from the jury that is reliable and relevant." The Court said, "reliability is the linchpin in determining the admissibility of identification testimony." Because the officer had sufficient time to observe the seller, was attentive, could accurately describe him, was certain of the identification, and had made the identification soon after the heroin sale, his testimony identifying Brathwaite was deemed reliable.

The *Brathwaite* ruling determined that the Supreme Court would not adopt a per se rule of exclusion for needlessly suggestive and unnecessary photographic identification. Given the Burger Court's disenchantment with the exclusionary rule generally, it was hardly unexpected that the Court chose not to impose the rule in *Brathwaite*. The Burger Court chose instead to base admissibility of identifications on their reliability and called reliability the "linchpin" of such testimony. The reliability focus brings into play the criteria discussed in *Neil v. Biggers* for evaluating confrontation identifications. In addition, *Brathwaite* holds that the suggestiveness of photographic identifications may be tempered by an inability to gather photographs of other persons. The Court recognized that an exigency may exist that requires a witness to examine only one photograph of a suspect, although the Court found that no such exigency existed in *Brathwaite*. Typically witnesses examine spreads of many photographs, as when "mugbooks" are used, and identifications that occur in this way are usually not suggestive. The *Brathwaite* holding provides greater latitude in photographic identification techniques in that it allows identifications deemed reliable to carry decisive weight against allegations of suggestive or unnecessary procedures.

Blood and Other Specimen Samples

There have long existed self-incrimination questions associated with evidence not in the form of words or testimony derived from an accused. The blood test to determine the presence of alcohol or other substances certainly occurs with great frequency. An instructive case on blood samples is *Schmerber v. California* (384 U.S. 757: 1966). The basic question in *Schmerber* was whether the self-incrimination protection covered defendant-derived evidence of a nontestimonial kind. *Schmerber* involved a conviction for driving while intoxicated. The principal evidence against Armande Schmerber came in the form of blood test results. The blood sample upon which the tests were performed was taken despite Schmerber's protest, and Schmerber subsequently challenged the conviction on a variety of grounds including self-incrimination. The Court was persuaded by none of his contentions, however. The justices held that taking the blood sample "constituted compulsion" for self-incrimination purposes, but also concluded that Schmerber had not really been made a "witness against himself." The Court ruled that the scope of the protection applied only to compelling evidence against the accused "from his own mouth," which means the evidence must be testimonial: the words or communications of the accused. The Court likened the blood sample to fingerprints and other means of identification and said that making the suspect provide "real or physical evidence does not violate" the privilege against self-incrimination. The Court found that in Schmerber's case, "not even a shadow of testimonial compulsion upon or enforced communication by the accused was involved either in extraction or in chemical analysis." Schmerber's "testimonial capacities were in no way implicated." In the Court's view, Schmerber himself, "except as a donor, is irrelevant to the results of the test."

Schmerber is the definitive ruling on blood samples. It simply held that blood samples, because they are not testimonial in character, are not covered by the privilege against self-incrimination. As long as the sample is not taken in a manner that "shocks the conscience," analysis conducted on the sample is admissible evidence. Seizure of evidence in a "shocking" manner is prohibited by the due process clause and may constitute an unreasonable seizure in violation of the Fourth Amendment. The Court also permitted states to admit into evidence a person's refusal to submit to a blood-alcohol test. In *South Dakota v. Neville* (459 U.S. 553: 1983), the Court held that since the offer of taking the test is "clearly legitimate," the action becomes "no less legitimate when the State offers a second option of refusing the test, with attendant penalties for making that choice."

Use of test results based on urine, skin, and other samples obtained from a suspect's body are also covered under the *Schmerber* decision. This includes bullets. In *Winston v. Lee* (470 U.S. 753: 1984), a suspect was compelled to have a bullet removed from his body. The Court found this to be an unreasonable search, however, because it could not be justified against the risk created by having to administer a general anesthetic to perform the surgery. Extending *Schmerber,* the Court held that samples of a person's handwriting or voice may be used for identification purposes. In *Gilbert v. California* (388 U.S. 263: 1967), the Court said that although one's voice and handwriting are a means of communication, a sample of handwriting or a voice exemplar, independent of the content of what is written or said, is an "identifying physical characteristic" outside the protection of the self-incrimination privilege. Warren Court decisions such as *Schmerber* and *Gilbert* clearly distinguish protected testimonial incrimination from unprotected nontestimonial evidence. The Burger and Rehnquist Courts have maintained that distinction.

Custodial Interrogation

Confessions obtained from suspects under physical or psychological duress have always been regarded as contrary to any concept of due process. Indeed, long before the Supreme Court extended self-incrimination protections to the state level, federal courts and to some extent state courts were prohibited from using any confession obtained by coercion. There are two fundamental problems with confessions extorted from persons held in police custody. First, the state should not be allowed to resort to force and violence when information is being sought from someone already detained. It is simply inhumane. Second, disclosures made under compulsion may have absolutely no value. If a person is subjected to sufficiently coercive techniques of interrogation, he or she may admit to anything the police want to hear. In other words, involuntary disclosures are likely to be unreliable.

Early rulings on coercive incidents at the state level came in such cases as *Brown v. Mississippi* (297 U.S. 278: 1936) and *Chambers v. Florida* (309 U.S. 227: 1940). In both cases, suspects were subjected to physical brutality and lengthy interrogation. In *Brown,* the Court said the states were generally free to do as they wished in the administration of criminal justice unless in doing so they offended "some principle of justice so rooted in the traditions and conscience of our people as to be ranked as fundamental." At that time, states were not required to provide jury trials on demand. The Court said that because a state may dispense with a jury trial, however, "it does not follow that it may substitute trial by ordeal." The "rack and torture chamber," the Court went on, "may not be substituted for the witness stand." The Court characterized the methods by which confessions were obtained in *Brown* as "revolting" and clearly amounting to a denial of due process. The message from cases such as these was clear: Coercion makes anything said by an accused inherently suspect, and any statements not freely and voluntarily given would be excluded.

The Court then built upon the free and voluntary requirement with rules focusing on prompt appearance before a judicial officer. Even in situations where claims of physical brutality did not arise, police would often question suspects for lengthy periods before a first court appearance. Delay of this kind was considered by the Court in *McNabb v. United States* (318 U.S. 332: 1943). The *McNabb* case involved "unremitting" questioning over a period of several days. Eventually, the suspects disclosed incriminating information. At no point were the suspects taken before a judicial officer as required by federal law. In addition, the McNabbs "had to submit to all this without the aid of friends or the benefit of counsel." The Supreme Court reversed their convictions, saying that a conviction based on evidence "secured through such a flagrant disregard" of procedure cannot be permitted "without making courts themselves accomplices in willful disobedience of the law." The rule of *McNabb* is that suspects must be arraigned "without unnecessary delay." The arraignment must not only deal with such matters as bail, but also advise the suspect of his or her rights with respect to custodial interrogation.

The Court reiterated this principle in *Mallory v. United States* (354 U.S. 449: 1957). The *Mallory* case involved the crime of rape, and delay from arrest to arraignment was approximately 20 hours. During the delay, Andrew Mallory confessed to the crime. The Supreme Court reversed the conviction and said it could not sanction this "extended delay" that produced a confession "without subordinating the general rule of prompt arraignment to the discretion of arresting officers in finding exceptional circumstances for its disregard." The Court concluded that the function of police is to arrest and not to "use an interrogation process at police headquarters in order to determine whom they should charge before a committing magistrate on 'probable cause.' "

Escobedo and *Miranda*

The Warren Court comprehensively reexamined criminal rights in the 1960s. One of the consequences of this review was the linking of several constitutional protections. The foremost example is the union of the right to assistance of counsel and the privilege to avoid self-incrimination. The principal decision on this subject is *Miranda v. Arizona* (384 U.S. 436: 1966), but there are many key supporting decisions as well. For instance, *Miranda* was preceded by another significant case, *Escobedo v. Illinois* (378 U.S. 478: 1964). Ernesto Escobedo was arrested for murder and taken to police headquarters for questioning. He was not allowed to consult with his attorney, and despite persistent efforts, Escobedo's counsel was not allowed to see him. Escobedo eventually made a statement that was used at his trial. The Supreme Court reversed his conviction, utilizing the "critical stage" rationale from several assistance-of-counsel cases of the period. The Court said that Escobedo had "become the accused," and the purpose of the police interrogation was to "get him to confess despite his constitutional right not to do so." Illinois argued that if counsel is afforded to defendants prior to indictment, the number of confessions will "diminish significantly." The fact that many confessions are obtained during this period, said the Court in response, "points up its critical nature as a stage when legal aid and advice are surely needed." The right to counsel "would indeed be hollow if it began at a period when few confessions are obtained."

Escobedo left a number of questions unanswered. Though Escobedo had sought to consult with his privately retained counsel, what of the suspect who did not specifically request counsel and did not have an attorney already? Further, there was the matter of the interrogation environment. The Warren Court believed it to be closed and inherently coercive. *Miranda* provided a response and also allowed the Warren Court to further develop other underlying themes from *Escobedo*. Chief Justice Earl Warren said, "Even without employing brutality . . . the very fact of custodial interrogation exacts a heavy toll on individual liberty and trades on the weaknesses of individuals." He added, "It is obvious that such an interrogation environment is created for no other purpose than to subjugate the individual to the will of the examiner. This atmosphere carries it own badge of intimidation."

The Court specified four rights that the accused must be made aware of at the time of arrest, prior to the beginning of interrogation. The *"Miranda* rules" require that an arrested person be told that (1) he or she may remain silent, (2) anything the accused says can be used against him or her in court, (3) he or she has a right to consult with an attorney prior to questioning and that failure to request counsel does not constitute a waiver of the right, and (4) counsel will be provided to the accused in the event that he or she cannot afford counsel. *Miranda* held that any statements made by a suspect before he or she has been advised of these rights are inadmissible in a trial.

The *Miranda* decision intensified criticism of the Warren Court's approach to defining the rights of the accused. The Court's detractors felt that *Miranda* made confessions virtually impossible to obtain and thus handcuffed law enforcement authorities. Many felt the Court had preempted legislative prerogatives in setting law enforcement standards as well. The negative feeling about *Miranda* was manifest in the Omnibus Crime Control Act of 1968. Provisions of this legislation softened some of the *Miranda* requirements, at least at the federal level. Federal judges, for example, were given greater latitude in determining the voluntariness of incriminating statements. It was essentially left to the Burger Court to determine how *Miranda* would affect state trials.

The Warren Court had attempted to define when a custodial interrogation begins in *Escobedo*. When the process "shifts from investigatory to accusatory—when its focus is on the accused and its purpose is to elicit a confession—our adversary system begins to operate, and the accused must be permitted to consult with his lawyer." This definition was reiterated in *Rhode Island v. Innis* (446 U.S. 291: 1980). Thomas Innis was arrested for his alleged involvement in the robbery of a cab driver. The robbery had been committed with the aid of a sawed-off shotgun. At the time of his arrest, Innis was not armed. He was fully advised of his rights under *Miranda*. While Innis was being transported to the police station, two officers discussed the yet unfound shotgun. Because Innis had been arrested near a school for handicapped children, one officer remarked that he hoped none of the children would find the gun and get hurt. Innis interrupted their conversation and indicated he would show them the location of the gun. They returned Innis to the scene and re-advised him of his rights, after which Innis disclosed the weapon's location. Innis tried to suppress the gun and his statements regarding its location at the trial. He essentially argued that he had been improperly interrogated without adequate waiver of his *Miranda* rights. The Court ruled that Innis had not been "interrogated." The conversation Innis overheard was not questioning. An interrogation, said the Court, occurs only when police know they are "reasonably likely to elicit an incriminating response from the suspect."

This issue was more recently considered in *Arizona v. Mauro* (481 U.S. 520: 1987). William Mauro was arrested for allegedly killing his son and advised of his rights. He indicated he did not wish to make any statement in the absence of his lawyer, at which point all questioning stopped. Mauro's wife, who had herself been questioned in another room, insisted on seeing her husband. A meeting was allowed in the captain's office on the condition that an officer remain in the room. The police used a plainly visible device to record Mauro's entire conversation with his wife. During the conversation, Mauro instructed his wife to answer no further questions in the absence of counsel. At the trial, the prosecutor used this recording to challenge Mauro's insanity defense, arguing that the instruction regarding counsel demonstrated Mauro's full understanding of the situation. The question in this case was whether the police actions in permitting and monitoring the meeting between Mauro and his wife constituted an interrogation or its functional equivalent. The Court ruled that they did not.

Interrogation includes any practice "reasonably likely to elicit an incriminating response." The purpose of the *Miranda* requirements is to prevent the government from capitalizing on the coercive nature of confinement to extract incriminating statements. Mauro was not subjected to compelling influences, psychological ploys, direct questioning, or any other practice of interrogation. The police had not initiated the meeting. Given various safety and security considerations, the Court considered the officer's presence at the meeting between Mauro and his wife to be legitimate. The Court also examined the situation from Mauro's perspective and concluded that it was unlikely he felt coerced to incriminate himself simply because he was allowed to speak with his wife. While the police might have been aware of the possibility that Mauro would say something incriminating during the meeting, an interrogation does not occur simply because the police may hope a suspect will confess.

Burger Court Modifications of *Miranda*

It was the Burger Court that dealt with the consequences of *Miranda*. A variety of questions developed, but most particularly around the issues of compliance and waiver. The first modification came in *Harris v. New York* (401 U.S. 222: 1971), which considered whether statements made by a defendant in violation of *Miranda* could be used to impeach that defendant's own testimony at his trial. *Miranda* established that defendants must be informed of their right against self-incrimination and their right to assistance of counsel. While Viven Harris was testifying at his own trial, he was asked during cross-examination whether he had made any statements immediately following his arrest. When he claimed he could not recall making any statements, the statements Harris had in fact made were introduced into evidence for the purpose of impeaching his credibility. The jury instruction attempted to differentiate between use of statements for impeachment purposes and their use as evidence of guilt. The jury was instructed it could not use the statements as the latter. Harris was subsequently convicted, and the Supreme Court rejected his appeal in a five to four decision.

The majority said that *Miranda* does not absolutely prohibit the use of statements taken without proper advisement of rights. The case does bar the prosecution from "making its case" with statements taken in violation of *Miranda*. But "it does not follow from *Miranda* that evidence inadmissible against an accused in the prosecutor's case in chief is barred for all purposes." Use of such evidence, however, must satisfy conditions of trustworthiness. Crucial to the outcome in *Harris* is the use of statements made in an adversary process, specifically impeachment of a witness during cross-examination. The "impeachment process here undoubtedly provided valuable aid to the jury in assessing petitioner's credibility." The majority of the Court felt that the information was of more value than guarding against the "speculative possibility" that police misconduct would be encouraged. The Court emphasized the need to maintain the integrity of the trial itself. A defendant can testify in his own defense, but does not have the "right to commit perjury." Once the defendant takes the witness stand, the prosecution can "utilize the traditional truth-testing devices of the adversary process." Chief Justice Burger concluded the opinion by saying, "The shield provided by *Miranda* cannot be perverted into a license to use the perjury by way of a defense, free from risk of confrontation with prior inconsistent utterances."

The Court ruled in *Michigan v. Harvey* (108 L. Ed. 2d 293: 1990) that although similar statements were properly suppressed from the prosecution case, the statements could be used to impeach the accused's testimony. The Court's reasoning was virtually identical to that found in *Harris*. The prosecution, said the Court, "must not be allowed to build its case . . . with evidence acquired in contravention of constitutional guarantees." Using such statements for impeachment purposes, however, "is a different matter." The Court said it has "consistently rejected" arguments that would allow an accused to turn the illegal method by which government evidence was obtained "to his own advantage, and provide himself with a shield against contradiction of his untruths." The Court held that the same rules apply in these Fifth and Sixth Amendment situations: The statements are inadmissible in the prosecutor's case-in-chief in both instances. At the same time, impeachment of a defendant's conflicting testimony should be allowed. Though a defendant may "sometimes later regret" the decision to make a statement, the Sixth Amendment "does not disable a criminal defendant from exercising his free will." The cases establishing "prophylactic rules that render some otherwise valid waivers of constitutional rights invalid" when they are the product of police-initiated interrogation should not be "perverted into a license to use perjury by way of a defense, free from the risk of confrontation with prior inconsistent utterances."

The question in *James v. Illinois* (107 L. Ed. 2d 676: 1990) was whether this principle extended to the impeachment of any other defense witness. Darryl James was arrested as he sat under a hair dryer at his mother's beauty salon on a charge of involvement in a shooting. James indicated at the time of arrest that he was attempting to change his appearance. He also described the color and style of his hair prior to alteration. His statements were subsequently suppressed as the product of an improper arrest. At James's murder trial, several witnesses identified him. Each witness described the style and color of James's hair at the time of the shooting, and these descriptions corresponded to James's own representation in the suppressed statement. James did not testify on his own behalf, but called a witness whose testimony differed as to James's hairstyle. The witness testified that James's hair before the shooting was the same as it appeared when James emerged from the hair dryer. After it was determined that James's statements about his hair had been obtained voluntarily, the prosecution was allowed to enter the statement to impeach the credibility of the defense witness.

The Supreme Court ruled that James's statements could not be used to impeach the defense witness. Justice William Brennan began for the majority by reiterating the reason for the defendant-impeachment exception to the exclusionary rule—furthering the "truth-seeking function" of the criminal trial. Expanding the exception to all defense witnesses, on the other hand, creates "different incentives affecting the behavior of both defendants and law enforcement officers." The defendant exception discourages perjured testimony because the defendant does not want to have the otherwise inadmissible statements used. The threat of a perjury prosecution creates a sufficient deterrent for the witness who is not also the defendant. The exception adds little to the likelihood of obtaining truthful testimony from other witnesses. More important, said the Court, the exception would have a "chilling effect" on the calling of certain defense witnesses. Defense could "reasonably fear" that a "hostile" or even "friendly" but inattentive defense witness would make some statement "in sufficient tension" with tainted evidence to allow introduction of that evidence for impeachment purposes. The defendant exception was intended to keep defendants from being able to "pervert" the exclusion of illegally obtained evidence as a "shield for perjury." In the Court's view, it is no more appropriate for the state to "brandish" illegally obtained evidence as a "sword with which to dissuade defendants from presenting a meaningful defense through other witnesses." The Court also feared that expansion of the impeachment exception would "significantly weaken the exclusionary rule's deterrent effect on police misconduct." The rule's deterrent effect works, notwithstanding the defendant exception, because police believe it "unlikely" that a defendant will open the door to the use of illegal evidence for impeachment purposes. Extending the exception to all witnesses, on the other hand, "vastly" increases the number of occasions during which illegal evidence could be used. Further, illegally obtained evidence would have even greater value to the prosecution because of the chilling effect. Prosecutorial access to impeachment evidence would more than deter perjury. It would also "deter defendants from calling witnesses in the first place." This encourages police misconduct because law enforcement officials "would recognize that obtaining evidence through illegal means stacks the deck heavily in the prosecutor's favor."

Harris modified the impact of *Miranda,* at least when the defendant seeks to testify. In *Harris,* the Court allowed statements and confessions defective under *Miranda* to be utilized to impeach a defendant. Though *Harris* did not permit the prosecution to use defective statements in making their primary case against the accused, the decision reflects the Burger Court's reluctance to fully embrace the *Miranda* holding. *Harris* also represents the Burger

Court's general unwillingness to disturb the dynamics of the adversary process. The basic thrust of *Harris* is that a jury ought to be given every opportunity to assess a defendant and the defense being advanced. The *Harris* rule does not apply, however, if statements are obtained involuntarily. In *Mincey v. Arizona* (437 U.S. 385: 1978), the Court ruled that interrogation of a defendant hospitalized in critical condition produced involuntary and untrustworthy responses that could not even be used for impeachment purposes. The Court also held that the fact of electing to remain silent after being read one's rights cannot be used to impeach a defendant. In *Doyle v. Ohio* (426 U.S. 610: 1976), two defendants offered explanations in their defense at their trial, explanations not previously shared with police or prosecutors. They were cross-examined about why they had withheld their stories until the trial. A six-justice majority concluded that "silence in the wake of these [*Miranda*] warnings may be nothing more than the arrestee's exercise of these *Miranda* rights." Similarly, the Court ruled in *Wainwright v. Greenfield* (474 U.S. 284: 1986) that the suspect's silence after he was advised of his rights could not be used as evidence to counter his insanity defense. A unanimous Court said the source of unfairness in this instance is the assurance contained in the *Miranda* warnings that silence will carry no penalty. It is fundamentally unfair to promise a person that silence will not be used against him and then breach that promise by using silence to overcome a defendant's plea of insanity.

In *Oregon v. Elstad* (470 U.S. 298: 1985), on the other hand, the Court held that a voluntary admission coming prior to *Miranda* warnings does not necessarily require suppression of a confession coming later. At the time of his arrest, Michael Elstad incriminated himself before he was advised of his rights. He made the statement voluntarily, in the presence of his mother, and in an environment that could be characterized as noncoercive. He was subsequently taken to the sheriff's office and advised of his rights. Elstad waived his rights and confessed again. While the initial statements were unquestionably inadmissible, Elstad later argued that his sheriff's office confession was tainted by the statements he made prior to being advised of his rights. The Supreme Court disagreed, saying that as long as the initial statements were voluntary, the later confession need not be suppressed. A defendant who responds to "unwarned yet uncoercive questioning is not disabled from waiving his warnings." In circumstances such as these, "thorough administration of *Miranda* warnings serves to cure the condition that rendered the unwarned statement inadmissible."

In like manner, silence occurring previous to receiving *Miranda* warnings can be used for impeachment purposes on the grounds that the silence was not "induced by the assurances contained in the *Miranda* warnings." *Harris* stemmed from a case in which *Miranda* had not been complied with at all. What course is appropriate for situations in which a suspect's rights are only partially conveyed? The controlling decision in this area is *Michigan v. Tucker* (417 U.S. 433: 1974). Thomas Tucker was questioned before *Miranda*, but his trial occurred after *Miranda* had been published. Tucker was advised that statements he made could be used against him but was not thoroughly advised about his right to access an attorney. In particular he was not told that counsel could be furnished him despite his indigent status. There was no way of knowing whether the defendant understood his right to an attorney. What is clear is that he was not told he could have a lawyer without cost. During the ensuing interrogation, Tucker named an alibi witness. The actual statements of the witness turned out to discredit Tucker's alibi, and Tucker was convicted. Thus, without assistance of counsel, Tucker provided the decisive evidence against himself through his own alibi witness. With only Justice William Douglas dissenting, the Court upheld Tucker's conviction.

The Court said *Miranda* precluded admission at trial of the statements made by Tucker during his interrogation. This did not cover, however, the naming of a third party, which was done voluntarily. The protection from self-incrimination is aimed at certain kinds of practices, none of which were involved in the naming of the alibi witness. The Court did find that *Miranda* was "disregarded" to the extent that the full warnings were not executed. In retrospect *Miranda* clearly applied, but the disregard was "inadvertent." More important, so long as "the police did not abridge respondent's constitutional privilege against self-incrimination, but departed only from the prophylactic standards set by this Court in *Miranda*," testimony from the witness named by the defendant could be used. The Court felt that use of the exclusionary rule in cases in which police actions were "pursued in complete good faith" did not serve to deter police misconduct. The Court emphasized the flexible character of *Miranda*. Failure to give full *Miranda* warnings "does not entitle the suspect to insist that statements made by him be excluded in every conceivable context." *Miranda* protections must be evaluated from a broader perspective. Justice Rehnquist remarked, "Just as the law does not require that a defendant receive a perfect trial, just a fair one, it cannot realistically require that police investigating serious crimes make no errors whatsoever." Furthermore, the information provided by the witness was reliable and subject to the "testing process" of an adversary trial. There was "no reason to believe that Henderson's [the witness's] testimony is untrustworthy simply because respondent [Tucker] was not advised of his right to appointed counsel."

Tucker determined that incomplete administration of *Miranda* warnings did not necessarily invalidate use of statements secured subsequent to the incomplete warnings. Whether or not the derived evidence could be used would depend on the reliability of the evidence itself. Generally, evidence culled from statements or confessions that are improperly obtained cannot be used. Such evidence is usually, but not necessarily, contaminated by the tainted confession. *Tucker* reiterated the Burger Court's strong predisposition for exposing the trial process to the fullest range of reliable evidence, even if the evidence was derived from a flawed and inadmissible confession. Since Tucker disclosed the witness voluntarily, and the witness's subsequent testimony was viewed as trustworthy, failure to fully advise Tucker of his *Miranda* protections was a subordinate interest.

The second major question stemming from *Miranda* involved waiver of its protections. Given the combination of self-incrimination and assistance of counsel interests at stake, waiver was not an option the Court wanted to have happen easily. An example of this can be readily seen in the Court's controversial decision in *Brewer v. Williams* (430 U.S. 387: 1977). Robert Williams was arrested, arraigned, and jailed in Davenport, Iowa, for abducting and murdering a young child in the city of Des Moines, Iowa. Williams consulted with attorneys in both cities and was advised to make no statements to the police. As Williams was being transported from Davenport to Des Moines, he indicated unwillingness to be interrogated until his attorney was present but said he would make a full statement at that time. Nonetheless, one of the officers, aware that Williams was a former mental patient and deeply religious, sought to elicit statements from Williams relative to the location of the child's body. The officer suggested to Williams that the parents were entitled to a "Christian burial" for their child. Williams eventually made a number of incriminating statements and directed the police to the location of the child's body; Williams was subsequently tried and convicted. Evidence relating to statements made during his transportation from Davenport to Des Moines were admitted at trial over his objections. The Supreme Court held in a five to four decision that the evidence was inadmissible and reversed the conviction.

The decision hinged on whether Williams had knowingly and intelligently waived his right to counsel. There was no dispute that the police officer had deliberately attempted to elicit information from Williams and that the "Christian burial speech" was "tantamount to interrogation." The majority concluded that the right to counsel had not been properly waived and said that waiver required "not merely comprehension but relinquishment." Evidence of Williams's unwillingness to waive his right to counsel could be seen in his heavy reliance on advice of counsel throughout, his consultation with attorneys at both ends of his trip, and his declaration that he would make a statement *after* completing the trip and again consulting with his attorney. The officer elicited incriminating statements "despite Williams' express and implicit assertions of his right to counsel." Regardless of the "senseless and brutal" character of the offense, what had occurred was "so clear a violation" of Williams's constitutional protection that it "cannot be condoned."

Williams highlights the relationship between assistance of counsel and the protection from compelled self-incrimination. The Court established in *Miranda* that preserving the privilege against self-incrimination is best accomplished by providing an accused with access to defense counsel. *Williams* conveyed that the Court is reluctant to allow waiver of counsel in interrogation situations and also raised questions about what constitutes interrogation. The Court found the "Christian burial speech" to be "tantamount to interrogation"—intentionally designed to elicit incriminating statements. The Court generally holds that *Miranda* safeguards apply when interactions occur that police know may reasonably be expected to elicit an incriminating response. Thus, warnings must be given whenever an officer, through any action—verbal or otherwise—is likely to prompt an incriminating response.

The Court has held firm on the counsel waiver issue. It will not accept a voluntary confession from a defendant made after he or she has requested counsel if counsel is not present when that confession is made. Police may continue to ask questions so long as the suspect understands his or her rights and voluntarily continues the discussion. Indication of a desire to initiate or continue conversations with police can be made in a number of ways by the person in custody. In *Oregon v. Bradshaw* (462 U.S. 1039: 1983), for example, the Court ruled that a prisoner's question, "Well, what is going to happen to me now?" constituted initiation of further conversation that could yield admissible statements against him. The Court has frequently reiterated, however, that once counsel is requested by a suspect, interrogation cannot continue or be resumed in the absence of counsel.

The decisive issue is whether or not police-initiated action is designed to elicit incriminating statements. The case of *Maine v. Moulton* (474 U.S. 159: 1985) illustrates this point. Perley Moulton, represented by retained counsel, was indicted with a co-defendant for several counts of theft. The co-defendant met separately with police, gave a full confession, and agreed to testify against Moulton. The police subsequently arranged to "wire" the co-defendant and have him meet with Moulton, ostensibly to plan defense strategy. Moulton made incriminating statements at this meeting that were later admitted at his trial. The Court reversed Moulton's conviction because he was denied assistance of counsel, and counsel was said to be essential to the safeguarding of other procedural rights, especially the right against self-incrimination. When the police had the co-defendant wear the wire to the meeting with Moulton, they knew Moulton would make statements he had a right not to make to their agent before consulting with counsel. By not telling Moulton that the co-defendant was their agent, the police denied him his right to assistance of counsel.

In *Edwards v. Arizona* (451 U.S. 477: 1981), the Court refused to allow admission of a confession obtained the day following a defendant's request for counsel. In this case, even a second reading of *Miranda* warnings was insufficient to overcome the failure to have counsel present. Once the right to assistance of counsel is invoked, no subsequent conversation may occur on the police's initiative; it may occur only if the defendent does the initiating. The reasoning in *Edwards* was also applied in *Michigan v. Jackson* (475 U.S. 625: 1986). Following his arraignment on a murder charge, Robert Jackson requested that counsel be appointed. Before he could meet with his lawyer, police officers administered *Miranda* warnings to Jackson and interrogated him. The Court said that when the officers initiated the interview after the defendant requested counsel "at an arraignment or similar proceeding," any subsequent waiver of the right to counsel for police-initiated interrogation is invalid.

As firm as the Court was in cases such as *Brewer* and *Edwards,* it still was willing to provide some flexibility. The waiver allowed in *North Carolina v. Butler* (441 U.S. 369: 1979), which considered whether the waiver of *Miranda* rights need be explicit, is a good example. Willie Butler was arrested and informed of his rights. He was given an "Advice of Rights" form that he read and said he understood. He refused to sign the waiver provision at the bottom of the form although he indicated he was "willing to talk." Butler subsequently tried to have statements made during the ensuing conversation suppressed. The case revolved around a determination of whether or not Butler had actually waived his rights. The Supreme Court decided that Butler's statements could be admitted. The majority held that although explicit waiver is usually strong proof of the validity of a waiver, it is not "inevitably either necessary or sufficient to establish a waiver." The Court said further, "the question is not one of form, but rather whether the defendant in fact knowingly and voluntarily waived the rights delineated in *Miranda*." The burden of demonstrating the adequacy of a waiver rests with the prosecution, and the prosecution's "burden is great." However, "in at least some cases waiver can be clearly inferred from the actions and words of the person interrogated." Waivers must be evaluated in terms of the facts and circumstances of each case. The Court's judgment was that Butler made a knowing and voluntary waiver even though it was not explicit. The majority clearly rejected the establishment of an "inflexible" rule requiring explicit waiver. The dissenters, justices William Brennan, Thurgood Marshall, and John Paul Stevens, argued that an affirmative or explicit waiver is required to satisfy *Miranda.*

Butler specifies what must be done by a defendant to waive the associated rights of assistance of counsel and protection from self-incrimination. The *Miranda* protections may be waived, but the waiver must be voluntary, knowing, and intelligent. It may not be the product of coercion, trick, threat, persuasion, or inducement. Though the waiver need not be written or explicit, it cannot be presumed from silence under any circumstances. The burden rests with the prosecution to demonstrate that a waiver was freely, knowingly, and intelligently made. Determinations of the adequacy of a waiver are to be based on the "totality of circumstances" in a particular case and may include such matters as the background and overall conduct of the defendant. *Butler* provides some latitude by not requiring a firm rule relative to explicit waiver. At the same time, it clarifies and maintains the general protections afforded by *Miranda,* which was intended to draw a clear line obviating the need for a case-by-case determination of voluntariness. *Butler* brought the Court full circle. The dissent recognized that *Butler* implicitly, if not explicitly, overruled part of *Miranda*'s clear holding.

The fundamental character of waiver adequacy is reflected in *Moran v. Burbine* (475 U.S. 412: 1986). Brian Burbine was arrested for breaking and entering. The police subsequently came to believe that he was involved in a murder in another community. Officers from the second community were notified, and they came to question Burbine about the murder. In the meantime, and unknown to Burbine, his sister was arranging for counsel on the breaking and entering charge. Neither Burbine's sister nor the public defender she obtained knew anything about the murder charge. Counsel contacted the police by phone, indicating that she was ready to represent Burbine if the police wished to question him. She was told he would not be questioned further until the next day. She was not told that police from the second community were present and ready to begin their questioning. Burbine was advised of his rights before each of three interview sessions. He signed waiver papers at each and eventually admitted to the murder. At no time was Burbine aware of his sister's arrangement of counsel or the attorney's telephone call. Yet, in a six to three decision, the Court allowed use of the confession.

The justices held that the police followed "with precision" the *Miranda* procedure for obtaining waivers. The failure to inform Burbine of the attorney's call did not deprive him of information essential to his ability to make a knowing and voluntary waiver. Events taking place outside his presence and unknown to him "can have no bearing on the capacity to comprehend and knowingly relinquish a constitutional right." As long as it could be shown that his waiver was uncoerced and that he knew he did not have to speak and could request counsel, the waiver was valid. The Court said *Miranda* would not be extended to require reversal of convictions if police are "less than forthright" in dealing with an attorney or if they fail to inform a suspect of the attorney's unilateral efforts to contact him or her. The purpose of *Miranda* is to "dissipate the compulsion inherent in custodial interrogation" and thus protect the suspect's Fifth Amendment rights. A rule that focuses on how police treat an *attorney*—conduct that has no relevance to the matter of compulsion of the defendant—would "ignore both *Miranda's* mission and its only source of legitimacy." ·

The Court fashioned a public safety exception to *Miranda* in *New York v. Quarles* (467 U.S. 649: 1984). The Court said that in some situations concern for public safety must take precedence over the need to administer *Miranda* warnings. In *Quarles,* arresting police officers first inquired about the location of a weapon Benjamin Quarles was known to have been carrying. After the weapon was found, the officers read Quarles his rights. The Court said that *Miranda* did not need to be applied in all its rigor when police conduct is reasonably prompted by such a concern for public safety. Finally, in *Berkemer v. McCarty* (468 U.S. 420: 1984), the Court ruled that although *Miranda* warnings are required for custodial interrogation of a person accused of a misdemeanor traffic offense, the warnings are not required for the roadside questioning of a motorist. In the latter instance, the motorist is not in custody, the questioning is of short duration, and it is public enough to reduce the potential for police misconduct.

A different kind of waiver issue was raised in *Colorado v. Connelly* (479 U.S. 157: 1986), in which the Court ruled that a defendant diagnosed as a schizophrenic is categorically unable to waive his *Miranda* rights. Francis Connelly approached a Denver police officer and said he had killed someone. He was immediately advised of his rights. He replied that he understood his rights and indicated that he wished to discuss the murder. A detective was summoned, and on his arrival Connelly was once again advised of his rights. He was taken to police headquarters, where he told his story in detail. The following morning, Connelly became disoriented and said he had been ordered by "the voice of God" to confess. Subsequent psychiatric examination revealed that Connelly suffered from a psychosis that interfered with his capacity to make free and rational choices. A psychiatrist said that Connelly's psychosis had motivated his confession. It was also the psychiatrist's view, however, that Connelly's condition had not impaired his ability to understand his rights. A trial court subsequently ruled that Connelly's initial statements, as well as his custodial confession, must be suppressed as involuntary. The Supreme Court reversed that decision, however.

In the majority opinion, Chief Justice Rehnquist wrote that coercive police conduct was required to reach a finding that *Miranda* had been violated. Despite the significance of one's mental condition as a factor regarding the voluntariness issue, that condition, "by itself and apart from its relation to official coercion," should never dispose of an inquiry into voluntariness. The purpose of suppression was to deter future violations, and the Court did not see that end served by excluding Connelly's statements in this case. Only if "we were to establish a brand new constitutional right—the right to confess only when totally rational and properly motivated" could Connelly's claim be supported. Coercive police conduct was seen as a necessary predicate to finding that a confession was not voluntary. In addition, mental illness would not invariably preclude a defendant from understanding and waiving his or her constitutional rights.

The question raised in *Illinois v. Perkins* (110 L. Ed. 2d 243: 1990) was whether *Miranda* applies to statements on other matters made by a suspect in custody to an undercover officer posing as a prisoner. With only Justice Marshall dissenting, the Court ruled that an officer can pose as a fellow inmate to elicit statements without a *Miranda* warning. The warning "mandated by *Miranda* was meant," wrote Justice Anthony Kennedy, to serve the privilege against self-incrimination during "incommunicado interrogation of individuals in a police-dominated atmosphere." On the other hand, conversations between suspects and undercover officers "do not implicate the concerns underlying *Miranda*." The "essential ingredients" of a "police-dominated atmosphere and compulsion are not present" when a suspect "speaks freely" to an officer "he believes to be a fellow inmate." When an individual believes he is in the company of cellmates and not the police, the "coercive atmosphere is lacking." The Court rejected the argument that *Miranda* warnings "are required whenever a suspect is in custody in a technical sense and converses with someone who also happens to be a government agent." *Miranda* forbids the use of coercion, not "mere strategic deception by taking advantage of a suspect's misplaced trust in one he supposes to be a fellow prisoner. . . . Ploys to mislead" a prisoner into a "false sense of security that do not rise to the level of compulsion or coercion to speak are not within *Miranda*'s concerns." *Miranda* was not meant, Kennedy concluded, "to prevent suspects from boasting about their criminal activities in front of persons they believe to be their cellmates." As a result, Lloyd Perkins spoke "at his own peril." *Baltimore City Department of Social Services v. Bouknight* (107 L. Ed. 2d 992: 1990) considered whether the privilege against self-incrimination applied to a woman who was ordered to surrender her child to juvenile authorities. The Baltimore City Department of Social Services sought to remove the child from Jacqueline Bouknight's custody. The child had been removed once before on grounds of child abuse and was only returned to Bouknight's custody subject to extensive conditions contained in a protective order. Bouknight was ordered to produce the child, but refused. She was held in civil contempt. The state court of appeals ruled that the order was unconstitutional on self-incrimination grounds because it compelled Bouknight to acknowledge control over the child in a situation where she could have "reasonable apprehension that she would be prosecuted."

The Supreme Court reversed the state court, however. Justice Sandra Day O'Connor wrote for the majority, first addressing the scope of the privilege against self-incrimination. It is generally reserved for testimonial communication, but O'Connor acknowledged that compliance with the production order might constitute a "limited testimonial assertion" for purposes of the privilege. The mere possibility of testimonial assertions, however, "does not, in all contexts, justify invoking the privilege to resist production." O'Connor did indicate that if the production order is complied with, parents such as Bouknight could assert self-incrimination protection if the government sought to prosecute on the basis of information derived from the production of the child. The Court ruled that Bouknight could not invoke the privilege in this case for two reasons. First, her prior abusive conduct had led to the requirement that she submit herself to assistance and supervision by juvenile authorities as a condition of custody. As a result, she could not invoke the privilege to prevent enforcement of those conditions. Second, the surrender of the child was not ordered in furtherance of the state's prosecutorial function. Rather, production of the child was required as part of a "noncriminal regulatory regime." The state has a legitimate interest in the well-being of children. When a person has control over items such as children that are the object of government's noncriminal regulatory control, "the ability to invoke the privilege is reduced." Viewing the use of custodial orders as part of a general, noncriminal regulatory scheme was key to rejecting Bouknight's contention that parents subjected to such orders were part of a "selective group inherently suspect of criminal activities."

One final self-incrimination issue arose out of a capital sentencing situation. It was resolved, however, on the basis of *Miranda. Estelle v. Smith* (451 U.S. 454: 1981) considered whether testimony by a psychiatrist who conducted a competency examination of a defendant prior to the trial can be offered at the penalty phase of the trial. Prior to Ernest Smith's murder trial, the prosecution made clear its intention to seek the death penalty. The trial court ordered a competency examination. Smith was found competent, and he was tried and convicted. A separate sentencing hearing is required for the death penalty. Under Texas law, a death sentence requires that it must be found, among other things, that the defendant is likely to commit more violent crime if given the opportunity. It was to this question that the psychiatrist's testimony was directed, and Smith was sentenced to death as a result of that testimony. The Supreme Court reversed the sentence in a unanimous decision.

The opinion by Chief Justice Burger made several statements about the right against self-incrimination. First, this right applies to the sentencing stage just as it does to the guilt adjudication stage of a trial. Its availability "does not turn on the type of proceeding, but on the nature of the statement or admission and the exposure which it invites." Second, the fact that the statements made by Smith were "uttered in the context of a psychiatric examination does not remove them from the reach of the Fifth Amendment." That they were nontestimonial in nature was irrelevant. Third, Smith should have been warned of his right to remain silent and that statements made to the psychiatrist could be used at a capital sentencing proceeding. The Court found Smith to be in the same position as a person subjected to a custodial interrogation by police. The psychiatrist may have been "neutral" in some respects, but when he went beyond simply reporting results of the examination and testified for the prosecution at the penalty stage, "his role changed and became essentially like that of an agent of the State recounting unwarned statements made in a post-arrest custodial setting." The Court reiterated that the protection against self-incrimination is as "broad as the mischief against which it seeks to guard." The Court also found a defect on right-to-counsel grounds, concluding that the right had attached to Smith prior to the examination and counsel should have been present at what proved to be a "critical stage of the aggregate proceedings against respondent [Smith]."

Estelle v. Smith was a strong statement by the Burger Court of its commitment to the interests protected by *Miranda. Smith* also reflects the wide scope to which self-incrimination coverage has evolved. The case refers to "exposure" in regard to the protection provided by the privilege against self-incrimination. This exposure is distinct from and more inclusive than protection based upon the type of legal proceeding taking place. Thus, self-incrimination coverage attaches to juvenile proceedings as well as to sentencing and competency examinations. By making it clear that exposure can exist in contexts other than trials and custodial interrogation, the *Smith* decision broadens the scope of the privilege. Recognition that statements need not be in the form of actual testimony is particularly significant in terms of the expanded scope of the privilege. *Smith* is one of the Burger Court's strongest pronouncements regarding self-incrimination.

The Sixth Amendment

T he Sixth Amendment mandates a fair trial for criminal defendants. It contains several specific kinds of fair trial protections. The Sixth Amendment states that in all criminal prosecutions, an accused "shall enjoy the right to a speedy and public trial, by an impartial jury of the State and district wherein the crime shall have been committed." Second, a criminal defendant is to be "informed of the nature and cause of the accusation." Third, the defendant is entitled to "be confronted with the witnesses against him." Fourth, like the prosecution, the accused is to "have compulsory process for obtaining witnesses in his favor." Finally, the defendant shall "have assistance of counsel for his defense." Like the Fifth Amendment, the Sixth Amendment is based on British common law tradition. Abuses of laws intended to safeguard the rights of criminal defendants were frequent in colonial America. As a result, the constitutions of most of the original 13 states contained language designed to prevent such abuses. The state constitutional ratifying conventions insisted, for example, that the principle of trial by jury is one of the most fundamental rights accruing to the citizens of a democracy.

We begin with a cursory overview of the component elements of the Sixth Amendment's provisions. The immediate cause of the framers' deep concern about fair trials was the British practice in colonial America of sending defendants to Britain for trial. Colonists believed to be guilty of violating trade laws or stamp acts, for example, were tried by British Admiralty Court in Britain without benefit of a jury. In 1774, the Continental Congress declared unequivocally that the "seizing of or attempting to seize any person in America in order to transport such person beyond the sea for trial of offenses committed within the body of a county in America, being against the law, will justify, and ought to meet with, resistance and reprisal." In that part of the Declaration of Independence containing the listing of "repeated injuries and injustices" suffered by the colonists, the following complaints appear: "For depriving us in many cases of the benefits of trial by jury; for transporting us beyond seas to be tried for pretended offenses."

The colonists also insisted that provisions of Magna Carta be remembered on the subject of speedy trials. A person accused of a crime must not be kept in prison an unreasonable period of time before trial of the facts. The founders were equally concerned that the Bill of Rights embody the British common law tradition holding that one accused of a criminal act should have available the full bill of indictment containing the charges against him. The assumption implicit in this clause of the Sixth Amendment is that if a defendant is aware of the precise charges levied against him or her, an appropriate defense can be mounted.

A clause of the Sixth Amendment that did not originate in the British common law tradition was the guarantee of compulsory process. Until 1798 it was well established in the conduct of British trials that persons accused of felonies or treason were not allowed to introduce witnesses on their own behalf. After 1787 this general law was abolished in Britain, but there were restrictions on the number and kinds of witnesses who could be summoned. Not only did the constitutional ratifying conventions have this immediate precedent before them in 1789, but they also had the U.S. tradition that "all criminals shall have the same privilege of witnesses as their prosecutors." The right of compulsory process is now an unchallenged part of U.S. criminal procedure, as is the right of access to counsel.

Prior to 1836, defendants in the British court system were allowed to access counsel only for cases in which the charge was treason. The U.S. tradition was different, however. The right to retain counsel, albeit at one's own expense, was codified in the Judiciary Act of 1789 and the Federal Crime Act of 1790. Thus, if a defendant could afford to retain counsel, his right to counsel was guaranteed. Several twentieth-century Supreme Court decisions dramatically reinterpreted this tradition. In *Powell v. Alabama* (287 U.S. 45: 1932), the Court determined that states were required to furnish counsel as an extension of the due process guarantee of the Fourteenth Amendment. In a series of subsequent decisions, assistance of counsel has been extended to all felony trials, some misdemeanor trials, and many pre-trial and post-trial proceedings including custodial interrogation. Thus, the evolution of the Sixth Amendment phrase "have the Assistance of Counsel for his defense" has made legal representation an absolute constitutional guarantee.

The Sixth Amendment provides rights that differentiate the U.S. system of jurisprudence from many other legal systems in the modern world. That part of the Sixth Amendment guaranteeing trial by jury emerged full-blown in the Plymouth Colony in 1623, where it was required that all criminal facts to be adjudicated should be tried by a jury of 12 "honest men to be impanelled by authority, in form of a jury upon their oaths." The Plymouth tradition that these 12 persons should unanimously agree on a verdict survives in federal criminal procedures to this day, although the Supreme Court has ruled in state actions that a unanimous jury is not always necessary to convict a criminal defendant. Similarly, later interpretations of what constitutes a fair trial and a proper jury have evolved according to the due process and equal protection standards of the Fourteenth Amendment. It is now Supreme Court doctrine that impartiality in the composition of a jury must reflect at least generally the sociological makeup of the trial district's population. By the same token, the idea of witness confrontation has evolved from the right of those accused of treason to confront witnesses against them (under Britain's Treason Act of 1696) to modern rules of procedure that take strongly into account a trial's reliance on evidence and testimony brought by witnesses. The Sixth Amendment's guarantee of the right to counsel assures that all other provisions of the amendment are monitored by persons with legal knowledge. The right to counsel has been extended to every corner and aspect of the criminal process, to the states, to the poor, and to persons immediately after being put in custody. In no other modern government have so many safeguards been assigned to the rights of persons accused of crimes.

Public Trial by Jury

Jury trials occur in only a small proportion of criminal cases, and yet the trial is regarded as the fairest way to determine the guilt or innocence of an accused. So important is the concept of trial that it comes first among the fairness protections contained in the Sixth Amendment. Access to jury trials is also mentioned in several other places in the Constitution. The principal objective of the jury is to safeguard the public from arbitrary conduct of government. The jury stands between the accused and unrestrained or capricious actions of police, prosecutors, and judges. Juries are a specified number of citizens called to render a judgment on various issues of fact in a legal proceeding. Two common jury forms are the grand jury and the petit, or ordinary trial, jury. A grand jury hears evidence and determines whether or not a person must stand trial on a criminal charge(s). A petit jury makes an actual determination of guilt in a criminal or civil trial. Article IV of the Constitution mandates jury trials for criminal cases, and the right is repeated in the Sixth Amendment.

The jury trial, like many other elements of the U.S. legal process, was inherited from Britain. The expectation that selected citizens should participate in making judgments about other citizens was deeply ingrained in British legal traditions and also has become so in the United States. The jury fosters citizen involvement in the justice system, and, specific case deviations notwithstanding, it brings a common-sense element into the legal process. Yet the quality of jury performance is occasionally questioned. The options the Supreme Court has recently permitted states regarding jury size and unanimity underscore performance concerns. Juries are to be composed of a representative cross-section of the community. Once the jury is in place, it becomes the paramount finder of fact in that particular case. Although the judge controls what the jury can consider by ruling on questions of law and evidence, the jury decides what value to assign to evidence and witness testimony. The use of juries reflects a fundamental commitment to the notion that administration of justice is produced by tempering legal rules with the common sense of citizens who are formally untrained in the law. At the same time, the several constitutional references to the jury including the language in the Sixth Amendment did not apply to state criminal cases. In the 1960s, however, the Warren Court extended most Bill of Rights protections for the accused to the state level through the due process clause of the Fourteenth Amendment. The jury trial was incorporated in the case of *Duncan v. Louisiana* (391 U.S. 145: 1968). In *Duncan,* the Court said the right to a jury trial was created to "prevent oppression by the Government." The constitutional authors knew from "history and experience that it was necessary to protect against unfounded criminal charges brought to eliminate enemies and against judges too responsive to the voice of [overzealous prosecutors' and his own] authority."

JURY SELECTION

Before a trial can begin, a jury must be selected. The first step in the three-step process is creating a master jury list. Procedures used to produce the master jury list must randomly select a representative cross-section of the community. Most jurisdictions have recently used lists of registered voters as their master list, although such a list certainly does not include all eligible jurors. Many states have turned to lists of licensed drivers since the 1970s either instead of or in addition to voter lists. Computers have allowed jury administrators to easily merge voter and driver lists to yield the most comprehensive list possible. In compiling the list of potential jurors, selection techniques may not discriminate. The pool of prospective jurors (called a venire) drawn from the master jury list can be challenged if it fails to contain members of particular racial groups or seriously underrepresents one gender or the other. The Court's first significant ruling on discriminatory jury selection came in *Norris v. Alabama* (294 U.S. 587: 1935), an appeal that grew out of the infamous *Scottsboro* trial, in which nine young, illiterate, and indigent blacks were convicted on capital rape charges in a court where the jury was chosen by means of racially discriminatory methods and the defendants were unrepresented by defense counsel. The *Norris* case prohibited systematic exclusion of persons from jury service based on race. In *Norris,* no witness could recall a black serving on any jury in the county of jurisdiction. This prompted the Court to say that for this "long continued, unvarying, and wholesale exclusion of Negroes from jury service we find no justification consistent with the constitutional mandate."

The *Norris* standard of systematic exclusion was quite insensitive to discrimination that did not totally exclude. As a result, the Court tightened its scrutiny and has struck down selection techniques that produce serious underrepresentation of particular groups on jury venires as well. Illustrative of this point is *Taylor v. Louisiana* (419 U.S. 522: 1975). Under Louisiana law, a woman could not serve on a jury without specially filing a declaration indicating her willingness to serve. Males were not required to take the same step to qualify for selection. As a result of the special requirement, only about 10 percent of prospective jurors in a particular jurisdiction were women despite the fact that women constituted 53 percent of the jurisdiction's population. The Court said that the system "does not disqualify women from jury service," but in operation produced a "systematic impact" where only a few women, "grossly disproportionate to the number of eligible women in the community," were actually summoned. The Court concluded by saying that "restricting jury service only to a special group or excluding identifiable segments playing major roles in the community cannot be squared with the constitutional concept of a jury trial."

Jurors for a particular case are selected from the venire, the jury pool randomly selected from the master list. Members of the venire undergo an examination process known as voir dire prior to actually qualifying for jury service. The idea of voir dire is to determine whether prospective jurors can serve impartially on a particular case. If a juror cannot fairly and impartially judge the facts of a case, he or she can be removed for cause. Questions about the nature of the voir dire examination have appeared before the Court. *Ristaino v. Ross* (424 U.S. 589: 1976), for example, considered the issue of whether a defendant is constitutionally entitled to ask questions specifically directed toward racial prejudice during the voir dire process. James Ross's motion to pursue race bias was denied by the trial court, and he was subsequently convicted of assaultive crimes against a white victim. The Supreme Court upheld the trial judge's decision. Justice Lewis Powell reasoned for the majority that the Constitution "does not always entitle a defendant to have questions posed during voir dire specifically directed to matters that conceivably might prejudice veniremen against him." Though circumstances might warrant specific questions about racial prejudice, these were matters to be handled through the exercise of "sound discretion" by the trial court, a function "particularly within the province of the trial judge." Ross had not shown that the prospective jurors were likely to be racially biased. According to the Court, the mere fact that the victim and the defendant were of different races was not in itself something that was "likely to distort the trial."

Ristaino is representative of the Burger Court's view of what kinds of questions a defendant is entitled to pursue during a voir dire examination. The supervision of voir dire rests with the trial judge. *Ristaino* determined that a trial judge's discretion has been properly exercised when a defendant is denied the opportunity to probe the racial prejudice of prospective jurors simply because the defendant and crime victim are of different races. *Ristaino* underscored the requirement that a defendant must demonstrate unusual circumstances, such as the presence of a racial issue, as an actual component of a particular case. In *Ham v. South Carolina* (409 U.S. 524: 1973), on the other hand, the Court concluded that questions relating to racial prejudice were appropriate given the defendant's visibility in the civil rights movement in the locality of his trial. *Ristaino* and *Ham* place the monitoring of the jury selection process, specifically the conduct of the voir dire examination, exclusively in the hands of the trial judge. This rule was subsequently modified for capital cases in *Turner v. Murray* (476 U.S. 28: 1986). In this case, the Court said a capital defendant accused of an interracial crime is entitled to have prospective jurors informed of the race of the victim and questioned on the issue of racial bias during voir dire. The Court believed the risk of racial prejudice infecting a capital sentencing proceeding is especially serious in light of the finality of the death sentence.

The issue of fitness to serve as an impartial juror has also arisen in a number of capital cases because of the strong attitudes people have about the punishment. Several cases have been before the Court, the most recent of which is *Lockhart v. McCree* (476 U.S. 1: 1986). Ardia McCree was tried for capital felony murder in a state proceeding. During the voir dire process, the judge removed for cause, prior to the guilt adjudication phase of the two-stage capital trial, all prospective jurors who indicated they could not impose a death penalty. A jury subsequently convicted McCree but rejected the death penalty at the sentencing stage. Instead it set punishment at life imprisonment without parole. McCree failed in his attempt for relief in the state courts and sought federal *habeas corpus* relief. He contended that the "death qualification" of the jurors remaining to determine his guilt or innocence deprived him of an impartial jury chosen from a representative cross-section of the community. The Supreme Court disagreed with McCree. The essence of a fair cross-section claim is the systematic exclusion of a distinctive group in the community. Groups defined solely in terms of shared attitudes that would substantially impair their functioning as jurors are not distinctive groups for fair cross-section purposes. Exclusion did not occur here for reasons completely unrelated to the ability of members of the group to function as jurors. This differentiated the *Lockhart* case from those in which exclusion of a distinctive group arbitrarily skewed the composition of a jury and denied defendants the benefits of community judgment.

PREJUDICIAL PRE-TRIAL PUBLICITY

The other issue that impacts the impartiality of prospective jurors is prejudicial pre-trial publicity. This can be a significant problem given the capacity of the media to reach a large proportion of the community from which a jury is to be selected. The problem is especially difficult because the First Amendment generally frees the media from regulation. The benchmark case on this subject is the famous case involving Dr. Sam Sheppard, *Sheppard v. Maxwell* (384 U.S. 333: 1966). In this case, the Court considered whether pervasive pre-trial publicity, most of which was highly adverse to Sheppard, deprived him of the fair trial mandated by the Sixth Amendment. Every stage of the *Sheppard* case was subjected to intensive media coverage, from inquest through indictment to trial itself. Even after jurors were selected, they were subjected to continued publicity about the case. Sheppard was eventually convicted of the murder of his wife, but the Supreme Court reversed the conviction.

The Court focused its discussion on the failures of the trial judge to adequately provide Sheppard with the "judicial serenity and calm to which he was entitled." Among other things, the judge should have tightened jury selection processes, kept jurors from contact with information from outside the courtroom, used stricter rules governing media in the courtroom, better insulated the witnesses from media representatives, limited the flow of information to the media from principals in the case, and admonished the media to monitor the accuracy of their reports. The Court found the failure to properly insulate the jury the most glaring error in the trial. Several jurors admitted hearing media broadcasts about the case while serving. The Court said Sheppard's trial turned into an avoidable "carnival" and deprived Sheppard of a fair trial.

The *Sheppard* case focused the tension existing between a defendant's right to a fair trial and the First Amendment right of a free press. The press has always possessed the capacity to impact the fairness of criminal proceedings, but technical developments in the broadcast media have increased that potential dramatically. Virtually an entire community can be reached with information that may have a prejudicial effect on a particular case. The *Sheppard* case reveals these prejudicial effects at their worst. The totality of circumstances of this case clearly demonstrated the possibility of prejudice, and that was sufficient for the Court to grant Sheppard relief. Even with the excesses that occurred in *Sheppard,* however, the Court resisted restricting the press and focused instead on the judge as the key figure in ensuring a fair trial. The justices talked about the option of delaying a trial until publicity had subsided or of changing the venue of a case. The Court emphasized how the voir dire examination could have been better used to determine whether prejudicial publicity existed. It also suggested sequestering or isolating juries in particularly visible trials. The caution the Court demonstrated in regulating press behavior prompted response from the industry itself. Discussions between representatives of trial courts and the media produced principles of conduct for media coverage of criminal cases, and much of the media now voluntarily complies with these principles.

A subsequent decision, *Murphy v. Florida* (421 U.S. 794: 1975), provided more clarity on the question of when reported information becomes prejudicial. The Court said in *Murphy* that prospective jurors need not be "totally ignorant" of a case. They need only to be able to "reach a verdict based on the evidence presented in court." The thrust of *Murphy* was reiterated in *Patton v. Yount* (467 U.S. 1025: 1984), in which the defendant challenged the jury selection for retrial following his successful appeal. Though extensive publicity had attended the first trial, the Court felt that the four-year period between trials had greatly reduced "any presumption of prejudice" that existed at the time of the initial trial. The Court said that when the matter of prejudice was examined, the relevant question was not whether the community remembered the case, but whether the prospective jurors for the new trial had such fixed opinions that they could not judge impartially. Press treatment of a case, especially when it is governed by self-imposed limits, does not necessarily mean the publicity is either prejudicial or adverse. The *Sheppard* case, however, clearly demonstrated the need for certain safeguards to ensure a fair trial for criminal defendants.

PEREMPTORY CHALLENGES

If a juror is not challenged for cause, the prosecution or the defense may remove a juror by means of a peremptory challenge or strike. A strike may remove a prospective juror without giving a reason. In this way, defense and prosecution may try to impanel jurors they believe will be more receptive to their case. For a long period, few restraints existed on peremptory challenges by either side. This included insulating prosecutors from regulation when use of strikes seemed racially motivated. The Warren Court examined this issue in *Swain v. Alabama* (380 U.S. 202: 1965). *Swain* was brought to the Court for consideration of more subtle forms of discriminatory jury selection that had developed since the *Norris* decision. The Court's decision in *Swain* did not abandon the basic thrust of *Norris* in terms of systematic exclusion, but it made the burden of proving discriminatory practices very difficult.

The Court said in *Swain* that the acknowledged underrepresentation of blacks in *Swain* did not amount to systematic exclusion, the standard derived from *Norris*. A defendant is not constitutionally entitled "to demand a proportionate number of his race on the jury which tries him nor on the venire or jury roll from which petit juries are drawn." The venire simply need not be a "perfect mirror of the community or accurately reflect the proportionate strength of every identifiable group." In *Batson v. Kentucky* (476 U.S. 79: 1986), the Court reconsidered the *Swain* standard and ruled that the equal protection clause precludes racially discriminatory use of peremptory challenges of potential jurors by prosecutors. During James Batson's burglary trial, the prosecutor used his peremptory challenges to remove all four black persons from the venire. Batson was subsequently convicted by an all white jury, and the Kentucky Supreme Court upheld his conviction based on the *Swain* decision. The Supreme Court used *Batson* to reexamine that part of *Swain* dealing with the burden of evidence a defendant must demonstrate in support of any claim of discriminatory use of peremptory challenges. The Court decided to shift much of the burden previously resting with the defendant to the prosecution.

First, the Court reaffirmed that exclusion of blacks from jury service was an evil the Fourteenth Amendment was designed to address. Purposeful racial discrimination violates a defendant's right to equal protection because it denies him or her the protection that a trial by jury is intended to secure. A defendant is entitled to a venire of jurors who are indifferently chosen. Beyond its impact on defendants, the Court observed that such discrimination unlawfully denies persons an opportunity to participate in jury service and "undermines public confidence in fairness of our system of justice." Second, the Court focused on the peremptory strike as the specific point of discrimination. Prosecutors are generally entitled to strike jurors "for any reason at all," although challenge exclusively on racial grounds is forbidden. Under *Swain*, a defendant was required to demonstrate an ongoing pattern of discrimination to get a conviction overturned. The Court in *Batson* viewed this requirement as a "crippling burden of proof" and one that left prosecutorial strikes "largely immune from constitutional scrutiny."

Accordingly, the Court concluded that a defendant may establish a prima facie case of intentional discrimination based exclusively on a prosecutor's use of peremptory challenges at the defendant's trial. Once a defendant establishes such a prima facie case, the burden shifts to the state to offer a neutral explanation for challenging black jurors. The explanation need not rise to the level of justifying exercise of a challenge for cause. The Court reiterated its recognition that the peremptory challenge "occupies an important position in our trial procedures." At the same time, however, the practice has been used as a means of discrimination. By requiring the courts to be sensitive to discriminatory use of the procedure, *Batson* "enforces the mandate of equal protection and furthers the ends of justice."

JURY SIZE AND UNANIMITY

Selection process questions have far outnumbered issues that stem from basic operating practices of juries. Though infrequent, issues relating to basic jury operations have come before the Court. The issue of jury size is a good example. Many believe that the Constitution simply requires twelve members, and historically most juries have had twelve members. In the early 1900s, however, several states started to reduce the number of jury members, first for civil cases and then for misdemeanors. Eventually, six-person juries in felony cases were authorized. The verdict from such a jury was challenged on the ground that a six-member jury simply did not satisfy the Sixth Amendment right to a jury trial. The Court considered this challenge in *Williams v. Florida* (399 U.S. 78: 1970).

The Court found that Florida's trial of Johnny Williams with a jury of six persons satisfied constitutional requirements. Justice Byron White concentrated on three key propositions in the majority opinion. First, although the jury is deeply rooted in U.S. legal history, he found nothing from the historical evidence to suggest that the authors of the Sixth Amendment intended either that exactly twelve persons should always serve on a jury or that the number twelve was an "indispensable component" of the Sixth Amendment. Second, juries should be large enough to promote group deliberation, free from "outside attempts at intimidation." The Court found nothing to lead it to believe that this goal was "in any meaningful sense less likely to be achieved when the jury numbers 6 than when it numbers 12." Third, juries must "provide a fair possibility for obtaining a representative cross-section of the community." The Court found the difference between twelve and six to be "negligible" in this regard. As long as selection processes prevent arbitrary or discriminatory exclusion, the Court felt "the concern that the cross-section will be significantly diminished if the jury is decreased in size from 12 to 6 seems an unrealistic one."

Williams represented an unexpected departure from British common law tradition, which clearly embraced a jury of twelve persons. When *Duncan* established the fundamental character of the jury trial at the state level, it was presumed that state juries would have twelve members as do federal juries. The *Williams* decision ruled to the contrary. The rationale offered by the Court in *Williams* has been seriously criticized, particularly as it relates to the deliberative and representative aspects of twelve- versus six-person juries. The Court subsequently established that six was the constitutional minimum. In *Ballew v. Georgia* (435 U.S. 223: 1978), the Court reviewed a conviction by a five-member jury in a state obscenity case. A unanimous Court, including all five members who had voted in the *Williams* majority eight years earlier, found a five-person jury to be constitutionally defective. The Court's opinion used as its rationale the reasons offered by critics of the *Williams* decision. The Court found that "effective group deliberation" and the ability to adequately represent a cross-section of the community were seriously threatened by a five-member jury. Critics say the difference between six and five appears to be entirely arbitrary. The *Williams* decision still provides the states with considerable discretion in determining the size of criminal juries.

Like jury size, the requirement of a unanimous jury decision to convict in a criminal case seemed beyond question. Once again, however, a number of states began to experiment by drawing away from the unanimity requirement, first in civil cases and then for misdemeanors. Finally, a small number of states established nine to three and ten to two conviction margins for at least some felonies. *Apodaca v. Oregon* (406 U.S. 404: 1972) gave the Court an opportunity to review these changes. Robert Apodaca was convicted in a state that allowed a jury decision by a ten to two margin. The Supreme Court upheld his conviction. The majority "perceived no difference" between the unanimous and non-unanimous jury decision. Both fulfilled the "interest of the defendant in having the judgment of his peers interposed between himself and the officers of the State." In response to the argument that non-unanimity detracted from the reasonable doubt standard, the majority replied that the standard of reasonable doubt "did not crystalize in this country until after the Constitution was adopted." Thus, it was not directly required by the Sixth Amendment.

Apodaca also argued that non-unanimity diminished the representativeness of a jury and allowed convictions "to occur without the acquiescence of minority elements within the community." The Court majority rejected this argument by saying it is not necessary that every "distinct voice in the community" be represented on every jury. The justices also rejected the notion that minority viewpoints would not be adequately represented even where convictions were obtained. They "found no proof for the notion that a majority will disregard its instructions and cast its vote for guilt or innocence based on prejudice rather than the evidence." Justices Harry Blackmun and Lewis Powell wrote separate concurring opinions. Justice Blackmun admitted "great difficulty" with the prospect of a seven to five jury decision. A nine to three decision was, however, a "substantial" enough jury majority for him.

Apodaca highlights the issue of confidence in jury decisions. Has the reasonable doubt standard been eroded and the likelihood of successful prosecutions increased with the *Apodaca* ruling? Some would answer yes to both questions. Like the twelve-person jury, the unanimity standard has been viewed as an integral part of the criminal process and still is regarded as such in the federal courts. If *Apodaca* is taken together with *Williams,* however, the Court leaves the jury trial a less effective right for state defendants than had been the case previously. The Court has established that conviction in a state criminal case coming on a five to one vote is unsatisfactory. In *Burch v. Louisiana* (441 U.S. 130: 1979), the unanimous opinion of the Court was that when a constitutional minimum of six jurors sits on a criminal case, nothing less than unanimity will suffice. *Apodaca* establishes that non-unanimous convictions on votes that may split as widely as nine to three are adequate, however. The sufficiency of margins less than nine to three for twelve-person juries, and split decisions from juries numbering more than six but less than twelve, remains to be defined. *Apodaca* and *Williams* opened doors relative to jury unanimity and size long thought to be closed; consequently, many states have accepted the Court's invitation to alter their jury policies.

Public Trials and the Media

Press coverage of criminal proceedings creates a number of problems. The fair trial interests of the criminal defendant necessarily conflict with the free press interests of the media. Certainly the media cannot report anything they wish without injuring the defendant. At the same time, restrictions on the media impinge on the First Amendment rights of a free press. A major problem occurs before a trial even begins because prejudicial pre-trial publicity can make it very difficult to draw an impartial jury. The problem is often compounded when the media cover and report pre-trial proceedings, which obviously take place before a jury is selected. One approach that has been tried is to enjoin the press from reporting what they observe, at least until the jury is chosen. *Nebraska Press Association v. Stuart* (427 U.S. 539: 1976) addressed the constitutional adequacy of this technique, which is known as the "gag rule."

The responsibility for maintaining a fair trial environment was placed with the judge in *Sheppard v. Maxwell* (384 U.S. 333: 1966). Judge Hugh Stuart sought to preserve the fair trial of a Nebraska murder defendent appearing in his court by restraining the media from "publishing or broadcasting accounts of confessions or admissions made by the accused or facts 'strongly implicative' of the accused" until such time as a jury had been impaneled. The crime itself was the murder of six persons. Compliance with the order was achieved, but the Nebraska Press Association sought a ruling from the Supreme Court even though the "gag order" had expired in this case. The Court rejected Judge Stuart's order though it noted that he had "acted responsibly, out of a legitimate concern, in an effort to protect the defendant's right to a fair trial." Nonetheless, the Court viewed the restraining order as excessive and suggested that truly extraordinary prejudicial publicity must be present to consider an action as severe as prior restraint. Given that the gag order was a denial of First Amendment rights, the Court said it must review carefully whether the record justified such an "extraordinary remedy." Included in such an examination are certain factors: (1) the "nature and extent" of the press coverage, (2) alternative measures and their likely impact on mitigating publicity, and (3) the effectiveness of the gag order in preventing damaging and prejudicial publicity. The Court concluded that the record was not sufficient on the last two factors in this instance. The criteria that must be addressed make such an order difficult to sustain under most circumstances.

Nebraska Press Association dealt with whether the press should be restricted from publishing what it already knows. This is a different problem from *Sheppard,* which focused on remedies after prejudicial publicity existed. Judge Stuart looked at the gag order as a means of stemming pre-trial publicity before the fact. The prior restraint issues raised in *Nebraska Press Association* had been understood for years, but a case on the point had not formally been decided. Though *Nebraska Press Association* stopped short of invalidating the gag rule approach altogether, the clear thrust of the decision was to impose conditions for use of the gag rule that are virtually impossible to meet. The case, then, is a kind of intermediate point between a policy that stresses after-the-fact remedies and an approach that would close judicial proceedings to the public and the media. It is apparent from *Nebraska Press Association* that prohibiting the media from reporting what they observe directly in open court is the least favored approach.

An alternative to the gag order is to keep the media from observing proceedings at all. This gives the media nothing to report, so there is no need to gag them. The closure of pre-trial stages to the media came before the Court in *Gannett Company v. DePasquale* (443 U.S. 368: 1979). The case posed the question of whether the media could be barred from a pre-trial suppression hearing. If the press is allowed to observe a judicial proceeding, it generally will be allowed to report what it observes. Because both the defense and prosecution agreed to close the proceeding in this case, the question before the Court really was whether or not the public (and the media) had an independent right to an open pre-trial hearing. The Court said no.

The majority reasoned that pre-trial suppression hearings, as distinct from trials, pose "special risks of unfairness." The objective of such hearings is to screen out unreliable or illegally obtained evidence. Pre-trial publicity about such evidence could "influence public opinion" and "inform potential jurors of inculpatory information wholly inadmissible at the actual trial." As for the public's independent right of access, the Court stressed two points. First, public interest in the application of the Sixth Amendment does not create "a constitutional right on the part of the public." The public interest is protected by the participants in the adversary process. Thus the public has no claim that could displace the defendant's desire to close the proceeding. Second, the common law tradition recognizes the difference between a pre-trial proceeding and the trial itself. "Pretrial proceedings, precisely because of concern for a fair trial, were never characterized by the degree of openness as were actual trials."

The situation in *Gannett* sidesteps the censorship question present in *Nebraska Press Association.* The media was not prohibited from publishing information it possessed by observing a court proceeding. Rather than focus on the free press rights of the media in *Gannett,* the Court considered whether a criminal defendant's interest in closing a pre-trial hearing supersedes the public's interest in an open proceeding. The *Gannett* decision clearly raised the possibility of all judicial proceedings, even trials, being closed at the initiative of the defense. The Court refused to take that step in *Richmond Newspapers, Inc. v. Virginia* (448 U.S. 555: 1980). In *Richmond,* defense counsel requested that a murder trial be closed to the public. The prosecutor expressed no objection, and the trial judge ordered the courtroom cleared. Under Virginia law a trial judge has the discretion to exclude from a trial any person whose "presence would impair the conduct of a fair trial." The Supreme Court, however, ruled that the closure order was a violation of the Sixth Amendment requirement of a public trial. Chief Justice Warren Burger began the majority opinion with a lengthy treatment of the history of the open trial. This "unbroken, uncontradicted history, supported by reasons as valid today as centuries past," forced the Court to conclude "that a presumption of openness inheres in the very nature of a criminal trial under our system of justice." The Court majority said that the open trial serves a therapeutic purpose for the community, especially in instances of shocking crimes. Open trials also offer protection against abusive or arbitrary behavior. They allow criminal processes "to satisfy the appearance of justice." Though access to trials is not specifically provided in the First Amendment, it is implicit in the amendment's guarantees. Without the freedom to attend trials, important aspects of free speech and a free press could be damaged. The chief justice returned to the specifics of the *Richmond* case in his conclusion, in which he stated that the closure order was defective because the trial judge made no particular finding to support such an order. Alternatives to closure were not explored, there was no recognition of any constitutional right for the press or the public to attend the proceeding, and there was no indication that problems with witnesses could not have been addressed otherwise.

Richmond Newspapers clearly distinguished the trial from pre-trial hearings and elevated press interests to prevailing weight in the former. In most instances, the Supreme Court has found a criminal defendant to be entitled to insulation from media coverage as a basic requirement of due process in pre-trial hearings. Consistent with the objective of minimizing adverse pre-trial publicity, the Court allowed closure of pre-trial proceedings in *Gannett*. In *Press-Enterprise Co. v. Superior Court of California* (464 U.S. 501: 1984), the Court added the detail that the voir dire examination must also be open to the public and the press. The presumption of openness can only be overcome by an "overriding interest" that meets protection through narrowly tailored closure. Two years later the Court softened the distinction between trials and pre-trial criminal proceedings in *Press-Enterprise Co. v. Superior Court of California II* (478 U.S. 1: 1986). The Court narrowed the scope of *Gannett* by saying that closure of pre-trial proceedings can only occur where such action is "essential to preserve higher values and is narrowly tailored to serve the interest," a standard that is likely to make closure of pre-trial proceedings more difficult.

Finally, the Court has responded to attempts to open the courtroom more widely to media coverage. Many states are permitting electronic and photographic coverage of various trial and appellate proceedings. The constitutionality of this kind of policy was examined by the Court in *Chandler v. Florida* (449 U.S. 560: 1981). The Florida Supreme Court fashioned a canon, as part of the Florida Code of Judicial Conduct, that permitted electronic media and still photographic coverage of trial and appellate proceedings. The canon gave authority over all media coverage to presiding trial judges. In its review of this case, the Supreme Court decided that, absent a specific showing of prejudice, the policy was constitutional. Chief Justice Burger wrote for the majority that the approach used by Florida was sufficient in that it provided safeguards for certain problem cases. The Florida guidelines placed on trial judges "positive obligations to be on guard to protect the fundamental right of the accused to a fair trial." The "mere presence" of the broadcast media does not "inherently" adversely affect the process. The burden is on the defendant to show that his or her case was influenced by the coverage. The Florida process allows review on appeal allegations of compromised proceedings because of media coverage. Noel Chandler, the defendant, could demonstrate no specific adverse impacts "on the trial participants sufficient to constitute a denial of due process."

Chandler reflects the Supreme Court's deference to the direction of trial judges in managing problems relating to media coverage of criminal trials. Just as in *Gannett* and *Richmond Newspapers,* the Court left critical assessments of possible adverse effects of coverage to the presiding judge. This approach squares with the Burger Court's preference for letting the "totality of circumstances" provide the basis for resolving questions of law. *Chandler* also represents a swing away from *Gannett,* a swing begun in *Richmond Newspapers.* Courtroom coverage by electronic media has the potential to be most problematic in terms of fair trial standards. Yet in *Chandler,* the Court refused to find such coverage inherently violative of due process. *Chandler* placed the burden of proof on the defendant by requiring the accused to demonstrate prejudice, whereas *Gannett* had allowed an accused simply to request closure. Absent a demonstration of adverse effect, a defendant cannot simply terminate coverage or achieve closure by request alone. The experiment in Florida warrants ongoing attention to determine whether any benefits or liabilities emerge as a result of more extensive media coverage.

Plea Bargaining

Plea bargaining is a process whereby the prosecutor and the accused negotiate a mutually acceptable settlement in a criminal case. Plea bargaining usually involves a defendant pleading guilty to a charge in exchange for a lessening of the charge, a reduction in the number of counts charged, and/or favorable sentencing recommendations. A proposed settlement must be accepted by the trial judge assigned to the case.

There is no constitutional provision dealing with plea bargaining. Rather, a plea involves the waiver of several constitutional protections. Foremost of these rights, of course, is the jury trial. As with any constitutional right, a person may waive it so long as the waiver is voluntary. Plea bargaining moves cases through the courts, relieving docket pressure that could not be handled through any other means. It also produces some certainty for the parties and gives both defendant and prosecutor some assurance about the final outcome. Plea bargaining is desirable because it produces prompt and largely final dispositions without lengthy pre-trial confinement. More prompt dispositions, in turn, diminish chances of additional criminal conduct by those on pre-trial release and enhance rehabilitative prospects. The procedures by which pleas are made are carefully prescribed. The Federal Rules of Criminal Procedure set forth the steps by which pleas are to be entered in federal courts, and most states have established similar guidelines. At minimum, no plea can be taken without a trial judge inquiring into the voluntary character of the plea. If a plea is determined to be freely and intelligently offered, all elements of the settlement agreement must be honored.

Plea bargaining is not a new practice. Defendants have been waiving their right to a trial from the outset of U.S. constitutional history. Approximately 90 percent of all current criminal cases are concluded by agreement, which means only one criminal case in ten is actually tried. Early in the twentieth century, the number of criminal cases concluded by trial was seldom above 15 percent. Since the 1960s, certain procedural safeguards have been developed to guide the plea process. The first significant Court decision on plea bargaining came in *Boykin v. Alabama* (395 U.S. 238: 1969). Edward Boykin pled guilty to five counts of robbery and was sentenced to death by a jury. The record showed that the trial judge asked no questions of Boykin at the time of the plea, that the defendant did not address the court in any way, and that the defendant did not testify at his sentencing proceeding. Boykin was represented by counsel throughout. A six-justice majority of the Supreme Court found the plea insufficient. The Court focused on the trial judge's error of accepting the plea without an "affirmative showing that it was intelligent and voluntary." The majority held that a plea is "more than a confession, it is a conviction." Waiver of such rights as trial by jury, confronting one's accusers, and the protection from self-incrimination simply cannot be presumed from a silent record.

A guilty plea constitutes more than a confession. It stands as a conviction equivalent to a jury finding of guilt. It also involves the waiver of several protections such as self-incrimination, jury trial, cross-examination of accusers, and forfeiture of the presumption of innocence. *Boykin* established minimum Sixth Amendment standards and federal-state uniformity regarding guilty pleas. Because of *Boykin,* no federal or state court can accept a guilty plea without questioning the defendant as to whether he or she understands the charge and the potential sentence that may result from pleading guilty to the charge, as well as whether promises or threats have been made. The defendant must be made aware that many constitutional protections are being waived. The basis of *Boykin* was to ensure that a plea of guilty was the defendant's knowing and voluntary choice. Although *Boykin* does not require it, some jurisdictions place a summary of the case against a defendant in the record. In the absence of satisfactory responses to any of the judge's inquiries, a trial judge has the discretion of refusing to accept a guilty plea and having the case scheduled for trial. Today in federal courts, a mandatory rule (Rule 11 of the Federal Rules of Criminal Procedure) stipulates the steps to be taken by the judge in considering a plea of guilty. The steps must comply with *Boykin*. Most state courts have similar code or rule requirements. Thus, the plea process takes considerably more time than it did before *Boykin,* but the *Boykin* type appeal rarely occurs anymore. It is thought that the *Boykin* process results in considerably greater protections to the criminal defendant.

It was inevitable after *Boykin* that the Court would impose performance requirements on the bargaining process itself. A defendant always has the option to withdraw from an agreement and exercise the right to a jury trial. Prosecution, on the other hand, does not have quite the same options. The lead case on this issue is *Santobello v. New York* (404 U.S. 257: 1971). Rudolph Santobello was indicted for two felonies and agreed to enter a guilty plea in exchange for no sentence recommendation by the prosecutor. At the sentencing hearing, delayed twice at defendant's initiative, a new prosecuting attorney appeared. Apparently ignorant of his colleague's promise, the new prosecutor recommended the maximum sentence. The trial judge imposed the maximum sentence, but said he was not influenced by the prosecutor's recommendation. The Supreme Court ruled that Santobello's sentence must be vacated.

On the basic sentencing question the Court said the condition of no sentence recommendation was an integral part of the bargain made with the prosecutor. The Court did not forgive the failure of one prosecutor to communicate the elements of the negotiation to his successor. The prosecutor's office has the "burden of 'letting the left hand know what the right hand is doing' or has done." The Court said further, "the breach of agreement was inadvertent," but that "does not lessen its impact." *Santobello* represented to the Court "another example of an unfortunate lapse in orderly prosecutorial procedures," presumably a product of excessively high caseloads. But although workload "may well explain these episodes, it does not excuse them." The plea process "must be attended by safeguards to insure the defendant what is reasonably due in the circumstances." The position of the Court was that where a plea "rests in any significant degree on a promise or agreement of the prosecutor, such promise must be fulfilled."

Santobello illustrates some of the problems characteristic of a congested court system. That system requires nontrial dispositions in order to keep pace with case volume. Most cases are passed from one assistant prosecutor to another within a prosecutor's office as the next stage of the process is reached. The left hand usually does not know what the right hand has done. Plea bargaining has long been a suspect practice, and such incidents as that in *Santobello* reinforce the suspicion. The National Advisory Commission on Criminal Justice Standards and Goals strongly urged the abolition of plea bargaining in the early 1970s. *Santobello* addresses several important issues related to the advisory commission's recommendations. First, the Court established the basic expectation that where promises are instrumental in achieving a plea, the integrity of the bargaining process must be maintained and the promises honored. *Santobello* defines a performance standard for prosecutors. Second, *Santobello* permits a defendant in a criminal case to enforce a plea agreement against the government. Although *Santobello* involved only a prosecutorial recommendation, it raised the specter of a prosecutor offering to dismiss other counts against a defendant and not prosecuting for similar offenses within a given time. The lower courts have frequently invoked *Santobello* when a defendant alleges and proves a plea agreement has been violated. It is not uncommon for courts to dismiss criminal proceedings when prosecutorial authorities are found to have reneged on a plea. This kind of specific enforcement may be the most important aspect of *Santobello*. Third, *Santobello* gave the Court an opportunity to speak generally to the practice of plea bargaining, which the Court strongly endorsed. The majority opinion referred to plea bargaining as an "essential component of the administration of justice. Properly administered, it is to be encouraged." The Court itemized several reasons that plea bargaining should be regarded not only as essential, but also as "highly desirable." The advantages included finality, elimination of pre-trial confinement, conservation of scarce resources, and enhancement of rehabilitative prospects because the accused would voluntarily admit guilt. Taken with the positive language found in several other plea cases, the *Santobello* decision can be viewed as foreclosing the possibility that the Court will declare plea bargaining constitutionally deficient in the near future.

But *Santobello* does not create an absolute right to have a plea bargain enforced. In *Mabry v. Johnson* (467 U.S. 504: 1984), a defendant, following a successful appeal, accepted a plea proposal offered by the prosecutor rather than chance a retrial. The proposal was subsequently withdrawn on the ground that it had been mistakenly tendered. An alternative proposal was offered and initially rejected, but later was accepted by the defendant. The defendant was sentenced under the second agreement, but he appealed again, arguing that the prosecutor was precluded from withdrawing the original offer once it had been accepted. The Supreme Court disagreed. The Court said George Johnson, the defendant, accepted the agreement knowing what the prosecutor would recommend. Further, he did so with the advice of competent counsel, and he was fully aware of the consequences. His plea was in no sense the product of governmental deception. The agreement did not rest on an unfulfilled promise, and it "fully satisfied the test for voluntariness and intelligence." Neither had Johnson been forced to accept the offer. In addition, had he thought the terms of the second offer to be unsatisfactory, Johnson could have gone to trial.

The prosecutor has substantial leverage in the bargaining process. So long as prosecutorial power is not used vindictively, a number of approaches are allowed in pursuing resolution of a case by agreement. The case of *Bordenkircher v. Hayes* (434 U.S. 357: 1978) is illustrative in this instance. After defendant Paul Lewis Hayes refused to plead to a particular felony indictment, the prosecutor carried out his threat to have the defendant re-indicted under Kentucky's habitual offender law. The statute included the possibility of a mandatory life sentence, and threat of this action was conveyed by the prosecutor during the course of plea negotiations. A jury subsequently convicted Hayes on the original charge and made an additional finding that he was eligible for a life term under the recidivist statute. Hayes appealed claiming violation of due process.

The Supreme Court upheld both convictions. The majority's opinion took two lines of argument. First, the Court acknowledged the breadth of prosecutorial discretion in the charging process. The majority saw little or no difference between the discretion to charge initially and discretion to drop the recidivist charge. Second, the Court said the plea bargaining process should be afforded substantial operating room. The bargaining process should entertain the whole range of options available to the defendant. In this case, Hayes was informed of what the prosecutor would do if he did not plead guilty, and since he was appropriately chargeable under the recidivist law, the prosecutor had not acted improperly. To the contrary, the Court concluded that the prosecutor "openly presented the defendant with the unpleasant alternatives of foregoing trial or facing charges on which he was plainly subject to prosecution." This was not viewed as a deprivation of due process. And, "in the 'give and take' of plea bargaining, there is no such element of punishment or retaliation so long as the accused is free to accept or reject the prosecutor's offer."

Plea bargaining will remain as a critical criminal justice practice because it benefits both prosecution and defense, creating a condition of mutual advantage. The negotiation itself occurs outside the scrutiny of the courts, so it is difficult for judges to detect agreements that might be suspect. But plea bargaining disposes of cases, and all the regular participants in the judicial system including defense attorneys assign that high priority. Since *Boykin,* at least, some formal requirements have been established in an attempt to minimize truly unjust outcomes.

Speedy Trial

The speedy trial provision of the Sixth Amendment is designed to move criminal cases through the courts in a timely fashion and to keep an accused from lengthy detention before trial. It also has the effect of safeguarding the capacity of the defendant to offer the best defense, as it ensures that the defendant's case will not deteriorate because of unwarranted delay. Of course, the guarantee has the same protective effect on the prosecution's case as well.

One important speedy trial question is when the protection begins: when the clock starts to run. *United States v. Marion* (404 U.S. 307: 1971) is instructive on this issue. William Marion was convicted for multiple counts of mail fraud, the last count of which was separated from the indictment by more than three years. He claimed the speedy trial protection applied to this period and that his rights had been violated by the delay. The Supreme Court would not extend the clause to the pre-indictment period, however, holding that the clock does not run until the charges have been formally brought, as through indictment, or the person has been taken into custody. Until actions of this sort occur, "a citizen suffers no restraint on his liberty and is not the subject of public accusations." Though delay before arrest or charge may "interfere with his ability to defend himself," this "possibility of prejudice" is itself insufficient reason to "wrench the Sixth Amendment from its proper context." The Court also pointed out that possible damage to a case is "inherent in any delay" but that this problem is shared with the prosecution. The *Marion* rationale was subsequently applied in *United States v. MacDonald* (456 U.S. 1: 1982), the "Green Beret" murder case that achieved national visibility through the television re-creation entitled "Fatal Vision." In *MacDonald,* the Court found that the time between dismissal of charges brought within the military system of justice and the subsequent filing of civilian charges is not subject to speedy trial protection.

Provided the right time period is measured, the criteria by which the Court assesses claims of speedy trial violations becomes the key component. The Court is currently operating by standards established in *Barker v. Wingo* (407 U.S. 514: 1972). Willie Barker was charged with murder and had a trial date set. Between the original trial date of 21 October 1958 and October 1963, Barker's trial was postponed 17 times. Barker did not object to the first 11 continuances because he was on pre-trial release through most of the period. When he was eventually tried, Barker was convicted and sentenced to life.

The Supreme Court unanimously upheld his conviction. Before fashioning the Court's speedy trial test in this case, Justice Powell considered the unique character of the speedy trial protection. He called it "generically different" from other constitutional protections because there is a "societal interest in providing a speedy trial which exists separate from, and at times in opposition to, the interests of the accused." The speedy trial concept is also "amorphous" and "vague," more so than other rights of the accused. In applying it, the Court rejected specific timetables and the "on demand" approach as too inflexible. Instead the Court devised a "balancing test" with four specific criteria for evaluating speedy trial claims: (1) length of delay; (2) reasons offered by the prosecution to justify the delay; (3) the defendant's assertion of his or her right to a speedy trial; and (4) prejudice to the defendant as measured by such things as pre-trial detention, anxiety, or impairment to the defense position itself. Applying these criteria to *Barker,* the Court concluded that despite the lengthy delay, Barker's defense was not demonstrably prejudiced or damaged. Further, he was on release throughout the period, and he failed to seriously assert his right to a speedy trial.

The criteria established in *Barker* provide a kind of two-edged speedy trial protection. The defendant must be protected from lengthy pre-trial detention and diminution of the capacity to advance a defense, but the state's case must be similarly protected from erosion by unwarranted delay. *Barker* creates several criteria for assessing constitutional violations based on delay. In fashioning the four criteria, the Court rejected both the fixed time and "demand-waiver" approaches. Instead the Court opted for a balance test compatible with the Burger Court's general preference for examining the "totality of circumstances." Thus, the burden of demonstrating violation of the speedy trial protection clearly rests with the defense. Cases such as *Marion* and *MacDonald* reflect the Court's preference for limiting the stages or time periods to which the protection applies. Meantime, Congress and the states have legislated speedy trial time periods for federal and state courts. Under the Speedy Trial Act of 1974 (as amended in 1979), 30 days are allowed from arrest to indictment in federal cases. Trial must occur within another 70 days. The time consumed for pre-trial motions and competency hearings is typically excluded. Most state speedy trial statutes demand comparable processing time, although the statutes do vary from state to state.

Standards set in such legislation are not constitutionally mandated, yet in *Barker* the Court clarified the constitutional requirements of the speedy trial clause.

Confrontation

The Sixth Amendment entitles a criminal defendant "to be confronted with the witnesses against him." The confrontation clause is often thought to be synonymous with the right to cross-examine accusers or adverse witnesses, but cross-examination is only one element of the clause's broader objective of fully exposing reliable evidence to the fact-finding process. The confrontation clause requires that witnesses be brought to open court and placed under oath and thereby under threat of perjury. Their testimony as well as their manner and presence are then assessed by jurors. The right to confront allows an accused to challenge the evidence against him or her in an attempt to present the best factual defense possible. The accused is given the opportunity to be present at all proceedings and may engage in a relatively restricted examination/cross-examination process. We examine the contours of the right to confront through a series of court decisions, several of which have an unusually direct connection to juveniles. We begin with *Pointer v. Texas* (380 U.S. 400: 1965), the decision that extended the right to confront to state cases.

Robert Pointer was charged with robbery. His chief accuser provided a detailed account of the crime at a preliminary hearing, a proceeding at which Pointer was unrepresented by defense counsel. At the trial, the prosecution used transcripts of this witness's testimony from the preliminary hearing because the witness had moved to another state. Pointer was convicted. On appeal, the Supreme Court reversed the conviction and said the right to cross-examine a witness was a central aspect of confrontation. Inclusion of the confrontation protection reflected the belief that "confrontation was a fundamental right essential to a fair trial." As for the practice in Texas of allowing use of a transcript, the Court said the confrontation protection would have been satisfied had the statements been made at a "full-fledged hearing" at which Pointer had been represented by counsel with a "complete and adequate opportunity to cross-examine." Absent that condition, what occurred was an unconstitutional denial of the right to confront.

The capability to cross-examine constitutes the center of the right to confront. This point was exemplified in *Pointer*. Soon after *Pointer,* the Court made it clear that there was no substitute for the right to subject a witness to cross-examination, in *Bruton v. United States* (391 U.S. 123:

1968). George Bruton was tried in federal court. A postal inspector gave testimony that described an oral confession by Bruton's co-defendant that implicated both the co-defendant and Bruton. The trial judge instructed the jury that the confession was inadmissible hearsay and must be disregarded in deciding Bruton's guilt. The Supreme Court held that the instruction was insufficient protection. The use of the co-defendant's confession "added substantial, perhaps even critical, weight to the Government's case in a form not subject to cross-examination, since the [co-defendant] did not take the stand." Though the Court conceded that some situations might be remedied by jury instructions, it held that the remedy did not apply in this case. The introduction of the confession "posed a substantial threat" to Bruton's capability to confront. "In the context of a joint trial we cannot accept limiting instructions as an adequate substitute for the petitioner's constitutional right of cross-examination. The effect is the same as if there has been no instruction at all."

In *Ohio v. Roberts* (448 U.S. 56: 1980), the Court reviewed a variation of the *Pointer* fact situation. After testifying at a preliminary hearing, a witness failed to appear at the trial despite several subpoenas. A state statute permitted use of preliminary hearing testimony by a witness who could not be produced at the trial. The defense objected to the use of the transcript despite the fact that the witness had originally been called by the defense, because the testimony had not turned out to be favorable to the defendant. The Supreme Court concluded that a sufficient good-faith effort had been made to locate the witness and that the prior testimony bore "sufficient indicia of reliability" to be used under these circumstances.

A different confrontation issue was addressed in *Delaware v. Fensterer* (88 L. Ed. 2d 15: 1985). In this case an expert witness for the prosecution was unable to recall the basis for an opinion he offered in testimony. The Court said this did not violate the defendant's right to confront the witness. The right to cross-examine is not denied "whenever the witness' lapse of memory impedes one method of discrediting him." The confrontation clause includes no guarantee that every witness "will refrain from giving testimony that is marred by forgetfulness, confusion, or evasion." To the contrary, the requirements of due process are generally satisfied when the defense has a full and fair opportunity to probe and expose these infirmities through cross-examination.

The right to confront has historically meant that both witness and defendant must be present in the courtroom for the various stages of the judicial process. Though that expectation generally holds, it is not inflexible. A defendant may waive the right to presence and choose not to attend any or all of the proceedings. A defendant's courtroom behavior may also become sufficiently disruptive to justify his or her removal from the courtroom as a requisite to continuing. In *Illinois v. Allen* (397 U.S. 337: 1970), for example, the Court specifically ruled that the right to be present at trial was not "absolute." The Sixth Amendment does not, said the Court, "so handicap a trial judge in conducting a criminal trial" as to require the defendant's presence regardless of his or her conduct. In addition to removal, the Court suggested in *Allen* that a trial judge can handle disruptive defendants by binding and gagging them or by citing them for contempt. Either is "constitutionally permissible" to protect the integrity of the judicial process.

Several other recent confrontation cases have involved the rights of juveniles or the rights of those accused of victimizing children. The pattern generally remains that defendants are entitled to the broadest opportunity to neutralize damaging evidence. In *Davis v. Alaska* (425 U.S. 308: 1974), the Court applied this principle to a case in which a defendant had been denied an opportunity to disclose and develop the juvenile record of a crucial prosecution witness. Although disclosure of the witness's status as a juvenile delinquent would conflict with the state's policy of preserving confidentiality of juvenile proceedings, the Court decided that disclosure was necessary to support the defendant's contention that the witness was biased. Whatever "temporary embarrassment might result" to the juvenile or his family, said the Court, is "outweighed by [the defendant's] right to probe the influence of possible bias on the testimony of a crucial witness."

The most controversial of the remaining decisions was *Coy v. Iowa* (487 U.S. 1012: 1988). A number of techniques have been tried to protect child witnesses in sexual misconduct prosecutions. Iowa sought to place a screen between the defendant and his child victims as they testified. The screen blocked the children's view of the defendant, but he could see and hear them through the screen. The Supreme Court, however, struck down the protective procedure as a confrontation violation. The Court said the confrontation protection "guarantees the defendant a face-to-face meeting" with witnesses. The protection has been essential to fairness "over the centuries" because a witness may "feel quite differently" when he "distort[s] or mistake[s] the facts" while looking at the defendant. The face-to-face confrontation, like the right to cross-examine, "ensures the integrity of the fact-finding process." The state, said the Court, cannot deny the "profound effect" the presence of the defendant may have on a witness because it is the "same phenomenon used to establish the potential trauma that allegedly justified the extraordinary procedure" used in this case. Face-to-face presence "may unfortunately upset the truthful rape victim or abused child," said the Court, but it may also "undo the false accuser, or reveal the child to be coached by a malevolent adult." Constitutional protections simply "have costs," the Court observed.

The state of Iowa had contended that the confrontation interest was "outweighed by the necessity of protecting victims of sexual abuse." It further argued that such necessity was established by the statute, which created a "legislative presumption of trauma." The Court ruled that this was not enough. Something more than the "generalized finding" underlying the law is required when an exception to a constitutional protection is not "firmly rooted in our jurisprudence." Since the state made no "individual findings" that the witnesses "needed special protection," the judgment in this case could not be "sustained by any conceivable exception." According to the *Coy* decision, no victim of child abuse is exempt from the face-to-face provision.

Although *Coy* held that physical courtroom confrontation is the principal component of the confrontation protection, it also held that in cases other than those involving child abuse exceptions would be considered in furtherance of important public policy. *Maryland v. Craig* (111 L. Ed. 2d 666: 1990) reflected the nonabsolute character of *Coy* by holding that, in special cases, states could protect victims—particularly child abuse victims—by allowing them to testify on closed-circuit television. Justice Sandra Day O'Connor wrote for a five-justice majority that neither *Coy* nor any previous ruling established that a defendant has an "absolute right to a face-to-face meeting" with witnesses. Although the confrontation clause "reflects a preference for face-to-face confrontation at trial, . . . we cannot say that such confrontation is an indispensable element of the Sixth Amendment guarantee." O'Connor rejected a "literal reading" of the clause and used hearsay exceptions as illustrative of instances in which "competing interests, if closely examined, may warrant dispensing with confrontation at trial." The "central concern" of the clause is to "insure the reliability of evidence . . . by subjecting it to rigorous testing in the context of an adversary proceeding." Maryland's procedure of using closed-circuit television does prevent the child witness from seeing the defendant, but it "preserves all the other elements of the confrontation right:" The child witness must be competent and testify under oath; the judge, jury, and defendant can view the witness's demeanor as he or she testifies; and the defendant "retains full opportunity for contemporaneous cross-examination." The presence of these other elements "adequately insures that the testimony is both reliable and subject to rigorous adversarial testing in a manner functionally equivalent to that accorded live, inperson testimony." As a result, O'Connor said the Court was "confident" that use of the television procedure, "where necessary to further an important state interest, does not impinge upon the truth-seeking or symbolic purposes of the confrontation clause." The "critical inquiry" in *Craig* then became whether use of the television procedure is needed to further an important state interest. The Court concluded that protection of minor victims of sex crimes from "further trauma and embarrassment is a compelling one." Further, the Court determined that the interest in the "physical and psychological well-being of child abuse victims may be sufficiently important to outweigh, at least in some cases, a defendant's right to face his or her accusers in court." The Court did not require use of closed-circuit television, but rather permitted it only in cases in which a trial court hears evidence and determines that the technique is "necessary to protect the welfare of the particular child witness who seeks to testify." In *Coy,* by contrast, the Iowa legislature had made the judgment in advance that all child witnesses must testify in a face-to-face situation.

In *Idaho v. Wright* (111 L. Ed. 2d 638: 1990), the Court said that states may not utilize hearsay exceptions that permit doctors or other adults to testify about their conversations with abuse victims. At issue in this case was the testimony of a pediatrician who represented statements made to him by a three-year-old girl. The Court concluded that the statements could not be admitted because they "lacked the particularized guarantees of trustworthiness necessary to satisfy the requirement of the Confrontation Clause." The state had contended that trustworthiness should be determined by considering the "totality of circumstances," including other evidence that "corroborates the truth of the statement," but the Court rejected this argument. To be admissible, said the Court, hearsay evidence "must possess indicia of reliability by virtue of its inherent trustworthiness, not by reference to other evidence at trial. . . . Corroboration of a child's allegation of sexual abuse by medical evidence of abuse, for example, sheds no light on the reliability of the child's allegations regarding the identity of the abuser." In these situations, the Court concluded, there is "very real danger that a jury will rely on partial corroboration to mistakenly infer the trustworthiness of the entire statement."

Compulsory Process

The Sixth Amendment provides that a criminal defendant is entitled to "have compulsory process for obtaining witnesses in his favor." This allows a defendant to use the legal process to compel a witness to appear. This compulsory process protects the defendant's right to present a defense that includes calling witnesses who may not want to appear. The compulsory process provision of the Sixth Amendment has been interpreted more broadly than the right to just subpoena witnesses, however. It has been interpreted to include preventing the state from denying access to certain categories of witnesses, such as co-participants in an alleged crime. Similarly, it prevents a state from creating a situation in which a witness for the defense is diminished in value by a judicial action or jury instruction. This protection establishes a substantial expectation that the defense will be able to present a full and unimpaired defense. The compulsory process protection was extended to the state level with *Washington v. Texas* (388 U.S. 14: 1967). In this case, the Court found the protection to be a fundamental right and one that "stands on no lesser footing than other Sixth Amendment rights." The specific question before the Court in *Washington* was whether or not a state could keep "principals, accomplices or accessories" in the same crime from being witnesses for each other. The law was enacted to prevent perjured testimony by co-participants. Jackie Washington, charged with murder, wished to use Charles Fuller as a defense witness. Fuller was a suspected co-participant with Washington in the alleged crime. Washington was denied use of Fuller as a witness by Texas statute. Fuller could testify for the prosecution under Texas law, however. On appeal, the Supreme Court reversed Washington's conviction.

Before addressing the specifics of the Texas law, the Court spoke generally on the nature of the compulsory process right. The right, said the Court, is "in plain terms the right to present a defense, the right to present the defendant's version of the facts as well as the prosecution's to the jury so it may decide where the truth lies." Just as a defendant may confront prosecution witnesses, the defendant is also entitled to "present his own witnesses to establish a defense." In this particular case, the defendant was denied the capacity to establish a defense because the state law prohibited use of his witness's testimony. Thus, the Court subordinated the trial court's interest in deterring perjury to the defendant's right to present a defense. The Court was also unconvinced that co-defendants would perjure themselves on behalf of accomplices. If a witness is convicted and awaiting sentence, or simply awaiting trial, "common sense would suggest that he often has a greater interest in lying in favor of the prosecution than against it." The Court concluded that to think that "criminals will lie to save their fellows but not to obtain favors from the prosecution for themselves is indeed to clothe the criminal class with more nobility than one might expect to find in the public at large." The ability to subpoena witnesses can be of paramount importance to a defense against criminal charges. In *Washington,* the Court ruled that Texas arbitrarily denied the defendant the right to have the material testimony of a witness, thus denying him the right to compulsory process.

The compulsory process provision of the Sixth Amendment has not been before the Court very often. The Burger Court, however, rendered two decisions on the issue, both of which were decided in favor of the defendant. *Webb v. Texas* (409 U.S. 95: 1972) involved judicial intimidation of a defense witness. The witness, serving a sentence on a prior conviction, was admonished by the trial judge about the "dangers of perjury," how perjury conviction would mean substantial supplement of the sentence being served, and how perjury would impair chances of parole. The witness decided not to testify, and Alfred Webb argued that his only witness had been coerced into not testifying by the trial judge. The Supreme Court agreed. It cited the judge's "threatening" remarks as effectively driving the witness from the stand and denying Webb due process. In *Cool v. United States* (409 U.S. 100: 1972), the Court again ruled for the defendant because the defense was impaired by an improper jury instruction. Defendant Marilyn Cool was relying on the testimony of a co-defendant. The witness, Robert Voyles, testified that he had committed the crime and that Cool had not been involved. The trial judge gave the jury a "lengthy 'accomplice instruction' to be used in evaluating Voyles' testimony." The judge suggested that the testimony was "open to suspicion" and that unless the jury believed the testimony "beyond a reasonable doubt," it should be discarded. The Supreme Court concluded that "the clear implication of the instruction was that the jury should disregard Voyles' testimony." An instruction of that kind "places an improper burden on the defense."

Decisions like *Washington, Webb,* and *Cool* established a basic expectation that the defense will be able to present a full and undeterred case. The Rehnquist Court recently encountered an intriguing variation on the right to present a defense in *Rock v. Arkansas* (483 U.S. 44: 1987). A state rule of evidence categorically disallowed the admission of hypnotically refreshed testimony. Vicki Lorene Rock was charged with shooting her husband. She twice underwent hypnosis to refresh her memory on the details of the incident. The trial court ruled that hypnotically refreshed testimony could not be permitted under state law and limited Rock's testimony to repeating statements she had made prior to hypnosis. In a five to four decision, the Court said the state rule that categorically excluded all hypnotically refreshed testimony impermissibly interfered with Rock's right to testify on her own behalf. Though the right to present relevant evidence is not without limitation, the restrictions "may not be arbitrary or disproportionate to the purposes they are designed to serve." The Court concluded that the Arkansas statute operated to the detriment of any defendant who undergoes hypnosis without regard to the reasons for the hypnosis, the circumstances under which it took place, or any independent verification of the information it produced. Although hypnosis may be unreliable in some situations, it has been found effective in obtaining certain kinds of information. In addition, hypnotically refreshed testimony is subject to verification by a variety of means, and any inaccuracies produced by the process can be reduced by the use of procedural safeguards.

Assistance of Counsel

The centerpiece of the fair trial guarantees of the Sixth Amendment has come to be the right to assistance of legal counsel. The counsel clause entitles any accused person to have "assistance of counsel for his defense." In its early construction this provision was confined to preventing the government from keeping an accused from securing his or her own counsel. There was no expectation that counsel was required or would be provided in the instance of defendant indigency. The Supreme Court has gradually expanded the counsel provision, however, to require the appointment of defense counsel in all federal and state felony cases and in all misdemeanors involving confinement to jail as a possible sentence. Since *In re Gault* (378 U.S. 1: 1967), juvenile delinquency proceedings also require appointment of counsel.

Assistance of counsel doctrine has developed around two somewhat different propositions. First, the aid provided by counsel is invaluable in criminal cases, and due process requires the "guiding hand of counsel" for an accused charged with a criminal offense. Justice Hugo Black remarked in the *Gideon* case, discussed below, that lawyers are "necessities, not luxuries." Second, a defendant should not be denied assistance of counsel because of his or her indigency. Any person who is charged with a criminal offense and is not able to afford counsel cannot have a fair trial unless counsel is provided.

COUNSEL AT STATE CRIMINAL TRIALS

The first significant counsel case to appear before the Supreme Court was *Powell v. Alabama* (287 U.S. 45: 1932), which raised a couple of major questions. The first was whether the Sixth Amendment counsel provisions, lodged in the federal Constitution, extended to state proceedings. Also, if the right did extend to state proceedings, it was not clear whether the state was required to provide counsel to indigent defendants. *Powell* arose out of the infamous *Scottsboro* trial in which nine black defendants were convicted of raping two white women in Alabama. Ozzie Powell and his co-defendants were on trial for their lives in a wholly hostile environment. They were indigent and illiterate. Trial counsel was not designated for the defendants until the morning of the trial, and even then, assigned counsel was the entire Bar of Alabama. All nine defendants were found guilty. The Supreme Court reversed the convictions and, in doing so, determined that the due process clause of the Fourteenth Amendment encompassed assistance of counsel because counsel was "fundamental" to the basic concept of due process. By this reasoning, the essence of the counsel provisions of the Constitution was extended to state trials, at least in capital cases. The trial judge in the *Scottsboro* case failed to give reasonable time and opportunity to secure effective counsel for the representation of the defense. Given the extreme circumstances of the case, this "failure of the trial court to make an effective appointment of counsel" constituted denial of due process within the meaning of the Fourteenth Amendment.

In a capital case in which the defendant is unable to employ counsel and is "incapable adequately of making his own defense because of ignorance, feeblemindedness, illiteracy or the like," the trial judge, whether requested to or not, must assign counsel for the defendant as a necessary requisite of due process. The assignment obligation can only be fulfilled if counsel is assigned in time to allow the "giving of effective aid in the preparation and trial of the case." A criminal defendant requires the "guiding hand of counsel at every step in the proceeding against him." Though the Court did not indicate every stage in which counsel might be required, *Powell* clearly demanded that counsel was at least required at the trial stage of capital cases.

Powell was a limited decision in that it involved only capital cases at the state level. It was the product of an unusual fact situation. Nonetheless, *Powell* impacted policy regarding assistance of counsel in two ways. First, it extended the Sixth Amendment counsel clause to the state level through the due process clause of the Fourteenth Amendment for the first time, albeit only in death penalty situations. Second, *Powell* changed the direction of the evolution of Court policy on assistance of counsel. For some time prior to *Powell,* many argued that the Sixth Amendment merely allowed a defendant to have counsel. From *Powell* on, it was recognized that states had an affirmative obligation to provide counsel when counsel could not be privately retained by a defendant. *Powell* also became the basis for establishing assistance of counsel as a requirement of fundamental fairness in all criminal cases. It was only a matter of time until the Court examined the question of providing counsel in noncapital felonies. In *Johnson v. Zerbst* (304 U.S. 458: 1938), the Court ruled that in all federal felony cases counsel must be provided to indigent defendants. Although limited to federal cases, *Zerbst* extended *Powell* beyond capital cases and established that without a knowing and voluntary waiver, counsel must be appointed for federal criminal trials. *Zerbst* also took *Powell* to the threshold of application of a parallel counsel policy at the state level, a position eventually taken in *Gideon.*

Gideon v. Wainwright (372 U.S. 335: 1963) considered whether or not states must provide counsel in all felony cases. Clarence Gideon was charged with a property felony in Florida. He was unable to secure his own counsel and requested appointment of counsel for his trial. The request was denied and Gideon was convicted and sentenced to five years in prison. The

Supreme Court reversed his conviction in a unanimous landmark decision. Had Gideon been prosecuted for a federal offense, he would have had counsel appointed under provisions of *Zerbst*. But the governing precedent in state cases was *Betts v. Brady* (316 U.S. 455: 1942), which required "special circumstances" in order to necessitate appointment of counsel. *Betts* had come before the Court when it was still extremely reluctant to use the federal Constitution to intervene in state affairs, especially those having to do with the criminal process. The Court said in *Betts* that each state court possessed the power to appoint counsel on a case-by-case basis and that the states should not be "strait-jacketed" by an interpretation of the counsel clause mandating appointment in every instance. *Gideon* gave the Court an opportunity to reconsider *Betts*. The Court ruled that *Betts* was wrong and that denial of counsel to indigent, noncapital felony defendants violated the basic concept of due process. The fundamental right to a fair trial "could not be realized if the poor man charged with a crime has to face his accuser without a lawyer to assist him." The Court said that *Betts* "had departed from the sound wisdom upon which the Court's holding in *Powell v. Alabama* rested" and should be overruled.

The Court's position in *Gideon* was unanimous and emphatic. Some of Justice Black's majority opinion deserves extended representation. He wrote that not only new precedents, but also

> Reason and reflection require us to recognize that in our adversary system of criminal justice, any person hailed into court, who is too poor to hire a lawyer, cannot be assured a fair trial unless counsel is provided for him. This seems to us to be an obvious truth. Governments, both state and federal, quite properly spend vast sums of money to establish machinery to try defendants accused of crime. Lawyers to prosecute are everywhere deemed essential to protect the public's interest in an orderly society. Similarly, there are few defendants charged with a crime, few indeed, who fail to hire the best lawyers they can get to prepare and present their defenses. That government hires lawyers to prosecute and defendants who have the money hire lawyers to defend are the strongest indications of the widespread belief that lawyers in criminal courts are necessities, not luxuries. The right of one charged with crime to counsel may not be deemed fundamental and essential to fair trials in some countries, but it is in ours. From the very beginning, our state and national constitutions and laws have laid great emphasis on procedural and substantial safeguards designed to assure fair trials before impartial tribunals in which every defendant stands equal before the law. This noble ideal cannot be realized if the poor man charged with crime has to face his accusers without a lawyer to assist him.

Gideon confirmed a position on counsel in state felony trials that had been evolving since *Betts* was decided. The evolution took two forms. First, *Betts* provided that trial courts find "special circumstances" before appointing counsel. Initially these special circumstances included capital cases, physical or mental handicap, or a very young defendant. Over time the Court broadened the concept of special circumstances and made it very difficult for trial judges not to appoint counsel under the standard. Between the late 1940s and the *Gideon* decision, no state conviction was affirmed by the Supreme Court over claims of denial of counsel. The Court was clearly moving toward a *Gideon* decision. Second, many states adopted a policy on their own of requiring counsel in all felony cases. By the time *Gideon* was decided, almost half the states had already embraced the *Gideon* position, at least for the trial stage of criminal proceedings. The attorneys general of 22 states submitted an amicus curiae brief to the Supreme Court on behalf of Gideon. Unlike some of the other Warren Court decisions dealing with rights of the accused, the *Gideon* holding was generally well received. It ended the uncertainties stemming from the special circumstances rule and established that all felony cases require defense counsel at the trial stage. With *Gideon* in place, the Court could move on to two other critical questions: Does the counsel requirement extend to misdemeanors, and are there other stages in the criminal process comparable to the trial stage that also require assistance of counsel? Thus, *Gideon* reshaped policy on assistance of counsel, but it also refocused other inquiry in a way that eventually produced such landmark decisions as *Miranda v. Arizona* (384 U.S. 436: 1984).

The Burger Court extended the *Gideon* rule to misdemeanors in *Argersinger v. Hamlin* (407 U.S. 25: 1972). Jon Argersinger was convicted of an offense punishable by up to six months' imprisonment. He was indigent and unrepresented by counsel. In a unanimous decision, the Supreme Court found his trial and conviction to be constitutionally defective. The opinion of the Court stressed three points. First, the Court found nothing historically to indicate that Sixth Amendment rights should be retractable in cases involving petty offenses. Second, the nature of the legal issues of a case should be the criterion for assessing necessity of counsel. Cases in which lesser terms of imprisonment result may not be any less complex than cases in which lengthy sentences may occur. Third, given the assembly-line character of misdemeanor proceedings, assistance of counsel may be especially important. The basic holding of *Argersinger* is that absent a "knowing and intelligent waiver," no defendant may receive jail or prison time unless he or she was represented by counsel at the trial.

The Court was not of one mind in *Argersinger* when it considered implementation. On the one hand, the justices wished to extend *Gideon* and did so in fairly strong terms. On the other hand, the Court was faced with implementing a policy where the court system is most congested and where pressures for "assembly-line justice" are most acute. *Argersinger* was a compromise. It required assistance of counsel in misdemeanor cases, recognizing that the legal needs of defendants in these cases may be equal to or greater than those of defendants in felony cases. At the same time, it also provided trial judges with the option of not appointing defense counsel at all, although in refusing to do so the trial judge might forfeit imprisonment as a sentence option. Despite the problems in implementing it, *Argersinger* has fundamentally altered the process of justice in misdemeanor courts, often called "city courts," "municipal courts," or "justice of the peace" courts. It has also produced important legislation at the state and local levels. Many cities, for example, now appoint or contract with private counsel to provide legal assistance to persons who desire to go to trial on misdemeanor charges. Some states have decriminalized most traffic offenses to avoid the consequences of *Argersinger*.

Argersinger was refined in *Scott v. Illinois* (440 U.S. 367: 1979), in which the Supreme Court held that a state court does not have to appoint counsel where imprisonment is authorized for a particular offense but not actually imposed. *Argersinger* and *Scott* together require greater caution by state and local governments in criminal proceedings. Many local judges are quite reluctant to imprison for misdemeanor convictions where counsel is not present, unless the defendant was made aware of his or her right to counsel before tendering a guilty plea.

The *Scott* emphasis on actual incarceration was reinforced in *Lassiter v. Department of Social Services* (452 U.S. 18: 1981), in which the Court held that counsel need not be provided to an indigent parent at a hearing that could terminate his or her status as a parent. The Court said an indigent litigant was entitled to counsel only when the litigant is threatened with the deprivation of physical liberty. On a related matter, the Court held in *Ake v. Oklahoma* (470 U.S. 68: 1985) that an indigent defendant seeking to utilize the insanity defense is entitled to court-appointed psychiatric assistance. Justice Thurgood Marshall said that a trial or sentencing proceeding is fundamentally unfair if the state proceeds against an indigent without ensuring that he or she has access to advice that is "integral to the building of an effective defense." The impact of *Ake* is limited in that the great majority of states already provided such aid to indigent defendants.

Finally, efforts to combat organized crime activities and narcotics trafficking have produced an interesting right-to-counsel question. Under provisions of such federal statutes as the Racketeer Influenced and Corrupt Organization (RICO) Act, the Continual Criminal Enterprise Act, and the Comprehensive Forfeiture Act, the federal government was authorized to seize assets that are the proceeds of criminal activities from criminal defendants. In 1989, in *United States v. Monsanto* (105 L. Ed. 2d 512: 1989) and *Caplin & Drysdale, Chartered v. United States* (105 L. Ed. 2d 528: 1989), the Supreme Court considered whether or not these forfeiture provisions could be used to seize assets intended to pay for defense counsel. By a vote of five to four, the Supreme Court ruled that assets intended to cover attorney fees are not exempt from seizure and that such seizure did not unconstitutionally interfere with the right to counsel. The language in the Comprehensive Forfeiture Act, said the Court, is "plain and unambiguous." Congress could not have chosen "stronger words to express its intent that forfeiture be mandatory" in these situations. Neither did the statute contain any language that "even hints" that assets used for attorney's fees are not included in seizable property. By enacting the Forfeiture Act, Congress "decided to give force to the old adage that 'crime does not pay.' " The Court found no evidence that Congress "intended to modify that nostrum to read, 'Crime does not pay, except for attorney's fees.' " The Court pointed out that the law did not prevent a defendant from "hiring the attorney of his [or her] choice or disqualify any attorney from serving as a defendant's counsel." A defendant with nonforfeitable assets remains free to retain "any attorney of his [or her] choosing."

There could be cases, however, in which a defendant is unable to retain an attorney of choice because forfeiture leaves him or her indigent. "Impecunious" defendants, said the Court, do not have the right to "choose their counsel." Neither do they have a "cognizable complaint" as long as they are "adequately represented by attorneys appointed by the court." Compulsory forfeiture of assets, even if such forfeiture renders a defendant unable to privately retain counsel, is not unconstitutional because defendants are not entitled to "spend another person's money for services rendered by an attorney." This proposition holds even if that money is the "only way that a defendant will be able to retain the attorney of his choice." The Court said there is a "compelling" public interest in "stripping criminals . . . of their undeserved economic power," and this interest "overrides any Sixth Amendment interest in permitting criminals to assets adjudged forfeitable to pay for their defense."

OTHER CRITICAL STAGES

The *Gideon* decision was based on the concept that assistance of counsel is critical to the trial stage. Once trial assistance was mandated for all felony prosecutions in *Gideon,* however, it was inevitable that other stages in the criminal process would be examined as well. The Court began reexamination of the prior process by redefining what was meant by a critical stage. A critical stage became a point in a criminal proceeding at which an accused person's constitutional protections come into play and at which the outcome of the criminal process might be affected. Under this definition, many stages were identified as critical. The Court then established that a person is entitled to assistance of counsel at each of these stages. Soon after *Gideon,* such pre-trial stages as custodial interrogation, post-indictment investigation, preliminary hearing, and post-indictment identification were found to be critical. Even prior to *Gideon,* assistance of counsel requirements had been extended to arraignments. The critical stages of post-trial proceedings have been defined as sentencing, probation revocation, and appeal. The large number of recognized critical stages reflects the high priority assigned to assistance of counsel by the Supreme Court. An accused must have access to legal counsel throughout the criminal process to satisfy due process requirements.

An example of how the Warren Court utilized the broadened critical stage concept is *United States v. Wade* (388 U.S. 218: 1967). Billy Joe Wade and two companions were indicted by a grand jury for bank robbery and were subsequently arrested. Counsel was appointed to represent Wade. Soon after, Wade appeared before two witnesses in a lineup, and both witnesses identified Wade as a participant in the robbery. The problem was that defense counsel had not been notified of the lineup and was not present as the witnesses observed and identified Wade. The issue in *Wade* was whether such a post-indictment lineup was a critical stage requiring presence of counsel. The Court vacated Wade's conviction and ordered a new trial, saying the post-indictment process was "peculiarly riddled with innumerable dangers and variable factors which might seriously, even crucially, derogate from a fair trial." Denial of counsel at this stage was seen as critical, as there exists "grave potential for prejudice, intentional or not, in the pre-trial lineup." The presence of counsel "can often avert prejudice and assure a meaningful confrontation at trial." The Court's conclusion was that there was "little doubt" that the lineup was a "critical stage" at which Wade was entitled to the aid of counsel.

Expansion of the concept of critical stage also occurred with respect to post-trial proceedings. In *Douglas v. California* (372 U.S. 353: 1963), the Court held that counsel was required for those appeals that are a matter of right. At the present time, counsel is not required for secondary or discretionary appeals. Counsel is required for juvenile proceedings, however, as held in *Re Gault* (387 U.S. 1: 1967), and at the sentencing stage of adult criminal proceedings. In *Mempa v. Rhay* (389 U.S. 128: 1967), the Court said an individual is entitled to counsel in a hearing at which probation is revoked and a sentence is to be imposed. These cases demonstrate the exceptionally high priority assigned by the Supreme Court to making legal counsel available to all persons at virtually all stages of the criminal process. They reflect the Court's recognition that other constitutional protections are best preserved through assistance of counsel. Assistance of counsel is also part of the civil trial process. Although such assistance is not constitutionally mandated for civil trials, federal appellate courts have held that less strict adherence to evidentiary rules and less formal compliance ought to be applied by trial courts when one of the parties is unrepresented by counsel. In the case of an unrepresented prisoner plaintiff in civil rights actions, counsel is often appointed by the trial judge to ensure fairness.

EFFECTIVENESS OF COUNSEL

Before the assistance of counsel protection was extended in *Gideon* and later cases, the issue of quality representation was not assigned great priority. The Court has never established precise standards by which to assess counsel performance. Basically, a standard known as "mockery of justice" was utilized. This standard was not stringent in that a claim of inadequacy could prevail only if the counsel's performance made the legal proceedings a "farce and a mockery of justice." A more demanding test was fashioned by the Court in *Strickland v. Washington* (466 U.S. 668: 1984).

Strickland developed from a death penalty proceeding that followed guilty pleas to three capital murder charges. During the plea colloquy, David Washington said he had no significant prior record and the crimes to which he was pleading were caused by extreme stress produced by his inability to provide for his family. Washington and his counsel discussed approaches to the sentencing hearing, and counsel decided it was inadvisable to call character witnesses or seek psychiatric examination. The decision reflected counsel's judgment that Washington was better off using his plea colloquy as sufficient evidence on these points. With this approach, the state would be unable to cross-examine Washington or to introduce its own evidence concerning his mental state. Counsel also chose not to request a pre-sentence report because it would have shown Washington's prior record to be extensive. Nevertheless, the trial judge sentenced Washington to death. Washington appealed on grounds of ineffective counsel, citing counsel's failure to request a pre-sentence report, seek psychiatric examination, and present character witnesses. In an eight to one decision, the Court said Washington had been effectively represented.

Justice O'Connor began the majority opinion by emphasizing the location of the right to counsel in the Sixth Amendment, which generally addresses the concept of fair trial. She said that a fair trial at minimum is one in which "evidence subject to adversarial testing is presented to an impartial tribunal for the resolution of defined issues." The benchmark for assessing a claim of ineffectiveness is "whether counsel's conduct so undermined the proper functioning of the adversarial process" that the proceeding cannot be relied upon as having produced a "just result." Reversal on grounds of ineffective counsel requires the consideration of two elements: that counsel performance is shown to be deficient and that the deficiency prejudiced the outcome. Counsel's representation must fall below an objective standard of reasonableness using prevailing professional norms. Judicial scrutiny of counsel performance should be highly deferential, O'Connor wrote, and should avoid the second-guessing of counsel judgment. The courts should indulge a strong presumption that counsel conduct falls within a wide range of reasonable professional assistance. Accordingly, strategic choices made after thorough investigation of plausible options are virtually unchallengeable.

Despite the deference recommended, some cases require reversal because their result was prejudiced. The defendant must show a reasonable probability that without the counsel's misrepresentation the result of the proceeding would have been different. Such a probability must be sufficient to undermine confidence in the result. Review of this issue must consider the totality of evidence entered at the proceeding. O'Connor concluded by saying that a number of practical considerations are crucial to applying the standards she discussed. Most important in reviewing claims of ineffectiveness is that the "principles we have stated do not create mechanical rules." The ultimate focus must be on the fundamental fairness of the proceeding. In examining Washington's case by these standards, the Court decided that had counsel offered the evidence Washington listed in his appeal, it would "barely have altered" the profile on which the sentence was based.

Strickland emphasized that the most important factor in assessing the effectiveness of counsel is whether the integrity of the adversary process is diminished. So long as counsel is "reasonably effective" and there is no "reasonable probability" of a different outcome, the quality of assistance is presumed to be adequate. Another example of a case in which the Court rejected claims of ineffective assistance is *Jones v. Barnes* (463 U.S. 745: 1983). The Court held that counsel assigned to handle an appeal for a convicted defendant need not raise every issue suggested by the defendant. For courts to "second guess reasonable professional judgments and impose on appointed counsel a duty to raise every 'colorable' claim suggested by a client" would not well serve the goal of vigorous and effective advocacy.

In *United States v. Cronic* (466 U.S. 648: 1984), the Court ruled that in assessing whether there had been a breakdown of the adversarial process, a court may not conclude by inference that circumstances surrounding representation constitute denial of effective assistance. Cronic contended that allowing his counsel only 25 days for trial preparation following appointment was unfair. The Court upheld his conviction, maintaining that the short period of time did not, in itself, demonstrate that his counsel had "failed to function in any meaningful sense." Two years later, the Court ruled in *Nix v. Whiteside* (475 U.S. 157: 1986) that an attorney does not deny a client effective assistance by insisting that the client testify truthfully. At a point where the client indicated an intention to perjure himself at his trial, the attorney threatened to inform the trial court and withdraw as counsel. The Court said that the attorney's duty to the client's cause is limited to "legitimate, lawful conduct compatible with the truth-seeking objective of a trial." The right to testify does not extend to testifying falsely, and the right to counsel "includes no right to have a lawyer who will cooperate with planned perjury."

Finally, there is the case of *Burger v. Kemp* (483 U.S. 776: 1987), which involved a claim of inadequate representation. Christopher Burger was represented by an experienced and well-respected local attorney, but was sentenced to death following a murder conviction. Burger contended he was ineffectively assisted because of a conflict of interest on the part of his attorney, who was the law partner of the attorney appointed to represent Burger's confederate in the crime. Burger also claimed that his counsel failed to adequately investigate the possibility of offering mitigating evidence at the sentencing hearing. The Supreme Court ruled that neither of Burger's claims had merit. The constitutional requirement of effective representation is not necessarily violated if partners or even a single attorney represents co-defendants. The Court was satisfied in this case that the overlap did not so infect counsel's conduct as to constitute an active representation of competing interests. The Court was also satisfied that the substance of the appellate briefs filed by Burger's attorney had a solid strategic basis even though a lesser culpability argument was not advanced on Burger's behalf. The justices said no part of the strategy was attributable to the fact that the lawyer's partner was the co-defendant's counsel. Finally, the lawyer's decision not to argue mitigating circumstances was suggested by reasonable professional judgment and well-established legal standards. Thus, the Court refused to second-guess the course of action taken.

Self-Representation

The Court paid inordinate attention in the 1960s and early 1970s to expanding the right to assistance of counsel. One of the more interesting decisions, however, came in a case in which the defendant wished to forgo assistance and represent himself. In *Faretta v. California* (422 U.S. 806: 1975), a six-justice majority held that Anthony Faretta could constitutionally defend himself. The majority recognized that self-representation may be an unwise course for a criminal defendant, but the Court said it is "one thing to hold that every defendant, rich or poor, has the right to the assistance of counsel, and quite another to say that a State may compel a defendant to accept a lawyer he does not want." Free choice was crucial to the Court's decision. The choice of a defense belongs to the defendant, including the question of counsel. Although the defendant's choice may be "ultimately to his own detriment, his choice must be honored." A trial judge must make the defendant "aware of the danger and disadvantages of self-representation" so the record can reflect that the defendant made the choice with "eyes open." The criterion by which the determination is to be made is not technical. The trial judge had denied Faretta's request to represent himself after quizzing him on aspects of the state law. It makes no difference "how well or poorly Faretta had mastered the intricacies of the hearsay rule and the California code provisions." The decision rested with his "knowing exercise of the right to defend himself." In this case, the majority concluded that Faretta had been denied a constitutional right to "conduct his own defense."

Faretta established the rule that a defendant has a right to carry on his or her own defense without violating the assistance of counsel requirement of the Sixth Amendment. The case runs absolutely counter to many recent Supreme Court decisions that found the "guiding hand of counsel" to be indispensable to due process. *Faretta* not only recognizes the option of self-representation but accords it the status of a protected right on par with assistance of counsel. *Faretta* holds in addition that a defendant need not demonstrate even minimal levels of legal skill to exercise this right of self-representation. Like any other constitutional provision, the right to counsel may be voluntarily waived. More recently, the Court examined the issue of unsolicited participation by standby counsel as it relates to the right of self-representation. In *McKaskle v. Wiggins* (465 U.S. 168: 1984), the Court said that the categorical silencing of standby counsel is not required as long as the defendant is able to retain control over the conduct of his or her own defense. The Court said that to determine whether *Faretta* rights have been preserved, "the primary focus must be on whether the defendant had a fair chance to present his case in his own way." As long as the jury perceives that the defendant is representing himself, even overzealous participation by standby counsel need not be absolutely barred.

The Eighth Amendment

T he Eighth Amendment contains two short clauses that focus on activities at opposite ends of the criminal process. The first applies to a person's status before criminal proceedings begin and directs that "excessive bail shall not be required." The second, which governs punishments imposed on those found guilty, prohibits infliction of "cruel and unusual punishments." Both are aimed at preventing the arbitrary detention of individuals. We begin by considering detention that occurs before a trial.

Excessive Bail

Bail refers to some form of security provided to a court to ensure the appearance of an accused at the several steps of the criminal process. The objective in seeking bail is to gain release for the accused until the matter of guilt is formally determined. Bail is set by a court as a condition of pre-trial release. Once the security is posted, the accused is released. Failure of the accused to appear at any proceeding brings with it forfeiture of the security and confinement in a county detention facility pending trial. The practice of permitting pre-trial release to persons accused of crimes had its origin in British common law. Such release was necessary because judges traveled widely and were not available to preside over trials for months at a time. In addition, criminal charges could be initiated by private citizens without screening by an independent agent such as a prosecutor. Thus, it was necessary to protect individuals from vindictively motivated criminal charges that might cause unreasonable and lengthy detention.

The concept of bail was brought to the United States, and the protection against "excessive" bail was eventually placed in the Bill of Rights. The language of the Eighth Amendment creates a general right to pre-trial release, but the right is not absolute. Rather, release is conditional, and both federal and state law contain significant limitations on pre-trial release. Those accused of capital crimes, for example, are not entitled to bail. Similarly, defendants determined by a judicial officer to be threats to the community or to be likely to flee may be refused bail. The key issue from a constitutional standpoint is determining whether or not conditions on release are excessive.

The Eighth Amendment language is general and cannot easily be reduced to a simple formula. The key to understanding the provision is to see bail as a guarantee of appearance. A defendant must stay in the jurisdiction and appear at any and all scheduled proceedings of the court. Thus, any consideration of excess must be related to the appearance objective. One of the Supreme Court's better statements of this notion is found in *Stack v. Boyle* (342 U.S. 1: 1951). *Stack* was not a typical criminal case in that the defendants, members of the U.S. Communist Party, were charged with violations of the Smith Act. Among other things, the Smith Act prohibited advocating overthrow of the government by violent means. Even though this was not a conventional criminal case, the pre-trial release issue was essentially the same as in other situations. Pre-trial release, said the Court, permits "unhampered preparation of a defense, and serves to prevent the infliction of punishment prior to conviction." Unless the right to bail is preserved, the "presumption of innocence, secured only after centuries of struggle, would lose its meaning."

The Court went on to define the basic function against which claims of excessiveness should be evaluated:

> The right to release before trial is conditioned upon the accused's giving adequate assurance that he will stand trial and commit to sentence if found guilty. . . . Like the ancient practice of securing the oaths of responsible persons to stand as sureties for the accused, the modern practice of requiring a bail bond or the deposit of a sum of money subject to forfeiture serves as additional assurance of the presence of an accused. Bail set at a figure higher than an amount reasonably calculated to fulfill this purpose is "excessive" under the Eighth Amendment.

Because the function of bail is a limited one, the determination of bail for any particular accused must be based on the standards directly related to the purpose of assuring appearance.

Congress and state legislatures have attempted to clarify the boundaries of the excessive bail clause by statute. In 1966, for example, Congress passed a bail reform act that listed criteria to be considered by judicial officers in making release judgments. Most state legislatures closely followed the federal lead, but for certain serious offenses and for defendants with extensive criminal records, state courts are empowered to deny bail altogether. Some, however, argue that to deny pre-trial release is to make bail "excessive." Pre-trial release also may be obtained without using money. Release on personal recognizance, for example, may be available to defendants who can show sufficient ties to such things as a family, a job, or other factors that relate to the likelihood that the defendant will appear at all remaining court proceedings.

Whether a person is likely to appear at the succeeding steps of the criminal process is the key issue in calculating bail. Bail cannot be used as a punishment. Neither can it be denied arbitrarily. Nonetheless, a number of states do not extend the right of bail to juveniles. This policy is a product of several factors. First, pre-trial release has not been constitutionally mandated for juvenile courts as have many other legal rights. Because states retain discretion in areas where constitutional obligations do not exist, many prefer not to extend to juveniles the Eighth Amendment protection on bail. Second, some states subscribe to the view that detention has rehabilitative qualities. Third, many feel that juveniles do not need a legal right to bail because every state allows juveniles to be released to their parents. The result of all of this is that little or no uniformity exists nationally as to juvenile eligibility for pre-trial release. As pointed out in chapter 3, however, a hearing must be held if a juvenile is to be detained before the adjudication of charges. When assessing likelihood of subsequent appearance, juvenile courts consider such factors as the charge, the juvenile's history at home and school, and the willingness of both the parents and the juvenile to return home.

Preventive Detention

An issue directly related to bail is preventive detention. This is a policy that, if used, changes the basis for deciding whether or not to release a person pre-trial. The practice of preventive detention keeps an accused in custody before trial to prevent him or her from engaging in further criminal conduct. Those who support preventive detention argue that it advances public safety because of data that show that some crime is committed by those on release. Opponents, on the other hand, assert that it imposes a punishment before guilt is proven. Most states allow judges to withhold pre-trial release from adult defendants for specified serious charges, especially if the person has previously committed crimes while on release. Every state permits the preventive detention of juveniles. The Supreme Court has examined and upheld the preventive detention approach for both adults and juveniles in two separate decisions. Though the constitutional question before the Court was similar, the rationales offered in support of these rulings differed somewhat.

The first case, *United States v. Salerno* (481 U.S. 739: 1987), required the Court to consider the preventive detention provisions of the Bail Reform Act of 1984. Among other things, the law permitted federal judges to order pre-trial detention of persons accused of serious crimes if appearance could not reasonably be assured and if the person was deemed sufficiently dangerous to other persons and the community. The law was challenged as a violation of due process and the excessive bail prohibition of the Eighth Amendment. In the majority opinion, which was signed by six justices, Chief Justice William Rehnquist began by setting aside the contention that the act was defective because it authorized punishment before trial. The history of the enactment, wrote Rehnquist, "clearly indicates that the Congress chose detention as a potential solution to the pressing societal problem of crimes committed by persons on release." Preventing danger to the community is a legitimate regulatory goal. Further, the incidents of detention are not excessive in relation to that goal.

The Court then unequivocally said that the due process clause did not prohibit preventive detention as such a regulatory measure. The government's regulatory interest in public safety can, under certain circumstances, outweigh an individual's liberty interest. The Court said the Bail Reform Act focused narrowly enough on the acute problem of crime by suspects in a situation where the government interest is overwhelming. In addition, the act contains extensive procedural safeguards that both limit the circumstances under which detention might be sought for the most serious crime and further the accuracy of deciding whether an arrestee is a likely danger to the community. Finally, the Court said the act did not violate the excessive bail prohibition. The law simply permitted bail to be set at an infinite amount for reasons not related to the risk of flight. Nothing in the Eighth Amendment, said the Court, limits the government's interest in setting bail solely for the prevention of flight. Where Congress has established detention on the basis of some other compelling interest—public safety in this case—the Eighth Amendment does not require release on bail.

Schall v. Martin (467 U.S. 253: 1984) upheld preventive detention for juveniles. *Schall* examined a New York law that authorized pre-trial detention of a juvenile if it could be shown that there was "serious risk" of the juvenile committing additional crimes if released. Gregory Martin brought suit challenging the constitutionality of the law. The Supreme Court upheld this law in a six to three vote, the same margin by which it approved the federal law in *Salerno*. Chief Justice Rehnquist wrote in the majority opinion that the question before the Court was whether or not preventive detention of juveniles is compatible with "fundamental fairness." To address this issue properly, the Court felt two inquiries were necessary: Is a legitimate state interest served by preventive detention, and are the procedural safeguards adequate to safeguard misuse of pre-trial detention?

The Court said that crime prevention is a "weighty social objective" and that a state's legitimate and compelling interest in protecting its citizenry from crime "cannot be doubted." That interest "persists undiluted in the juvenile context." The harm caused by crime is not dependent on the age of the perpetrator, and the harm to society generally may be even greater given the high rate of recidivism among juveniles. In addition, the juvenile's liberty interest may be subordinated to the state's "*parens patriae* interest in preserving and promoting the welfare of the child." Rehnquist argued that society has a legitimate interest in protecting a juvenile from the consequences of his or her criminal activity. This includes the potential injury that may occur when a victim resists and the "downward spiral of criminal activity into which peer pressure may lead the child" persists. The Court saw the state interest as substantial and legitimate, a view "confirmed by the widespread use and judicial acceptance of preventive detention for juveniles." Rehnquist observed that "mere invocation of a legitimate purpose" will not justify particular restrictions and conditions of confinement amounting to punishment. The Court found the statute in question to have nonpunitive objectives, however. The detention was "strictly limited in time," and it entitled the juvenile to an expedited hearing. The Court then addressed the procedural issue of whether there was "sufficient protection against erroneous and unnecessary deprivation of liberty." The Court ruled that the statute provided "far more predetention protection" than required for probable cause determinations in the adult criminal process. Though the initial appearance is informal, full notice is given and records are kept. The juvenile is accompanied by a parent or guardian and is informed of his or her constitutional rights, including the right to remain silent and be represented by counsel. Finally, the Court rejected the contention that the statute's standard for detention—serious risk that additional criminal conduct would take place—was "fatally vague." Prediction of future criminal conduct is a judgment based on "a host of variables which cannot be readily codified." Nonetheless, the decision on detention is based on "as much information as can reasonably be obtained at the initial appearance" and therefore is not impermissibly vague.

The Court's decision in *Schall* was its first treatment of preventive detention. Prior to *Schall,* the Court had let preventive detention statutes stand without review, silently agreeing with their view of pre-trial release. Although bail should have the effect of ensuring an appearance at subsequent proceedings, those persons released also constitute a continuing threat to society. The policy of preventive detention is aimed at confining defendants who present a serious threat of additional criminal conduct. Such a policy may be effective as a crime prevention strategy, but it also runs counter to the presumption of innocence. For many, it constitutes punishment before trial. The *Schall* ruling suggested that the Court would be receptive to preventive detention statutes for adults, a position the Court actually took in *Salerno* three years later. Although *Schall* gives juvenile courts the authority to detain juveniles before adjudication, the decision did establish a due process standard for juvenile detention hearings that includes proper notice and substantial justification for detention.

Cruel and Unusual Punishment

Like the language on excessive bail and fines, the language of the Eighth Amendment clause proscribing cruel and unusual punishment also comes from the reign of William and Mary. In 1689 the British Parliament was forced to adopt a Bill of Rights as the result of widespread abuses of individual liberties during the reign of the Stuarts. The Bill of Rights was a direct result of the cruel and unusual punishments imposed during the days of the infamous Court of the Star Chamber. A major difference between the British and the U.S. Bill of Rights was that the former had only legislative standing, whereas the latter had constitutional status. The authors of the Eighth Amendment also chose to substitute the words "shall not" in the U.S. Bill of Rights for the words "ought not" in the British Bill of Rights. The change made the amendment enforceable by the courts and not subject to future legislative modification. The Virginia, North Carolina, and New York ratifying conventions urged the inclusion of the Eighth Amendment in the Bill of Rights, knowing full well of the violations of the safeguards supposedly contained in the British Bill of Rights. Punishments in the colonies during the years prior to the American Revolution were quite severe, a factor that underscored concerns about criminal punishments.

The most critical cruel and unusual punishment question is the standard to be applied when assessing a particular sentence. If the standard in place at the time the Bill of Rights was adopted were used, rather harsh punishments would be permitted. That standard, however, has been modified to fit the times. Substantive criteria are drawn from "evolving standards of decency," which means the status of a particular punishment may change as society's values change.

The cruel and unusual punishment doctrine holds that punishment must "comport with human dignity." Sentences cannot involve torture or cruelty. Neither can punishments be imposed on a status, such as being a juvenile, or condition, such as being addicted to narcotics, and sentences must be proportionate to the offense. The death penalty, a punishment unique in terms of its severity and irrevocability, does not automatically offend the Eighth Amendment. Procedural flaws may make the imposition of the death penalty impermissible, however. For example, it may not be imposed without a two-stage trial and sentencing process. The sentencer must also be provided with sufficient guidance for making a determination of death. One useful way to illustrate the process by which cruel and unusual punishment standards have developed is to look at specific situations.

The Eighth Amendment principally applies to legislative actions by which crimes are defined and punishments devised for violations. The amendment does not permit legislatures to punish conduct that is not deemed sufficiently antisocial; the *Robinson* case, discussed below, develops this rationale more fully. Neither can legislatures impose punishments that are excessively cruel or "barbaric." Included in the evaluation of the punishment is its relationship to the crime. There must be a proportionality between crime and punishment. A 10-year sentence imposed on a first-time shoplifter would be excessive, whereas the same 10-year sentence for some assaultive crime would not. In *Weems v. United States* (217 U.S. 349: 1910), the Court found a 15-year sentence at hard labor for falsifying public documents to be excessive. Aside from the physically punishing nature of the sentence, the Court found it unconstitutionally cruel because it was not "graduated and proportional" to the offense. It was in *Weems* that the Court emphasized the "expansive and vital" character of the meaning of the cruel and unusual punishment clause. The Court spoke of the need for evolutionary growth in the standards and specifically said the standards to be used were not to be those from the eighteenth century. Using this adaptive approach, the Court concluded in *Trop v. Dulles* (356 U.S. 2: 1958) that taking a person's citizenship away as punishment for wartime desertion was an unusually degrading form of punishment, and thus not constitutional.

The issue of proportionality is considered more carefully a little later. Obviously, one very interesting issue is how these evolving standards apply in the instance of capital punishment. We start, however, with application of the clause to penalties less severe than death, beginning with *Robinson v. California* (370 U.S. 660: 1962). Until this time, the cruel and unusual punishment clause applied only to sentences in federal courts. The question before the Warren Court in this case was whether the Eighth Amendment prohibition against cruel and unusual punishment precluded a state from making narcotics addiction a crime. Lawrence Robinson had been convicted of addiction to narcotics, a misdemeanor, and sentenced to 90 days in jail. Robinson was not under the influence of drugs at the time of his arrest, and the only evidence against him was the testimony of the arresting officer, who observed scars and needle marks on Robinson's arms. The California courts upheld the conviction, and Robinson appealed to the Supreme Court. In a six to two decision (Justice Felix Frankfurter not participating), the Court struck down the California statute as one that punished an individual based solely on the presence of a particular condition or status, rather than on conviction of an overt criminal act. In doing so, the Court ruled that the cruel and unusual punishment clause applies to the states through the due process clause of the Fourteenth Amendment.

The majority opinion, written by Justice Potter Stewart, said that a statute making a chronic condition a criminal "offense" renders a person "continuously guilty of the offense." As the Court viewed it, the statute subjected an individual to potential prosecution "at any time prior to [that individual's] reform." Further, the statute's focus on this "status of addiction" reached in scope to a person who might never have used or possessed narcotics or have been engaged in any other "antisocial behaviors" in the state. The criminal offense approach to the problem of narcotics addiction could not stand because addiction was not unlike other illnesses, such as venereal disease and mental illness. The Court reasoned that legislation making the contracting of an illness a criminal offense would "doubtless be universally thought to be an infliction of cruel and unusual punishment." The majority concluded that the 90-day jail sentence imposed on Robinson was not a problem in an abstract sense, but that the particular penalty had to be considered in the context of the particular offense. Justice Stewart wrote, "Even one day in prison would be cruel and unusual punishment for the 'crime' of having a common cold." The Court's emphasis, therefore, was not focused on the method of punishment so much as the nature of the "crime" for which the punishment was considered.

Robinson was important because it clarified the relationship of the cruel and unusual punishment prohibition to the states. Because the states administer the overwhelming majority of criminal sanctions, placing the states under the same constitutional limitations as the federal government was significant. *Robinson* also established that prohibitions envisioned in the cruel and unusual punishment clause include restraints on the kinds of behavior and conditions that can be properly considered criminal. The decision in *Robinson* integrated the concepts of criminal intent and overt criminal acts into the cruel and unusual punishment clause. Criminal punishment therefore requires criminal behavior. The broader immediate effect was to place in jeopardy all laws that focused on a particular condition or status. Vagrancy ordinances became suspect, for example, and many states decriminalized certain kinds of conduct in which the victim of the crime and the person charged with the crime were the same person. Some states reduced from felonies to misdemeanors certain types of antisocial behavior. Other states opened treatment facilities for substance abusers while simultaneously abolishing the previously construed criminal nature of the condition.

Robinson also raised questions about the constitutionality of punishments for crimes that were based on a condition or status. In *Powell v. Texas* (392 U.S. 514: 1968), for example, the Court considered whether a chronic alcoholic could be convicted of public intoxication. In this case the Court did not extend *Robinson* to include symptomatic behavior. The Court distinguished *Powell* from *Robinson* because Leroy Powell was convicted "not for being a chronic alcoholic but for being in public while drunk." Texas had not, said the Court, sought to penalize Powell's status or attempted to regulate his conduct in the privacy of his home. Rather, it punished him for "public behavior which may create substantial health and safety hazards, both for [Powell] and members of the general public, and which offends the moral and esthetic sensibilities of a large segment of the community." In the Court's view, this was a "far cry" from convicting Powell for his condition as an alcoholic.

Consideration of the proportionality of sentences that impose terms of confinement has been approached by the Court with great caution. States have traditionally exercised substantial control over defining crimes and punishments, which is seen as an outgrowth of the basic police power each state retained when the Constitution was ratified. The Court has been quite reluctant to sit in judgment of state decisions on how to use that power, especially when noncapital sentences are involved. Again, some cases serve to illustrate this point. Note the Court's almost total deference to the states in the first two cases.

Rummel v. Estelle (445 U.S. 263: 1980) assessed a Texas policy whereby all third-time offenders would automatically receive life sentences. William Rummel was sentenced to life imprisonment under this law (known as a recidivist law), which provided that a third felony conviction mandated such a penalty. Rummel's three convictions came over a ten-year period and were for property offenses totaling $239.11. Rummel argued that life imprisonment was excessive given his crime and that it was so disproportionate as to constitute cruel and unusual punishment. A five-justice Supreme Court majority rejected Rummel's arguments. Justice Rehnquist focused on three points in the majority opinion. First, he argued that outside the issue of capital punishment, the disproportionality argument should seldom apply. Second, he suggested that Rummel's likelihood of parole must be considered. Parole is "an established variation on imprisonment," and a "proper assessment of Texas' treatment of Rummel could hardly ignore the possibility that he will not actually be imprisoned for the rest of his life." Finally, Rehnquist said that Texas ought to have latitude in dealing with repeat offenders. The Eighth Amendment does not require Texas to "treat him in the same manner it might treat him were this his first 'petty property offense.' " The duration of imprisonment is a matter "largely within the discretion of the punishing jurisdiction." Though the justices noted that Texas had the most severe habitual offender statute in the country, the Court concluded that it differed only in degree rather than in kind from those of other states. Short of differences of kind, the Eighth Amendment should not be used to invalidate judgments that are "peculiarly" matters for legislatures.

Two years later, in *Hutto v. Davis* (454 U.S. 370: 1982), the Court upheld the imposition of two consecutive 20-year prison terms and two $10,000 fines for the crime of possession and distribution of 9 ounces of marijuana. Building on the *Rummel* rationale, the Court said there was no way to "make any constitutional distinction between one term of years and a shorter or longer term of years." Though expressing some concern about the severity of the sentence received by Roger Davis, the Court refrained from finding for him. To have done so would be "invariably a subjective decision," and courts should be "reluctant to review legislatively mandated terms of imprisonment."

Rummel and *Davis* seemed to suggest that Eighth Amendment challenges of prison sentences would not be successful. But in *Solem v. Helm* (463 U.S. 277: 1983), the Court invalidated a life sentence without possibility for parole as imposed under South Dakota's recidivist statute. Justice Harry Blackmun joined the four dissenting justices from *Rummel* (William Brennan, Thurgood Marshall, Lewis Powell, and John Paul Stevens) to form a new five to four majority that embraced some of the arguments rejected in *Rummel*. Among those was the argument that the proportionality principle applies to noncapital cases. The constitutional language, said the Court, "suggests no exception for imprisonment." Rather than directly overturn *Rummel,* however, the Court found *Helm* "clearly distinguishable." The Court noted the nonconfrontational character of Jerry Helm's crime, which was issuing a "no account" check in the amount of $100, and the relatively minor nature of his previous offenses. Also key to distinguishing *Helm* was the impossibility of parole. Whereas Rummel could have reasonably expected to become eligible for early parole, Helm stood little chance of having his sentence commuted. The Court also developed some comparative criteria in *Helm* to be used to assess claims of disproportionate punishment. First, of course, the Court said the "gravity of the offense and the harshness of the penalty" must be considered. This standard applies in any of the cases under discussion. The Court said it may also be "helpful" to compare sentences imposed on other defendants within the jurisdiction. If more serious crimes are subject to the same or lesser penalties, that is "some indication that the punishment at issue may be excessive." Finally, the Court said there was utility in comparing the sentences imposed for the same crime in other jurisdictions. In this case, the Court found that nowhere in the country would a defendant have received as severe a sentence as Helm had received in this case.

Capital Punishment

The most visible Eighth Amendment issue has been the death penalty, even though very few criminal defendants face the possibility of that sentence. The important developments in capital punishment doctrine came almost exclusively from the Burger Court. The Supreme Court historically chose to hear very few capital punishment cases prior to the 1970s, and the ones that were reviewed were very narrowly focused. For example, the Court considered whether death by firing squad was a "humane" form of execution in *Wilkerson v. Utah* (99 U.S. 130: 1878) and ruled that it was. Electrocution as a mode of execution was similarly upheld in *In re Kemmler* (136 U.S. 436: 1890). These cases did not examine the underlying issue of constitutionality of the death penalty as such. Even the Warren Court, for all its activism in the area of criminal rights, did not take on the issue despite having the opportunity. The first issue to come before the Burger Court actually came twice, and it received two different responses. The issue revolved around the exercise of discretion by sentencers (a judge, a jury, or some combination of the two). Not everyone convicted of a capital crime is actually sentenced to death. Rather, only a small fraction are, and the large remainder receive a prison sentence of some length. The question that came before the Court was how the determination is made of who gets the death penalty and who does not. The contention was that the choices were being made arbitrarily or possibly in a discriminatory fashion. Those challenging the laws allowing such broad discretion argued that states needed to specify some factors to be considered in all capital cases before making the death penalty decision. There was demand for some structure upon which to base sentencing decisions.

The Court's first response to this issue came in *McGautha v. California* (402 U.S. 183: 1971). The Court refused in *McGautha* to find the procedure of unlimited discretion unconstitutional. On the basis of "history, experience, and the present limitations of human knowledge," the Court found it "quite impossible" to say that giving a jury complete discretion to decide capital sentences is "offensive to anything in the Constitution." The states, the Court went on, are "entitled to assume" that persons serving on juries will "act with due regard for the consequences of the decisions" in death penalty situations. The Court was also satisfied that a "variety of factors" would be considered by juries in meeting the "truly awesome responsibility of decreeing death for a fellow human." The Court rejected the suggestion that specific guidelines be prepared. To "catalog" appropriate considerations could "inhibit rather than expand" deliberations. The Court concluded that cataloging or structuring factors was virtually impossible as well as undesirable.

The question of sentencer discretion returned to the Court within a year in *Furman v. Georgia* (408 U.S. 238: 1972). The response was different, however, as the Court invalidated statutes that allowed for unguided sentencer discretion in a five to four decision. There was no single majority opinion in *Furman*. Rather, the case produced a total of 133 pages of individual opinions including the dissents. Justice Stewart emphasized the arbitrariness of unstructured discretion. He found the lack of definition in the state statutes to be the key problem because it left an unlimited amount of discretion in the hands of jurors or judges. The resulting judgments could be very subjective and, as a result, cruel and unusual. Justice Stewart found the death penalty in such cases to be cruel "in the same way that being struck by lightning is cruel." Those receiving the death sentence became a "capriciously selected, random handful," and a "freakishly imposed" penalty is cruel and unusual. Justice Byron White cited the infrequency of the imposition of capital punishment as a factor in its diminished impact as a deterrent. He found the death penalty to be cruel and unusual by virtue of its infrequent use. Justice William Douglas suggested the death penalty was not only capriciously imposed, but also imposed in a racially discriminatory manner. Justices Brennan and Marshall said capital punishment was cruel and unusual punishment in any form. Those in the minority stressed three main points. First, the dissenters criticized the judicial activism of the majority. They viewed the decision as an "act of will" rather than a proper interpretation of law. Second, the dissenters maintained that capital punishment did not offend contemporary standards of humaneness. Third, the minority felt that competent jurors were capable of rendering reasonable decisions even in the absence of specific statutory guidance. This opinion essentially characterized the Court's decision in *McGautha*. The infrequency of the imposition of the death penalty was emphasized as a reflection of the proper exercise of "sensitivity and caution" by judges and juries. The minority saw unlimited discretion as something positive rather than as a liability.

The Court believed unguided sentencer discretion to be the principal defect of many state statutes, and *Furman* signaled the states to make significant revisions. The states could use two approaches in addressing the discretion issue. One was to provide guidance to sentencers by a more careful definition of those offenses and accompanying factors for which the death penalty might be imposed. The other was to remove sentencer discretion by imposing a mandatory death sentence as an automatic result of conviction for certain crimes. By 1976, 35 state legislatures had taken one or the other of these options as they revised their statutes that had been invalidated by the *Furman* ruling.

GUIDING SENTENCER DISCRETION

The Court had been asked in *Furman* to find capital punishment unconstitutional in and of itself, but it did not do so. Rather, it found the process by which the sentence had been imposed to be cruel and unusual. Thus, the justices never addressed the underlying question of the constitutionality of the death penalty as such. As states attempted to remedy the defects pointed out in *Furman,* the basic question of the constitutionality of capital punishment was again present. In 1976, the Court decided three cases that upheld state revisions that attempted to provide some guidelines for sentencers. These three cases were *Gregg v. Georgia* (428 U.S. 128: 1976), *Proffitt v. Florida* (428 U.S. 242: 1976), and *Jurek v. Texas* (428 U.S. 262: 1976). The Court also said for the first time that the death penalty "does not invariably violate the Constitution." So long as some basic procedural guidelines are followed, the death penalty is a permissible criminal sentence. Justice Stewart, writing for a majority of seven, said that the Court may not "require the legislature to select the least severe penalty possible so long as the penalty selected is not cruelly inhumane or disproportionate." He found society willing to embrace the death penalty, as 35 state legislatures had reenacted their capital punishment statutes after *Furman;* thus, contemporary standards were not offended. Justice Stewart also said retribution was a sufficient legislative motive to support the death penalty. He viewed capital punishment as an "expression of society's moral outrage at particularly offensive conduct."

The Court also considered whether death was an excessive penalty in itself and decided that when a life has been taken, death is not invariably "disproportionate." It is an "extreme sanction, suitable to the most extreme crimes." As for the statutory flaws found in *Furman,* Stewart concluded that the revisions contained in the new state laws adequately remedied those defects. Arbitrariness was eliminated through several procedural revisions; all the statutes contained two-stage (bifurcated) trial-sentence processes in which the guilt determination stage was separated from the sentencing stage; and the statutes all required mandatory appellate review and structured sentencer discretion through defined aggravating and mitigating circumstances. A sentencer could not consider imposing death in the absence of aggravating circumstances (aggravation and mitigation are discussed in greater detail below). *Gregg, Proffitt,* and *Jurek* clarified several central issues regarding capital sentencing. First, the Court held that death is a constitutional penalty for murder given certain conditions of aggravation. Second, *Gregg* acknowledged that retribution was a legitimate objective of criminal sentencing. Third, *Gregg* determined that structuring sentencer discretion by means of the concepts of aggravation and mitigation could be accomplished sufficiently to satisfy constitutional standards.

MANDATORY CAPITAL PUNISHMENT

Several states responded to *Furman* by revising their capital punishment statutes to make the death sentence a requirement upon conviction for a particular crime. A five-justice majority of the Supreme Court ruled in *Woodson v. North Carolina* (428 U.S. 280: 1976) that the mandatory approach was "unduly harsh and unworkably rigid." The justices said allowing some discretion in sentencing was more compatible with evolving standards of societal decency, a frequently mentioned criterion in cruel and unusual punishment cases. The fact that juries possessing discretion infrequently impose capital punishment suggests that the penalty is viewed as "inappropriate" in a large number of cases. A second defect cited was that mandatory sentences did not remedy *Furman* flaws. The mandatory approach "papers over" the problem of jury discretion. There are no standards by which to determine "which murderer shall live and which shall die"; neither does the mandatory approach allow a review of arbitrary death sentences. The third flaw in the mandatory approach was its undifferentiating character. The statutes did not allow for contemplation of circumstances particular to the crime and the defendant, which precluded considering "compassion or mitigating factors." Instead, the statutes treated all convicted persons as "members of a faceless, undifferentiated mass to be subjected to the blind infliction of the penalty of death." The four dissenters were troubled by the majority's process focus. Justice Rehnquist, in the dissenting opinion, wrote that the Court should confine itself to the simple dimension of whether or not a punishment is cruel, a question already decided in *Gregg*.

Woodson gave the Court an opportunity to choose between two approaches to capital punishment, and it clearly reflects the Court's preference for retaining some discretion for sentencers in capital cases. To implement capital punishment reasonably, the sentencer must evaluate the specific details of a particular case against criteria defined by state legislatures. The mandatory approach precludes consideration of the factors that make a case unique, and that was its fatal flaw. The Court has since underscored the inadequacy of the mandatory approach. In *Roberts v. Louisiana* (431 U.S. 633: 1977), the Court struck down a Louisiana statute that called for the death penalty for the deliberate killing of a police officer or firefighter. The Court said "it is incorrect to suppose that no mitigating circumstances can exist when the victim is a police officer." The Court said that if the victim was someone performing a public duty, that may be set forth by the state as an aggravating circumstance, but a state cannot preclude consideration of mitigating circumstances, something "essential" to the capital sentencing decision.

The mandatory death sentence reappeared in *Sumner v. Shuman* (483 U.S. 66: 1987). Under Nevada law, a prisoner serving a life term without the possibility of parole could receive an automatic death sentence upon conviction for first-degree murder. The Court held that even under this unique circumstance, there could be no exception to the ban on mandatory capital punishment. Nevada argued that only such a mandatory sentence would effectively deter prisoners who had no hope of release, but the Court responded that the death sentence could be arrived at more reasonably by demonstrating aggravating circumstances. Just as involvement in other crime varies, so can level of involvement vary in a violent prisoner incident. Therefore, mitigation may still be an issue.

The Court reviewed additional cases during the 1989 term that involved mandatory actions for sentencing juries. Pennsylvania requires the death penalty if a jury unanimously finds aggravation in the absence of mitigation or aggravation that outweighs mitigation. The Court upheld this method in *Blystone v. Pennsylvania* (108 L. Ed. 2d 255: 1990). The justices distinguished this approach from those in cases such as *Woodson* by pointing out that the sentence was not automatically imposed upon conviction, but only after a consideration of aggravating and mitigating factors. An aggravating factor "serves the purpose of limiting the class of death-eligible defendants," and the mitigating factor satisfies the requirement that a capital sentencing jury be able to "consider and give full effect to all relevant mitigating evidence." North Carolina had a death penalty law similar to Pennsylvania's, but it maintained that mitigation only existed when all jurors agreed upon its presence. It also required a jury to unanimously find, beyond a reasonable doubt, that aggravating factors were sufficiently substantial to warrant the death penalty when considered along with any mitigating factors. The Court struck down these provisions in *McKoy v. North Carolina* (108 L. Ed. 2d 369: 1990) because the unanimity requirement precluded giving full effect to mitigating factors. Although the law allowed a jury to choose a penalty other than death, the jury was required to make its choice based only on mitigating circumstances for which there was unanimity. As a result, "one juror can prevent the others from giving effect to evidence they feel calls for a lesser sentence." Further, even if all the jurors agree that *some* mitigating factors exist, "they cannot give effect to evidence supporting any of those circumstances unless they agree unanimously on the *same* circumstances." For example, if the defendant asserted that he participated in the crime under duress, under North Carolina law all of the jurors would have to agree that duress existed in order for it to qualify as a mitigating circumstance.

REFINEMENTS TO *GREGG*

The Court ruled in *Gregg* that states could use the death penalty so long as they provided some guidance for sentencers. The most critical problem, of course, is identifying that small fraction of offenders who will be sentenced to death. Most states chose to guide sentencers by addressing factors that either aggravate or mitigate an offender's crime. One or more aggravating circumstances would heighten the severity of the crime to possible death eligibility, whereas mitigating circumstances, if present, would diminish a person's culpability. The presence of an aggravating circumstance thus helps isolate the most serious offenders. Itemization of such aggravating factors is a legislative prerogative. Though a number of different factors have been adopted, there are several factors on which there is consensus. Among these is the commission of a capital offense in the course of another felony. A lengthy record of assaultive crime is also usually included in many capital punishment statutes. So long as one or more such circumstance can be proven beyond a reasonable doubt, a sentencer may properly consider imposition of the death penalty. Without such a condition, the offender is not a candidate for execution. Thus, aggravating factors assist in distinguishing between cases appropriate for the death penalty and those that are not.

A state legislature is generally free to adopt any aggravating factor it wishes so long as it is neither vague nor ambiguous. The sentencer, however, cannot amend the list of factors assembled by the legislature even if a factor is reasonable. Florida, for example, did not include prior criminal record as an aggravating condition. Nonetheless, a trial judge mentioned an offender's record as one of the several factors used to justify a death sentence. The Supreme Court ruled in *Barclay v. Florida* (463 U.S. 939: 1983) that sentencers are not free to depart from statutory guidelines on aggravation. Allowing sentencers to utilize their own factors would render meaningless the structure provided by statute.

For similar reasons, the Court ruled in *Booth v. Maryland* (482 U.S. 496:

1987) that victim impact statements (VISs) could not be used in capital cases. The VISs, required in this case by state law, were based on interviews with the victim's family. They contained descriptions of the impact of the crime on the family, characterizations of the victim(s), and family opinions of both the crime and the defendant. John Booth sought to suppress the VISs, contending that their introduction was inflammatory. The Supreme Court agreed in a five to four decision. The Court said the information contained in a VIS may be "wholly unrelated to the blameworthiness" of the defendant. Rather, VISs may cause the sentencing decision to turn on such factors as the degree to which the victim's family is willing and able to articulate its grief or the relative worth of the victim's character. Use of family members' emotionally charged opinions could "serve no other purpose than to inflame the jury and divert it from deciding the case on the relevant evidence concerning the crime and the defendant."

Booth was overruled by the Rehnquist Court in 1991 in the case of *Payne v. Tennessee* (115 L. Ed. 2d 720: 1991). The Court ruled that evidence reflecting the character of the victim and effects on the surviving family of a victim could be introduced at the sentencing stage of a murder trial. Justice William Rehnquist noted that although, through a series of decisions, the Court removed virtually all limits on the mitigating evidence a defendent can introduce, none of those cases ever said that a defendant is entitled to consideration "wholly apart from the crime he committed." *Booth* "unfairly weighted the scales in capital trial," said Rehnquist, by keeping the state from either offering a "glimpse of the life" the defendant chose to end or from characterizing the "loss to the victim's family and to society." States have the authority to devise new methods for dealing with capital cases. Victim impact evidence is "simply another form or method of informing the sentencing authority about the specific harm caused by the crime in question." The Court in *Booth* was "wrong in stating this kind of evidence leads to the arbitrary imposition of the death penalty." To the contrary, victim impact evidence generally serves "entirely legitimate" purposes.

The Court has handled mitigating circumstances differently from aggravating factors. Once again, most states set forth a list of factors recognized as mitigating. Generally the Court has not allowed lists of mitigating factors to be restrictive. Neither has the Court permitted trial judges discretion to disallow evidence offered in mitigation by a defendant. Several cases are quite consistent on this point. The first is *Lockett v. Ohio* (438 U.S. 586: 1978). Sandra Lockett was found guilty of capital murder. She wished to argue at the sentencing stage that she deserved other than the death penalty because, among other things, she was young, had no prior criminal record, and had played only a minor role in the crime. These factors could not be used in mitigation, however, because they were not among the three factors recognized under Ohio law. Finding none of the three specified factors applicable to Lockett, the trial judge sentenced her to death. The Supreme Court reversed the sentence and said that a sentencer must have a "full opportunity" to consider mitigating circumstances in capital cases. A law that prevents consideration of any aspect of a defendant's character or record "creates the risk that the death penalty will be imposed in spite of factors which call for a less severe penalty." The Court characterized the risk as "unacceptable" when the choice is life or death.

A capital defendant, thus, is afforded the opportunity to offer virtually anything in mitigation. The circumstance may be wholly unpersuasive, but the defendant must have the opportunity to have it considered. This is true even when a sentencer incorrectly understands a legal restriction to apply. A case in point involved a juvenile in Oklahoma. Monty Lee Eddings offered a plea of no contest to a first-degree murder charge. He was 16 years old, but was tried as an adult. He was entitled to present evidence supporting "any" mitigating circumstance under law. He submitted a great deal of evidence of a "turbulent" family history, physical abuse, and "severe" emotional distur-bance. The judge considered Eddings's age as a mitigating factor, but erroneously ruled that, as a matter of law, he could not consider the other circumstances as mitigating and proceeded to sentence Eddings to death. The Supreme Court, in *Eddings v. Oklahoma* (455 U.S. 104: 1982), disallowed the sentence, reiterating that nothing could exclude any relevant mitigating evidence from consideration by the sentencer.

WHERE DEATH IS EXCESSIVE PUNISHMENT

The capital punishment cases examined to this point have largely focused on procedural matters. The procedural issues were the first to appear before the Court and largely dominated capital punishment considerations at the outset. However, substantive questions of proportion or excessiveness were inevi-table. Cases containing this issue created great difficulty for the Burger Court. Most of its justices were not inclined toward judicial activism and generally felt uncomfortable ruling against legislative judgments, but that is the kind of question contained in these challenges. The first significant test case was *Coker v. Georgia* (433 U.S. 584: 1977), in which the Court ruled that the death penalty could not be imposed for the rape of an adult victim.

In *Coker,* a seven-justice majority developed two lines of argument against the death penalty for rape. Writing for the majority was Justice White, who said, first, that society did not endorse capital punishment for rape. This was reflected in the refusal of 32 of the 35 states making post-*Furman* revisions to their capital punishment laws to include rape of an adult as a capital crime. Even in Georgia, where the penalty was allowed, juries did not frequently impose the penalty, which suggested that juries found the sanction excessive. Justice White also argued that the death penalty was excessive on other grounds. Because the death penalty is unique in its "severity and irrevocability," it is excessive for a defendant "who does not take a human life." He said rape is "without doubt deserving of serious punishment," but in terms of "moral depravity and of the injury to the person and to the public, it does not compare with murder."

Coker produced a substantive limitation on the imposition of the death penalty, and the Court attempted to establish a set of criteria by which excess could be evaluated. The Court suggested that public attitudes toward a particular offense were germane and used both legislative judgments and the behavior of juries as reflective of these attitudes. Using much the same disproportionality rationale, the Court extended *Coker* to persons who aid and abet felony murder in *Enmund v. Florida* (458 U.S. 782: 1982). As in *Coker*, the Court looked at the number of states authorizing the death penalty for Earl Enmund's offense and found it minimal. This was evidence, in the Court's view, that society generally wished to withhold the death penalty from accomplices in felony murders. The Court was also convinced that the death sentence for the aider and abetter was excessive. Putting Enmund to death to "avenge two killings that he did not commit and had no intention of committing or causing does not measurably contribute to the retributive end of ensuring that the criminal gets his just desserts."

A variation on the proportionality question is whether there are certain categories of offenders for whom capital punishment is unconstitutional. One obvious category is juveniles. The Court ruled in *Thompson v. Oklahoma* (487 U.S. 815: 1988) that a person may not be executed for a crime committed before he or she reaches 16 years of age. The Court said that the "contours" of the cruel and unusual punishment protection are determined by judges, who are to be guided by the "evolving standards of decency that mark the progress of a maturing society." As in other cases, measures of these "evolving standards" are present in legislative judgments as well as in jury decisions in particular cases. The Court then looked at numerous examples of where state law recognizes differences "which must be accommodated in determining the rights and duties of children as compared with those of adults." The Court found "near unanimity" in the judgment that a person under the age of 16 has not yet reached adulthood. It was seen as "most relevant" that every state had established a juvenile court system to adjudicate those 16 and under. The Court then examined the statutes authorizing capital punishment and found that of the 18 states that established a minimum age, all required the defendant to have "attained at least the age of 16 at the time of the capital offense." The Court concluded from this that it was offensive to "civilized standards of decency" to execute a juvenile. It was pointed out that this conclusion was also held by "respected" professional organizations such as the American Bar Association, and other nations that "share our Anglo-American heritage." The Court then turned to the second "societal factor" to be used in assessing the "acceptability of capital punishment to the American sensibility": jury behavior. Department of Justice data on homicide for the years 1982–1986 revealed that about 1,400 persons were sentenced to death from a group of more than 82,000 arrested for homicide. Only 5 of that number (including William Thompson) were under 16 at the time of the offense. This led the Court to the "unambiguous conclusion" that the death penalty for a 15-year-old is now "generally abhorrent to the conscience of the community."

The Court then addressed the issue of the juvenile's comparative culpability. It was sufficiently apparent to the Court that because less culpability attaches to a crime committed by a juvenile, "extended explanation" was not necessary. More attention was paid to the question of whether or not the juvenile death penalty "measurably contributes to the societal purposes" of retribution or deterrence. The Court responded that less experience and education makes the juvenile "less able to evaluate the consequences of his or her conduct." Rather, the juvenile is more likely to be "motivated by mere emotion or peer pressure" than an adult is. The reason juveniles are not "trusted with the privileges and responsibilities of an adult also explain why their irresponsible conduct is not as morally reprehensible as an adult." Given the lesser culpability, retribution serves no purpose in the context of juveniles and is "simply inapplicable" to the execution of a juvenile. Similarly, deterrence is an "unacceptable" rationale in the case of the juvenile. Juveniles constitute such a small proportion of those eligible to receive the penalty that excluding them will not "diminish the deterrent value of capital punishment." The Court was unpersuaded that the use of the penalty with juveniles made any "measurable contribution to the goals that capital punishment is intended to achieve," and, therefore, referred to the punishment in this instance as "nothing more than the purposeless and needless imposition of pain and suffering."

The Court further examined capital punishment for juveniles the following year in *Stanford v. Kentucky* and *Wilkins v. Missouri* (492 U.S. 361: 1989). Stanford and Wilkins were both convicted of murder, and both were over the age of 16 at the time of the crimes: Kevin Stanford was 17 years and 4 months of age, and Heath Wilkins was 16 years and 6 months old. The Court ruled in these cases, both by votes of five to four, that imposing the death penalty on Stanford and Wilkins did not constitute cruel and unusual punishment. Deciding whether or not the execution of juveniles violates the Eighth Amendment requires determining whether such action is contrary to "evolving standards of decency that mark the progress of a maturing society." In assessing this question, the Court must look to "conceptions of modern American society" as reflected by "objective evidence" as opposed to "its own subjective conceptions." As the Court said in *Thompson,* the "most reliable" reflection of "national consensus" is the actions of state legislatures and Congress. The Court concluded that the "settled" consensus against executing those 15 or younger did not extend to 16-year-olds. Only 15 of the states that permit capital punishment forbid its application to 16-year-olds. The number of states restricting the death penalty decreases to 12 when the age is elevated to 17. This finding does not "establish the degree of national agreement" necessary to "label" a punishment cruel and unusual. Neither does the jury behavior involving 16- or 17-year-olds reveal a "categorical aversion" to the penalty. Justice Antonin Scalia rejected the relevance to the capital punishment question of 18 as a minimum legal age for such activities as "drinking alcoholic beverages and voting." Such laws, he said, "operate in gross" and do not require individualized tests for application. The death sentence, by contrast, is highly selective, and "individualized consideration is a constitutional requirement."

Justice Scalia then addressed measures other than legislative actions and jury behavior purported to be "indicia" of national consensus. Scalia said public opinion data and the positions of interest groups and professional associations are "too uncertain a foundation for constitutional law." He characterized "socioscientific or ethicoscientific" evidence or arguments as similarly inadequate. One such argument is that the death penalty does not deter 16- or 17-year-olds because they have a "less highly developed fear of death." Similarly, it is argued that the death penalty fails to achieve retribution when a juvenile is involved because, being less "mature and responsible," juveniles are "less morally blameworthy." Scalia said the "audience for such arguments is not this Court but the citizenry."

In a case decided the same day as *Stanford* and *Wilkins,* the Court ruled that the death penalty for convicted murderers who are mentally retarded is not necessarily cruel and unusual punishment. At the same time, the Court reversed the sentence in *Penry v. Lynaugh* (106 L. Ed. 2d 256: 1989), because the jury had not been properly instructed regarding how it might give effect to the defendant's retardation and other mitigating factors. Under Texas law, a defendant convicted of capital murder is sentenced to death if a jury unanimously finds at least one of three "special issues." These issues are (1) that the murder was committed deliberately and with the expectation that (the victim's) death would occur, (2) that the defendant would continue to pose a threat to society in the future, and (3) that the murder was an "unreasonable" response to victim provocation.

Johnny Paul Penry submitted various evidence in mitigation including his IQ (between 50 and 63), his learning age (estimated as that of a six- to seven-year-old child), his social maturity (estimated as that of a nine-year-old), and evidence that he had been severely abused as a child. The defense asked for jury instructions that defined the key terms in the special issues in relation to the mitigating evidence introduced. The trial judge refused to provide such instructions, and the jury found that each of the special issues delineated in the statute existed. Penry consequently was sentenced to death. On review, the Supreme Court decided that Penry's death sentence must be vacated.

An established principle for capital cases is that the punishment must relate directly to the defendant's "personal culpability." Failure to elaborate on or further define the key terms in the special issues to "give effect" to the defendant's mitigating evidence "compels the conclusion" that the jury was not fully enabled to give a "reasoned moral response" to the evidence submitted at the sentencing stage of the trial. The jury was required to find that the murder had been committed "deliberately." Penry requested special instructions that defined the term *deliberately* in a manner that would direct jurors to consider the mitigating evidence as it pertained to moral culpability. Without the special instructions, a juror who was persuaded by the mitigating evidence that the death penalty should not be imposed would be unable to give effect to that judgment if the juror also believed the crime to have been committed deliberately.

Penry's retardation and history of childhood abuse also furnished a "two-edged sword" with respect to the special issue of future dangerousness. On the one hand, those factors may have diminished his "blameworthiness," but on the other hand, Penry's "inability to learn from his mistakes" because of his retardation and his history of abuse also indicated a "probability that he will be dangerous in the future." The same kind of defect existed on the third special issue, regarding victim provocation. The Court did not find satisfactory the broad instruction that the jury could simply decline to impose the death penalty on Penry. Such an instruction was too unfocused and gave the sentencing jury the kind of "unbridled discretion" prohibited under *Furman v. Georgia*.

On the broader question, the Court concluded that the Eighth Amendment does not categorically preclude execution of mentally retarded murderers. The Court agreed that the "profoundly retarded" person lacks the "capacity to appreciate the wrongfulness" of his or her conduct and, thus, cannot be sentenced to death. The profoundly retarded person is "unlikely" to face the prospect of the death penalty, however, because he or she is rarely found competent to stand trial or can advance an insanity defense based on "mental defect." People such as Penry do not fit in that classification. The jury found him competent to be tried and rejected his insanity defense, "reflecting the conclusion that he knew his conduct was wrong" and that he was "capable of conforming it to the requirements of law." The Court was also unconvinced that any "national consensus" existed against executing mentally retarded murderers. Indeed, only one state had enacted a prohibition on the practice. The Court agreed that retardation may diminish culpability and therefore warrants consideration as a mitigating factor. Nonetheless, the Court concluded that not all retarded persons, by virtue of that "retardation alone" and separate from any individual consideration of personal responsibility, "inevitably lack the cognitive, volitional, and moral capacity to act with the degree of culpability associated with the death penalty." In other words, the Court found "insufficient basis" for a "categorical" Eighth Amendment ban on the death penalty for retarded murderers.

CAPITAL PUNISHMENT AND RACE DISCRIMINATION

One of the issues included in the original *Furman* case was race discrimination. It was asserted that if sentencers were allowed to impose the death penalty at their discretion, race would invariably be drawn into the sentencing decision. The Court said in *Furman* that sentencers could no longer exercise unguided discretion, which made it unnecessary to directly address the issue of discrimination at that time. A number of changes in capital sentencing followed *Furman,* but the issue of discrimination did not go away. The Court examined the issue in *McCleskey v. Kemp* (481 U.S. 279: 1987). Following sentencing and unsuccessful appeals in the state courts, Warren McCleskey sought *habeas corpus* relief in the federal courts. He claimed that Georgia's death penalty process was administered in a racially discriminatory manner. McCleskey supported his claim by submitting statistical data developed by Professor David C. Baldus and others (the Baldus study) based on more than 2,000 Georgia murder cases tried in the 1970s. The study revealed that blacks whose victims were white had the greatest probability of receiving the death sentence.

In a five to four decision, the Court ruled that the Baldus study did not sufficiently demonstrate unconstitutional discrimination. For McCleskey to prevail, said the Court, it was necessary to show that the decisionmakers in his specific case had acted with discriminatory intent. The Baldus study data offered concerning McCleskey's claim was insufficient to support such an inference. The statistics, said the Court, must be viewed in the context of

McCleskey's legal challenge, one aimed at the core of Georgia's criminal justice process. Implementation of capital punishment laws simply requires some discretionary judgments. Because discretion has a legitimate role, the Court needed to find exceptionally clear proof before concluding that the process had been abused. Similarly, the Court rejected McCleskey's claim that the data revealed that Georgia had violated the equal protection clause by adopting and retaining a death penalty law that discriminated in effect. The Court said McCleskey was required to show that Georgia's legislature had enacted or maintained the law because of an anticipated racially discriminatory result, but the Baldus study could not prove such intent.

The Court also rejected McCleskey's Eighth Amendment contentions. The statistics did not show that Georgia's death penalty law was arbitrary or capricious in application because they did not show that race drives capital punishment decisions in general or was a motivating factor in McCleskey's own case. The likelihood of prejudice allegedly shown did not provide the constitutional measure of an unacceptable risk of racial prejudice. The inherent lack of predictability of jury decisions does not justify their condemnation. All the study showed, said the Court, was a "discrepancy that appears to correlate with race, but this discrepancy does not constitute a major systemic defect." Any process for determining guilt or sentence has its weaknesses and the potential for misuse. Despite such imperfections, the Constitution's requirements are satisfied when the techniques used have been designed with safeguards to make them as fair as possible. The Constitution does not require that a state "eliminate any demonstrable disparity that correlates with a potentially irrelevant factor in order to operate a criminal justice system that includes capital punishment."

CAPITAL PUNISHMENT TODAY

It is unlikely that the Supreme Court will significantly modify capital punishment policy for some time to come. From a substantive standpoint, the Court has essentially reserved the death penalty for the most heinous murders. Short of finding the punishment unacceptable in all situations, the Court will have little opportunity to adjust policy otherwise. Similarly, the Court has fashioned a basic procedural structure for capital punishment over the years, and it is unlikely the justices will choose to deviate from that structure in the near future. The Court has also indicated that some variation between states is acceptable. Two recent decisions illustrate this point.

One of the elements many states built into their post-*Furman* capital punishment statutes was a requirement for comparative review of cases, which means state supreme courts were required to conduct, as part of the mandatory appeals process, a comparison between a particular sentence and punishments imposed on others convicted of the same crime. California failed to include this comparative review, and its statute was challenged in *Pulley v. Harris* (465 U.S. 37: 1984). Although the Court had upheld the step as part of the Georgia revision in *Gregg,* the justices said here that to find comparative review reasonable and constitutional "does not mean that it is indispensable." Though such review as found in *Gregg* was considered an "additional safeguard against arbitrary or capricious sentencing," the Court did not see it as so critical that without the review the statute would not have been sufficient. The Court concluded that there was no basis for saying that a proportionality review is required in every case. The *Pulley* ruling made it clear that so long as a state procedure generally conformed to *Gregg* as modified, state policies need not be uniform. The Eighth Amendment is not violated, said the Court, "every time a state reaches a conclusion different from a majority of its sisters over how best to administer its criminal law." Decisions such as *Pulley* indicate that the Court feels the death penalty statutes now in place are generally free of constitutional defect. Although varying processes can be found from state to state, the differences no longer are critical enough to warrant the Court's frequent intervention.

Equal Protection and Privacy

Most of the cases in this chapter involve the matter of equality. No equal protection language existed in the Constitution until the addition of the Fourteenth Amendment. This amendment is a useful point of departure for the consideration of equal protection. Added to the Constitution in 1868, the Fourteenth Amendment was designed to do several things. It was certainly intended to expand upon the Thirteenth Amendment and provide additional basis for federal civil rights authority. It was also aimed at forcing southern compliance with newly established political rights for blacks. The provisions of Section 1 are the heart of the amendment.

The amendment first declares that "all persons born or naturalized in the United States, and subject to the jurisdiction thereof, are citizens of the United States and the State wherein they reside." This language reversed the citizenship ruling in *Dred Scott v. Sandford* (60 U.S. 393: 1857). Next comes the privileges and immunities provision, which was intended to allow federal authority to be used to protect and advance the civil rights of black citizens and to combat the effects of the Black Codes, which were laws, found primarily in the South, that regulated slavery and established segregation by race and condition of servitude. The *Slaughterhouse Cases* decision (83 U.S. 36: 1873) neutralized this thrust through the use of the dual citizenship doctrine. Dual citizenship allowed the Supreme Court to ascribe civil and political rights of major consequence to the states.

Section 1 also says that no state shall deprive any person of life, liberty, or property without due process of law. The due process clause eventually allowed the Supreme Court to extend most Bill of Rights guarantees from the U.S. Constitution to the state level in a process known as incorporation. The clause also enabled the Court to engage in a substantive review of state policies, particularly those regulating private property rights. Section 1 concludes by saying that no state shall deny to any person within its jurisdiction the equal protection of the laws. The function of this provision was to prohibit unjustified classifications that might unreasonably discriminate. Section 5 of the amendment empowers Congress to "enforce by appropriate legislation, the provisions of this article." Early attempts to do so were unsuccessful because the Supreme Court held that congressional power might be used in a remedial fashion only in cases where the state was itself an active participant in impermissible discrimination. The state action requirement survives, although the scope of federal legislative power conferred by the Fourteenth Amendment has been expanded considerably.

Early Fourteenth Amendment decisions from the Supreme Court were quite restrictive. In 1883, the Court struck down the Civil Rights Act of 1875, ruling that the equal protection clause applied only to state or public discrimination. Essentially, the Court's judgment in the *Civil Rights Cases* (109 U.S. 3: 1883) categorically rejected the view that the equal protection clause authorized Congress to create a "code of municipal law for the regulation of private rights." Soon thereafter a comprehensive network of state segregation statutes was enacted. The Court found the segregative approach to be constitutional in *Plessy v. Ferguson* (163 U.S. 537: 1896) and justified its decision with the separate but equal doctrine. The Court said such statutes made a legal distinction only between races and had "no tendency to destroy the legal equality of the two races." Little attention was paid to the equivalent treatment under separate circumstances dimension until certain graduate-level educational cases came to the Court in the late 1940s. Separate but equal was eventually struck down in the landmark decision of *Brown v. Board of Education I* (347 U.S. 483: 1954). These cases are examined in more detail shortly. In the meantime, we turn to *Dred Scott*.

Dred Scott v. Sandford was decided before the Fourteenth Amendment was added to the Constitution, but the case's linkage to that amendment is direct and substantial. Dred Scott, a slave from Missouri, had been taken by his master to the free state of Illinois and then to the Louisiana Territory, an area designated "free" under terms of the Missouri Compromise of 1820. Scott ultimately returned to Missouri, where he brought suit claiming his residency in free areas had ended his status as a slave. The Missouri Supreme Court held that Missouri law governed despite Scott's interim residence elsewhere. Scott then pressed his suit in a federal court. The case could have been resolved by a Supreme Court ruling that Scott's status was a matter of state law. Indeed, the Court had said just that in another case a few years earlier. Instead, the Court chose to address the merits of the specific case, largely because two justices wanted to make it an occasion to examine the institution of slavery. The remainder of the Court decided against Scott in a seven to two decision, with each justice entering a separate opinion.

Chief Justice Roger Taney wrote in the majority opinion that Scott was not entitled to sue because he was not a citizen. He was not a citizen because he was black and a slave. The chief justice contended that at the time the Constitution was written, blacks were regarded as "beings of an inferior order and altogether unfit to associate with the white race, either in social or political relations"; blacks were property. Chief Justice Taney then invoked the concept of dual citizenship to foreclose Scott's claims. Federal citizenship is conferred only through federal action, he said, and no matter how extensive the privileges and immunities conferred elsewhere, they neither carried over to Missouri nor could they affect Scott's ineligibility for federal citizenship. Taney said no state can "introduce a new member into its political community created by the Constitution of the United States. It cannot make him a member of this community by making him a member of its own." Neither can a state "introduce any person, or description of persons, who were not intended to be embraced in this new political family, which the Constitution brought into existence, but here intended to be excluded from it." Scott's noncitizen status also flowed from his being a slave. Taney asserted that Scott had never achieved free status under provisions of the Missouri Compromise because that enactment was unconstitutional. In the Court's view, Congress did not have the authority to designate certain territories as free, because to do so would deprive slaveholders of their due process property rights.

The Fourteenth Amendment was ratified a decade after *Dred Scott* and, among other things, reversed the effect of that decision. The Supreme Court's first significant ruling on the equal protection clause of the Fourteenth Amendment came in the *Civil Rights Cases*. These cases were an aggregated suit that challenged the constitutionality of the Civil Rights Act of 1875. The act provided that all persons "shall be entitled to the full and equal enjoyment of the accommodations, advantages, facilities, and privileges of inns, public conveyances and theaters," and it was passed on authority conferred by Section 5 of the Fourteenth Amendment. The parties to these cases challenged Congress's power to regulate private acts of racial discrimination. In addition to its prohibition of private discriminatory behavior in public accommodations, the act also allowed federal control over situations in which state and local governments failed to protect citizens from discrimination by other citizens. Over the vigorous dissent of Justice John Harlan, the Court struck down the act. Justice Joseph Bradley's opinion for the Court stressed that the Fourteenth Amendment did not extend to

Congress an unlimited source of legislative power. Rather, the amendment was intended only to "provide modes of relief against State legislation, or State action" in which the state (government, law, public official, or policy) is party to or helps accomplish a discriminatory end. The Fourteenth Amendment did not "invest Congress with power to legislate upon subjects which are within the domain of State legislation" or authorize Congress to "create a code of municipal law for the regulation of private rights." Congress was only authorized to enact corrective rather than general legislation that "may be necessary and proper for counteracting such laws as the States may adopt or enforce, and which, by the amendment, they are prohibited from making or enforcing."

The state action requirement established by the *Civil Rights Cases* remains in force, but discrimination in privately owned public accommodations can now be addressed. The Court eventually became receptive to arguments that a close relationship exists between state authority and discriminatory activity. In *Burton v. Wilmington Parking Authority* (365 U.S. 715: 1961), for example, the Court found that the state had become a party to discrimination by a restaurant that leased space in a municipal parking facility. The state had not required equal access to all patrons. Granting a liquor license to a racially exclusive private club, however, was held not to alter the club's private character in *Moose Lodge #107 v. Irvis* (407 U.S. 163: 1972). Congress was also able to bypass the state action requirement by regulating access to public accommodations through the commerce clause in the Civil Rights Act of 1964. The Court upheld the public accommodations portions of the statute, provisions of which looked very much like those of the Civil Rights Act of 1875.

Separate but Equal

The doctrine of separate but equal holds that a legal distinction between the black and white races does not destroy the legal equality of the two races. Separate but equal was a reaction to the equal protection clause's prohibition against discriminatory state conduct. Following ratification of the Fourteenth Amendment, many southern states enacted statutes requiring racial segregation in a wide variety of situations and argued that such segregation did not constitute impermissible discrimination. The separate but equal doctrine had its origin in *Plessy v. Ferguson* (163 U.S. 537: 1896), which addressed the question of state-mandated segregation. Louisiana enacted a statute that compelled all railroads operating within the state to "provide equal but separate accommodations for the white and colored races." Homer

Plessy, a black passenger on a railway car, was subjected to criminal penalties for his refusal to leave the white section. Plessy appealed his conviction on Thirteenth and Fourteenth Amendment grounds, but the Court rejected his arguments in an eight to one decision.

In the Court's view, the Fourteenth Amendment was intended to provide both races with equality before the law, but it was also limited to legal equality. The amendment was not designed to "abolish distinctions based upon color, or to enforce social, as distinguished from political, equality, or a commingling of the two races upon terms unsatisfactory to either." The Court asserted that statutory segregation did not necessarily imply the inferiority of either race to the other and was a policy option within the competency of the state legislatures as they exercised police power. Legislatures must have discretion to act with reference to "established usages, customs, and traditions of the people" as they reasonably attempt to promote the people's comfort and preserve public peace and good order. The Court categorically rejected the proposition that "social prejudices may be overcome by legislation, and that equal rights cannot be secured to the Negro except by an enforced commingling of the two races." Such equality could only occur as the result of natural affinities, because the Constitution cannot put social inequality "upon the same plane." With such reasoning, the Court established the separate but equal doctrine. For several decades, the Court used the separate but equal doctrine without paying attention to whether or not facilities were actually equivalent. Prior to 1954, the only successful challenges to segregation on public carriers typically involved interstate travelers, which allowed the Court to base its holdings on the impermissible burdens segregation imposed on the free flow of interstate commerce. When the Court renounced the separate but equal doctrine in *Brown v. Board of Education,* it also extended the public education desegregation requirement of *Brown* to state-mandated segregation in transportation, public accommodations, and municipal facilities.

SEPARATE BUT EQUAL DOCTRINE AND PUBLIC EDUCATION

Court support for separate but equal began to erode in the 1940s. The first cases to reveal the Court's changing views came out of the public education arena, with the initial focus on graduate education. A representative decision is *Sweatt v. Painter* (339 U.S. 629: 1950), which held that intangible factors may be considered in determining whether educational programs are comparable under the separate but equal doctrine. The case involved a comparison of the educational facilities at two state law schools in Texas. The equivalence of segregated facilities had not been seriously examined by the

Court for several decades following *Plessy*. Herman Sweatt was denied admission under terms of state law to the University of Texas Law School because he was black. Sweatt's state court suit was postponed to give Texas time to establish a separate law school for blacks. However, Sweatt persisted in his effort to enter the white law school even after a black law school was opened. The Supreme Court unanimously reversed the finding of the state court that the facilities were equivalent and ordered that Sweatt be admitted to the white law school. Sweatt had argued that the Court should reverse separate but equal as a constitutional doctrine, but instead the Court chose to focus on the narrower issue of the institutional equivalence of the two law schools. Chief Justice Fred Vinson began the Court's opinion with obvious and easily measured items such as the size of the faculties, the breadth of course offerings, the number and quality of volumes in the libraries, and opportunities for specialization. On the basis of these factors, the Court concluded there was not "substantial equality in the educational opportunities offered white and Negro law students by the State." More important to the Court, however, were the differences between the two schools "in qualities which are incapable of objective measurement." Chief Justice Vinson included among the intangibles such items as faculty reputation, the position and influence of alumni, and tradition and prestige. Although the decisions involving graduate education had been focused narrowly, it was clear from such cases as *Sweatt* that the stage was being set for a full-scale reexamination of the separate but equal doctrine. Less than two years later, the Court agreed to examine segregation in elementary- and secondary-level public education.

BROWN V. BOARD OF EDUCATION

Sweatt opened the door for the direct reconsideration of the separate but equal doctrine that came in the decision of *Brown v. Board of Education I* (347 U.S. 483: 1954). *Brown I* was a Kansas case, but there were also companion cases from Delaware, Virginia, South Carolina, and the District of Columbia. Each was premised on different facts and different local conditions, but all raised the common question of the constitutionality of racial segregation in public schools. After hearing arguments in December 1952, the Court postponed a decision and ordered re-argument of the issues in December 1953. During the intervening year, Earl Warren succeeded Fred Vinson as chief justice. The decision that came the following year was unanimous, and the opinion was written by the new chief justice.

Warren began by considering whether those persons who proposed the Fourteenth Amendment intended it to apply to school segregation. He found the amendment's history to be illusive and the evidence generally inconclusive. He declared that the resolution of the issue must come from an examination of the "effect of segregation itself on public education." This could not be done by turning the clock back to 1868, when the Fourteenth Amendment was adopted, or even to 1896, when *Plessy v. Ferguson* was decided. Rather, the Court was obliged to consider public education in the light of its full development and its present place in U.S. life. The chief justice spoke of the importance of education, calling it the basis of good citizenship. He said it was instrumental in awakening a child to cultural values and that it was the key to success in life. In fact, education was "perhaps the most important function of state and local government." Given the fundamental importance of education, therefore, opportunity to acquire it must be made available to all on equal terms. The controlling question was whether segregation deprived minority children of equal educational opportunity; the Court concluded that it did. The basis of the Court's judgment was extensive psychological evidence that segregation negatively affected the educational development of minority students. "To separate them from others of similar age and qualification solely because of their race generates a feeling of inferiority as to their status in the community that may affect their hearts and minds in a way unlikely ever to be undone." The Court asserted that the doctrine of separate but equal has no place in public education, as separate educational facilities are "inherently unequal."

Brown I held that the equal protection clause of the Fourteenth Amendment prohibits the segregation of public schools anywhere in the United States. Having found constitutional violations in all of the five cases involving official, or de jure, segregation, the Court then separated the remedy questions and docketed them for later argument. *Brown v. Board of Education II* (349 U.S. 294: 1955) addressed enforcement of the decision in *Brown I*. The broad implications of the decisions were apparent immediately, however. Although *Brown I* had focused on segregation in public education, it had the effect of establishing a constitutional prohibition on race as a classification in any context. Soon thereafter, the Court extended the *Brown I* ruling to other areas, such as transportation and municipal facilities. Yet the question of whether segregation that existed unofficially (de facto segregation) was subject to the same relief as de jure segregation remained unanswered for several years following *Brown I*.

Brown II established guidelines by which public school desegregation could begin and was exclusively devoted to implementation of the desegregation of public schools as mandated by *Brown I*. The Supreme Court chose to remand (or send back) all five of the original cases to the lower courts from which they had come because "full implementation may require solution of varied local school problems." The Court felt that the primary responsibility for assessing and solving these problems rested with local school authorities. The role of the courts was defined as considering "whether the action of school authorities constitutes good faith implementation of the governing constitutional principles." Lower federal courts were to be guided by principles of equity in fashioning specific decrees. Recourse to equity law allowed lower courts some flexibility in shaping their remedies and the power to adjust to and reconcile public and private needs. The Court urged prompt implementation of remedies but did not specify deadlines. Local authorities were expected to make a "prompt and reasonable start toward full compliance." Additional time might be available presuming that school districts could establish that such time is "necessary in the public interest and is consistent with good faith compliance at the earliest practicable date." The Court said that constitutional violations must be relieved "with all deliberate speed."

Reaction to *Brown II* was both intense and varied. Widespread support existed for abandoning separate but equal in public education, and the temperate character of the order in *Brown II* defused much of the potential opposition. Nonetheless, substantial resistance developed. In some places the reactions were violent. The situation in Little Rock, Arkansas, exemplifies this point. The state legislature passed a constitutional amendment registering opposition to the desegregation decisions and enacted legislation "relieving school children from compulsory attendance at racially mixed schools." Because school was to begin in the fall of 1957 under a desegregation plan designed by the Little Rock School Board, the governor of Arkansas, Orval Faubus, sent units of the Arkansas National Guard to Central High School in Little Rock and placed the school "off limits" to black students. Crowds gathered and violence was threatened. The school board sought postponement of *Brown* implementation because of the "extreme public hostility." In *Cooper v. Aaron* (358 U.S. 1: 1958), the Court unanimously found the situation "directly traceable" to provocative actions by state officials and rejected the request to postpone. The justices firmly indicated that the constitutional rights of black students were "not to be sacrificed or yielded to the violence and disorder which have followed upon the actions of the Governor and Legislature."

Another form of resistance in segregated areas was to close the public schools altogether. One such attempt was made in Prince Edward County, Virginia, a school district involved in one of the original suits decided in *Brown I*. Under a freedom of choice provision of state law, local authorities closed the public schools. Education was made available to white students through private schools financed by means of a complex mixture of state monies and local tuition grants. In *Griffin v. County School Board of Prince Edward County* (377 U.S. 218: 1964), the Court upheld a lower court injunction against this strategy. The Court said it had "no doubt of the power of the court to give this relief to enforce the discontinuance of the county's racially discriminatory practices." The most common form of resistance, however, was simply to delay any change from the dual (segregated) school system. In *Green v. County School Board of New Kent County* (391 U.S. 430: 1968), the Court termed "intolerable" local plans that "at this late date fail to provide meaningful assurance of prompt and effective disestablishment of a dual school system." The following year, in *Alexander v. Holmes County Board of Education* (396 U.S. 19: 1969), the Court abandoned the "all deliberate speed" proviso of *Brown II* and ordered operation of only unitary schools systems "at once." These two cases clearly established an affirmative obligation for local authorities to desegregate public schools with no further delay. Among the options for lower court judges was the busing of students.

SCHOOL BUSING

The first busing case to appear before the U.S. Supreme Court was *Swann v. Charlotte-Mecklenburg Board of Education* (402 U.S. 1: 1971). *Swann* examined the scope and character of remedies to be used by federal judges in eliminating public school segregation under the equal protection clause. It became the first case in which the Court said that busing was a reasonable approach to achieving racially integrated public schools. In 1965, the Charlotte-Mecklenburg School District was required to devise a desegregation plan. The plan, approved by a federal court, had a substantial number of black students still attending schools identifiable as "black." Various Supreme Court decisions, such as *Holmes County,* had spoken of the obligation to eliminate all vestiges of a dual school system, and so more extensive desegregation was sought. Finding the Charlotte-Mecklenburg School District plan inadequate, another federal court had a plan of its own prepared by a court-appointed desegregation expert. The new plan involved extensive transportation of elementary-level students and was adopted by the district court as part of the desegregation order. The school board appealed, arguing the remedy was excessive. The Supreme Court unanimously rejected the school board's argument and upheld the lower court's entire remedy order, including the busing component. Chief Justice Warren Burger said the controlling objective was the elimination of all vestiges of state-imposed segregation. Judicial authority may be invoked, he said, if local school authorities fail in their affirmative obligation to eliminate all segregation. The scope of judicial authority to remedy past wrongs was seen as broad in order for courts to fashion equitable remedies. Such power is not unlimited, however, and may be exercised "only on the basis of a constitutional violation." Remedial authority does not automatically put judges in the shoes of school authorities, whose powers are plenary. Judicial authority enters only when local authority defaults. The Court believed the district court had appropriately taken corrective action in this case. In reviewing the student assignment element of the remedy order, the Court found the use of racial population ratios to be a "useful starting point in shaping a remedy" rather than an inflexible requirement.

The Court upheld an extensive busing order in *Swann*. The justices made it clear, however, that busing was not an absolute ingredient of desegregation orders and that mathematical ratios were to be used only to dismantle segregated districts and not to achieve racial balance as such. The outer limits of judicial power to order interdistrict busing as a remedy for school segregation were established in *Milliken v. Bradley* (418 U.S. 717: 1974). *Milliken* addressed the critical question of whether desegregation orders could cross district lines and combine urban districts with outlying suburban districts. This question was outside the scope of *Swann*. The decision would determine the extent to which school districts outside the South could be desegregated. Suit was brought by Ronald Bradley and others charging that the Detroit school system had been racially segregated by action of local as well as state school authorities. The district court found violations and considered several desegregation plans. It rejected one plan involving only Detroit because so few white students were available for reassignment that the plan would only "accentuate the racial identifiability of the district as a black school system." Instead, the court chose a plan that involved busing students between the Detroit district and 53 suburban districts. The Supreme Court, however, overturned the multidistrict remedy in a five to four decision. Chief Justice Burger said such a consolidation would "give rise to an array of other problems in financing and operating the new school system." The new "super-district" would require that the federal court become a de facto legislative authority to resolve many complex questions as well as give the courts substantial executive control. The chief justice felt that few judges could effectively fulfill these roles. The Court found a more fundamental flaw, however, in the district court's remedial order: The scope of the order exceeded the scope of the demonstrated violation. The chief justice said that before a consolidation or cross-district order could be issued, it must be shown that a "constitutional violation within one district produces a significant segregative effect in another district." The Court concluded that without an interdistrict violation, and interdistrict effect, there is no constitutional wrong calling for an interdistrict remedy.

The troublesome question of the status of de facto segregation had continued to escape direct response. In *Keyes v. School District No. 1* (413 U.S. 189: 1973), the Supreme Court finally held that actions undertaken in support of de facto segregated schools constituted de jure segregation. In two cases from Ohio, *Columbus Board of Education v. Penick* (443 U.S. 449: 1979) and *Dayton Board of Education v. Brinkman* (443 U.S. 526: 1979), the Court upheld systemwide busing as a remedy because both systems were officially segregated at the time *Brown I* was decided. Given the encompassing interpretation the Court put on the concept of de jure segregation in these cases, the need to determine the constitutionality of de facto segregation has diminished significantly.

Employment Discrimination

Solving the problem of racial segregation is extremely complex, and employment opportunity has been one of the critical policy battlegrounds. Pursuit of greater employment opportunities for minorities has essentially taken two forms: federal laws that prohibit racial discrimination in the workplace and minority preference programs. The first initiatives, which date from during World War II, were presidential executive orders that either attempted to increase minority employment or established special commissions to address the problem. In the 1960s, presidents John F. Kennedy and Lyndon Johnson issued executive orders that sought to equalize employment opportunities for jobs in the federal government and with those employers in the private sector who received federal contracts. The Civil Rights Act of 1964 was passed soon thereafter. Title VII of the act categorically prohibited discrimination on the basis of race, national origin, religion, or gender. The first important Title VII case was *Griggs v. Duke Power Company* (401 U.S. 424: 1971), which established disproportionate impact as the governing standard. In *Griggs,* the Court refused to permit an employer to use a high school diploma and scores on an intelligence test as qualifying conditions for employment. Unanimously the Court held that once a plaintiff shows unequal or disproportionate impact, the employer must demonstrate a relationship between the challenged practice and job performance.

Washington v. Davis (426 U.S. 229: 1976) considered the question of whether statutory standards prohibiting racial discrimination in employment under Title VII of the Civil Rights Act of 1964 are the same as those for adjudicating claims of invidious racial discrimination. The Court held that the latter required not only a showing of impact, but intent as well. *Davis* involved a written personnel test that was administered to all prospective federal employees, including those who, like Alfred Davis, sought positions with the Washington, D.C., police force. The test, called Test 21, was ostensibly used to measure verbal aptitude. Four times more black than white applicants failed the test. Davis claimed that the test was not reasonably related to one's performance as a police officer and that it discriminated against black applicants. In a seven to two decision, the Supreme Court upheld use of the test. *Davis* distinguished situations involving constitutional provisions such as equal protection from those based upon federal civil rights statutes. Although certain practices may be found to be in violation of a federal law such as Title VII, those practices may not be constitutional violations.

In *Watson v. Fort Worth Bank and Trust* (487 U.S. 977: 1988), the Court ruled that measures of "disparate impact," as distinct from demonstration of "disparate treatment," could be used in examining subjective employment criteria in job discrimination challenges. Clara Watson, a black bank teller, was denied promotion four times. She brought suit in federal court and established a prima facie case of discrimination. Such a case offers sufficient proof to demonstrate the likelihood of illegal discrimination, but the case is preliminary and subject to further examination. The trial court, however, found that the bank had sufficiently justified its reasons for each denial. In so finding, the court refused to consider certain statistical evidence offered by Watson addressing the bank's subjective evaluations and the effects of its decisions on blacks as a class. The Supreme Court reversed the trial court's decision on that point. In finding for Watson, the Court extended for the first time the disparate impact test of *Griggs* to subjective employment decisions. Previously, *Griggs* had applied only to standardized tests or criteria. In other words, the *Watson* decision altered the evidentiary standards that apply in cases flowing from Title VII of the Civil Rights Act of 1964, and it applied the disparate impact test to the discretionary judgments of supervisors. The Court basically agreed with Watson's contentions that subjective criteria are as likely to have discriminatory effects as objective tests and that, by confining disparate impact analysis to only objective criteria, employers could substitute subjective criteria and render *Griggs* a "dead letter."

Several Rehnquist Court rulings made job discrimination more difficult to demonstrate, however. One such decision was *Wards Cove Packing Company, Inc. v. Atonio* (104 L. Ed. 2d 733: 1989). *Wards Cove* involved Title VII complaints brought by nonwhite workers at two fish canneries in Alaska. Employment was divided into two classes: cannery and noncannery jobs. The cannery jobs were unskilled and were largely held by local and nonwhite employees. Noncannery jobs were skilled, higher paying, and held by white workers hired at company offices in Washington and Oregon. The minority workers filed an action claiming the company's practices unfairly divided the workforce on racial bases. The Supreme Court was highly critical of the data used by the lower courts to establish a prima facie case of disparate impact. A simple comparison of percentages of nonwhite workers in the two job classes was seen by the Court as "nonsensical." The "proper" comparison is between the racial composition of the "at issue jobs" and the "qualified population in the relevant labor market." In the Court's view, the cannery workforce "in no way reflected the pool of *qualified* job applicants or the *qualified* labor force population" relevant with respect to the skilled noncannery jobs. Accordingly, the methods of recruiting workers or other employment practices "cannot be said to have disparate impact on nonwhites" if the absence of nonwhites holding such skilled jobs reflects a "dearth of qualified nonwhite applicants for reasons that are not the [employers'] fault."

In addition, the Court did not find percentages of nonwhite workers in other positions relevant to workforce composition for cannery jobs. As long as there are no "barriers to applying," the selection process probably has no disparate impact on minorities if the percentage of nonwhites hired is "not significantly less than the percentage of qualified nonwhite applicants." Under the comparative method used by the court of appeals, any employer having a "racially imbalanced segment of its workforce could be hauled into court and made to undertake the expensive and time-consuming task of defending the business necessity of its selection methods." The Court also clarified the burden of proof issue. If the nonwhite workers can establish a prima facie case of disparate impact for any of the employers' practices by making the appropriate statistical comparisons, the burden of justifying those practices shifts to the employer. The "ultimate burden of persuasion," however, will remain "at all times" with those challenging the employment practices. Such a rule "conforms with the usual method for allocating persuasion and production burdens in the federal courts."

Affirmative Action

One method that has been used to address discrimination is affirmative action programs, be they mandated by government or fashioned by private parties. Such programs typically offer some kind of advantage or preference to a designated group. An absolutely necessary precondition of such programs is that the advantaged group has suffered substantial discrimination previously. Racial minorities and women are most often targeted. This approach is advocated by those who wish to offer some kind of compensation for long-standing patterns of discrimination. The programs raise constitutional questions because classification by race or gender serves as their foundation, and it is because of this characteristic that opponents of affirmative action refer to it as "reverse discrimination." The affirmative action approach differs from equal opportunity laws in that it requires particular remedial measures, whereas equal opportunity laws such as Title VII simply prohibit discriminatory conduct.

The Supreme Court's first important affirmative action ruling came in *Regents of the University of California v. Bakke* (438 U.S. 265: 1978). The medical school at University of California–Davis admitted 100 students annually. In an attempt to assure minority representation within the student body, 16 places were reserved for minority applicants. Allan Bakke, a white applicant, was twice denied admission although his credentials were better than those of some of the minority applicants admitted under the affirmative action policy. Bakke brought suit arguing that the racially sensitive quota system at Davis violated Title VI of the Civil Rights Act of 1964. Title VI prohibited discrimination in programs receiving federal funding.

The Court resolved the issues in *Bakke* by essentially finding for both sides. In a five to four split, the Court ruled that the Davis quota system was impermissible and ordered that Bakke be admitted. At the same time, the Court also held, by a five to four vote, that a state university may take race into account in allowing for a diverse student body. Each issue split the Court into two blocs of four members each, with Justice Lewis Powell providing the decisive vote on each component of the ruling. Justice Powell joined Chief Justice Burger and Justices William Rehnquist, Potter Stewart, and John Paul Stevens on the quota question, but aligned himself with Justices William Brennan, Thurgood Marshall, Byron White, and Harry Blackmun on the issue of limited affirmative action efforts. Justice Powell's opinion rejected the quota approach and the injustice of racial classifications generally. The Fourteenth Amendment confers protection to individuals, he said, and the "guarantee of equal protection cannot mean one thing when applied to one individual and something else when applied to a person of another color." Justice Powell rejected the view that race was not a suspect classification when applied to the white majority because the purpose of such classification was benign. Individuals within that class "are likely to find little comfort in the notion that the deprivation they are asked to endure is merely the price of membership in the dominant majority and that its imposition is inspired by the supposedly benign purpose of aiding others." Noting that the white majority itself was composed of various minority groups, Justice Powell feared that courts would forever be asked to assess the degree of discrimination each has suffered and the redress each was due. By "hitching the meaning of the Equal Protection Clause to these traditional considerations, we would be holding, as a constitutional principle, that judicial scrutiny of classifications touching on racial and ethnic background may vary with the ebb and flow of political forces."

Justice Powell did, however, recognize attainment of a diverse student body as a constitutionally permissible goal for an institution of higher education. Indeed, he said the nation's future depends on leaders trained through wide exposure, which comes about partly through a diverse student body. He referred to the Harvard University admissions program, which assigns a plus to particular racial or ethnic backgrounds but still treats each applicant as an individual in the admissions process. In striking down the Davis quota system, the Court said it did not need to address the broader constitutional question of race as a factor for admissions decisions. It was enough to say that Title VI required Bakke's admission and the elimination of Davis's reserved seat policy. A majority of the Court saw the Davis program as educationally sound and sufficiently important to justify the use of race-conscious admissions programs. The Davis approach did not "stigmatize any discrete group or individual" and thus was adequate as a means of "remedying the effects of past societal discrimination."

The affirmative action focus then changed to policies mandated by Congress that gave preference to minorities. The "set-aside" approach to federal funding on construction projects was spotlighted in *Fullilove v. Klutznick* (448 U.S. 448: 1980). The Public Works Employment Act of 1977 contained a minority business enterprise (MBE) section that required at least 10 percent of federal monies designated for local public works projects to be set aside for businesses owned by minorities. Implementation of the policy was designed to come through grant recipients, who were expected to seek out MBEs and provide whatever assistance or advice might be necessary to negotiate bonding, bidding, or any other historically troublesome process. The policy was challenged by a number of nonminority contractors, but was upheld by the Supreme Court in a six to three decision. Chief Justice Burger said the MBE section must be considered against the background of ongoing efforts directed toward delivering the century-old promise of economic opportunity. The chief justice noted that a program using racial or ethnic criteria, even in a remedial context, calls for close examination, "yet we are bound to approach our task with appropriate deference." The Court's analysis involved two steps: the constitutionality of Congress's objectives and the permissibility of the means chosen to pursue those objectives. The Court ruled that Congress had ample evidence to conclude that minority businesses had impaired access to public contracting opportunities, that their impaired access had an effect on interstate commerce, and that the pattern of disadvantage and discrimination was a problem of national scope. Thus, Congress had the authority to act.

The Court then turned to the means used. Racial or ethnic criteria may be used in a remedial fashion as long as the program is narrowly tailored to achieve the corrective purpose. The Court rejected the view that in developing remedies Congress must act in a wholly color-blind fashion. No organ of government has more comprehensive remedial power than Congress. Where Congress can prohibit certain conduct, "it [also] may, as here, authorize and induce state action to avoid such conduct." The Court recognized that some nonminority contractors who may not themselves have acted in a discriminatory manner may lose some contracts but said that such a result, outside the legislative purpose, is an unfortunate but incidental consequence. As Congress attempts to devise a limited and properly tailored remedy to cure the effect of prior discrimination, such a sharing of the burden by innocent parties is not impermissible.

The local parallel to *Fullilove* was examined in *City of Richmond v. J. A. Croson Company* (488 U.S. 469: 1989). The city of Richmond, Virginia, adopted an affirmative action plan requiring prime contractors receiving city construction contracts to subcontract at least 30 percent of the dollar value of the contract to businesses owned or controlled by one (or more) of a number of specified minorities. The plan was designed to "promote wider participation by minority business enterprises in the construction of public projects" and was characterized by the Richmond City Council as "remedial." The Supreme Court disallowed the Richmond plan. The principal defect was that Richmond failed to show past discrimination either in the city's contract-letting practices or in the conduct of prime contractors toward minority subcontractors. Rather, the city had relied on data that showed that although the city's population was 50 percent black, less than 1 percent of the large construction projects had been awarded to minority businesses. The Court viewed claims based on such data as "generalized" and "amorphous" and ruled that these data could not justify the use of an "unyielding" race-based quota approach. The plan was aimed, said the Court, at remedying the effects of discrimination in the entire construction industry. The data on which the plan was based provided "no guidance for a legislative body to determine the precise scope of the injury it seeks to remedy"; it had no "logical stopping point." Using these kinds of data to define "identified discrimination" would allow local government "license to create a patchwork of racial preferences based on statistical generalizations about any particular field of endeavor."

The Court also refused to defer to the city's own designation of the plan as remedial, saying that "mere recitation of a 'benign' or legitimate purpose for a racial classification is entitled to little or no weight." Racial classifications are "suspect," so "legislative assurances of good intention cannot suffice" in themselves. The Court also found the Richmond plan defective with respect to its scope. The justices said it was "almost impossible to assess" whether or not the plan was narrowly tailored to remedy prior discrimination because it was not "linked to identified discrimination in any way." Two other aspects of the *Croson* decision are worth noting. First, the Court emphasized that this decision does not preclude state and local governments from "taking action to rectify the effects of identified discrimination." Also, the Court made it clear that striking down the Richmond plan had absolutely no effect on the federal set-aside law upheld in *Fullilove*, after which the Richmond plan had been fashioned. The Court asserted that a different standard applies to congressional action. Although the Fourteenth Amendment bars state and local units from discriminating on the basis of race, Congress has a "specific constitutional mandate to enforce the dictates of the Fourteenth Amendment." This power includes authority to define situations that Congress determines threaten principles of equality and to adopt prophylactic rules to deal with such situations. Thus, Congress may "identify and redress the effects of society-wide discrimination." States and their political subdivisions are not, on the other hand, "free to decide that such remedies are appropriate."

At issue in *United States v. Paradise* (480 U.S. 149: 1987) was the use of promotion quotas as a race-based remedy for past discrimination. A federal district court had found that the Alabama Department of Public Safety had systematically excluded blacks from employment as state police officers. An order was issued in 1972 calling for the end of such discrimination and establishing a hiring quota. A number of years later it was discovered that none of the blacks recruited under the quota had been promoted. The department agreed to fashion a plan to resolve the problem, but after two years no blacks yet had been promoted. A test was subsequently devised for promotions, but it was found to have an adverse impact on blacks. When the department failed to submit a satisfactory promotion plan, the Court ordered that blacks and whites be promoted on a one-for-one basis until such time as acceptable promotion policies were in place. The Supreme Court, in a five to four decision, upheld the one-for-one plan against the claim that the approach was race-conscious and violated both the equal protection clause and the Civil Rights Act of 1964.

The remedy devised in this case was seen by the Supreme Court as effective, temporary, and flexible. The order came from the considered judgment of the district court, which, with its knowledge of the parties and their resources, properly determined that strong measures were required in light of the department's "long and shameful" record of delay and resistance. Similarly, the Court upheld the use of an affirmative action plan giving preference to women in *Johnson v. Transportation Agency* (480 U.S. 616: 1987). The Santa Clara County Transportation Agency designed an affirmative action plan for employee promotions. The plan authorized the agency to consider the gender of a qualified applicant for promotion to positions within traditionally gender-segregated job classifications. In upholding the plan, which made consideration of gender a factor in promotion decisions, the Court drew heavily from the rationale in *United Steelworkers v. Weber* (443 U.S. 193: 1979)—a case in which the Court allowed a private employer to give preference to unskilled black employees over white employees for training programs designed to elevate unskilled workers to skilled levels. The *Weber* Court permitted the preferential treatment because prior discrimination had demonstrably disadvantaged black workers in the past. In *Johnson,* Justice Brennan wrote that the Court must be particularly mindful of the value of voluntary efforts to further the objectives of the law when evaluating an affirmative action plan against Title VII's objectives. In this case, the agency identified a conspicuous imbalance in a traditionally segregated job class and undertook a "voluntary effort in full recognition of both the difficulties and the potential for intrusion on males and nonminorities."

Protection of Civil Rights

Several of the provisions of the U.S. Constitution are dedicated to protecting civil rights. Much of the previous discussion has involved situations in which individuals used the courts in an effort to demonstrate constitutional violations and obtain appropriate relief for such violations. The Constitution also enables the Congress to enact legislation designed to further the end of protecting civil rights. The Thirteenth, Fourteenth, and Fifteenth amendments each have a specific section authorizing congressional initiatives pursuant to the content of each respective amendment. Drawing on power conveyed by these amendments, Congress enacted several civil rights laws in the period between 1866 and 1875. The value of this early legislation was minimal for several reasons. First, the Reconstruction mentality that drove Congress during this time abated, and Congress lost its resolve. As a result, Congress itself repealed some of the protections previously enacted. Second, enforcement of civil rights was not a priority of presidential administrations during this period; thus, existing protections in law were not utilized. Third, the Supreme Court interpreted the legislative power granted by the three post–Civil War amendments narrowly and struck down provisions of some of these laws. Illustrative of this point is the Court's decision in the previously discussed *Civil Rights Cases,* which invalidated the Civil Rights Act of 1875.

Legislative enactments aimed at protecting civil rights do exist, however, and the remainder of this section examines them in greater detail.

The substance of the Civil Rights Act of 1875 was repackaged and adopted by Congress as Title II of the Civil Rights Act of 1964. The Supreme Court's framework in reviewing the constitutionality of the later statute differed from that in the *Civil Rights Cases* because Congress had based the 1964 enactment on its power to regulate interstate commerce. By 1964, this power had become established. The critical case is *Heart of Atlanta Motel v. United States* (379 U.S. 241: 1964). Title II of the Civil Rights Act of 1964 prohibited racial discrimination in "public accommodations," such as lodging, restaurants, and entertainment. In *Heart of Atlanta Motel,* provisions of the act were applied to a motel, a large proportion of whose guests were from outside the state. A companion case, *Katzenbach v. McClung* (379 U.S. 294: 1964), examined the prohibition on discrimination in restaurants. The Heart of Atlanta Motel appealed a district court injunction that required it to allow black travelers to stay in its facilities. U.S. Attorney General Nicholas Katzenbach appealed in the *McClung* case following a lower court judgment that the act could not be applied to Ollie McClung's restaurant. The Supreme Court unanimously ruled that Congress could use the interstate commerce power to prohibit discrimination in facilities that serve interstate travelers.

Justice Tom Clark reviewed instances in which congressional power to protect interstate commerce was used. The interest in protecting commerce let Congress, for example, deal with segregation in interstate carriers, prohibit white slave traffic, and regulate deceptive sales practices. That Congress was legislating "against moral wrongs" in these instances "rendered its enactments no less valid." That Congress considered discrimination a "moral problem" did not "detract" from the "overwhelming evidence" of the "disruptive effect" of discrimination in interstate traffic. The only questions the Court can raise are whether the Congress had a "rational basis" for its finding that discrimination affected commerce and whether the means chosen to address the matter were "reasonable and appropriate."

The landmark Civil Rights Act of 1964 was one of several congressional initiatives during the period from 1957 to 1968. In 1957 and 1960, two civil rights acts were adopted. These laws largely focused on voting practices, although a Civil Rights Commission was created by the 1957 act. The commission was designed to investigate discriminatory practices and report findings to Congress. The Civil Rights Act of 1964 was followed by the Voting Rights Act of 1965 and the Civil Rights Act of 1968. The Voting Rights Act, which is discussed later in this chapter, was an inventive and expansive application of congressional power stemming from the Fifteenth Amendment. The 1968 law was primarily aimed at addressing discrimination in housing. The volume of legislative activity during this period resembled that of the Reconstruction period. As mentioned above, much of that early activity did not produce significant results, at least initially. Some provisions of the Reconstruction civil rights laws did survive, however, and have played an important role in modern civil rights protection. The Enforcement Act of 1870, for example, establishes criminal penalties for civil rights violations. In *United States v. Guest* (383 U.S. 745: 1966), the Court upheld use of this law to punish conspiracies to violate Fourteenth Amendment rights. Section 241 of Title 18 of the U.S. Code (taken directly from language of the 1870 law) provides for fine and imprisonment of persons who conspire to "injure, oppress, threaten, or intimidate any citizen in the free exercise or enjoyment of any right or privilege secured to him by the Constitution or laws of the United States." The *Guest* case involved the murder of a black citizen on a Georgia highway. Herbert Guest was one of two persons allegedly involved in the conspiracy who had been acquitted in a state murder proceeding. Subsequently, Guest and others were indicted for conspiracy to violate Section 241.

The principal issue in the case was whether Congress possessed the authority to protect more than a narrow range of "secured" rights that flow directly from national citizenship against infringement by private persons. Prior to *Guest,* it was required that the state be shown to be a party to any acts of discrimination to be within the legislative reach of the Fourteenth Amendment. A majority of the Court felt such state involvement was present in this case. Part of the conspiracy involved private parties causing the false arrest of blacks, so the Court determined that the state was drawn into the conspiracy sufficiently to allow the indictments to stand. The majority also cited the right to travel as one of those fundamental rights of federal citizenship to be secured from violation even by private parties. Thus, under a liberal construction of the state involvement provision, the Court found the conspiracy in this case to be within reach using traditional Fourteenth Amendment standards.

Guest held that Congress had the power to punish private conspiracies to deprive persons of their right to travel interstate. The utility of Section 241 as a means of preventing conspiracies had been limited because it was felt that the provisions applied only to a narrow class of civil rights, but *Guest* dramatically broadened the scope of Section 241. In addition, the effect of the Court's holding in *Guest* needs to be seen in a broader context of Warren Court decisions affecting congressional power to protect civil rights. In a companion case to *Guest, United States v. Price* (383 U.S. 787: 1966), the Court upheld indictments allowing federal prosecution for the murders of three civil rights workers in Mississippi. These indictments were brought under Section 242 of Title 18 of the U.S. Code, provisions growing out of the

Civil Rights Act of 1866. Section 242 required that discriminatory acts be committed by public officials acting under the authority of the state in order for them to merit federal intervention. Nonetheless, it protected an extensive range of rights, not just those derived from federal citizenship. The holding in *Price* allowed the federal government to intervene if civil rights were violated and state prosecutions were unsuccessful. Coupled with the decision in *Jones v. Alfred Mayer Company* (392 U.S. 409: 1968), which acknowledged comprehensive legislative power through the Thirteenth Amendment, the Warren Court's decisions in aggregate left Congress with substantial authority to protect civil rights. Indeed, the Civil Rights Act of 1968 prohibits "willful" interference with various civil rights whether the conspirator acts "under color" of law or privately.

The early civil rights laws also contained language paralleling the criminal sanctions that authorized civil damage suits for civil rights violations. A provision of the Civil Rights Act of 1866 guaranteed blacks the right to "make and enjoy contracts." Section 1981 of Title 42 of the U.S. Code provides for civil actions as a means of enforcing those contractual rights. For a long period, this language was thought to be applicable only against state action or public discrimination. In the case of *Runyon v. McCrary* (427 U.S. 160: 1976), however, the Court extended Section 1981 to private discrimination. Since *Runyon,* this section has become a common basis of actions seeking damages for employment discrimination.

Brenda Patterson brought such an action against her employer claiming racial harassment. Following argument of her case before the Supreme Court in February 1988, the Court ordered that the case be re-argued. The question to be considered in re-argument was whether *Runyon* ought to be overruled. Although it ruled that the law could be used in private actions, the Court decided in *Patterson v. McLean Credit Union* (105 L. Ed. 2d 132: 1989), by a vote of five to four, that the statute had limited application in the employment setting and did not extend to Patterson's racial harassment claim. Justice Anthony Kennedy began with the broader question of retaining *Runyon,* arguing from the standpoint of *stare decisis* (Latin for "let it stand"), which holds that once a principle of law is established for a particular situation, the Court should adhere to that principle in future cases of a similar nature. Though "our precedents are not sacrosanct," Kennedy wrote, "departure from the doctrine of *stare decisis* demands special justification." The Court concluded that no such "special justification" had been demonstrated to necessitate the overruling of *Runyon.* The most common reason for a court to shift position on a precedent is the "intervening development of the law." *Runyon,* wrote Kennedy, has not been "undermined by subsequent changes or development in the law." Kennedy noted that *Runyon* remains "entirely consistent with our society's deep commitment to the eradication of discrimination based on a person's race."

Kennedy then turned to Patterson's specific allegation of discriminatory harassment. He reviewed the language of Section 1981 and pointed out that its "most obvious feature" is the restriction on the scope of the law. If a discriminatory act does not involve "impairment" of one of its specific provisions, Section 1981 "provides no relief." The section cannot, wrote Kennedy, "be construed as a general proscription of racial discrimination in all aspects of contract relations," for it expressly prohibits discrimination only in the making and enforcement of contracts. The section prohibits refusal to enter into a contract because of race or making contracts only on discriminatory terms. The right to make contracts does not extend, "as a matter of either logic or semantics, to conduct by the employer after the contract relation has been established." That limitation includes breaching the contract terms or imposing "discriminatory working conditions." Such "post-formation conduct" does not involve the right to make a contract. Instead, performance of established contract obligations is involved, which is a matter "more naturally governed by state contract law and Title VII" of the Civil Rights Act of 1964. *Patterson* limited the reach of Section 1981 by confining it to those discriminatory employment decisions occurring before someone is hired. Once a person is employed, discriminatory treatment falls under the purview of Title VII of the Civil Rights Act of 1964. *Patterson* can be seen as a decision that retreats from previous civil rights rulings, but it is also important for what it did not do. It did not overrule *Runyon v. McCrary* (427 U.S. 160: 1976). *Runyon* had held that Section 1981 reaches private contracts. When the Court agreed to review *Patterson* it indicated a reconsideration of *Runyon* would be included. *Patterson* affirmed *Runyon;* thus, Section 1981 continues to cover private contracts.

Section 1981 is confined to contractual situations. Section 1983 of Title 42 of the U.S. Code provides for civil suits against any person "acting under color of any statutes, ordinance, regulation, custom or usage" who violates the constitutional rights of a citizen. A large number of cases are presently brought under this section, which also says that liability shall attach to the "deprivation of any right, privileges or immunities secured by the Constitution and laws." This provision remained largely unused for almost a century because it was believed to extend only to official authorized misconduct. The Warren Court broadened the reach of Section 1983 as a remedy in *Monroe v. Pape* (365 U.S. 167: 1961), ruling that persons are subject to damage suits anytime their conduct violates federal or state law. Under Section 1983, defendants may be liable not only for compensatory damages, but punitive damages as well. The latter requires a finding that the action was reckless or "callously indifferent" to a person's rights. *Monroe* opened the door for a great many damage suits, and the Court has frequently faced questions about such litigation. From *Monroe* on, civil rights actions seeking damages or other relief became more numerous. The trend has been to bring state and local governments under closer federal scrutiny; illustrative is the decision of *Maine v. Thiboutot* (448 U.S. 1: 1980). In this case, the Court held that Section 1983 suits may be brought against state and local governments for alleged denial of *any* federal law. The controversy in *Thiboutot* arose over loss of certain benefits under the Aid to Families with Dependent Children provisions of the Social Security Act. Cases like *Thiboutot* proved to have a powerful impact on the old doctrine of dual federalism. Given the degree to which federal laws, especially those involving entitlement programs, intertwine with state and local governmental activities, officials responsible for these activities have become more and more subject to direct legal action.

Section 1983 actions are not without limit, however. Consider the case of *DeShaney v. Winnebago County Department of Social Services* (103 L. Ed. 2d 249: 1989). Joshua DeShaney was physically abused on a regular basis by his biological father. The Winnebago County Department of Social Services (DSS) received numerous complaints about the abuse and made some effort to protect the child. However, DSS took no steps to remove Joshua from his father's custody. A final beating of Joshua, age four at the time of the incident, was sufficiently severe to leave the child permanently brain damaged and "profoundly" retarded. Action was brought under Section 1983 against DSS by Joshua and his mother for failure to protect him from his father's abusive conduct. It was asserted that DSS's failure to remove Joshua from his father's custody deprived him of the physical safety to which he was entitled under the substantive component of the due process clause of the Fourteenth Amendment.

The Supreme Court ruled that the agency did not violate Joshua's rights under the due process clause because the clause is aimed at limiting the state's power to act and is not a "guarantee of certain minimal levels of safety and security." It forbids deprivation of life, liberty, and property by the state, but cannot be expanded to impose an "affirmative obligation on the state to ensure that those interests do not come to harm by other means." An argument was also presented on behalf of Joshua that, even if there were no due process obligation to act to protect the general public, the state had a particular duty in Joshua's case because of a "special relationship" of DSS to client in this instance. DSS was aware that Joshua "faced a special danger of abuse," and caseworkers had specifically indicated an intention to "protect him against that danger." Having recognized the need to protect Joshua from his father, the state acquired an "affirmative duty," through the due process clause, to do so in a "reasonably competent fashion." The Court rejected these contentions, arguing that the state assumes responsibility for a person's "safety and general well-being" only when it formally takes custody of a person and holds that individual against his or her will. The affirmative duty to protect arises "not from a State's knowledge of an individual's predicament or from its expressions of intent to help him, but from the limitation which it has imposed on his freedom to act on his own behalf." The harm suffered by Joshua in this case occurred while he was in the custody of his father, "who was in no sense a state actor." Although the state may have been aware of the "dangers that Joshua faced in the free world," the state "played no part in their creation," nor did it "do anything to render him any more vulnerable to them."

THE "NEW" EQUAL PROTECTION

Initially, the equal protection clause had only limited impact. It was reserved exclusively for racial discrimination and was seldom aggressively applied even in that context. The character of equal protection began to change in the post–New Deal period, however, as the Court generally became more extensively involved with civil liberties matters. The Warren Court in particular began to consider application of the equal protection clause to other classifications in addition to race. The expanding scope of the clause is sometimes called the "new" equal protection. Because most legislation engages in some form of classification, the clause became an attractive vehicle for challenges to those classificatory schemes.

The equal protection clause does not preclude the use of classifications but merely requires that a classification be reasonable. The main problem of the new equal protection is that of distinguishing reasonable and permissible classifications from arbitrary and impermissible ones. Even under the new equal protection, the Court does not wish to make all classificatory schemes equally vulnerable to challenge. Legislatures are generally afforded wide discretion in making classifications, so legislative classifications are typically evaluated by the rationality test, a standard reflecting the Court's understanding that drawing lines that create distinctions is peculiarly a legislative task as well as an unavoidable task. Classifications are presumed to be valid under this approach, and they need not function perfectly. If the legislative objective is legitimate, a classification may be used as long as it rationally relates to its objective. This doctrine places the burden of proof on the party claiming the classification has no rational or reasonable basis.

Under certain circumstances, more may be required of the state to sustain a classification than mere rationality. Some classifications may be subject to closer examination or scrutiny. The strict scrutiny standard requires a state to show more than reasonableness for a classificatory policy. The state must demonstrate a critical need or a compelling interest that can be addressed only by use of the challenged classification. Thus, the burden of proof shifts to the state in cases in which strict scrutiny is undertaken. The strict scrutiny standard applies when the classification impinges on a fundamental or expressly protected right, such as freedom of speech, religious exercise, or the right to vote. A fundamental right also may extend to rights fashioned by implication, such as the right to cross state lines or the right to political association. In *Shapiro v. Thompson* (394 U.S. 618: 1969), for example, the Court struck down a residency requirement for public assistance benefits because the classification inhibited movement of people from state to state. The Court said such a classification, which touches on the fundamental right of interstate movement, is "patently unconstitutional." Similarly, interference with the fundamental right of an unimpaired vote prompted the Court to develop the "one person, one vote" principle in legislative apportionment cases.

The strict scrutiny standard also applies if the classification affects a "suspect" group or class. A suspect class is a class that is saddled with such disabilities, is the recipient of such purposeful unequal treatment over time, or occupies such a politically powerless position as to require extraordinary protection within the political process. Classifications based on race and alienage are considered to be inherently suspect. The racially conscious affirmative action policies upheld by the Court have demonstrated a compelling interest being served by the classification. If a classification is to be used in such situations, it must also be precisely drawn or carefully tailored, and it must employ the least drastic means possible to achieve its particular legislative objectives. The Court has stricken down a number of gender-based classifications, but to date has not found gender to be a suspect class. Some members of the Court have suggested that gender receive heightened scrutiny at a level between strict scrutiny and the rationality standard. It is clear that challenges to classification schemes are more likely to succeed if a fundamental right or suspect class is involved, and it is for this reason that arguments are entered urging the Court to find either or both of these conditions present. Even though the Court has been reluctant to find other than race or alienage to be suspect, the new equal protection has substantially altered the scope of the equal protection clause.

GENDER

Prior to the 1970s, the Supreme Court found no constitutional defect in gender-based classifications. That view changed beginning with such decisions as *Frontiero v. Richardson* (411 U.S. 677: 1973). *Frontiero* involved a female air force lieutenant who sought higher housing and medical allowances by having her husband declared a dependent. Such benefits were automatically granted with respect to the wife of a male member of the uniformed services. Sharron Frontiero argued that the policy was discriminatory in two ways. First, she argued the process was unfair because only female members were required to demonstrate spouse dependency. Second, a male member of the armed services received the benefits even if he provided less than half of his wife's support, whereas a similarly situated female would not receive such benefits. With only Justice Rehnquist dissenting, the Court invalidated the statutory provisions. The eight-justice majority was fragmented, however, on the standard by which gender classification ought to be evaluated.

Justices Brennan, Douglas, Marshall, and White viewed sex classifications, like those of race, alienage, and national origin, to be suspect and therefore subject to close judicial scrutiny. Justice Brennan noted a long history of sex discrimination, rationalized by an attitude of romantic paternalism that, "in practical effect, put women not on a pedestal, but in a cage." Sex is an "immutable characteristic determined solely by the accident of birth." To impose special disabilities on women because of their sex runs counter to the concept that legal burdens should bear some relationship to individual responsibility. What gives gender classification its suspect status, argued Justice Brennan, is that the "sex characteristic frequently bears no relation to ability to perform or contribute to society." The result is that women are often invidiously relegated to inferior legal status without regard to actual capabilities. Policies achieving nothing more than administrative convenience through different treatment by gender is the "very kind of legislative choice forbidden by the Equal Protection Clause." Chief Justice Burger and Justices Stewart, Powell, and Blackmun also found the statute impermissibly discriminatory, but refused to go so far as to label gender an inherently suspect class. They resolved the case using the less stringent rational basis test. Justice Powell said that an expansion to suspect status had far-reaching implications, but that it was also preemptive and premature given that the Equal Rights Amendment was under consideration at the time.

Frontiero was preceded by *Reed v. Reed* (404 U.S. 71: 1971), a case in which the Court struck down an Idaho law giving preference to males over females in administering estates. Using the rationality test, the Court unanimously concluded that the equal protection clause does not permit states to place persons into different classes on the basis of criteria wholly unrelated to the objective of the statute. In *Craig v. Boren* (429 U.S. 190: 1976), the Court struck down an Oklahoma statute that permitted females to buy 3.2

percent beer at age 18 while prohibiting males from doing so until the age of 21. The Court said gender classifications must serve important governmental objectives and be substantially related to reaching those objectives. The Oklahoma statute could not survive those criteria.

Five years later, the Court ruled in *Rostker v. Goldberg* (453 U.S. 57: 1981) that Congress could exclude women from registering for a possible military draft without violating the due process limitations of the Fifth Amendment. The Military Selective Service Act gave the president power to require "every male citizen" and male resident aliens of appropriate age to register for potential conscription. Suit was brought by Robert Goldberg, and a number of others subject to the registration order, claiming gender discrimination. The Court disagreed in a six to three decision. Justice Rehnquist wrote for the majority that congressional judgments warrant particular deference when the issues involve raising and regulating the armed forces. Indeed, congressional authority is greatest in this policy area. Against that background, the Court turned to the issue of gender-based registration.

Unlike other sex discrimination cases, this one involved an enactment in which the legislative body "did not act unthinkingly or reflexively." The decision to exempt women from registration was not the accidental byproduct of a traditional way of thinking about women. On the contrary, the policy was considered at great length, and Congress clearly expressed its purpose and intent. The Court upheld the classification primarily because males and females were not viewed as similarly situated with respect to combat duty. Women are statutorily restricted from such duty. By viewing the draft of combat-ready troops in time of national emergency and registration for that draft as part of the same function, the Court found basis for distinguishing the situations of males and females. Justice Rehnquist wrote that the Constitution "requires that Congress treat similarly situated persons similarly, not that it engage in gestures of superficial equality." Therefore, Congress was entitled to focus on the question of military need rather than equity.

Despite decisions like *Frontiero* and *Reed*, the Burger Court more typically was found in the position taken in *Rostker*. In *Personnel Administrator v. Feeney* (442 U.S. 256: 1979), for example, the Court upheld a state policy extending preferential status to military veterans for state employment. It found no discriminatory intent in the advantage given veterans over nonveterans, a class composed of both men and women, despite the policy's adverse impact on women. And in *Michael M. v. Superior Court of Sonoma County* (450 U.S. 464: 1981), the Court upheld a statutory rape law prohibiting sexual intercourse with a female under 18 years of age. The statute in this case was permissible because it addressed a substantial inequality between men and women based on "harmful and inescapably identifiable consequences of teenage pregnancy." Further, the risk of pregnancy "constitutes a substantial deterrence to young females." The law creating criminal sanctions for males "serves roughly to equalize the deterrent on the sexes."

GENDER DISCRIMINATION IN EMPLOYMENT

As with race, a key gender discrimination battleground has become the workplace. We return to Title VII and start with two recent decisions that favored the female litigants. In *Hishon v. King & Spalding* (467 U.S. 69: 1984), the Court unanimously held that law firms may not discriminate on the basis of gender in making decisions on promotion to partnership. The Court rejected two arguments advanced by the law firm. First, the firm contended that such promotion decisions as this—partnership status—were exempt from the job discrimination provisions of Title VII. Second, the firm maintained that the right of association insulated partnership decisions. While its purpose was not necessarily discriminatory, the firm wanted to reserve partnership judgment for itself. The Court disagreed on both points made by the defendant.

A similar decision came in *Price Waterhouse v. Hopkins* (490 U.S. 228: 1989). Ann Hopkins was an officer in an office of Price Waterhouse, a national accounting firm. She was proposed for partnership, but the decision was postponed for a year. At the end of the year, her partnership was never reconsidered. She resigned from the firm and filed suit under Title VII of the Civil Rights Act of 1964 claiming gender discrimination. Title VII, said the Court, "eliminates certain bases for distinguishing among employees while otherwise preserving employers' freedom of choice." This "balance" of employee rights and employer prerogatives "turns out to be decisive" in this case. Though an employer may not take gender into account in making employment decisions, the employer must be "free to decide against a woman for other reasons." Accordingly, once a plaintiff in a Title VII action "shows that gender played a motivating part" in a decision, the defendant "may avoid a finding of liability only by proving that it would have made the same decision even if it had not allowed gender to play such a role."

We now add the ingredient of the Equal Pay Act of 1963, which prohibited wage differentials based on sex for persons performing equivalent work. Title VII contained a reference to the Equal Pay Act through a provision of the Bennett amendment, which exempted from the Equal Pay Act differences in wage stemming from seniority, merit, or work quantity. *County of Washington v. Gunther* (450 U.S. 907: 1981) held that Title VII challenges of sex-based wage discrimination are not limited to claims of unequal pay for equal work. Though the Court explicitly said that its decision did not embrace the comparable worth concept, *Gunther* did mean that women bringing wage discrimination suits need only show that gender was used in a discriminatory fashion in setting rate of pay. *Gunther* also reflected the broadening view of the Burger Court about what constitutes sex discrimination. Three additional decisions are illustrative. In *Newport News Shipbuilding and Dry Dock Company v. Equal Employment Opportunity Commission* (462 U.S. 669: 1983), the Court struck down a health plan that did not provide the same pregnancy coverage for the wives of male employees as it provided for female employees. In *Los Angeles Department of Water and Power v. Manhart* (435 U.S. 702: 1978), the Court held that requiring female employees to make higher contributions to retirement programs than men violated Title VII despite the statistical probability that a woman would collect more retirement benefits because of greater longevity. The counterpart to *Manhart* came in *Arizona Governing Committee for Tax Deferred Annuity and Deferred Compensation Plans v. Norris* (463 U.S. 1073: 1983), in which the Court invalidated an employer-sponsored retirement plan that provided smaller benefits to women by using sex-based actuarial tables reflecting greater longevity for women. The Court said the classification of employees on the basis of sex was no more permissible at the pay-out stage of a retirement plan than at the pay-in stage. It is evident from decisions such as these that the Supreme Court has used the equal protection clause to reach gender-based discrimination even in the wake of the failure to ratify the Equal Rights Amendment.

Finally, the Court held in *University of Pennsylvania v. Equal Employment Opportunity Commission* (107 L. Ed. 2d 571: 1990) that universities can be compelled to disclose previously confidential peer reviews in cases in which discrimination is charged in the making of tenure and promotion decisions. Title VII of the Civil Rights Act of 1964 prohibits employment discrimination and empowered the Equal Employment Opportunity Commission (EEOC) to investigate claims of such discrimination. The EEOC was given the power to subpoena needed documents as part of its enforcement authority. Here, the EEOC requested materials relating to an allegedly discriminatory tenure decision, and the Court unanimously declined to protect the peer review process from such examination. The Court said that the process is not entitled to privileged status unless it "promotes sufficiently important interests to outweigh the need for probative evidence." Justice Blackmun, writing for the Court, noted a particular reluctance to recognize a privilege in an area in which Congress itself had thoroughly considered the possibility and chosen against it. He referred to congressional judgment to extend Title VII to educational institutions and provide the EEOC with broad subpoena power. The Court agreed that the role of universities is significant and that confidentiality is important to the peer review process. The "costs that ensue from disclosure, however, constitute only one side of the balance." The costs associated with racial and gender discrimination are "a great if not compelling governmental interest." Often, peer review documents are indispensable in determining the presence of illegal discrimination. "Indeed, if there is a 'smoking gun' to be found that demonstrates discrimination in tenure decisions, it is likely to be tucked away in peer review files."

A different kind of Title VII issue is considered in *California Federal Savings and Loan Association v. Guerra* (479 U.S. 272: 1987), which upheld a state law requiring employers to grant maternity leave and job reinstatement to women employees. California Federal Savings and Loan (Cal Fed) refused to reinstate Lillian Garland following her pregnancy disability leave. Garland then sought to invoke state law by filing a complaint with the state agency authorized to enforce the law. Cal Fed brought action in U.S. district court claiming the state law was inconsistent with and preempted by Title VII of the Civil Rights Act of 1964 as amended by the Pregnancy Disability Act (PDA) of 1978. The PDA declared that discrimination on the basis of pregnancy constituted illegal gender discrimination. The PDA also required that pregnant women be treated the same as any other disabled employee. Cal Fed asserted that the PDA therefore prohibited the preferential treatment of pregnant women. The trial court granted summary judgment for Cal Fed, but the court of appeals reversed. The Supreme Court also ruled against Cal Fed in a six to three decision.

The question presented in the *Guerra* case was whether Title VII, as amended by the PDA, preempted California law. In making such a determination the Court's task was to ascertain the intent of Congress. Federal law may supersede state law by simply stating that in expressed terms. State law is also superseded where the scheme of federal regulation is sufficiently comprehensive to support the inference that Congress left no room for supplementary state regulation. A third preemptive situation exists in policy areas in which Congress has not completely displaced state regulation and in which federal law may actually conflict with state law. The last was the situation involved in *Guerra*. Upon examining the Civil Rights Act of 1964, the Court found that the preemptive effect of Title VII was narrow in scope and severely limited. The Court said this reflected the importance Congress attached to state antidiscrimination laws in achieving Title VII objectives. The provisions added by the PDA accomplished the same purpose. The PDA was intended to illustrate how discrimination against pregnancy is to be remedied. Congress intended the PDA to be a "floor beneath which pregnancy disability benefits may not drop—not a ceiling above which they may not rise." In addition, the Court found it significant that Congress was aware of state laws similar to California's, but apparently did not consider them inconsistent with the PDA. In the Court's view, Title VII as amended by the PDA and California's pregnancy disability leave statute shared a common goal. Both sought to promote equal employment opportunity. By requiring reinstatement after pregnancy leave, the California law ensures that women will not lose their jobs because of pregnancy disability. By taking pregnancy into account, California's leave statute allows both men and women to have families without losing their jobs. The state law does not compel employers to treat pregnant workers better than other disabled employees. Rather, it establishes benefits that employers must, at a minimum, provide to pregnant workers.

The issue of gender discrimination by private organizations was taken up in *Roberts v. United States Jaycees* (468 U.S. 609: 1984). The Court upheld the application of a state antidiscrimination law in *Roberts* that forced an organization to accept women into its membership. The Court found that the state's interest in promoting gender equality prevailed over the organization's First Amendment expression and association interests. The balance between regulations designed to combat discrimination and the associational rights of private clubs was again considered in *New York State Club Association, Inc. v. City of New York* (487 U.S. 1: 1988). New York City adopted a human rights law in 1965 that prohibited discrimination of virtually all kinds. The law specifically exempted clubs and institutions of a "distinctly private" nature. A 1984 amendment to the law provided that a club shall not be considered "distinctly private" and therefore exempt from the original law if it has "more than four hundred members, provides regular meal service and regularly receives payment . . . directly or indirectly from or on behalf of nonmembers for the furtherance of trade or business." Benevolent orders and religious corporations were not included in the narrowed exemption language of the 1984 amendment. The New York State Club Association, a nonprofit consortium of private clubs and associations, challenged the amendments on First and Fourteenth Amendment grounds but was unsuccessful. A unanimous Supreme Court also upheld the constitutionality of the amended law. A number of the large clubs were clearly subject to antidiscrimination regulation under the holding in *Roberts*. The Court did not find any infringement on club members' rights. Absent evidence demonstrating special circumstances, the Court was satisfied that large clubs could "effectively advance their desired viewpoints without confining their memberships to persons having the same sex, for example, or the same religion." Neither was there evidence to demonstrate that the law actually impaired the "ability to associate or to advocate public or private viewpoints." Finally, the Court rejected the equal protection challenge aimed at the exemption extended to benevolent orders and religious organizations. The Court said that the city council could have reasonably distinguished among the groups "in the crucial respect of whether business activity is prevalent among them." The law reflects a legislative judgment that benevolent orders and religious corporations are "unique," a finding that provides a rational basis for their exemption, and the Court concluded that the association had not shown such a judgment to be erroneous.

ALIENAGE

Alienage, like race, is a suspect classification. An example of how the Court has handled alienage in the equal protection context is provided by *Graham v. Richardson*. Carmen Richardson was a lawfully admitted resident alien who had become permanently and totally disabled. She applied for public assistance benefits under provisions of the Social Security Act that offer financial assistance to persons with the disabilities she had. She met all the requirements except for a 15-year residency requirement for aliens established under state law in Arizona. The Supreme Court ruled the requirement to be unconstitutional. Justice Blackmun's opinion for the unanimous Court said that states generally have been accorded broad discretion to classify, especially in the areas of "economics and social welfare." Yet "classifications based on alienage, like those based on nationality or race, are inherently suspect and subject to close judicial scrutiny." Aliens are a prime example of a discrete and insular minority for whom such heightened judicial solicitude is appropriate. The Arizona requirement was defective because it created two classes of needy persons, indistinguishable except with respect to whether they are or are not citizens of the United States. Arizona sought to justify its classification on the basis of a "special public interest in favoring its own citizens over aliens in the distribution of limited resources such as welfare benefits." The Court disagreed that such a special interest existed even though Arizona had a "valid interest in preserving the fiscal integrity of its programs." But a state cannot accomplish even valid purposes by invidious distinctions, and the "saving of welfare costs cannot justify an otherwise invidious classification." Unlike the situation in *Shapiro,* however, this justification is "particularly inappropriate where the discriminated class consists of aliens." Aliens, like citizens, pay taxes and may be called into the armed forces. Finally, the Court held that the federal government has overriding and superior authority in this field. Federal power is preemptive of state regulation, and Congress "has not seen fit to impose any burden or restriction on aliens who become indigent after their entry into the United States."

In *Sugarman v. Dougall* (413 U.S. 634: 1973), the Court used the *Graham* rationale to strike down a state civil service statute precluding aliens from competing for state civil service jobs. Alienage does not retain suspect status in all situations, however. In *Matthews v. Diaz* (426 U.S. 67: 1976), the Court unanimously upheld a Social Security Act provision denying Medicare supplemental medical insurance to aliens unless they had been admitted for permanent residence and had resided in the United States for at least five years. The Court deferred to the federal government's comprehensive authority regarding immigration and citizenship and evaluated the classification using the less stringent rationality test. Alienage classifications are also subject to the rational standard test rather than the compelling state interest test associated with strict scrutiny when vital governmental functions are involved. In *Foley v. Connelie* (435 U.S. 291: 1978), the Court upheld a New York State regulation limiting state police appointments to citizens. Suggesting that it would be inappropriate to require every statutory exclusion of aliens to clear the high hurdle of strict scrutiny, the Court held that the police function is a basic governmental responsibility and therefore may be reserved to citizens.

WEALTH

Differences in levels of economic well-being may also pose equal protection questions. Two such questions were raised in *San Antonio Independent School District v. Rodriguez* (411 U.S. 1: 1973). The first question was whether or not access to public education is one of the fundamental rights that a state can limit only by a showing of compelling interest. The second question was whether or not indigence constitutes a suspect class under evolving equal protection standards. The San Antonio case involved a challenge to the funding mechanisms for public education in Texas. A portion of the educational costs was provided by state appropriations, with local districts supplementing these revenues by locally levied property taxes. Suit was brought asserting that this funding approach created inequities among school districts because some were disadvantaged by low or limited property-tax bases. It was argued that the differences in property-tax yields produced impermissible disparities in per-pupil expenditures. In a five to four decision, the Court rejected the argument that wealth discrimination had occurred or that a fundamental right had been violated.

The Court distinguished *Rodriguez* from prior cases involving indigence. Indigents are unable to pay for a particular benefit so that an "absolute deprivation of a meaningful opportunity to enjoy that benefit occurs." Even in the poorest of school districts, however, children were receiving some kind of public education. This led the Court to conclude that the Texas system "does not operate to the particular disadvantage of any suspect class." Even showing wealth discrimination would not have provided "an adequate basis for invoking strict scrutiny." Neither is education a fundamental right. Although it noted historical dedication to public education in the United States, the Court said the importance of a service performed by the state does not determine whether or not it must be regarded as fundamental for purposes of examination under the equal protection clause. The Court also thought the Texas system was implemented in an effort to extend public education and improve its overall quality. That differentiated it from other situations in which the Court had applied strict scrutiny. Furthermore, for the Court to void the educational financing system in Texas would require it to intrude into an area in which it had traditionally deferred to state legislatures. The Court said it was impossible to devise a scheme of taxation that is free of all discriminatory impacts. Although the Texas system "provides less freedom of choice with respect to expenditures from some districts than for others, the existence of some inequality in the manner in which the state's rationale is achieved is not alone a sufficient basis for striking down the entire system." Insofar as wealth was concerned, the equal protection clause "does not require absolute equality or precisely equal advantages."

ILLEGITIMACY

Many states condition policies on legitimacy. Children are considered legitimate if they are born to married parents or paternity is legally acknowledged. Like other classificatory bases, legitimacy has been subject to equal protection challenges. Illustrative is the case of *Weber v. Aetna Casualty and Surety Company* (406 U.S. 164: 1972). The Court ruled in *Weber* that a state may not disadvantage the unacknowledged illegitimate child of a deceased worker when distributing worker's compensation benefits. Henry Stokes had died from employment-related injuries. At the time of his death, Stokes was living with four legitimate minor children, one unacknowledged minor, and Willie Mae Weber, the mother of the unacknowledged minor. After Stokes's death, a second illegitimate child of Stokes and Weber was born. The Louisiana worker's compensation law placed unacknowledged illegitimate children in a class of "other dependents," a class of lower status than that of "children." The "other dependents" class may recover worker's compensation benefits only if the higher class of survivors does not exhaust the maximum benefits. The four legitimate offspring of Stokes were awarded the statutory maximum, leaving nothing to the two unacknowledged illegitimate children. In an eight to one decision, the Supreme Court said this statutory scheme violated the equal protection clause.

Justice Powell's opinion declared the statute to be unacceptable even though it was limited to unacknowledged illegitimate children and did not prohibit recovery altogether. The less favorable position into which the unacknowledged illegitimate child was placed was said to be fatal because "such a child may suffer as much from the loss of a parent as a child born within wedlock or any illegitimate acknowledged later." Louisiana law precluded acknowledgement of the illegitimate child even if the father had wished to do so. Justice Powell observed that "the burden of illegitimacy, already weighty, becomes doubly so when neither parent nor child can legally lighten them." He suggested the Court's inquiry into such cases turned on two questions: What legitimate state interest does the classification promote, and what fundamental personal rights might the classification endanger? The Court did not take issue with Louisiana's interest in protecting legitimate family relationships, but it did not feel the challenged statute promoted that interest. "Persons will not shun illicit relations because their offspring may not one day reap the benefits of workmen's compensation."

Though the Court ruled in *Weber* that a state could not deny equal benefit recovery opportunities to unacknowledged illegitimate children, it did not establish more generally the level of scrutiny that illegitimacy deserves. The Court has examined the problem more closely than the rationality test would require, but has never found illegitimacy to be a suspect class deserving strict scrutiny. The Court's path in dealing with this classification has not followed a straight line, as illustrated by the following examples. In *Levy v. Louisiana* (391 U.S. 68: 1968), the Court struck down a law that denied unacknowledged illegitimate children opportunity to recover damages in the event of their mother's wrongful death. The statute was viewed as sufficiently arbitrary that impermissible discrimination could be found by use of standards less demanding than strict scrutiny. In *Labine v. Vincent* (401 U.S. 532: 1972), however, the Court upheld a state succession law that denied illegitimate children inheritance rights equal to those of legitimate children. The Court said a state had the power to protect and strengthen family life as well as to regulate the disposition of property. *Weber* was next in sequence and resembled more closely the approach taken in *Levy*. The ruling in *Matthews v. Lucas* (427 U.S. 495: 1976) then held that a requirement demanding proof of dependency by illegitimate children seeking Social Security death benefits was a rational means of protecting against survivor benefits being paid to children who were not dependent. The Court noted in *Lucas* that statutory classifications based on illegitimacy fall into "a realm of less than strict scrutiny." Claiming that such less-than-strict-scrutiny was not "toothless," the Court a year later struck down an Illinois statute that precluded illegitimate children from inheriting property from their fathers in *Trimble v.*

Gordon (430 U.S. 762: 1977). Using a rationale closely resembling that of *Weber,* the Court found the classification too remote from a legitimate state purpose to pass review.

AGE

Age is a common method of classification. As we saw in chapter 3, the Court permits states to set minimum ages for a wide variety of things such as driving, purchase of alcohol, and acquisition of debt. As a general rule, such minimum ages are not seen as either arbitrary or unreasonable. Most constitutional challenges to the use of age as a means of classification relate to older people. A good example is the mandatory retirement case of *Massachusetts Board of Retirement v. Murgia* (427 U.S. 307: 1976). In *Murgia* the Court used the least stringent standard, known as the rationality test. This test invalidates classifications only if they are arbitrary and have no demonstrable justification. A provision of Massachusetts State law required that uniformed state police officers retire at age 50. Key to the Court's ruling in this case was the criteria used to assess the mandatory retirement policy. Robert Murgia argued that the age classification creates a "suspect class" and therefore is entitled to a "strict scrutiny" review, a more demanding review than that associated with the rationality test. The Court disagreed and held that Murgia did not belong to a suspect class. In a seven to one decision, the Court upheld the mandatory retirement law. Under the rationality approach, legislative actions are presumed valid, and "perfection in making the necessary classification is neither possible nor necessary." In this instance, the legislature sought "to protect the public by assuring the physical preparedness of its uniformed police." Given the fact that physical ability generally declines with age, the Court found the mandatory retirement policy rationally related to the state's objective. The Court did not say the policy chosen by Massachusetts was necessarily the best or most humane, but only that under terms of the rationality criterion the enactment did not deny equal protection.

Murgia stated that a mandatory retirement policy for uniformed police officers was rational. Soon after *Murgia,* the Court upheld a mandatory retirement policy for Foreign Service officers in *Vance v. Bradley* (440 U.S. 93: 1979). Again the Court found the retirement policy rationally related to the legislative goal of assuring the professional capacity of people holding critical public service positions. In this case, Foreign Service officers have to undergo special rigors associated with overseas duty. Justice Marshall dissented and reiterated his call for a more demanding standard in reviewing such legislation. Not all age discrimination suits have been unsuccessful, however. In *Trans World Airlines, Inc. v. Thurston* (469 U.S. 111: 1984), the Court unanimously held that an airline's policy of not permitting the automatic transfer of age-disqualified captains to other positions with the company was a violation of the Age Discrimination in Employment Act of 1967. The *Thurston* decision was soon followed by two other important rulings on the same federal law. In *Western Air Lines, Inc. v. Criswell* (472 U.S. 400: 1985), the Court unanimously held that an airline could not require mandatory retirement of flight engineers at age 60. Unlike the situation of pilots and copilots, where age was considered a bona fide occupational qualification, the Court felt that flight engineers could be individually assessed rather than subjected to blanket early retirement rules. In *Equal Employment Opportunity Commission v. Wyoming* (460 U.S. 226: 1983), the Court ruled that state and local governments are not immune from provisions of the Age Discrimination in Employment Act. The act prohibits employer discrimination against any employee or potential employee because of age. The Court made it clear, however, that this judgment did not compel a state to abandon policies that can demonstrate age as a bona fide occupational qualification. Central to the decisions in both *Murgia* and *Bradley* was the holding that compulsory retirement would better ensure good job performance by limiting the age of employees. The retirement policies in both cases sought to maximize the physical capabilities of persons performing certain functions.

RESIDENCY

Finally, we consider classification by residency. The foundation case is *Shapiro v. Thompson* (394 U.S. 618: 1969). *Shapiro* was a pivotal case in the development of the expanded, or "new," equal protection. Once the Court decided that the equal protection clause might apply to classifications other than race, it was forced to examine the scope of the protection afforded and the standards by which classifications might be assessed. It determined that legislative classifications that interfered with "fundamental" rights demanded strict judicial scrutiny. *Shapiro* involved a woman trying to obtain support under the Aid to Families with Dependent Children (AFDC) public assistance program. She was denied assistance because she could not satisfy the state's one-year residency requirement. The Court struck down the requirement in a six to three decision. The Court said the effect of the waiting period requirement was to create two classes of needy resident families indistinguishable from each other except that one is composed of people who have resided in the state a year or more and the other is composed of people who have resided there less than a year. The purpose of the requirement was to deter migration of needy people into the state and thus preserve the fiscal integrity of state public assistance programs. But the Court said inhibiting migration is constitutionally impermissible. It is a long recognized right of citizens to be "free to travel throughout the length and breadth of our land uninhibited by statutes, rules, or regulations which unreasonably burden or restrain this movement." The right of interstate travel was held to be a fundamental right, and a classification that would "chill" the assertion of such a right is "patently unconstitutional." Classifications such as this that touch on the fundamental right of interstate movement must be assessed by the stricter standard of whether they promote a compelling state interest. In the Court's view, the arguments submitted by the state in this case were not compelling.

Shapiro led to the elimination of many residency requirements where provisions of public services are involved, and it reduced voting registration requirements to a short duration. Some residency requirements have survived, however, as in the cases of state university tuition and establishing jurisdiction to obtain a divorce. *Shapiro* was the first of a series of cases involving access to public assistance as a matter of right, although the case did not directly address the question of whether welfare was to be protected as a fundamental right. Soon after *Shapiro,* the Court again refused to address that problem in *Dandridge v. Williams* (397 U.S. 471: 1970). In this case, the justices upheld a ceiling on monthly aid to be received by any one family. The ceiling policy was challenged as overbroad, but the Court said the concept of overreaching "has no place in cases which establish social and economic regulations." Though some aid payment disparities may be produced, the imperfection of classifications does not necessarily produce equal protection violations as long as there is a reasonable basis for the regulation. In *Hicklin v. Orbeck* (437 U.S. 518: 1978), the Court struck down an Alaska law reserving jobs in the oil and gas development industry for qualified state residents. Similarly, the Court said a municipal ordinance requiring hiring preference for city residents on all city construction projects was subject to privileges and immunities limitations. This was true even though a state did not discriminate against citizens of another state because a political subdivision of a state cannot discriminate against state residents not living within that political subdivision—in this case, a city.

VOTING RIGHTS

The Fifteenth Amendment was added to the Constitution in 1870. It provides that the "right of the citizens of the United States to vote shall not be denied or abridged by the United States or by any State on account of race, color, or previous condition of servitude." A second section of the amendment empowers Congress to pass appropriate enforcement legislation. The Fifteenth Amendment did not extend the right to vote per se but did prohibit racial discrimination in voting. The amendment essentially left control over voting to the states, which placed qualifications for voting within the purview of state legislation. Early Supreme Court decisions recognized that federal power could be exercised if citizens were denied the opportunity to vote in state elections on racial grounds. It was not until World War II, however, that the Supreme Court used the Fifteenth Amendment to reach the more sophisticated discriminatory techniques used in several states, such as the white primary and qualifying tests.

Broad congressional initiatives based on the Fifteenth Amendment did not appear until the Voting Rights Act of 1965. That act abolished devices such as the literacy test and accumulated poll taxes by which citizens had been disqualified from voting. The act also provided for extensive federal supervision of elections and required that any new conditions of voter eligibility be reviewed by the attorney general before implementation. Provisions of the act were triggered if less than 50 percent of citizens of voting age were registered to vote or where fewer than 50 percent of the voting population had participated in the 1964 presidential election. The Supreme Court unanimously upheld the act in *South Carolina v. Katzenbach* (383 U.S. 301: 1966).

Chief Justice Warren, writing for the Court, pointed out that the purpose of the act was to "banish the blight of racial discrimination in voting, which has infected the electoral process in parts of our country for nearly a century." The Court accorded great deference to an act dedicated to such a purpose even if the Congress had exercised power in an inventive manner. Referring to the stringent remedies and their implementation without prior adjudication, the Court said litigation was inadequate when discrimination was widespread and persistent. Following nearly 100 years of systematic resistance to the Fifteenth Amendment, Congress might well decide to shift the advantage of time and inertia from the perpetrators of the evil to its victims. The targeted nature of the act's coverage was a reasonable legislation option in the Court's view. Congress determined that voting discrimination "presently occurs in certain sections of the country," and in acceptable legislative fashion, Congress chose to limit its attention to the geographic areas where immediate action seemed necessary. In sum, the Court viewed the act as an array of potent weapons marshalled to combat the evil of voting discrimination and felt that these weapons constituted a "valid means for carrying out the commands of the Fifteenth Amendment." The Voting Rights Act also targeted, for the first time, voting practices involving non-English-speaking voters. The act had provisions intended for the large Spanish-speaking population in New York City, and these provisions were upheld in *Katzenbach v. Morgan* (384 U.S. 641: 1966).

The act was initially adopted to run for five years, but it was extended in 1970, 1975, and 1982. The 1970 extension banned use of literacy tests and set the minimum voting age at 18 throughout the country. The Court held in *Oregon v. Mitchell* (400 U.S. 112: 1970), however, that Congress could establish age qualifications only for federal elections and that states retained control over state and local elections. Ratification of the Twenty-sixth Amendment in 1971 superseded the Court's decision in *Oregon v. Mitchell*. Primary elections also have attained constitutional status. After several decisions to the contrary, the Court held in *United States v. Classic* (313 U.S. 299: 1941) that the federal government could regulate primaries because of their integral role in the overall election process. In *Smith v. Allwright* (321 U.S. 649: 1944), the Court found that political parties conducting racially exclusive primaries were acting as agents of the states and thus were in violation of the Fifteenth Amendment. The Court also outlawed the poll tax for state elections in *Harper v. Virginia State Board of Elections* (383 U.S. 663: 1966), holding that such a tax discriminated in an invidious fashion.

APPORTIONMENT

Beyond the question of discriminatory voting practices, the equal protection clause has been used in situations involving legislative apportionment. Apportionment is the process by which representation for a legislative body is allocated. Apportionment is based on population, and it is now a requirement of equal protection that legislatures have districts of substantially equal populations. Prior to 1962 the Supreme Court considered legislative apportionment to be a matter inappropriate for judicial intervention. Apportionment was one of those issues that posed a "political question," a question more appropriately resolved by one or both of the elective branches of government. In *Baker v. Carr* (369 U.S. 186: 1962), however, the Warren Court held apportionment to be a justiciable issue. Although *Baker* did not itself establish a standard for apportionment, it created the expectation of population equivalence for single-member legislative districts. The "one person, one vote" standard now applies to all levels of government, including local units. We begin our examination of apportionment with *Baker*.

By the middle of the twentieth century, gross malapportionment existed for most state legislatures as well as for Congress. Years of inattention to shifting populations had produced highly inequitable representation. Some legislative districts were several times larger than others. Charles Baker and others brought suit in federal court in Tennessee claiming that despite significant growth and shifts in the population of Tennessee, legislative districts were still apportioned on the basis of a 1901 statute. Prior decisions directed that the Court should not intervene. *Colegrove v. Green* (328 U.S. 549: 1946), for example, held that the enjoining of an election because of malapportionment was beyond the competence of the judiciary.

Baker allowed the matter of reapportionment to be brought to federal courts, but it did not set forth particular standards for reapportionment. Rather, the case generated a great deal of follow-up reapportionment litigation. It had merely opened the door to judicial intervention by finding reapportionment to be a justiciable issue. The Court's first indication of a standard that could guide redistricting came in *Gray v. Sanders* (372 U.S. 368: 1963). The voting practice at issue was the unit system, a technique by which statewide officials were nominated in Georgia. Although the Court distinguished this process from legislative districting, it held that the equal protection clause required people to have an equal vote. Specific reference to "one man, one vote" was made in *Gray,* and the following year the Court applied the "one man, one vote" standard to apportionment of congressional districts, in *Wesberry v. Sanders* (376 U.S. 1: 1964).

Reynolds v. Sims (377 U.S. 533: 1964) established the requirement for the apportionment of bicameral state legislatures. *Reynolds,* accompanied by several companion cases from other states, held that the one person, one vote principle applied to both houses of state legislatures. *Reynolds* challenged the apportionment of Alabama House and Senate districts, a districting system allegedly based on the 1900 census. A six-justice majority struck down both the existing districts and a proposal based on the federal concept, a plan that apportioned only one house on the basis of population. The Court's opinion was written by Chief Justice Warren, who saw the central question as being whether any constitutionally cognizable principles would justify departures from the basic standard of equality among voters in the apportionment of legislative seats. The gravity of the issue was reflected in the observation that the "right of suffrage can be denied by a debasement or dilution of the weight of a citizen's vote just as effectively as by wholly prohibiting the free exercise of the franchise." Warren declared that legislators represent people, not trees or acres, and that legislators are elected by voters, not by farms or cities or economic interests. People must have an unimpaired capacity to elect representatives, and the weight of a citizen's vote cannot be made to depend on where he or she lives. Population is of necessity the starting point for consideration of, as well as being the controlling criterion for judgment in, legislative apportionment controversies. The constitutional demands of equal protection require that a legislative vote is not diluted when compared with the vote of other citizens living in a less populated district, where a citizen's vote carries more weight. Equal protection also demands that both chambers of state legislatures be apportioned on the basis of population.

Reynolds established stringent population guidelines for the apportionment of legislative districts. The extent to which the Warren Court would tolerate deviation from the one person, one vote standard became quite evident in *Lucas v. Forty-Fourth General Assembly* (377 U.S. 713: 1964), one of the companion cases to *Reynolds.* In *Lucas,* the Court rejected a plan with a 3.6 to 1 largest-to-smallest variance in the House and a 1.7 to 1 variance in the Senate. The ruling was made despite approval of the plan in a statewide referendum. Subsequently, the Burger Court permitted deviations of slightly more than 16 percent in *Mahan v. Howell* (410 U.S. 315: 1973). This variance was permitted because it was done to "advance the rational state policy of respecting the boundaries of political subdivisions" and did not otherwise exceed constitutional limitations.

Following *Reynolds,* the Court was asked to consider whether the one person, one vote principle applied to local units of government. In *Avery v. Midland County* (390 U.S. 474: 1968), the justices held that when local government elects representatives from single-member districts, good faith attempts must be undertaken to make those districts equal in population. The considerations given to equal protection in apportioning legislative districts also carried over to other electoral situations. In *Kramer v. Union Free School District* (395 U.S. 621: 1969), the Court held that a state could not restrict participation in school district elections to district property owners and parents of children in the school system. Despite the original controversy and the contention that representation might effectively be calculated on a basis other than population, the democratic premise underpinning *Reynolds* has been generally accepted.

The apportionment question becomes even more complex when the dimension of racial discrimination is also involved. The case of *Mobile v. Bolden* (446 U.S. 55: 1980) upheld a municipal at-large election process against claims that such a system diluted minority group voting influence. *Bolden* considered whether malapportionment of legislative districts violated the Constitution because it debased the value of an individual's vote. A federal district court found a constitutional violation in the election process in Mobile, Alabama, and ordered that a single-member district structure replace the at-large system. The Supreme Court found the at-large plan to be constitutionally adequate, however, and reversed the lower court decision. Critics of the at-large or multimember district approach argued that some elements of the electorate were unrepresented. The Court noted that criticism of the at-large election is rooted in its winner-take-all aspect and its tendency to submerge minorities.

The specific question posed in *Bolden* was whether the at-large scheme had been established for the express purpose of reducing the impact of black voters. Constitutional violations occur in apportionment systems only "if their purpose were invidiously to minimize or cancel out the voting potential of racial or ethnic minorities." To demonstrate such a violation, a plaintiff must prove that the disputed plan was conceived or operated as a purposeful device to further racial discrimination. A showing that a particular group has not elected representatives in proportion to its members is not sufficient. The Court said that although black candidates in Mobile have been defeated, that fact alone does not indicate a constitutional deprivation. The Court also rejected the relevance of discrimination by the city in the context of municipal employment and the dispensing of public services. Evidence of possible discrimination by city officials in other contexts is "tenuous and circumstantial evidence of the constitutional invalidity of the electoral system under which they attained their offices." The Burger Court concluded that past cases show "the Court has sternly set its face against the claim, however phrased, that the Constitution somehow guarantees proportional representation."

The Voting Rights Act of 1965 also requires that any changes in voting procedures or conditions that impact voting practices are subject to pre-clearance by the attorney general of the United States. The full impact of this requirement was seen in *City of Pleasant Grove v. United States* (479 U.S. 462: 1987). Pleasant Grove, a nearly all-white city in Alabama, was denied clearance to annex a then uninhabited area on the ground that it had refused to annex adjacent black neighborhoods despite petitions by the neighborhood residents. The Supreme Court said an annexation is subject to pre-clearance under the law. Even the annexation of vacant land on which residential development is anticipated must be pre-cleared. Allowing the pre-clearance requirement to be circumvented when annexing vacant land intended for white development was seen as inconsistent with congressional intent to reach the subtle as well as the obvious official actions that have the effect of denying voter groups based on race. Further, pre-clearance depends on a showing that both discriminatory purpose and effect are absent. The burden of proving absence of discriminatory intent and effect, said Justice White, rests with the governmental unit seeking pre-clearance. Pleasant Grove argued that there were no black voters in the city at the time the annexation decision was made, so the proposals did not deny or reduce existing black voter representation. The Court rejected this contention, saying it was based on an incorrect assumption that relevant provisions of the act can relate only to present circumstances and that the act's provisions look not only at present effects, but at future effects as well.

Finally, the Court ruled in *Davis v. Bandemer* (478 U.S. 109: 1986) that claims of political gerrymandering are justiciable. *Bandemer* focused on a challenge to Indiana's reapportionment plan devised after the 1980 census. The plan called for a mixture of single-member and multimember districts to elect the state House of Representatives. Democrats challenged the plan, alleging it was intentionally disadvantageous and thus violated their right to equal protection. Results from the 1982 election did show a dilution of the Democratic vote. Democratic House candidates received 51.9 percent of the vote cast statewide but won only 43 of the 100 seats in the House. A federal district court invalidated the plan and enjoined the state from holding further elections using it. The Supreme Court reversed the lower court in a seven to two decision, but it ruled six to three that gerrymandering claims are justiciable even if the plan under challenge meets the one person, one vote standard.

Justice White said the case presented none of the identifying characteristics of a nonjusticiable political question. Neither did it present issues in which there were no judicially discernible and manageable standards by which to decide the case. The suit claimed that "each political group in the state should have the same chance to elect representatives of its choice as any other political group." Even though the one person, one vote standard does not apply, the issue is one of representation, and "we decline to hold that such claims are never justiciable." Justice White said that an equal protection violation requires a threshold showing of discriminatory vote dilution. The mere fact that an apportionment plan makes it more difficult for a particular group in a particular district to elect the representatives of its choice does not render that scheme constitutionally infirm. Unconstitutional vote dilution, either on an individual district or statewide level, requires demonstration beyond a mere lack of proportional representation. Unconstitutional discrimination occurs "only when the electoral system is arranged in a manner that will consistently degrade a voter's or a group of voters' influence on the political process as a whole." The principal question in reviewing gerrymandering allegations is whether a particular group has been "unconstitutionally denied its chance to effectively influence the political process." A finding of unconstitutionality must be supported by evidence of either "continued frustration of the will of a majority of the voters" or a showing of "effective denial [of] a fair chance to influence the political process." Relying on a single election to prove unconstitutional discrimination was viewed as unsatisfactory.

The Right of Privacy

The right of privacy is a protection drawn from several constitutional provisions that places certain aspects of life beyond the reach of government.

The right of privacy was first acknowledged by the Supreme Court in *Griswold v. Connecticut* (381 U.S. 479: 1965). The view that the Constitution afforded such protection had existed for some time, however. As early as 1928, in the wiretapping case of *Olmstead v. United States* (277 U.S. 438), Justice Louis Brandeis offered a classic dissent, stating that the Fourth and Fifth Amendments conferred the "right to be let alone." Justice Brandeis regarded this as the "most comprehensive of rights and the right most valued by civilized men." Although Brandeis found the Fourth and Fifth Amendments to be a sufficient source for the right of privacy, the rest of the Court had more difficulty finding a constitutional mandate for the protection of privacy.

Several additional possibilities have been suggested by individual justices in subsequent cases. The First Amendment has been cited, for example, as providing some insulation for privacy interests. In *Stanley v. Georgia* (394 U.S. 557: 1969), a case involving privately possessed obscene materials, Justice Thurgood Marshall said regulation of obscenity cannot "reach into the privacy of one's own home." He added that "if the First Amendment means anything, it means that a state has no business telling a man, sitting alone in his own house, what books he may read or what films he may watch." In another obscenity case, *Paris Adult Theatre I v. Staton* (413 U.S. 49: 1973), Justice Brennan also looked to the First Amendment as a protection for "sexually oriented materials" for consenting adults. The First Amendment has also been used to protect the anonymity of a voluntary association. In *NAACP v. Alabama* (357 U.S. 449: 1957), Justice John Marshall Harlan cited the "vital relationship between freedom to associate and privacy in one's associations."

Justice Harlan argued in *Griswold* that the due process clause of the Fourteenth Amendment also offered protection against invasions of privacy. In his view, the Connecticut prohibition on the distribution of contraceptives violated basic values "implicit in the concept of ordered liberty" and thus contravened the protection of the clause. Justice Harlan said that although other constitutional provisions also might be relevant in this instance, the due process clause was sufficient in itself. It stands "on its own bottom" when a right as fundamental as privacy is concerned. The due process clause must not, in Justice Harlan's opinion, be limited to merely procedural safeguards. Rather, the clause is a "rational continuum which includes a freedom from all substantial arbitrary impositions and purposeless restraints." *Roe v. Wade* (410 U.S. 113: 1973), the landmark abortion decision, also grounded its privacy holding on due process considerations.

Justice Brennan has also argued that privacy is secured by the equal protection clause in certain situations. *Eisenstadt v. Baird* (405 U.S. 438:

1972) involved a state prohibition on the sale of contraceptives to unmarried persons. The Court struck down the statute. *Griswold* had already established that such regulation could not be applied to married persons because the right of privacy inhered in the marital relationship. *Eisenstadt* was based on the view that married couples were "two individuals with a separate intellectual and emotional make-up." Given that, if the right of privacy "means anything," it must mean that the "individual, married or single, is to be free from unwarranted governmental intrusion into matters so fundamentally affecting a person as the decision whether to bear or beget a child."

Finally, the Ninth Amendment has been mentioned as supporting a constitutional right to privacy. This amendment states that the "enumeration in the Constitution of certain rights shall not be construed to deny or disparage others retained by the people." In his concurring opinion in *Griswold,* Justice Arthur Goldberg argued for the recognition of privacy as a constitutionally protected right by saying that the Ninth Amendment "lends strong support" to the proposition that the liberty protected by the Fifth and Fourteenth Amendments is "not restricted to rights specifically mentioned in the first eight amendments." The Court's approach in the pivotal *Griswold* decision indirectly drew from most of those arguments for privacy.

The Court was presented with the occasion to consider the privacy issue in *Griswold,* in which it reviewed a Connecticut statute that made it a crime to use birth control devices or provide counsel on their use. Estelle Griswold was arrested and convicted for violation of the statute. The Supreme Court voided the statute in a seven to two decision, although members of the majority differed in their views about the constitutional source of the privacy protection. The opinion of the Court was offered by Justice Douglas, who disclaimed that the Court should act as a "super-legislature" making determinations about the "wisdom, need, and propriety of laws that touch economic problems, business affairs, or social conditions." At the same time, however, the justices held that the Connecticut statute "operates directly on an intimate relation of husband and wife and their physician's role in one aspect of the relation." The Court could intervene because "various guarantees create zones of privacy."

These zones are formed by emanations from "penumbras" of specific Bill of Rights guarantees. Douglas developed the freedom of association as an example. In several cases, such as *NAACP v. Alabama,* the Court protected the privacy of association as a right peripheral to the First Amendment. The protection of association came from a First Amendment penumbra under which privacy is protected from governmental intrusion. The emanations that cast the penumbras draw from Bill of Rights guarantees and give them life and substance. The several guarantees involved here include the First

Amendment, the privacy of the home that comes from the Third and Fourth Amendments, the self-incrimination provision of the Fifth Amendment, and the Ninth Amendment. Justices Harlan and White used the due process clause of the Fourteenth Amendment to find that the "enactment violates basic values implicit in the concept of ordered liberty." *Griswold* defined privacy as a constitutionally protected right. The key question remaining after *Griswold* was the scope of the protection and where the boundaries and criteria for application of the right were located. The Court first enlarged upon the privacy protection defined in *Griswold,* particularly as it affected procreation in *Eisenstadt,* as it struck down a Massachusetts statute that limited distribution of contraceptives to married persons. *Eisenstadt* became the cornerstone of the highly controversial abortion decision of *Roe v. Wade* (410 U.S. 113: 1973).

The *Roe* decision said state laws that make abortion a crime impermissibly encroach upon a person's right of privacy, and it was by far the most controversial outgrowth of the privacy protection doctrine. *Roe* involved a Texas statute that made it a crime to perform an abortion except to preserve the mother's life. The statute was typical of many nineteenth-century criminal abortion laws. In a seven to two decision, the Court struck down the prohibition. Justice Blackmun's opinion began with a historical survey of laws proscribing abortion followed by a three-part rationale for the prohibition. The objectives of such statutes were to discourage illicit sexual conduct, protect pregnant women from the hazardous abortion procedure, and protect prenatal life. Only the final justification, protection of prenatal life, offered any possibility of being a sufficiently compelling interest for the state. The Court, however, saw that interest as very limited because the language and meaning of the Fourteenth Amendment apply "only postnatally." The term *person* as used in the amendment "does not include the unborn." Furthermore, the privacy protection is broad enough to encompass a woman's decision whether or not to terminate her pregnancy. It might appear, therefore, that the woman's choice was to be absolutely insulated from regulation. That is not quite so, for there comes a time in every pregnancy when the state's interests "become sufficiently compelling to sustain regulation of the factors that govern the abortion decision." Justice Blackmun established a timetable for these interests based upon the three trimesters of a pregnancy. During the first trimester, a state has no interest whatsoever. Throughout the second trimester, the state can regulate the conditions under which abortions occur, but the pregnant woman, in consultation with her physician, is still free to determine, without regulation by the state, whether or not to terminate the pregnancy. The state's interest in protecting potential life begins with the final trimester, when the fetus becomes viable or has the capability of meaningful life outside the mother's womb. This approach allowed Justice Blackmun to suggest that the Court need not resolve the difficult question of when life begins. When doctors, philosophers, and theologians "are unable to arrive at any consensus, the judiciary is not in a position to speculate as to the answer."

The cases that followed *Roe v. Wade* examined particular restrictions imposed on the exercise of the right to abortion. Illustrative is *Thornburgh v. American College of Obstetricians and Gynecologists* (476 U.S. 747: 1986), a case that essentially reaffirmed *Roe*. The authors of the statute under review in *Thornburgh* did not dispute the fact that the law was designed to discourage elective abortions. Suit was brought by an organization of obstetricians and gynecologists as well as various individuals who alleged the statute was incompatible with *Roe*. The challenged provisions fell into three main categories. The first required that all women give informed consent before an abortion. This required that a woman be told of the comparative risks of abortion and full-term pregnancy, the medical assistance benefits available for full-term pregnancies, the legal recourse for obtaining support from the father, and the possible detrimental physical and psychological effects of having an abortion. The woman was also to be told of the characteristics of the fetus in two-week gestational increments. The second category of regulations involved reporting. All physicians were required to report a variety of information about the woman, the abortion, and the nonviability of the fetus. Though these reports were not to be deemed public records, they were accessible for public inspection and copying. Third, the law required all physicians performing abortions after a point when the fetus could be viable to exercise the degree of care required to preserve the fetus. The attendance of a second physician was mandated in all instances in which viability was possible.

The Supreme Court found the law unconstitutional. Justice Blackmun again spoke for the majority and began by reaffirming the basic positions taken in *Roe v. Wade*. Despite the numerous attempts to restrict the exercise of a woman's right of choice, Blackmun said the constitutional principles that provided the basis for *Roe* "still provide the compelling reason for recognizing the constitutional dimensions of a woman's right to decide whether to end her pregnancy." The states are simply not free, under the guise of protecting either maternal health or potential life, to intimidate women into continuing pregnancies. Close analysis of the statute's provisions shows that they wholly subordinate constitutional privacy interests and concerns with maternal health in an effort to deter a woman from making a decision that, with her physician, is hers to make. Blackmun characterized the informational requirements as "poorly disguised elements of discouragement for the abortion decision." He called the provision requiring dissemination of specific printed material an "outright attempt to wedge" the state's anti-abortion message into the privacy of the patient-physician dialogue. The reporting requirements were found impermissible because they "raise the specter of public exposure." The decision to terminate a pregnancy is an intensely private one that must be protected in a way that assures anonymity. A woman and her physician will be more reluctant to choose an abortion if the possibility exists that her decision and her identity will become public. The second-physician attendance requirement where possible fetus viability exists was struck down because it addressed no medical emergency but simply chilled the performance of late abortions. Blackmun concluded by saying that the Constitution recognizes that a certain private sphere of individual liberty will be kept largely beyond the reach of government. Few decisions are more "personal and intimate, more properly private, and more basic to human dignity and autonomy" than the abortion decision.

The statute reviewed in *Thornburgh* closely resembled the law struck down in *Akron v. Akron Center for Reproductive Health, Inc.* (462 U.S. 416: 1983). In *Akron*, however, the margin against state regulation of abortion was six to three, with Chief Justice Burger voting with the majority. Between *Akron* and *Thornburgh,* the Reagan administration strongly urged the overruling of *Roe v. Wade.* Although reversal did not happen in *Thornburgh,* the margin became extremely thin. Most enactments imposing restrictions on abortions have been invalidated. In *Planned Parenthood of Central Missouri v. Danforth* (428 U.S. 52: 1976), the Court rejected spousal consent, or parental consent in the case of an unmarried minor, for all abortions. It said the state cannot delegate a veto power that the state itself is absolutely and totally prohibited from exercising. The Court reiterated its position on consent requirements in *Bellotti v. Baird* (443 U.S. 622: 1979) by rejecting a parental consent requirement because it provided no process by which the minor's own capacity to make the decision could be examined. Regulations in two companion cases to *Akron* were upheld, however. In *Planned Parenthood Association v. Ashcroft* (462 U.S. 476: 1983), statutory provisions involving parental consent, mandatory pathological examination of all aborted tissue, and attendance of a second physician for abortions after 12 weeks were upheld. The Missouri parental consent provision was approved because, unlike that in *Akron,* it contained a process by which a minor could be determined mature enough to make the decision, thus bypassing parental or judicial consent. In *Simopoulos v. Virginia* (462 U.S. 506: 1983), a hospital requirement confining second-trimester abortions to hospitals or other licensed facilities was upheld because licensure was available for outpatient clinics. The Court also sustained legislation requiring notification of parents prior to a minor having an abortion. In *H. L. v. Matheson* (450 U.S. 398: 1981), the Court specified the difference between notification and consent, saying the latter was not required.

As support for *Roe v. Wade* has seemed to erode on the Court, cases reviewing state regulations of abortion have become more critical because each is seen as a possible vehicle for the reversal of *Roe*. The most important of these cases is *Webster v. Reproductive Health Services* (106 L. Ed. 2d 410: 1989). The Court's decision in *Webster* substantially modified *Roe* but did not explicitly overrule it. The origin of the case was a Missouri statute enacted in 1986. Several components of the statute were challenged in federal court by a number of doctors and nurses and two nonprofit medical corporations, one of which was Reproductive Health Services (RHS). The challenged provisions included (1) a preamble that states that life begins at conception and that the "unborn" have life interests requiring protection; (2) a requirement that before an abortion can be performed on any woman whom a physician has "reason to believe" is 20 or more weeks pregnant, the physician must determine whether the fetus is "viable" by performing specified medical examinations and tests; (3) an informed consent section that required provision of information on abortion alternatives; and (4) prohibitions on use of public funds, public facilities, or public employees in "performing or assisting" an abortion. This restriction included public employees counseling pregnant women to have abortions for reasons other than medical necessity.

A U.S. district court upheld only the viability testing, but in doing so eliminated many of the viability tests specified in the law. Missouri, through its attorney general, William Webster, challenged each element of the district court decision except for the portion that struck down the informed consent requirement. The Court of Appeals for the 8th Circuit affirmed the district court decision, relying on *Roe v. Wade*. In a fragmented five to four decision, the Supreme Court allowed the restrictions but did not explicitly reverse *Roe*. The opinion of the Court was delivered by Chief Justice Rehnquist. The Court did not rule on the preamble, which was seen as an "abstract proposition" rather than an operating regulation. Because the preamble did not restrict the activities of RHS in "some concrete way," the Court concluded that RHS had no standing to challenge the preamble language. This ruling was a rejection of the RHS argument that the preamble was an "operative part" of the statute intended to "guide the interpretation of other provisions of the Act." Rehnquist then turned to the ban on the use of public funds, facilities, and employees. The court of appeals had seen this regulation as possibly preventing a woman's doctor from performing an abortion if the doctor did not have privileges in another hospital. Increased costs and possible delay were also attributed to the regulation. The Supreme Court disagreed, using much of the same analysis as that found in Medicaid cases such as *Maher v. Roe* (432 U.S. 464: 1977) and *Harris v. McRae* (448 U.S. 297: 1980). As with those cases, the Court recognized the state's decision to "encourage childbirth over abortion" and asserted that this policy preference "places no governmental obstacle in the path of a woman who chooses to terminate her pregnancy." Missouri's refusal to allow public employees to perform abortions or to allow abortions to be performed in public facilities leaves a pregnant woman "with the same choices as if the State had chosen not to operate any public hospitals at all." As the Court had already ruled that state refusal to fund abortions (in *Maher* and *Harris*) does not violate *Roe v. Wade,* it "strains logic to reach a contrary result for the use of public facilities and employees."

Rehnquist then turned to the most critical aspect of the decision, the viability testing requirements. Rehnquist said the statute required physicians to perform "only those tests that are useful to making subsidiary findings as to viability." Key, however, was the presumption of viability at 20 weeks, which must be directly rebutted by viability test results before an abortion can be performed. The *Roe v. Wade* decision is based on a concept of trimesters. Under *Roe,* the interests of the fetus are not recognized until the final trimester, which occurs about 24 weeks into the pregnancy. Specification in the Missouri law of methods for determining viability "does superimpose state regulation on the medical determination of viability," and this section was struck down by the court of appeals on this basis. The Supreme Court was less convinced that the law was flawed, however. Rather, Rehnquist said the problem was the "rigid trimester analysis of the course of a pregnancy enunciated in *Roe.*" The "rigid *Roe* framework is hardly consistent with the notion of a Constitution cast in general terms." The Court simply should not function as the "country's ex officio medical board with powers to approve or disapprove medical and operative practices and standards." Thus, the "web of legal rules" developed through application of *Roe* could be loosened. More important, the Court did not see "why the State's interest in protecting potential human life should come into existence only at the point of viability" or why there should be a "rigid line allowing state regulation after viability but prohibiting it before viability." The Court acknowledged that the tests "increase the expense of abortion and regulate the discretion of the physician in determining viability of the fetus." Nonetheless, the Court was "satisfied" that the requirement "permissibly furthers the State's interest in protecting potential human life" and therefore is constitutional. Justice O'Connor agreed that the viability testing requirement was constitutional, but came to that conclusion because she did not see the requirement as incompatible with

Roe v. Wade. Justice Scalia was also among the majority but said in his concurring opinion that *Roe* had been effectively overruled. Indeed, he was critical of Rehnquist for not acknowledging that result. By hanging on to *Roe,* Scalia said, the Court "needlessly" prolonged its "self-awarded sovereignty over a field where it has little proper business," as responses to most of the critical questions are "political and not juridical."

Webster signaled state legislatures that the Court would be receptive to additional restrictions on abortion. Two additional abortion decisions followed shortly thereafter. *Hodgson v. Minnesota* (111 L. Ed. 2d 344: 1990) and *Ohio v. Akron Center for Reproductive Services* (111 L. Ed. 2d 405: 1990) examined parental notification statutes in Minnesota and Ohio. The Minnesota statute had two key parts. First, the state required notification of both biological parents when a minor daughter sought an abortion. In a five to four decision, the Court struck down this requirement. The statute contained contingency language that if a court enjoined enforcement of the notification requirement, the statute would be amended automatically to provide a judicial bypass as an alternative to parental notification. This alternative allowed a minor to petition a court for permission to obtain an abortion without notifying her parents. The Court upheld this alternative, again by a five to four vote. Justice O'Connor provided the decisive vote in both instances. She joined Justices Marshall, Brennan, Blackmun, and Stevens in striking down the statute without judicial bypass, and she was joined by Chief Justice Rehnquist and Justices Kennedy, White, and Scalia in upholding the alternative. The Ohio statute required notification of only one parent. It also contained judicial bypass language, but the Court upheld the one-parent notice requirement on its own by a six to three vote, with Justice Stevens joining the five justices who had upheld the Minnesota alternative. The defect with the Minnesota statute absent the judicial bypass arose from the fact that only about half of Minnesota's minors resided with both biological parents. Justice Stevens spoke of the "particularly harmful effects" of the two-parent notification requirement on "both the minor and custodial parent when parents were divorced or separated." In addition, the Court concluded that the requirement "does not reasonably further any legitimate state interest." The principal justification for notification is that it "supports the authority of a parent who is presumed to act in the minor's best interest and thereby assures that the minor's decision to terminate her pregnancy is knowing, intelligent, and deliberate." To the extent "such an interest is legitimate," it could be "fully served" by the notification of one parent who can then seek counsel from the other parent or anyone else.

The state has no legitimate interest in questioning the one parent's judgment on whether to seek wider counsel. The Court concluded that the two-parent requirement actually "disserves" any state interest in protecting a minor in "dysfunctional families" and that two-parent notice in such situations is "positively harmful to the minor and her family." As in cases involving judicial hearings as an alternative to securing parental consent for an abortion, the Court found the bypass alternative constitutionally sufficient for notification as well. The judicial bypass feature allows a minor to demonstrate she is fully capable of making the abortion decision. The Court decided the Ohio case without actually ruling on whether the judicial bypass provision is necessary in the one-parent notice situation. Rather, it upheld the one-parent notification requirement as a "rational way" for a state to assist a pregnant minor who is considering abortion. "It would deny all dignity to the family," said Justice Kennedy, "to say that the State cannot take this reasonable step . . . to ensure that, in most cases, a young woman will receive guidance and understanding from a parent." In the Court's view, Ohio's requirement did not impose an "undue, or otherwise unconstitutional, burden on a minor seeking an abortion."

Finally, there is the question of whether public funds are to be used to cover costs of elective abortions. The definitive case is *Harris v. McRae* (448 U.S. 297: 1980). More precisely, this case examined the constitutionality of congressional restrictions on Medicaid reimbursements for abortion costs. The restrictions, known as the Hyde amendment, limited federal funds for abortions to those cases in which the mother's life was jeopardized by full-term pregnancy or for rape or incest victims, provided "such rape or incest has been reported promptly to a law enforcement agency or public health service." The Supreme Court upheld the Hyde amendment against equal protection and due process challenges in a five to four decision. The Court concluded that the right to have an abortion as established in *Roe v. Wade* carried with it no entitlement to federal funding to cover an abortion's costs. The funding limitation imposed no restriction on access to abortions, and though indigence may make it more difficult, perhaps impossible, for some women actually to have abortions, the enactment did not create or affect the indigent.

The Hyde amendment merely reflected a value choice favoring childbirth over abortion and placed no governmental obstacle in the path of a woman who chooses to terminate her pregnancy. By means of unequal subsidization of abortion and other medical services it encourages the alternative of childbirth. The Hyde amendment leaves an indigent woman with at least the same range of choices in deciding whether to obtain a medically necessary abortion as she could have if Congress had chosen to subsidize no health care costs at all. The freedom to be protected from governmental interference in such personal decisions as abortion does not also confer an entitlement to such funds as may be necessary to realize all the advantages of that freedom. Finally, the majority concluded that the Hyde amendment was rationally related to a legitimate governmental objective. The incentives that make childbirth a more attractive alternative bear a direct relationship to the legitimate congressional interest in protecting potential life. That abortion was singled out for more extensive restriction than other medical services was viewed as rational in that abortion is inherently different from other medical procedures. No other procedure involves the purposeful termination of potential life.

THE RIGHT TO TERMINATE MEDICAL TREATMENT

No other issue has dominated the right of privacy debate in the way that abortion has. The issue of the right to die and the related matter of refusal of medical treatment have recently been before the Court, however, and may approach the abortion question in importance. We consider the highly visible case of Nancy Cruzan. In *Cruzan v. Director, Missouri Department of Health* (111 L. Ed. 2d 224: 1990), the Court ruled that a person has a right to discontinue life-sustaining medical treatment. At the same time, the Court ruled five to four that a state can require maintenance of such treatment in the absence of "clear and convincing" evidence that the person being sustained would want the treatment stopped. Nancy Cruzan was injured in an automobile accident in 1983. Since that time, she has remained in a "persistent vegetative" state. She is administered food and water through a tube in her stomach. Cruzan's parents, acting as legal guardians, requested that the life-sustaining feedings be stopped. The hospital refused to stop the feedings, and the Cruzans initiated legal action. A state trial court found that a person had a right to refuse procedures that were "death prolonging," but Nancy, of course, was incapable of stopping the feedings herself. The issue then became whether statements uttered by Nancy prior to the accident constituted sufficient evidence of her desire to discontinue medical treatment under the post-accident circumstances.

The trial court concluded that all medical treatment should be terminated. The Missouri Supreme Court reversed, however, and ruled that Missouri's "living will" statute favored "preservation of life" in the absence of "clear and convincing" evidence for withdrawal of treatment. The "clear and convincing" standard is the highest standard of evidence used in a civil proceeding. The Missouri Supreme Court decided that Cruzan's pre-accident statements were "unreliable" for determining her intent. The issue before the U.S. Supreme Court was whether the federal Constitution precludes a state "from choosing the rule of decision which it did." The Court rested its decision on Fourteenth Amendment due process grounds rather than on the right of privacy. It was the Court's view that a "competent person has a constitutionally protected liberty interest in refusing unwanted medical treatment." That, however, said Chief Justice Rehnquist, "does not end our inquiry." Whether constitutional rights have been violated requires that liberty interests be weighed against the "relevant state interests." The problem in this case was that Nancy Cruzan was herself incompetent to "make an informed and voluntary choice." Rather, the right "must be exercised for her . . . by some sort of surrogate." Missouri recognizes actions by surrogates, but also has "established a procedural safeguard to assure that the actions of the surrogate conform as best it may to the wishes expressed by the patient while competent."

A five-justice majority held that Missouri's requirement of proof by clear and convincing evidence in such cases was not forbidden by the Constitution. This procedural requirement was established in furtherance of the state's interest in the "protection and preservation of human life, and there can be no gainsaying this interest." Furthermore, the state has an even "more particular interest" in situations like Cruzan's. The choice between "life and death is a deeply personal decision of obvious and overwhelming finality." Accordingly, Missouri may "legitimately seek to safeguard the personal element of this choice through the imposition of heightened evidentiary requirements." Rehnquist concluded by focusing on the issue of surrogate decision making, and in doing so characterized the Cruzans as "loving and caring parents." Were the Constitution to require states to "repose a right of 'substituted judgment' with anyone, the Cruzans would surely qualify." But, he said, the Court does not think the Fourteenth Amendment "requires the state to repose the judgment on these matters with anyone but the patient herself." Family members may possess a "strong feeling—a feeling not at all ignoble or unworthy, but not entirely disinterested, either—that they do not wish to witness the continuation of the life of a loved one which they regard as hopeless, meaningless, and even degrading." But there is no automatic assurance that the view of the close family members will "necessarily be the same as the patient's would have been had she been confronted with the prospect of her situation while competent." That being the case, the Court concluded that Missouri could reasonably defer to the patient's own wishes rather than those of close family members by imposing a clear and convincing standard of evidence.

OTHER MATTERS OF FAMILY

Several other privacy issues also have come before the Court since 1970. It is necessary to briefly represent them to complete the discussion of the right of privacy. The most important of these have involved the definition of family. In *Moore v. East Cleveland* (431 U.S. 494: 1977), the Court ruled that a municipality did not have authority to restrict occupancy of a private home to persons defined as a family. *Moore* involved a zoning ordinance that limited occupancy of a dwelling unit to members of a "single family." Most successful applications of the invasion of privacy approach have been situations in which matters of family were involved in some way. In the East Cleveland ordinance, "family" was defined very narrowly to include essentially parents and children. Inez Moore lived in her home with her son and two grandsons. She was found in violation of the ordinance because the grandsons were cousins rather than brothers. Although the Court could not agree on common language, a five-justice majority found the ordinance unconstitutional.

The opinion of the Court was written by Justice Powell, who characterized the ordinance as "slicing deeply into the family itself." He said such an enactment compels the Court to act aggressively. "When a city undertakes such an intrusive regulation of the family," the usual judicial deference to the legislature is "inappropriate." That posture was demanded because the Court had long recognized that freedom of personal choice in matters of marriage and family life is one of the liberties protected by the due process clause of the Fourteenth Amendment. Justice Powell acknowledged that the family is not beyond regulation, but governmental interest in doing so must be very carefully examined, as well as the means chosen to advance those interests. The interests asserted by East Cleveland were served only marginally by the ordinance. Justice Powell noted the risk involved when the "judicial branch gives enhanced protection to certain substantive liberties without the guidance of more specific provisions of the Bill of Rights." Although history counsels caution and restraint as a general rule, it does not counsel abandonment. Nor does it require what the city urged in this case: cutting off any protection of family rights at the first convenient boundary of the nuclear family.

Prior to *Moore*, the Court had upheld a zoning ordinance in *Belle Terre v. Boraas* (416 U.S. 1: 1974) that limited land use to single-family dwellings. The ordinance defined family more broadly than the ordinance in *Moore*, and the Court deferred to the permissible legislative objectives of regulating population density and preventing congestion and noise. In *Zablocki v. Redhail* (434 U.S. 374: 1978), the Court found that the right of privacy precluded interference with a person's desire to marry. A state law required any person under an order to pay child support to obtain authorization to marry. Permission was contingent on showing that support obligations were current and that the children involved "would not likely thereafter become public charges." Roger Redhail was denied a marriage license because he had failed to make support payments for a previously fathered child. The Court held the statute unconstitutional because it barred certain classes from ever marrying. They were "coerced into foregoing the right to marry."

The right of privacy is limited to traditional marital relationships as seen in *Doe v. Commonwealth's Attorney for Richmond* (425 U.S. 901: 1976). The Court summarily affirmed a three-judge district court dismissal of a privacy challenge to the use of a state sodomy statute against homosexuals. The lower court found that homosexuality was "obviously no portion of a marriage, house, or family life" and that a state may impose criminal sanctions on conduct "even when committed in the home, in the promotion of morality and decency." The refusal to extend the right of privacy to homosexual conduct was amplified in the highly controversial ruling of *Bowers v. Hardwick* (478 U.S. 186: 1986). In this case, the Court upheld a state law that criminalized consensual sodomy. The Court said that homosexuals had no right to engage in sodomy. In addition, the Court said that none of the previous right of privacy rulings involving family relationships, marriage, and procreation "bear any resemblance to the claimed constitutional right of homosexuals to engage in acts of sodomy that is asserted in this case." The Court also categorically rejected the contention that the previous right of privacy cases insulated private sexual conduct between consenting adults from state regulation. Neither does the fact that the conduct occurred in the privacy of a home immunize otherwise illegal conduct. Victimless crimes such as possession and use of illegal drugs, said the Court, "do not escape the law when they are committed at home." The same is true for sexual conduct. It would be difficult to limit the asserted right to homosexual conduct "while leaving exposed to prosecution adultery, incest, and other sexual crimes even though they are committed in the home. We are unwilling to start down that road."

 # Constitution of the United States

PREAMBLE

We the People of the United States, in Order to form a more perfect Union, establish Justice, insure domestic Tranquility, provide for the common defence, promote the general Welfare, and secure the Blessings of Liberty to ourselves and our Posterity, do ordain and establish this Constitution for the United States of America.

Article I

Section 1. All legislative Powers herein granted shall be vested in a Congress of the United States, which shall consist of a Senate and House of Representatives.

Section 2. The House of Representatives shall be composed of Members chosen every second Year by the People of the several States, and the Electors in each State shall have the Qualifications requisite for Electors of the most numerous Branch of the State Legislature.

No Person shall be a Representative who shall not have attained to the age of twenty five Years, and been seven Years a Citizen of the United States, and who shall not, when elected, be an Inhabitant of that State in which he shall be chosen.

Representatives and direct Taxes shall be apportioned among the several States which may be included within this Union, according to their respective Numbers, which shall be determined by adding to the whole Number of free Persons, including those bound to Service for a Term of Years, and excluding

Indians not taxed, three fifths of all other Persons. The actual Enumeration shall be made within three Years after the first Meeting of the Congress of the United States, and within every subsequent Term of ten Years, in such Manner as they shall by Law direct. The Number of Representatives shall not exceed one for every thirty Thousand, but each State shall have at Least one Representative; and until such enumeration shall be made, the State of New Hampshire shall be entitled to chuse three, Massachusetts eight, Rhode-Island and Providence Plantations one, Connecticut five, New-York six, New Jersey four, Pennsylvania eight, Delaware one, Maryland six, Virginia ten, North Carolina five, South Carolina five, and Georgia three.

When vacancies happen in the Representation from any State, the Executive Authority thereof shall issue Writs of Election to fill such Vacancies.

The House of Representatives shall chuse their Speaker and other Officers; and shall have the sole Power of Impeachment.

Section 3. The Senate of the United States shall be composed of two Senators from each State, chosen by the Legislature thereof, for six Years; and each Senator shall have one Vote.

Immediately after they shall be assembled in Consequence of the first Election, they shall be divided as equally as may be into three Classes. The Seats of the Senators of the first Class shall be vacated at the Expiration of the second Year, of the second Class at the Expiration of the fourth Year, and of the third Class at the Expiration of the sixth Year, so that one third may be chosen every second Year; and if Vacancies happen by Resignation, or otherwise, during the Recess of the Legislature of any State, the Executive thereof may make temporary Appointments until the next Meeting of the Legislature, which shall then fill such Vacancies.

No Person shall be a Senator who shall not have attained to the Age of thirty Years, and been nine Years a Citizen of the United States, and who shall not, when elected, be an Inhabitant of that State for which he shall be chosen.

The Vice President of the United States shall be President of the Senate, but shall have no Vote, unless they be equally divided.

The Senate shall chuse their other Officers, and also a President pro tempore, in the Absence of the Vice President, or when he shall exercise the Office of President of the United States.

The Senate shall have the sole Power to try all Impeachments. When sitting for that Purpose, they shall be on Oath or Affirmation. When the President of the United States is tried the Chief Justice shall preside: And no Person shall be convicted without the Concurrence of two thirds of the Members present.

Judgment in Cases of Impeachment shall not extend further than to removal from Office, and disqualification to hold and enjoy any Office of honor, Trust or Profit under the United States: but the Party convicted shall nevertheless be liable and subject to Indictment, Trial, Judgment and Punishment, according to Law.

Section 4. The Times, Places and Manner of holding Elections for Senators and Representatives, shall be prescribed in each State by the Legislature thereof; but the Congress may at any time by Law make or alter such Regulations, except as to the Places of chusing Senators.

The Congress shall assemble at least once in every Year, and such Meeting shall be on the first Monday in December, unless they shall by Law appoint a different Day.

Section 5. Each House shall be the Judge of the Elections, Returns and Qualifications of its own Members, and a Majority of each shall constitute a Quorum to do Business; but a smaller Number may adjourn from day to day, and may be authorized to compel the Attendance of absent Members, in such Manner, and under such Penalties as each House may provide.

Each House may determine the Rules of its Proceedings, punish its Members for disorderly Behaviour, and, with the Concurrence of two thirds, expel a Member.

Each House shall keep a Journal of its Proceedings, and from time to time publish the same, excepting such Parts as may in their Judgment require Secrecy; and the Yeas and Nays of the Members of either House on any question shall, at the Desire of one fifth of those Present, be entered on the Journal.

Neither House, during the Session of Congress, shall, without the Consent of the other, adjourn for more than three days, nor to any other Place than that in which the two Houses shall be sitting.

Section 6. The Senators and Representatives shall receive a Compensation for their Services, to be ascertained by Law, and paid out of the Treasury of the United States. They shall in all Cases, except Treason, Felony and Breach of the Peace, be privileged from Arrest during their Attendance at the Session of their respective Houses, and in going to and returning from the same; and for any Speech or Debate in either House, they shall not be questioned in any other Place.

No Senator or Representative shall, during the Time for which he was elected, be appointed to any civil Office under the Authority of the United States, which shall have been created, or the Emoluments whereof shall have been increased during such time; and no Person holding any Office under the United States, shall be a Member of either House during his Continuance in Office.

Section 7. All Bills for raising Revenue shall originate in the House of Representatives; but the Senate may propose or concur with amendments as on other Bills.

Every Bill which shall have passed the House of Representatives and the Senate, shall, before it become a Law, be presented to the President of the United States; If he approve he shall sign it, but if not he shall return it, with his Objections to that House in which it shall have originated, who shall enter the Objections at large on their Journal, and proceed to reconsider it. If after such Reconsideration two thirds of that House shall agree to pass the Bill, it shall be sent, together with the Objections, to the other House, by which it shall likewise be reconsidered, and if approved by two thirds of that House, it shall become a Law. But in all such Cases the Votes of both Houses shall be determined by yeas and Nays, and the Names of the Persons voting for and against the Bill shall be entered on the Journal of each House respectively. If any Bill shall not be returned by the President within ten Days (Sunday excepted) after it shall have been presented to him, the Same shall be a Law, in like Manner as if he had signed it, unless the Congress by their Adjournment prevent its Return, in which Case it shall not be a Law.

Every Order, Resolution, or Vote to which the Concurrence of the Senate and House of Representatives may be necessary (except on a question of Adjournment) shall be presented to the President of the United States; and before the Same shall take Effect, shall be approved by him, or being disapproved by him, shall be repassed by two thirds of the Senate and House of Representatives, according to the Rules and Limitations prescribed in the Case of a Bill.

Section 8. The Congress shall have Power To lay and collect Taxes, Duties, Imposts and Excises, to pay the Debts and provide for the common Defence and general Welfare of the United States; but all Duties, Imposts and Excises shall be uniform throughout the United States;

To borrow Money on the credit of the United States;

To regulate Commerce with foreign Nations, and among the several States, and with the Indian Tribes;

To establish an uniform Rule of Naturalization, and uniform Laws on the subject of Bankruptcies throughout the United States;

To coin Money, regulate the Value thereof, and of foreign Coin, and fix the Standard of Weights and Measures;

To provide for the Punishment of counterfeiting the Securities and current Coin of the United States;

To establish Post Offices and post Roads;

To promote the Progress of Science and useful Arts, by securing for limited Times to Authors and Inventors the exclusive Right to their respective Writings and Discoveries;

To constitute Tribunals inferior to the supreme Court;

To define and punish Piracies and Felonies commit[t]ed on the high Seas, and Offences against the Law of Nations;

To declare War, grant Letters of Marque and Reprisal, and make Rules concerning Captures on Land and Water;

To raise and support Armies, but no Appropriation of Money to that Use shall be for a longer Term than two Years;

To provide and maintain a Navy;

To make Rules for the Government and Regulation of the land and naval Forces;

To provide for calling forth the Militia to execute the Laws of the Union, suppress Insurrections and repel Invasions;

To provide for organizing, arming, and disciplining the Militia, and for governing such Part of them as may be employed in the Service of the United States, reserving to the States respectively, the Appointment of the Officers, and the Authority of training the Militia according to the discipline prescribed by Congress;

To exercise exclusive Legislation in all Cases whatsoever, over such District (not exceeding ten Miles square) as may, by Cession of Particular States, and the Acceptance of Congress, become the Seat of the Government of the United States, and to exercise like Authority over all Places purchased by the Consent of the Legislature of the State in which the Same shall be, for the Erection of Forts, Magazines, Arsenals, dock-Yards, and other needful Buildings;

—And

To make all Laws which shall be necessary and proper for carrying into Execution the foregoing Powers, and all other Powers vested by this Constitution in the Government of the United States, or in any Department or Officer thereof.

Section 9. The Migration or Importation of such Persons as any of the States now existing shall think proper to admit, shall not be prohibited by the Congress prior to the Year one thousand eight hundred and eight, but a Tax or duty may be imposed on such Importation, not exceeding ten dollars for each Person.

The Privilege of the Writ of Habeas Corpus shall not be suspended, unless when in Cases of Rebellion or Invasion the public Safety may require it.

No Bill of Attainder or ex post facto Law shall be passed.

No capitation, or other direct, Tax shall be laid, unless in Proportion to the Census of Enumeration herein before directed to be taken.

No Tax or Duty shall be laid on Articles exported from any State.

No Preference shall be given by any Regulation of Commerce or Revenue to the Ports of one State over those of another; nor shall Vessels bound to, or from, one State, be obliged to enter, clear or pay Duties in another.

No Money shall be drawn from the Treasury, but in Consequence of Appropriations made by Law; and a regular Statement and Account of the Receipts and Expenditures of all public Money shall be published from time to time.

No Title of Nobility shall be granted by the United States: And no Person holding any Office of Profit or Trust under them, shall, without the Consent of the Congress, accept of any present, Emolument, Office, or Title, of any kind whatever, from any King, Prince or foreign State.

Section 10. No State shall enter into any Treaty, Alliance, or Confederation; grant Letters of Marque and Reprisal; coin Money; emit Bills of Credit; make any Thing but gold and silver Coin a Tender in Payment of Debts; pass any Bill of Attainder, ex post facto Law, or Law impairing the Obligation of Contracts, or grant any Title of Nobility.

No State shall, without the Consent of the Congress, lay any Imposts or Duties on Imports or Exports, except what may be absolutely necessary for executing it's inspection Laws: and the net Produce of all Duties and Imposts, laid by any State on Imports or Exports, shall be for the Use of the Treasury of the United States; and all such Laws shall be subject to the Revision and Controul of the Congress.

No State shall, without the Consent of Congress, lay any Duty of Tonnage, keep Troops, or Ships of War in time of Peace, enter into any Agreement or Compact with another State, or with a foreign Power, or engage in War, unless actually invaded, or in such imminent Danger as will not admit of delay.

Article II

Section 1. The executive Power shall be vested in a President of the United States of America. He shall hold his Office during the Term of four Years, and, together with the Vice President, chosen for the same Term, be elected, as follows.

Each State shall appoint, in such Manner as the Legislature thereof may direct, a Number of Electors, equal to the whole Number of Senators and Representatives to which the State may be entitled in the Congress: but no Senator or Representative, or Person holding an Office of Trust or Profit under the United States, shall be appointed an Elector.

The Electors shall meet in their respective States, and vote by Ballot for two Persons, of whom one at least shall not be an Inhabitant of the same State with themselves. And they shall make a List of all the Persons voted for, and of the Number of Votes for each; which List they shall sign and certify, and transmit sealed to the Seat of the Government of the United States, directed to the President of the Senate. The President of the Senate shall, in the Presence of the Senate and House of Representatives, open all the Certificates, and the Votes shall then be counted. The Person having the greatest Number of Votes shall be the President, if such Number be a Majority of the whole Number of Electors appointed; and if there be more than one who have such Majority, and have an equal Number of Votes, then the House of Representatives shall immediately chuse by Ballot one of them for President; and if no Person have a Majority, then from the five highest on the list the said House shall in like Manner chuse the President. But in chusing the President, the Votes shall be taken by States, the Representation from each State having one Vote; a quorum for this Purpose shall consist of a Member or Members from two thirds of the States, and a Majority of all the States shall be necessary to a Choice. In every Case, after the Choice of the President, the Person having the greatest Number of Votes of the Electors shall be the Vice President. But if there should remain two or more who have equal Votes, the Senate shall chuse from them by Ballot the Vice President.

The Congress may determine the Time of chusing the Electors, and the Day on which they shall give their Votes; which Day shall be the same throughout the United States.

No Person except a natural born Citizen, or a Citizen of the United States, at the time of the Adoption of this Constitution, shall be eligible to the Office of President; neither shall any Person be eligible to that Office who shall not have attained to the Age of thirty five Years, and been fourteen Years a Resident within the United States.

In Case of the Removal of the President from Office, or of his Death, Resignation, or Inability to discharge the Powers and Duties of the said Office, the Same shall devolve on the Vice President, and the Congress may by Law provide for the Case of Removal, Death, Resignation or Inability, both of the President and Vice President, declaring what Officer shall then act as President, and such Officer shall act accordingly, until the Disability be removed, or a President shall be elected.

The President shall, at stated Times, receive for his Services, a Compensation, which shall neither be encreased nor diminished during the Period for which he shall have been elected, and he shall not receive within that Period any other Emolument from the United States, or any of them.

Before he enter on the Execution of his Office, he shall take the following Oath or Affirmation:—"I do solemnly swear (or affirm) that I will faithfully execute the Office of President of the United States, and will to the best of my Ability, preserve, protect and defend the Constitution of the United States."

Section 2. The President shall be Commander in Chief of the Army and Navy of the United States, and of the Militia of the several States, when called into the actual Service of the United States; he may require the Opinion, in writing, of the principal Officer in each of the executive Departments, upon any Subject relating to the Duties of their respective Offices, and he shall have Power to grant Reprieves and Pardons for Offenses against the United States, except in Cases of Impeachment.

He shall have Power, by and with the Advice and Consent of the Senate, to make Treaties, provided two thirds of the Senators present concur; and he shall nominate, and by and with the Advice and Consent of the Senate, shall appoint Ambassadors, other public Ministers and Consuls, Judges of the supreme Court, and all other Officers of the United States, whose Appointments are not herein otherwise provided for, and which shall be established by Law: but the Congress may by Law vest the Appointment of such inferior Officers, as they think proper, in the President alone, in the Courts of Law, or in the Heads of Departments.

The President shall have Power to fill up all Vacancies that may happen during the Recess of the Senate, by granting Commissions which shall expire at the End of their next Session.

Section 3. He shall from time to time give to the Congress Information of the State of the Union, and recommend to their Consideration such Measures as he shall judge necessary and expedient; he may, on extraordinary Occasions, convene both Houses, or either of them, and in Case of Disagreement between them, with Respect to the Time of Adjournment, he may adjourn them to such Time as he shall think proper; he shall receive Ambassadors and other public Ministers; he shall take Care that the Laws be faithfully executed, and shall Commission all the Officers of the United States.

Section 4. The President, Vice President and all Civil Officers of the United States, shall be removed from office on Impeachment for, and Conviction of, Treason, Bribery, or other high Crimes and Misdemeanors.

Article III

Section 1. The judicial Power of the United States shall be vested in one supreme Court, and in such inferior Courts as the Congress may from time to time ordain and establish. The Judges, both of the supreme and inferior Courts, shall hold their Offices during good Behaviour, and shall, at stated Times, receive for their Services, a Compensation, which shall not be diminished during their Continuance in Office.

Section 2. The judicial Power shall extend to all Cases, in Law and Equity, arising under this Constitution, the Laws of the United States, and Treaties made, or which shall be made, under their Authority;—to all Cases affecting Ambassadors, other public Ministers and Consuls;—to all Cases of admiralty and maritime Jurisdiction;—to Controversies to which the United States shall be a Party;—to Controversies between two or more States;—between a State and Citizens of another State;—between Citizens of different States;—between Citizens of the same State claiming Lands under Grants of different States, and between a State, or the Citizens thereof, and foreign States, Citizens or Subjects.

In all Cases affecting Ambassadors, other public Ministers and Consuls, and those in which a State shall be Party, the supreme Court shall have original Jurisdiction. In all the other Cases before mentioned, the supreme Court shall have appellate Jurisdiction, both as to Law and Fact, with such Exceptions, and under such Regulations as the Congress shall make.

The Trial of all Crimes, except in cases of Impeachment, shall be by Jury; and such Trial shall be held in the State where the said Crimes shall have been committed; but when not committed within any State, the Trial shall be at such Place or Places as the Congress may by Law have directed.

Section 3. Treason against the United States shall consist only in levying War against them, or in adhering to their Enemies, giving them Aid and Comfort. No Person shall be convicted of Treason unless on the Testimony of two Witnesses to the same overt Act, or on Confession in open Court.

The Congress shall have Power to declare the Punishment of Treason, but no Attainder of Treason shall work Corruption of Blood, or Forfeiture except during the Life of the Person attainted.

Article IV

Section 1. Full Faith and Credit shall be given in each State to the public Acts, Records, and judicial Proceedings of every other State. And the Congress may by general Laws prescribe the Manner in which such Acts, Records and Proceedings shall be proved, and the Effect thereof.

Section 2. The Citizens of each State shall be entitled to all Privileges and Immunities of Citizens in the several States.

A Person charged in any State with Treason, Felony, or other Crime, who shall flee from Justice, and be found in another State, shall on Demand of the executive Authority of the State from which he fled, be delivered up, to be removed to the State having Jurisdiction of the Crime.

No Person held to Service or Labour in one State, under the Laws thereof, escaping into another, shall, in Consequence of any Law or Regulation therein, be discharged from such Service or Labour, but shall be delivered up on Claim of the Party to whom such Service or Labour may be due.

Section 3. New States may be admitted by the Congress into this Union; but no new State shall be formed or erected within the Jurisdiction of any other State; nor any State be formed by the Junction of two or more States, or Parts of States, without the Consent of the Legislatures of the States concerned as well as of the Congress.

The Congress shall have Power to dispose of and make all needful Rules and Regulations respecting the Territory or other Property belonging to the United States; and nothing in this Constitution shall be so construed as to Prejudice any Claims of the United States, or of any particular State.

Section 4. The United States shall guarantee to every State in this Union a Republican Form of Government, and shall protect each of them against Invasion; and on Application of the Legislature, or of the Executive (when the Legislature cannot be convened) against domestic Violence.

Article V

The Congress, whenever two thirds of both Houses shall deem it necessary, shall propose Amendments to this Constitution, or, on the Application of the Legislatures of two thirds of the several States, shall call a Convention for proposing Amendments, which, in either Case, shall be valid to all Intents and Purposes, as Part of this Constitution, when ratified by the Legislatures of three fourths of the several States, or by Conventions in three fourths thereof, as the one or the other Mode of Ratification may be proposed by the Congress; Provided that no Amendment which may be made prior to the Year One thousand eight hundred and eight shall in any Manner affect the first and fourth Clauses in the Ninth Section of the first Article; and that no State, without its Consent, shall be deprived of its equal Suffrage in the Senate.

Article VI

All Debts contracted and Engagements entered into, before the Adoption of this Constitution, shall be as valid against the United States under this Constitution, as under the Confederation.

This Constitution, and the Laws of the United States which shall be made in Pursuance thereof; and all Treaties made, or which shall be made, under the Authority of the United States, shall be the supreme Law of the Land; and the Judges in every State shall be the supreme Law of the Land; and the

Judges in every State shall be bound thereby, any Thing in the Constitution or Laws or any State to the Contrary notwithstanding.

The Senators and Representatives before mentioned, and the Members of the several State Legislatures, and all executive and judicial Officers, both of the United States and of the several States, shall be bound by Oath or Affirmation, to support this Constitution; but no religious Test shall ever be required as a Qualification to any Office or public Trust under the United States.

Article VII

The Ratification of the Conventions of nine States, shall be sufficient for the Establishment of this Constitution between the States so ratifying the Same.

Amendments

AMENDMENT I

[First ten amendments ratified 15 December 1791]

Congress shall make no law respecting an establishment of religion, or prohibiting the free exercise thereof; or abridging the freedom of speech, or of the press; or the right of the people peaceably to assemble, and to petition the Government for a redress of grievances.

AMENDMENT II

A well regulated Militia, being necessary to the security of a free State, the right of the people to keep and bear Arms, shall not be infringed.

AMENDMENT III

No Soldier shall, in time of peace be quartered in any house, without the consent of the Owner, nor in time of war, but in a manner to be prescribed by law.

AMENDMENT IV

The right of the people to be secure in their persons, houses, papers, and effects, against unreasonable searches and seizures, shall not be violated, and no Warrants shall issue, but upon probable cause, supported by Oath or affirmation, and particularly describing the place to be searched, and the persons or things to be seized.

AMENDMENT V

No person shall be held to answer for a capital, or otherwise infamous crime, unless on a presentment or indictment of a Grand Jury, except in cases arising in the land or naval forces, or in the Militia, when in actual service in time of War or public danger; nor shall any person be subject for the same offence to be twice put in jeopardy of life or limb; nor shall be compelled in any criminal case to be a witness against himself, nor be deprived of life, liberty, or property, without due process of law; nor shall private property be taken for public use, without just compensation.

AMENDMENT VI

In all criminal prosecutions, the accused shall enjoy the right to a speedy and public trial, by an impartial jury of the State and district wherein the crime shall have been committed, which district shall have been previously ascertained by law, and to be informed of the nature and cause of the accusation; to be confronted with the witnesses against him; to have compulsory process for obtaining witnesses in his favor, and to have the Assistance of Counsel for his defence.

AMENDMENT VII

In Suits at common law, where the value in controversy shall exceed twenty dollars, the right of trial by jury shall be preserved, and no fact tried by a jury, shall be otherwise re-examined in any Court of the United States, than according to the rules of the common law.

AMENDMENT VIII

Excessive bail shall not be required, nor excessive fines imposed, nor cruel and unusual punishments inflicted.

AMENDMENT IX

The enumeration in the Constitution, of certain rights, shall not be construed to deny or disparage others retained by the people.

AMENDMENT X

The powers not delegated to the United States by the Constitution, nor prohibited by it to the States, are reserved to the States respectively, or to the people.

AMENDMENT XI

[Ratified 7 February 1795]

The Judicial power of the United States shall not be construed to extend to any suit in law or equity, commenced or prosecuted against one of the United States by Citizens of another State, or by Citizens or Subjects of any Foreign State.

AMENDMENT XII

[Ratified 15 June 1804]

The Electors shall meet in their respective states and vote by ballot for President and Vice-President, one of whom, at least, shall not be an inhabitant of the same state with themselves; they shall name in their ballots the person voted for as President, and in distinct ballots the person voted for as Vice-President, and they shall make distinct lists of all persons voted for as President, and of all persons voted for as Vice-President, and of the number of votes for each, which lists they shall sign and certify, and transmit sealed to the seat of the government of the United States, directed to the President of the Senate;—The President of the Senate shall, in the presence of the Senate and House of Representatives, open all the certificates and the votes shall then be counted;—The person having the greatest number of votes for President, shall be the President, if such number be a majority of the whole number of Electors appointed; and if no person have such majority, then from the persons having the highest numbers not exceeding three on the list of those voted for as President, the House of Representatives shall chuse immediately, by ballot, the President. But in chusing the President, the votes shall be taken by states, the representation from each state having one vote; a quorum for this purpose shall consist of a member or members from two-thirds of the states, and a majority of all the states shall be necessary to a choice. And if the House of Representatives shall not chuse a President whenever the right of choice shall devolve upon them, before the fourth day of March next following, then the Vice-President shall act as President, as in the case of the death or other constitutional disability of the President—The person having the greatest number of votes as Vice-President, shall be the Vice-President, if such number be a majority of the whole number of Electors appointed, and if no person have a majority, then from the two highest numbers on the list, the Senate shall chuse the Vice-President; a quorum for the purpose shall consist of two-thirds of the whole number of Senators, and a majority of the whole number shall be necessary to a choice. But no person constitutionally ineligible to the office of President shall be eligible to that of Vice-President of the United States.

AMENDMENT XIII

[Ratified 6 December 1865]

Section 1. Neither slavery nor involuntary servitude, except as a punishment for crime whereof the party shall have been duly convicted, shall exist within the United States, or any place subject to their jurisdiction.

Section 2. Congress shall have power to enforce this article by appropriate legislation.

AMENDMENT XIV

[Ratified 9 July 1868]

Section 1. All persons born or naturalized in the United States and subject to the jurisdiction thereof, are citizens of the United States and of the State wherein they reside. No State shall make or enforce any law which shall abridge the privileges or immunities of citizens of the United States; nor shall any State deprive any person of life, liberty, or property, without due process of law; nor deny to any person within its jurisdiction the equal protection of the laws.

Section 2. Representatives shall be apportioned among the several States according to their respective numbers, counting the whole number of persons in each State, excluding Indians not taxed. But when the right to vote at any election for the choice of electors for President and Vice President of the United States, Representatives in Congress, the Executive and Judicial officers of a State, or the members of the Legislature thereof, is denied to any of the male inhabitants of such State, being twenty-one years of age, and citizens of the United States, or in any way abridged, except for participation in rebellion, or other crime, the basis of representation therein shall be reduced in the proportion which the number of such male citizens shall bear to the whole number of male citizens twenty-one years of age in such State.

Section 3. No person shall be a Senator or Representative in Congress, or elector of President and Vice President, or hold any office, civil or military, under the United States, or under any State, who, having previously taken an oath, as a member of Congress, or as an officer of the United States, or as a member of any State legislature, or as an executive or judicial officer of any

State, to support the Constitution of the United States, shall have engaged in insurrection or rebellion against the same, or given aid or comfort to the enemies thereof. But Congress may by a vote of two-thirds of each House, remove such disability.

Section 4. The validity of the public debt of the United States, authorized by law, including debts incurred for payment of pensions and bounties for services in suppressing insurrection or rebellion, shall not be questioned. But neither the United States nor any State shall assume or pay any debt or obligation incurred in aid of insurrection or rebellion against the United States, or any claim for the loss or emancipation of any slave; but all such debts, obligations and claims shall be held illegal and void.

Section 5. The Congress shall have power to enforce, by appropriate legislation, the provisions of this article.

AMENDMENT XV

[Ratified 3 February 1870]

Section 1. The right of citizens of the United States to vote shall not be denied or abridged by the United States or by any State on account of race, color, or previous condition of servitude.

Section 2. The Congress shall have power to enforce this article by appropriate legislation.

AMENDMENT XVI

[Ratified 3 February 1913]

The Congress shall have power to lay and collect taxes on incomes, from whatever source derived, without apportionment among the several States, and without regard to any census or enumeration.

AMENDMENT XVII

[Ratified 8 April 1913]

The Senate of the United States shall be composed of two Senators from each State, elected by the people thereof, for six years; and each Senator shall have one vote. The electors in each State shall have the qualifications requisite for electors of the most numerous branch of the State legislatures.

When vacancies happen in the representation of any State in the Senate, the executive authority of such State shall issue writs of election to fill such vacancies: *Provided,* That the legislature of any State may empower the executive thereof to make temporary appointments until the people fill the vacancies by election as the legislature may direct.

This amendment shall not be so construed as to affect the election or term of any Senator chosen before it becomes valid as part of the Constitution.

AMENDMENT XVIII

[Ratified 16 January 1919]

Section 1. After one year from the ratification of this article the manufacture, sale, or transportation of intoxicating liquors within, the importation thereof into, or the exportation thereof from the United States and all territory subject to the jurisdiction thereof for beverage purposes is hereby prohibited.

Section 2. The Congress and the several States shall have concurrent power to enforce this article by appropriate legislation.

Section 3. This article shall be inoperative unless it shall have been ratified as an amendment to the Constitution by the legislatures of the several States, as provided in the Constitution, within seven years from the date of the submission hereof to the States by the Congress.

AMENDMENT XIX

[Ratified 18 August 1920]

The right of citizens of the United States to vote shall not be denied or abridged by the United States or by any State on account of sex.

Congress shall have power to enforce this article by appropriate legislation.

AMENDMENT XX

[Ratified 23 January 1933]

Section 1. The terms of the President and Vice President shall end at noon on the 20th day of January, and the terms of Senators and Representatives at noon on the 3d day of January, of the years in which such terms would have ended if this article had not been ratified; and the terms of their successors shall then begin.

Section 2. The Congress shall assemble at least once in every year, and such meeting shall begin at noon on the 3d day of January, unless they shall by law appoint a different day.

Section 3. If, at the time fixed for the beginning of the term of the President, the President elect shall have died, the Vice President elect shall become President. If a President shall not have been chosen before the time fixed for the beginning of his term, or if the President elect shall have failed to qualify, then the Vice President elect shall act as President until a President shall have qualified; and the Congress may by law provide for the case wherein neither a President elect nor a Vice President elect shall have qualified, declaring who shall then act as President, or the manner in which one who is to act shall be selected, and such person shall act accordingly until a President or Vice President shall have qualified.

Section 4. The Congress may by law provide for the case of the death of any of the persons from whom the House of Representatives may choose a President whenever the right of choice shall have devolved upon them, and for the case of the death of any of the persons from whom the Senate may choose a Vice President whenever the right of choice shall have devolved upon them.

Section 5. Sections 1 and 2 shall take effect on the 15th day of October following the ratification of this article.

Section 6. This article shall be inoperative unless it shall have been ratified as an amendment to the Constitution by the legislatures of three-fourths of the several States within seven years from the date of its submission.

AMENDMENT XXI

[Ratified 5 December 1933]

Section 1. The eighteenth article of amendment to the Constitution of the United States is hereby repealed.

Section 2. The transportation or importation into any State, Territory or possession of the United States for delivery or use therein of intoxicating liquors, in violation of the laws thereof, is hereby prohibited.

Section 3. This article shall be inoperative unless it shall have been ratified as an amendment to the Constitution by conventions in the several States, as provided in the Constitution, within seven years from the date of the submission hereof to the States by the Congress.

AMENDMENT XXII

[Ratified 27 February 1951]

Section 1. No person shall be elected to the office of the President more than twice, and no person who has held the office of President, or acted as President, for more than two years of a term to which some other person was elected President shall be elected to the office of the President more than once. But this Article shall not apply to any person holding the office of President when this Article was proposed by the Congress, and shall not prevent any person who may be holding the office of President, or acting as President, during the term within which this Article become[s] operative from holding the office of President or acting as President during the remainder of such term.

Section 2. This Article shall be inoperative unless it shall have been ratified as an amendment to the Constitution by the legislatures of three-fourths of the several States within seven years from the date of its submission to the States by the Congress.

AMENDMENT XXIII

[Ratified 29 March 1961]

Section 1. The District constituting the seat of Government of the United States shall appoint in such manner as the Congress may direct:

A number of electors of President and Vice President equal to the whole number of Senators and Representatives in Congress to which the District would be entitled if it were a State, but in no event more than the least populous State; they shall be in addition to those appointed by the States, but they shall be considered, for the purposes of the election of President and Vice President, to be electors appointed by a State; and they shall meet in the District and perform such duties as provided by the twelfth article of amendment.

Section 2. The Congress shall have power to enforce this article by appropriate legislation.

AMENDMENT XXIV

[Ratified 23 January 1964]

Section 1. The right of citizens of the United States to vote in any primary or other election for President or Vice President, for electors for President or Vice President, or for Senator or Representative in Congress, shall not be denied or abridged by the United States or any State by reason of failure to pay any poll tax or other tax.

Section 2. The Congress shall have power to enforce this article by appropriate legislation.

AMENDMENT XXV

[Ratified 10 February 1967]

Section 1. In case of the removal of the President from office or of his death or resignation, the Vice President shall become President.

Section 2. Whenever there is a vacancy in the office of the Vice President, the President shall nominate a Vice President who shall take office upon confirmation by a majority vote of both Houses of Congress.

Section 3. Whenever the President transmits to the President pro tempore of the Senate and the Speaker of the House of Representatives his written declaration that he is unable to discharge the powers and duties of his office, and until he transmits to them a written declaration to the contrary, such powers and duties shall be discharged by the Vice President as Acting President.

Section 4. Whenever the Vice President and a majority of either the principal officers of the executive departments or of such other body as Congress may by law provide, transmit to the President pro tempore of the Senate and the Speaker of the House of Representatives their written declaration that the President is unable to discharge the powers and duties of his office, the Vice President shall immediately assume the powers and duties of the office as Acting President.

Thereafter, when the President transmits to the President pro tempore of the Senate and the Speaker of the House of Representatives his written declaration that no inability exists, he shall resume the powers and duties of his office unless the Vice President and a majority of either the principal officers of the executive department or of such other body as Congress may by law provide, transmit within four days to the President pro tempore of the Senate and the Speaker of the House of Representatives their written declaration that the President is unable to discharge the powers and duties of his office. Thereupon Congress shall decide the issue, assembling within forty-eight hours for that purpose if not in session. If the Congress, within twenty-one days after receipt of the latter written declaration, or, if Congress is not in session, within twenty-one days after Congress is required to assemble, determines by two-thirds vote of both houses that the President is unable to discharge the powers and duties of his office, the Vice President shall continue to discharge the same as Acting President; otherwise, the President shall resume the powers and duties of his office.

AMENDMENT XXVI

[Ratified 1 July 1971]

Section 1. The right of citizens of the United States, who are eighteen years of age or older, to vote shall not be denied or abridged by the United States or by any State on account of age.

Section 2. The Congress shall have power to enforce this article by appropriate legislation.

(Source: Congressional Quarterly Inc. *CQ Guide to Current American Government*. Spring 1991.)

Justices of
the Supreme Court

	TENURE	APPOINTED BY	REPLACED
JOHN JAY	1789–1795	Washington	
John Rutledge	1789–1791	Washington	
William Cushing	1789–1810	Washington	
James Wilson	1789–1798	Washington	
John Blair	1789–1796	Washington	
James Iredell	1790–1799	Washington	
Thomas Johnson	1791–1793	Washington	Rutledge
William Paterson	1793–1806	Washington	Johnson
JOHN RUTLEDGE	1795	Washington	Jay
Samuel Chase	1796–1811	Washington	Blair
OLIVER ELLSWORTH	1796–1800	Washington	Rutledge
Bushrod Washington	1798–1829	John Adams	Wilson
Alfred Moore	1799–1804	John Adams	Iredell
JOHN MARSHALL	1801–1835	John Adams	Ellsworth
William Johnson	1804–1834	Jefferson	Moore
Brockholst Livingston	1806–1823	Jefferson	Paterson
Thomas Todd	1807–1826	Jefferson	(new judgeship)
Gabriel Duval	1811–1835	Madison	Chase
Joseph Story	1811–1845	Madison	Cushing
Smith Thompson	1823–1843	Monroe	Livingston
Robert Trimble	1826–1828	John Q. Adams	Todd
John McLean	1829–1861	Jackson	Trimble
Henry Baldwin	1830–1844	Jackson	Washington
James Wayne	1835–1867	Jackson	Johnson

	TENURE	APPOINTED BY	REPLACED
ROGER B. TANEY	1836–1864	Jackson	Marshall
Phillip P. Barbour	1836–1841	Jackson	Duval
John Catron	1837–1865	Jackson	(new judgeship)
John McKinley	1837–1852	Van Buren	(new judgeship)
Peter V. Daniel	1841–1860	Van Buren	Barbour
Samuel Nelson	1845–1872	Tyler	Thompson
Levi Woodbury	1846–1851	Polk	Story
Robert C. Grier	1846–1870	Polk	Baldwin
Benjamin R. Curtis	1851–1857	Fillmore	Woodbury
John A. Campbell	1853–1861	Pierce	McKinley
Nathan Clifford	1858–1881	Buchanan	Curtis
Noah H. Swayne	1862–1881	Lincoln	McLean
Samuel F. Miller	1862–1890	Lincoln	Daniel
David Davis	1862–1877	Lincoln	Campbell
Stephen J. Field	1863–1897	Lincoln	(new judgeship)
SALMON CHASE	1864–1873	Lincoln	Taney
William Strong	1870–1880	Grant	Grier
Joseph P. Bradley	1870–1892	Grant	Wayne
Ward Hunt	1872–1882	Grant	Nelson
MORRISON R. WAITE	1874–1888	Grant	Chase
John Marshall Harlan	1877–1911	Hayes	Davis
William B. Woods	1880–1887	Hayes	Strong
Stanley Matthews	1881–1889	Garfield	Swayne
Horace Gray	1881–1902	Arthur	Clifford
Samuel Blatchford	1882–1893	Arthur	Hunt
Lucius Q. C. Lamar	1888–1893	Cleveland	Woods
MELVILLE W. FULLER	1888–1910	Cleveland	Waite
David J. Brewer	1889–1910	Harrison	Matthews
Henry B. Brown	1890–1906	Harrison	Miller
George Shiras, Jr.	1892–1903	Harrison	Bradley
Howell E. Jackson	1893–1895	Harrison	Lamar
Edward D. White	1894–1910	Cleveland	Blatchford
Rufus W. Peckham	1895–1909	Cleveland	Jackson
Joseph McKenna	1898–1925	McKinley	Field
Oliver Wendell Holmes	1902–1932	T. Roosevelt	Gray
William R. Day	1903–1922	T. Roosevelt	Shiras
William H. Moody	1906–1910	T. Roosevelt	Brown
Horace H. Lurton	1909–1914	Taft	Peckham
Charles Evans Hughes	1910–1916	Taft	Brewer

	TENURE	APPOINTED BY	REPLACED
EDWARD D. WHITE	1910–1921	Taft	Fuller
Willis VanDevanter	1910–1937	Taft	White
Joseph R. Lamar	1910–1916	Taft	Moody
Mahlon Pitney	1912–1922	Taft	Harlan
James McReynolds	1914–1941	Wilson	Lurton
Louis D. Brandeis	1916–1939	Wilson	Lamar
John H. Clark	1916–1922	Wilson	Hughes
WILLIAM H. TAFT	1921–1930	Harding	White
George Sutherland	1922–1938	Harding	Clarke
Pierce Butler	1922–1939	Harding	Day
Edward T. Sanford	1923–1930	Harding	Pitney
Harlan F. Stone	1925–1941	Coolidge	McKenna
CHARLES EVANS HUGHES	1930–1941	Hoover	Taft
Owen J. Roberts	1932–1945	Hoover	Sanford
Benjamin N. Cardozo	1932–1938	Hoover	Holmes
Hugo L. Black	1937–1971	F. Roosevelt	Van Devanter
Stanley F. Reed	1938–1957	F. Roosevelt	Sutherland
Felix Frankfurter	1939–1962	F. Roosevelt	Cardozo
William O. Douglas	1939–1975	F. Roosevelt	Brandeis
Frank Murphy	1940–1949	F. Roosevelt	Butler
James F. Byrnes	1941–1942	F. Roosevelt	McReynolds
HARLAN F. STONE	1941–1946	F. Roosevelt	Hughes
Robert H. Jackson	1941–1954	F. Roosevelt	Stone
Wiley B. Rutledge	1943–1949	F. Roosevelt	Byrnes
Harold H. Burton	1945–1958	Truman	Roberts
FRED M. VINSON	1946–1953	Truman	Stone
Tom C. Clark	1949–1967	Truman	Murphy
Sherman Minton	1949–1956	Truman	Rutledge
EARL WARREN	1954–1969	Eisenhower	Vinson
John M. Harlan	1955–1971	Eisenhower	Jackson
William J. Brennan	1957–1990	Eisenhower	Minton
Charles E. Whittaker	1957–1962	Eisenhower	Reed
Potter Stewart	1959–1981	Eisenhower	Burton
Byron R. White	1962–	Kennedy	Whittaker
Arthur J. Goldberg	1962–1965	Kennedy	Frankfurter
Abe Fortas	1965–1969	Johnson	Goldberg
Thurgood Marshall	1967–1991	Johnson	Clark
WARREN E. BURGER	1969–1986	Nixon	Warren
Harry A. Blackmun	1970–	Nixon	Fortas

	TENURE	APPOINTED BY	REPLACED
Lewis F. Powell	1971–1988	Nixon	Black
William H. Rehnquist	1971–	Nixon	Harlan
John Paul Stevens	1975–	Ford	Douglas
Sandra Day O'Connor	1981–	Reagan	Stewart
WILLIAM H. REHNQUIST	1986–	Reagan	Burger
Antonin Scalia	1986–	Reagan	Rehnquist
Anthony M. Kennedy	1988–	Reagan	Powell
David H. Souter	1990–	Bush	Brennan
Clarence Thomas	1991–	Bush	Marshall

Composition of the U.S. Supreme Court since 1900

The table below represents the members of the Supreme Court since 1900. By locating the term in which a particular case was decided, the names of the justices on the Court at the time of the decision may be readily determined.

THE FULLER COURT (1900–1909)

1900–1901	Fuller	White	Gray	Peckham	Brown	Shiras	Brewer	Harlan	McKenna
1902	Fuller	White	Holmes	Peckham	Brown	Shiras	Brewer	Harlan	McKenna
1903–1905	Fuller	White	Holmes	Peckham	Brown	Day	Brewer	Harlan	McKenna
1906–1908	Fuller	White	Holmes	Peckham	Moody	Day	Brewer	Harlan	McKenna
1909	Fuller	White	Holmes	Lurton	Moody	Day	Brewer	Harlan	McKenna

THE WHITE COURT (1910–1920)

1910–1911	White	VanDevanter	Holmes	Lurton	Lamar	Day	Hughes	Harlan	McKenna
1912–1913	White	VanDevanter	Holmes	Lurton	Lamar	Day	Hughes	Pitney	McKenna
1914–1915	White	VanDevanter	Holmes	McReynolds	Lamar	Day	Hughes	Pitney	McKenna
1916–1920	White	VanDevanter	Holmes	McReynolds	Brandeis	Day	Clarke	Pitney	McKenna

THE TAFT COURT (1921–1929)

1921	Taft	VanDevanter	Holmes	McReynolds	Brandeis	Day	Clarke	Pitney	McKenna
1922	Taft	VanDevanter	Holmes	McReynolds	Brandeis	Butler	Sutherland	Pitney	McKenna
1923–1924	Taft	VanDevanter	Holmes	McReynolds	Brandeis	Butler	Sutherland	Sanford	McKenna
1925–1929	Taft	VanDevanter	Holmes	McReynolds	Brandeis	Butler	Sutherland	Sanford	Stone

THE HUGHES COURT (1930–1940)

1930–1931	Hughes	VanDevanter	Holmes	McReynolds	Brandeis	Butler	Sutherland	Roberts	Stone
1932–1936	Hughes	VanDevanter	Cardozo	McReynolds	Brandeis	Butler	Sutherland	Roberts	Stone
1937	Hughes	Black	Cardozo	McReynolds	Brandeis	Butler	Sutherland	Roberts	Stone
1938	Hughes	Black	Cardozo	McReynolds	Brandeis	Butler	Reed	Roberts	Stone
1939	Hughes	Black	Frankfurter	McReynolds	Douglas	Butler	Reed	Roberts	Stone
1940	Hughes	Black	Frankfurter	McReynolds	Douglas	Murphy	Reed	Roberts	Stone

THE STONE COURT (1941–1945)

1941–1942	Stone	Black	Frankfurter	Byrnes	Douglas	Murphy	Reed	Roberts	Jackson
1943–1944	Stone	Black	Frankfurter	Rutledge	Douglas	Murphy	Reed	Roberts	Jackson
1945	Stone	Black	Frankfurter	Rutledge	Douglas	Murphy	Reed	Burton	Jackson

THE VINSON COURT (1946–1952)

| 1946–1948 | Vinson | Black | Frankfurter | Rutledge | Douglas | Murphy | Reed | Burton | Jackson |
| 1949–1952 | Vinson | Black | Frankfurter | Minton | Douglas | Clark | Reed | Burton | Jackson |

THE WARREN COURT (1953–1968)

1953–1954	Warren	Black	Frankfurter	Minton	Douglas	Clark	Reed	Burton	Jackson
1955	Warren	Black	Frankfurter	Minton	Douglas	Clark	Reed	Burton	Harlan
1956	Warren	Black	Frankfurter	Brennan	Douglas	Clark	Reed	Burton	Harlan
1957	Warren	Black	Frankfurter	Brennan	Douglas	Clark	Whittaker	Burton	Harlan
1958–1961	Warren	Black	Frankfurter	Brennan	Douglas	Clark	Whittaker	Stewart	Harlan
1962–1965	Warren	Black	Goldberg	Brennan	Douglas	Clark	White	Stewart	Harlan
1965–1967	Warren	Black	Fortas	Brennan	Douglas	Clark	White	Stewart	Harlan
1967–1969	Warren	Black	Fortas	Brennan	Douglas	Marshall	White	Stewart	Harlan

THE BURGER COURT (1969–1985)

1969	Burger	Black	Fortas	Brennan	Douglas	Marshall	White	Stewart	Harlan
1969–1970	Burger	Black		Brennan	Douglas	Marshall	White	Stewart	Harlan
1970	Burger	Black	Blackmun	Brennan	Douglas	Marshall	White	Stewart	Harlan
1971–1974	Burger	Powell	Blackmun	Brennan	Douglas	Marshall	White	Stewart	Rehnquist
1975–1980	Burger	Powell	Blackmun	Brennan	Stevens	Marshall	White	Stewart	Rehnquist
1981–1985	Burger	Powell	Blackmun	Brennan	Stevens	Marshall	White	O'Connor	Rehnquist

THE REHNQUIST COURT (1986–)

1986	Rehnquist	Powell	Blackmun	Brennan	Stevens	Marshall	White	O'Connor	Scalia
1987–1989	Rehnquist	Kennedy	Blackmun	Brennan	Stevens	Marshall	White	O'Connor	Scalia
1990	Rehnquist	Kennedy	Blackmun	Souter	Stevens	Marshall	White	O'Connor	Scalia
1991	Rehnquist	Kennedy	Blackmun	Souter	Stevens	Thomas	White	O'Connor	Scalia

Index